Honoré de Balzac

The Celibates and Other Stories

Honoré de Balzac

The Celibates and Other Stories

ISBN/EAN: 9783744751384

Printed in Europe, USA, Canada, Australia, Japan

Cover: Foto ©Thomas Meinert / pixelio.de

More available books at **www.hansebooks.com**

H. DE BALZAC

THE COMÉDIE HUMAINE

PIERRETTE AND HE——HAD SKETCHED THEIR CHILDISH
DREAMS ON THE VEIL OF THE FUTURE.

THE CELIBATES

AND OTHER STORIES

TRANSLATED BY

CLARA BELL

WITH A PREFACE BY

GEORGE SAINTSBURY

PHILADELPHIA

THE GEBBIE PUBLISHING CO., Ltd.

1898

CONTENTS.

LIST OF ILLUSTRATIONS.

Drawn by *W. Boucher.*

PREFACE.

"Les Célibataires" (The Celibates), the longest number of the original "Comédie" under a single title, next to "Illusions Perdues" (Lost Illusions), is not, like that book, connected by any unity of story. Indeed, the general bond of union is pretty weak; and though it is quite true that bachelors and old maids are the heroes and heroines of all three,* it would be rather hard to establish any other bond of connection, and it is rather unlikely that any one unprompted would fix on this as a sufficient ground of partnership.

Two at least of the component parts, however, are of very high excellence. I do not myself think that "Pierrette," which opens the series, is quite the equal of its companions. Written, as it was, for Countess Anna de Hanska, Balzac's step-daughter of the future, while she was still very young, it partakes necessarily of the rather elaborate artificiality of all attempts to suit the young person, of French attempts in particular, and it may perhaps be said of Balzac's attempts most of all. It belongs, in a way, to the Arcis series—the series which also includes the fine "Ténébreuse Affaire," and the unfinished "Député d'Arcis"—but is not very closely connected therewith. The picture of the actual "Celibates," the brother and sister Rogron, with which it opens, is in one of Balzac's best-known styles, and is executed with all his usual mastery both of the minute and of the at least partially repulsive, showing also that strange knowledge of the *bourgeois de Paris* which, somehow or other, he seems to have attained by

* The third part, "A Bachelor's Establishment," constitutes the title story of another volume.

(ix)

dint of unknown foregatherings in his ten years of apprentice-ship.

The other and shorter constituent of the series, "The Abbé Birotteau," is certainly on a higher level, and has attracted the most magnificent eulogies from some of the novelist's admirers. I think both Mr. Henry James and Mr. Wedmore have singled out this little piece for detailed and elaborate praise, and there is no doubt that it is a happy example of a kind in which the author excelled. The opening, with its evident but not obtruded remembrance of the old and well-founded superstition—derived from the universal belief in some form of Nemesis—that an extraordinary sense of happi-ness, good-luck, or anything of the kind, is a precursor of misfortune, and calls for some instant act of sacrifice or humiliation, is very striking; and the working out of the ven-geance of the goddess by the very ungoddess-like though feminine hand of Mademoiselle Gamard has much that is commendable. Nothing in its well-exampled kind is better touched off than the Listomère coterie, from the shrewdness of Monsieur de Bourbonne to the selfishness of Madame de Listomère. I do not know that the old maid herself—cat, and far worse than cat as she is—is at all exaggerated, and the sketch of the coveted *appartement* and its ill-fated *mobilier* is about as good as it can be. And the battle between Madame de Listomère and the Abbé Troubert, which has served as a model for many similar things, has, if it has often been equaled, not often been surpassed.

"The Abbé Birotteau" strikes some good judges as of ex-ceptional character, while no one can refuse it merit in a high degree. I should not, except for the opening, place it in the very highest class of the "Comédie," but it is high beyond all doubt in the second.

"Pierrette," which was earlier called "Pierrette Lorrain," was issued in 1840, first in the *Siècle*, and then in volume form, published by Souverain. In both issues it had nine chapter or book divisions with headings. With the other "Celibates" it entered the "Comédie" as a "Scène de la Vie de Province" in 1843.

"The Abbé Birotteau" (which Balzac had at one time intended to call by the name of the curé's enemy, and which at first was simply called by the general title "Les Célibataires") is much older than its companions, and appeared in 1832 in the "Scènes de la Vie Privée." It was soon properly shifted to the "Vie de Province," and as such in due time joined the "Comédie," bearing the title of "Le Curé de Tours."

The short stories added to the volume are contemporaneous in point of time, and for this reason have been placed in their present position. "Colonel Chabert," which would well have deserved a place in those "Scènes de la Vie Militaire," so scantily represented in the "Comédie," has other attractions. It reminds us of Balzac's sojourn in the tents of Themis, and of the knowledge that he brought therefrom ; it gives an example of his affection for the *idée fixe*, for the man with a mania ; and it is also no inconsiderable example of his nature.

"The Vendetta" ranked with the "Scènes de la Vie Privée" from their first edition, but had an earlier separate publication in part, for it is one of those stories which Balzac originally divided into chapters and afterwards printed without them. The first of these, which appeared in the *Silhouette* of April, 1830, was entitled "L'Atélier," and the others were "La Désobéissance," "La Mariage," and "La Châtiment." G. S.

THE CELIBATES.

I.

PIERRETTE.

To Mademoiselle Anna de Hanska.

Dear Child :—You, the joy of a whole house, you whose white or rose-colored cape flutters in the summer like a will-o'-the-wisp through the arbors of Wierzchownia, followed by the wistful eyes of your father and mother—how can I dedicate to you a tale full of sadness ? But is it not well to tell you of sorrows such as a girl so fondly loved as you are will never know ? For some day your fair hands may take them comfort. It is so difficult, Anna, to find in the picture of our manners any incident worthy to meet your eye, that an author has no choice ; but perhaps you may discern how happy you are from reading this tale, sent by

Your old friend,

DE BALZAC.

IN October, 1827, at break of day, a youth of about sixteen, whose dress proclaimed him to be what modern phraseology insolently calls a proletarian, was standing on a little square in the lower part of the town of Provins. At this early hour he could, without being observed, study the various houses set round the plazza in an oblong square. The mills on the streams of Provins were already at work. Their noise, repeated by the echoes from the upper town, and harmonizing with the sharp air and the clear freshness of the morning, bewrayed the perfect silence—so complete that the clatter of a diligence was audible still a league away on the high-road.

The two longer rows of houses, divided by an arched avenue of lime trees, are artless in style, confessing the peaceful and circumscribed life of the townsfolk. In this part of the town there are no signs of trade. At that time there was hardly a carriage-gate suggesting the luxury of the rich—or, if there were, it rarely turned on its hinges—excepting that of Monsieur Martener, a doctor who was obliged to keep and use a cab. Some of the fronts were graced by a long vine stem, others with climbing roses growing up to the second floor, and scenting the windows with their large scattered bunches of flowers. One end of this square almost joins the High Street of the lower town ; the other end is shut in by a street parallel with the High Street, and the gardens beyond run down to one of the two rivers that water the valley of Provins.

At this end, the quietest part of the plazza, the young workman recognized the house that had been described to him—a front of white stone, scored with seams to represent joints in the masonry, and windows with light iron balconies, decorated with rosettes painted yellow, and closed with gray Venetian shutters. Above this front — a first floor and a second floor only—three attic windows pierce a slate-roof, and on one of the gables twirls a brand-new weather-cock. This modern weather-cock represents a sportsman aiming at a hare. The front door is reached by three stone steps. On one side of the door an end of leaden pipe spouts dirty water into a little gutter, revealing the kitchen ; on the other, two windows, carefully guarded by gray wooden shutters in which heart-shaped holes are cut to admit a little light, seemed to our youth to be those of the dining-room. In the basement secured by the three steps, under each window is an air-opening into the cellars, closed by painted iron shutters pierced with holes in a pattern. Everything was then quite new. An observer, looking at this house freshly repaired, its still raw splendor contrasting with the antique aspect of all the rest, would at once have seen in it the mean ideas and perfect contentment of a retired tradesman.

The young fellow gazed at every detail with an expression of pleasure mingled with sadness ; his eyes wandered from the kitchen to the garret with a look that denoted meditation. The pink gleams of sunshine showed in one of the attic windows a cotton curtain which was wanting to the others. Then the lad's face brightened completely ; he withdrew a few steps, leaned his back against a lime tree, and sang, in the drawling tones peculiar to the natives of the west, this ballad of Brittany, published by Bruguière, a composer to whom we owe some charming airs. In Brittany the young swains of the villages sing this song to newly-married couples on their wedding-day :

> *"We come to wish you every happiness,*
> *To th' maister at your side,*
> *As well as to the bride.*

> *"You, mistress bride, are bound for life and death,*
> *With a bright golden chain,*
> *That none may break in twain.*

> *"Now you to fairs and junkets go no more ;*
> *Nay, you must stay at home,*
> *While we may dance and roam.*

> *"And do you know how trusty you must be,*
> *And faithful to your mate,*
> *To love him rathe and late ?*

> *"Then take this posy I have made for you.*
> *Alack ! for happy hours*
> *Must perish like these flowers."*

This national air, as sweet as that arranged by Chateaubriand to the words *Ma sœur, te souvient-il encore ?* sung in a little town of La Brie in Champagne, could not fail to arouse irresistible memories in a native of Brittany, so faithfully does it paint the manners, the simplicity, the scenery of that noble old province. There is in it an intangible melancholy, caused by the realities of life, which is deeply touching. And is not this power to awaken a whole world of grave, sweet, sad things by a familiar and often cheerful strain characteristic of those popular airs which are the superstitions of music, if we accept the word superstition as meaning what remains from the ruin of nations, the flotsam left by revolutions ?

As he ended the first verse, the workman, who never took his eyes off the curtain in the attic, saw no one astir. While he was singing the second, it moved a little. As he sang the words, "Take this posy," a young girl's face was seen. A fair hand cautiously opened the window, and the girl nodded to the wanderer as he ended with the melancholy reflection contained in the two last lines :

"Alack ! for happy hours
Must perish like these flowers."

The lad suddenly took from under his jacket, and held up to her, a golden-yellow spray of a flower very common in Brittany, which he had picked no doubt in a field in La Brie, where it is somewhat rare—the flower of the furze.

"Why, is it you, Brigaut ? " said the girl in a low voice.

"Yes, Pierrette, yes. I am living in Paris ; I am walking about France ; but I might settle down here, since you are here."

At this moment the window-fastening of the room on the first floor, below Pierrette's, was heard to creak. The girl showed the greatest alarm, and said to Brigaut, "Fly ! "

The young fellow jumped like a frog to a bend in the street, round a mill, before entering the wider street that is the artery of the lower town ; but in spite of his agility, his hobnailed shoes, ringing on the paving-cobbles of Provins, made a noise easily distinguished from the music of the mill, and heard by the individual who opened the window.

This person was a woman. No man ever tears himself from the delights of his morning slumbers to listen to a minstrel in a round jacket. None but a maid is roused by a love song. And this was a maid—and an old maid. When she had thrown open her shutters with the action of a bat, she looked about her on all sides, and faintly heard Brigaut's steps as he made his escape. Is there on earth anything more hideous than the matutinal apparition of an ugly old maid at her window? Of all the grotesque spectacles that are the amusement of travelers as they go through little towns, is it not the most unpleasing? It is too depressing, too repulsive to be laughed at.

This particular old maid, whose ear was so keen, appeared bereft of the artifices of all kinds that she used to improve herself; she had no front of false hair, and no collar. Her headgear was the frightful little caul of black sarsnet which old women draw over their skull, showing beyond her night-cap, which had been pushed aside in her sleep. This untidiness gave her head the sinister appearance ascribed by painters to witches. The temples, ears, and nape, scarcely concealed, betrayed their withered leanness, the coarse wrinkles were conspicuous for a redness that did not charm the eye, and that was thrown into relief by the comparative whiteness of a bedgown tied at the throat with twisted tapes. The gaps where this bedgown fell open revealed a chest like that of some old peasant-woman careless of her ugliness. The fleshless arm might have been a stick covered with stuff. Seen at the window, the lady appeared tall by reason of the strength and breadth of her face, which reminded the spectator of the extravagant size of some Swiss countenances. The chief characteristic of the features, which presented a singular lack of harmony, was a hardness of line, a harshness of coloring, and a lack of feeling in the expression which would have filled a physiognomist with disgust. These peculiarities, visible now, were habitually modified by a sort of business smile, and a vulgar stupidity which aped good-nature so successfully that the people among whom she lived might easily have supposed her to be a kind woman.

She and her brother shared the ownership of this house. The brother was sleeping so soundly in his room that the opera-house orchestra would not have roused him; and the power of that orchestra is famous! The old maid put her head out of the window, and raised her eyes to that of the attic—eyes of a cold, pale blue, with short lashes set in lids that were almost always swollen. She tried to see Pierrette; but recognizing the futility of the attempt, she withdrew into her room with a movement not unlike that of a tortoise hiding its head after putting it out of its shell. The shutters were closed again, and the silence of the square was no more disturbed but by peasants coming into the town, or early risers. When there is an old maid in the house a watch-dog is not needed; not the smallest event occurs without her seeing it, commenting on it, and deducing every possible consequence. Thus this incident was destined to give rise to serious inferences, and to be the opening of one of those obscure dramas which are played out in the family, but which are none the less terrible for being unseen—if indeed the name of drama may be applied to this tragedy of home-life.

Pierrette did not get into bed again. To her Brigaut's arrival was an event of immense importance. During the night—the Eden of the wretched—she escaped from the annoyances and fault-finding she had to endure all day. Like the hero of some German or Russian ballad, to her sleep seemed a happy life, and the day a bad dream. This morning, for the first time in three years, she had had a happy waking. The memories of infancy had sweetly sung their poetry to her soul. She had heard the first verse in her dreams; the second had roused her with a start; at the third she had doubted

—the unfortunate are of the school of Saint Thomas; at the fourth verse, standing at her window, barefoot, and in her shift, she had recognized Brigaut, the friend of her earlier childhood.

Yes, that was indeed the short square jacket with quaint little tails and pockets swinging just over the hips, the classical blue-cloth jacket of the Breton; the coarse-knit waistcoat, the linen shirt buttoned with a golden heart, the wide-rolled collar, the earrings, heavy shoes, trousers of blue drill, mottled in streaks of lighter shades; in short, all the humble and durable items of a poor Breton's costume. The large white horn buttons of the jacket and waistcoat had set Pierrette's heart beating. At the sight of the branch of furze the tears had started to her eyes; then a spasm of terror clutched her heart, crushing the flowers of remembrance that had blossomed for a moment. It struck her that her cousin might have heard her rise and go to the window. She knew the old woman, and made the signal of alarm to Brigaut, which the poor boy had hastened to obey without understanding it. Does not this instinctive obedience betray one of those innocent and mastering affections such as are to be seen once in an age, on this earth where they bloom, like the aloe trees on Isola Bella, but two or three times in a century. Any one seeing Brigaut fly would have admired the artless heroism of a most artless love.

Jacques Brigaut was worthy of Pierrette Lorrain, who was now nearly fourteen—two children! Pierrette could not help weeping as she saw him take to his heels with the terror inspired by her warning gesture.

She then sat down in a rickety armchair, in front of a looking-glass above a little table. On this she set her elbows, and remained pensive for an hour, trying to recall Le Marais, the hamlet of Pen-Hoël, the adventurous voyages on a pond in a boat untied from an old willow tree by little Jacques; then the old faces—her grandmother and grandfather, her

mother's look of suffering, and General Brigaut's handsome
head; a whole childhood of careless joy! And this again
was a dream—the lights of happiness against a gray background.

She had fine light-brown hair, all in disorder, under a little
nightcap tumbled in her sleep, a little cambric cap with frills
that she herself had made. On each side curls fell over her
temples, escaping from their gray papers. At the back of her
head a thick plait hung down to her shoulders. The excessive pallor of her face showed that she was a victim to a girlish
ailment to which medical science gives the pretty name of
chlorosis, which robs the blood of its natural hue, disturbing
the appetite, and betraying much disorderment of the whole
system. This waxen hue was apparent in all the flesh-tints.
The whiteness of her neck and shoulders, the colorlessness of
an etiolated plant, accounted for the thinness of her arms
crossed in front of her. Pierrette's feet even looked weak and
shrunken by disease; her shift, falling only to her calf, showed
the relaxed sinews, blue veins, and bloodless muscles. As
the cold air chilled her, her lips turned purple. The mourn-
ful smile that parted her fairly delicate mouth showed teeth
of ivory whiteness, even and small, pretty transparent teeth,
in harmony with well-shaped ears and a nose that was elegant,
if a little sharp; her face, though perfectly round, was very
sweet. All the life of this charming countenance lay in the
eyes; the iris, of a bright snuff-brown mottled with black,
shone with golden lights round a deep bright retina. Pierrette ought to have been gay; she was sad. Her vanished
gaiety lingered in the vivid modeling of her eyes, in the in-
genuous form of her brow, and the moulding of her short chin.
The long eyelashes lay like brushes on the cheeks worn by
debility; the whiteness, too lavishly diffused, gave great
purity to the lines and features of her countenance. The ear
was a little masterpiece of modeling; it might have been of
marble.

Pierrette suffered in many ways. Perhaps you would like to have her story? Here it is.

Pierrette's mother was a Demoiselle Auffray of Provins, half-sister to Madame Rogron, the mother of the present owners of this house. Monsieur Auffray, after marrying for the first time at the age of eighteen, took a second wife at the age of sixty-nine. The child of his first marriage was an only daughter, ugly enough, who, when she was sixteen, married an innkeeper of Provins named Rogron. By his second marriage old Auffray had another daughter, but she was very pretty. Thus the quaint result was an enormous difference in age between Monsieur Auffray's two daughters. The child of his first wife was fifty when the second was born. By the time her father gave her a sister Madame Rogron had two children of her own, both of full age.

The uxorious old man's younger child was married for love, at eighteen, to a Breton officer named Lorrain, a captain in the Imperial Guard. Love often begets ambition. The captain, eager to get his colonelcy, exchanged into the line. While the major and his wife, comfortable enough with the allowance given them by Monsieur and Madame Auffray, were living handsomely in Paris, or running about Germany as the Emperor's wars or truces might guide them, old Auffray, a retired grocer at Provins, died suddenly, before he had time to make his will. The good man's estate was so cleverly manipulated by the innkeeper and his wife that they absorbed the larger part of it, leaving to old Auffray's widow no more than the house in the little square and a few acres of land. This widow, little Madame Lorrain's mother, was but eight-and-thirty when her husband died. Like many other widows, she had an unwholesome wish to marry again. She sold to her stepdaughter, old Madame Rogron, the land and house she had inherited under her marriage settlement, to marry a young doctor named Néraud, who ran through her fortune, and she died of grief in great poverty two years afterwards.

Thus Madame Lorrain's share of the Auffray property had in great part disappeared, being reduced to about eight thousand francs.

Major Lorrain died on the field of honor at Montereau, leaving his widow, then one-and-twenty, burthened with a little girl fourteen months old, and with no fortune but the pension she could claim from the government, and whatever money might come to her from Monsieur and Madame Lorrain, tradespeople at Pen-Hoël, a town of La Vendée, in the district known as Le Marais. These Lorrains, the parents of the deceased officer, and Pierrette's paternal grandfather and grandmother, sold building-timber, slates, tiles, cornices, pipes, and the like. Their business was a poor one, either from their incapacity or from ill luck, and brought them in a bare living. The failure of the great house of Colinet at Nantes, brought about by the events of 1814, which caused a sudden fall in the price of colonial produce, resulted in a loss to them of eighty thousand francs they had placed on deposit. Their daughter-in-law was therefore warmly received; the major's widow brought with her a pension of eight hundred francs, an enormous sum at Pen-Hoël. When her half-sister and brother-in-law Rogron sent her the eight thousand francs due to her, after endless formalities, prolonged by distance, she placed the money in the Lorrain's hands, taking a mortgage, however, on a little house they owned at Nantes, let for a hundred crowns a year, and worth, perhaps, ten thousand francs.

Young Madame Lorrain died there after her mother's second and luckless marriage, in 1819, and almost at the same time as her mother. This daughter of the old man and his young wife was small, fragile, and delicate; the damp air of Le Marais did not agree with her. Her husband's family, eager to keep her there, persuaded her that nowhere else in the world would she find a place healthier or pleasanter than Le Marais, the scene of Charette's exploits. She was so well taken care of, nursed, and coaxed that her death brought honor to the Lorrains.

Some persons asserted that Brigaut, an old Vendéen, one of those men of iron who served under Charette, Mercier, the Marquis de Montauran, and the Baron du Guénic in the wars against the Republic, counted for much in young Madame Lorrain's submission. If this were so, it was certainly for the sake of a most loving and devoted soul. And, indeed, all Pen-Hoël could see that Brigaut, respectfully designated as the major—having held that rank in the Royalist army— spent his days and his evenings in the Lorrains' sitting-room by the side of the Emperor's major's widow. Towards the end the curé of Pen-Hoël allowed himself to speak of this matter to old Madame Lorrain; he begged her to persuade her daughter-in-law to marry Brigaut, promising to get him an appointment as justice of the peace to the district of Pen-Hoël, by the intervention of the Vicomte de Kergarouët. But the poor woman's death made the scheme useless.

Pierrette remained with her grandparents, who owed her four hundred francs a year, naturally spent on her maintenance. The old people, now less and less fit for business, had an active and pushing rival in trade, whom they could only abuse, without doing anything to protect themselves. The major, their friend and adviser, died six months after young Madame Lorrain, perhaps of grief, or perhaps of his wounds; he had had seven-and-twenty. Their bad neighbor, as a good man of business, now aimed at ruining his rivals, so as to extinguish all competition. He got the Lorrains to borrow on their note of hand, foreseeing that they could never pay, and so forced them in their old age to become bankrupt. Pierrette's mortgage was second to a mortgage held by her grandmother, who clung to her rights to secure a morsel of bread for her husband. The house at Nantes was sold for nine thousand five hundred francs, and the costs came to fifteen hundred francs. The remaining eight thousand francs

came to Madame Lorrain, who invested them in a mortgage
in order to live at Nantes in a sort of almshouse, like that of
Sainte-Périne in Paris, called Saint-Jacques, where the two
worthy old people found food and lodging at a very moderate
rate.

As it was impossible that they should take with them their
little destitute grandchild, the old Lorrains bethought them
of her uncle and aunt Rogron, to whom they wrote. The
Rogrons of Provins were dead. Thus the letter from the
Lorrains to the Rogrons would seem to be lost. But if there
is anything here below which can take the place of Providence, is it not the General Postoffice? The genius of the
post, immeasurably superior to that of the public, outdoes in
inventiveness the imagination of the most brilliant novelist.
As soon as the post has charge of a letter, worth, on delivery,
from three to ten sous, if it fails at once to find him or her
to whom it should be delivered, it displays a mercenary solicitude which has no parallel but in the boldest duns. The
post comes, goes, hunts through the eighty-six departments.
Difficulties incite the genius of its officials, who, not unfrequently, are men of letters, and who then throw themselves
into the pursuit with the ardor of the mathematicians at the
National Observatory; they rummage the kingdom. At the
faintest gleam of hope the Paris offices are on the alert again.
You often sit amazed as you inspect the scrawls that meander
over the letter, back and front—the glorious evidence of the
administrative perseverance that animates the postoffice. If
a man were to undertake what the post has accomplished,
he would have spent ten thousand francs in traveling, in time
and in money, to recover twelve sous. The post certainly
has more intelligence than it conveys.

The letter written by the Lorrains to Monsieur Rogron,
who had been dead a year, was transmitted by the post to
Monsieur Rogron, his son, a haberdasher in the Rue Saint-
Denis, Paris. This is where the genius of the postoffice

shines. An heir is always more or less puzzled to know
whether he has really scraped up the whole of his inheritance,
whether he has not forgotten some debt or some fragments.
The Revenue guesses everything; it even reads character.
A letter addressed to old Rogron of Provins was bound to
pique the curiosity of Rogron, *junior*, of Paris, or of Mademoiselle Rogron, his heirs. So the Revenue earned its sixty
centimes.

The Rogrons, towards whom the Lorrains held out be-
seeching hands, though they were in despair at having to part
from their granddaughter, thus became the arbiters of Pierrette Lorrain's fate. It is indispensable, therefore, to give
some account of their antecedents and their character.

Old Rogron, the innkeeper at Provins, on whom Old Auffray had bestowed the child of his first marriage, was hot-
faced, with a purple-veined nose, and cheeks which Bacchus
had overlaid with his crimson and bulbous blossoms. Though
stout, short, and pot-bellied, with stumpy legs and heavy
hands, he had all the shrewdness of the Swiss innkeeper, resembling that race. His face remotely suggested a vast hail-
stricken vineyard. Certainly he was not handsome; but his
wife was like him. Never were a better matched couple.
Rogron liked good living, and to have pretty girls to wait on
him. He was one of the sect of egoists whose ways are
brutal, and who give themselves up to their vices and do their
will in the face of Israel. Greedy, mercenary, and by no
means refined, obliged to be the purveyor to his own fancies,
he ate up all he earned till his teeth failed him. Then avarice
remained. In his old age he sold his inn, collected, as we
have seen, all his father-in-law's leavings, and retired to the
little house in the square, which he bought for a piece of
bread from old Auffray's widow, Pierrette's grandmother.

Rogron and his wife owned about two thousand francs a
year, derived from the letting of twenty-seven plots of land
in the neighborhood of Provins, and the interest on the price

of their inn, which they had sold for twenty thousand francs.
Old Auffray's house, though in a very bad state, was used as
it was for a dwelling by the innkeepers, who avoided repair-
ing it as they would have shunned the plague; old rats love
cracks and ruins. The retired publican, taking a fancy for
gardening, spent his savings in adding to his garden; he
extended it to the bank of the river, making a long square
shut in by two walls, and ending with a stone embankment,
below which the water plants, left to run wild, displayed their
abundant flowers.

Early in their married life the Rogron couple had a son
and a daughter, with two years between them; everything
degenerates; their children were hideous. Put out to nurse
in the country as cheaply as possible, these unhappy little
ones came home with the wretched training of village life,
having cried long and often for their foster-mother, who went
to work in the fields, and who left them meanwhile shut up
in one of the dark, damp, low rooms which form the dwelling
of the French peasant. By this process the children's features
grew thick, and their voices harsh; they were far from flattering their mother's vanity, and she tried to correct them of
their bad habits by a severity which, by comparison with their
father's, seemed tenderness itself. They were left to play in
the yards, stables, and outhouses of the inn, or to run about
the town; they were sometimes whipped; sometimes they
were sent to their grandfather Auffray, who loved them little.
This injustice was one of the reasons that encouraged the
Rogrons to secure a large share of the "old rascal's" leavings. Meanwhile, however, Rogron sent his boy to school;
and he paid a man, one of his carters, to save the lad from
the conscription. As soon as his daughter Sylvie was twelve
years old, he sent her to Paris as an apprentice in a house of
business. Two years later, his son, Jérôme-Denis, was packed
off by the same road. When his friends the carriers, who
were his allies, or the inn customers asked him what he meant

to do with his children, old Rogron explained his plans with a brevity which had this advantage over the statements of most fathers, that it was frank—

"When they are of an age to understand me, I shall just give them a kick you know where, saying, 'Be off and make your fortune,' " he would reply, as he drank, or wiped his mouth with the back of his hand. Then looking at the inquirer with a knowing wink, "Ha, ha!" he would add, "they are not greater fools than I am. My father gave me three kicks, I shall give them but one. He put a louis into my hand, I will give them ten; so they will be better off than I was. That's the right way. And after I am gone, what is left will be left; the notaries will find them fast enough. A pretty joke, indeed, if I am to keep myself short for the children's sake! They owe their being to me; I have brought them up; I ask nothing of them; they have not paid me back, heh, neighbor? I began life as a carter, and that did not hinder me from marrying that old rascal Auffray's daughter."

Sylvie was placed as an apprentice, with a premium of a hundred crowns for her board, with some tradespeople in the Rue Saint-Denis, natives of Provins. Two years later she was paying her way; though she earned no money, her parents had nothing to pay for her food and lodging. This, in the Rue Saint-Denis, is called being "at par." Two years later Sylvie was earning a hundred crowns a year. In the course of that time her mother had sent her a hundred francs for pocket-money. Thus, at the age of nineteen, Mademoiselle Sylvie Rogron was independent. When she was twenty, she was second "young lady" in the house of Julliard, raw-silk merchants, at the sign of the *Ver chinois* (or Silkworm), in the Rue Saint-Denis.

The history of the brother was like the sister's. Little Jérôme-Denis Rogron was placed with one of the largest wholesale mercers in the Rue Saint-Denis, the *Maison Guépin* at the *Trois Quenouilles*. While Sylvie, at twenty-one, was forewoman with a thousand francs a year, Jérôme-Denis, better served by luck, was, at eighteen, head store-clerk, earning twelve hundred, with the Guépins, also natives of Provins. The brother and sister met every Sunday and holiday, and spent the day in cheap amusements. They dined outside Paris; they went to St. Cloud, Meudon, Belleville, or Vincennes.

At the end of 1815 they united the money they had earned by the sweat of their brow, and bought of Madame Guénée the business and good-will of a famous house, the *Sœur de famille*, one of the best-known retail haberdashers. The sister kept the cash, the store, and the accounts; the brother was both buyer and head-clerk, as Sylvie was for some time her own forewoman. In 1821, after five years' hard work, competition had become so lively in the haberdashery business that the brother and sister had scarcely been able to pay off the purchase-money and keep up the reputation of the house.

Though Sylvie Rogron was at this time but forty, her ugliness, her constant toil, and a peculiarly crabbed expression, arising as much from the shape of her features as from her anxieties, made her look like a woman of fifty. Jérôme-Denis Rogron, at the age of thirty-eight, had the most idiotic face that ever bent over a counter to a customer. His low forehead, crushed by fatigue, was seamed by three arid furrows. His scanty gray hair, cut very short, suggested the unutterable stupidity of a cold-blooded animal; in the gaze of his blue-gray eyes there was neither fire nor mind. His round, flat face aroused no sympathy, and did not even bring a smile to the lips of those who study the varieties of Parisian physiognomy; it was depressing. And while, like his father, he was short and thick, his shape, not having the coarse obesity of the innkeeper, showed in every detail an absurd flabbiness. His father's excessive redness gave place in him to the flaccid lividness acquired by people who live in airless backstores, in the barred coops that serve as counting-houses, always folding and unfolding skeins of thread, paying or receiving money, harrying clerks, or repeating the same phrases to customers. The small intelligence of this brother and sister had been completely sunk in mastering their business, in debit and credit, and in the study of the rules and customs of the Paris market. Thread, needles, ribbon, pins, buttons, tailors' trimmings, in short, the vast list of articles constituting Paris haberdashery, had filled up their memory. Letters to write and answer, bills and stock-taking, had absorbed all their capabilities.

Outside their line of business they knew absolutely nothing; they did not even know Paris. To them Paris was something spread out round the Rue Saint-Denis. Their narrow nature found its field in their store. They knew very well how to nag their assistants and shop-girls and find them at fault. Their joy consisted in seeing all their hands as busy on the counters as mice's paws, handling the goods or folding up the pieces. When they heard seven or eight young voices of lads and girls simpering out the time-honored phrases with which shop-assistants reply to a customer's remarks, it was a fine day, nice weather. When ethereal blue brought life to Paris, and Parisians out walking thought of no haberdashery but what they wore, "Bad weather for business," the silly master would observe. The great secret, which made Rogron the object of his apprentices' admiration was his art in tying, untying, re-tying, and making up a parcel. Rogron could pack a parcel and look out at what was going on in the street, or keep an eye on his store to its farther depths; he had seen everything by the time he handed it to the buyer, saying, "Madame—nothing more this morning?"

But for his sister, this simpleton would have been ruined. Sylvie had good sense and the spirit of trade. She advised

2

her brother as to his purchases from the manufacturers, and
relentlessly sent him off to the other end of France to make a
sou of profit on some article.   The shrewdness, of which
every woman possesses more or less, having no duty to do for
her heart, she had utilized it in speculation.   Stock to be
paid for! this thought was the piston that worked this
machine and gave it appalling energy.   Rogron was never
more than head-assistant; he did not understand his business
as a whole; personal interest, the chief motor of the mind,
had not carried him forward one step.   He often stood dis-
mayed when his sister desired him to sell some article at a
loss, foreseeing that it would go out of the fashion; and
afterwards he guilelessly admired her.   He did not reason
well or ill; he was incapable of reasoning; but he had sense
enough to submit to his sister, and he did so for a reason that
had nothing to do with business.   "She is the eldest," he
would say.   Physiologists and moralists may possibly find in
such a persistently solitary life, reduced to satisfy mere needs,
and deprived of money and pleasure in youth, an explanation of the animal expression of face, the weak brain, and
idiotic manner of this haberdasher.   His sister had always
hindered his marrying, fearing perhaps that she might lose
her influence in the house, and seeing a source of expense
and ruin in a wife certainly younger, and probably less hideous, than herself.

Stupidity may betray itself in two ways—it is talkative or
it is mute.   Mute stupidity may be endured; but Rogron's
was talkative.   The tradesman had fallen into the habit of
scolding his assistants, of expatiating to them on the minutiæ
of the haberdashery business and selling to "the trade,"
ornamenting his lectures with the flat jokes that constitute
the *bagout*, the gab of the store.   (This word *bagout*, used
formerly to designate the stereotyped repartee, has given way
before the soldier's slang word *blague* or humbug.)   Rogron,
to whom his little domestic audience was bound to listen;

Rogron, very much pleased with himself, had finally adopted a set of phrases of his own. The chatterbox believed himself eloquent. The need for explaining to customers the thing they want, for finding out their wishes, for making them want the thing they do not want, loosens the tongue of the counter-jumper. The retail dealer at last acquires the faculty of pouring out sentences in which words have no meaning, but which answer their purpose. Then he can explain to his customers methods of manufacture unknown to them, and this gives him a sort of short-lived superiority over the purchaser; but apart from the thousand and one explanations necessitated by the thousand and one articles he sells, he is, so far as thought is concerned, like a fish on straw in the sunshine.

Rogron and Sylvie—a pair of machines illicitly baptized —had neither potentially nor actively the feelings which give life to the heart. These two beings were utterly dry and tough, hardened by toil, by privations, by the remembrance of their sufferings during a long and wearisome apprenticeship. Neither he nor she had pity for any misfortune. They were not implacable, but impenetrable with regard to anybody in difficulties. To them virtue, honor, loyalty, every human feeling was epitomized in the regular payment of their accounts. Close-fisted, heartless, and sordidly thrifty, the brother and sister had a terrible reputation among the traders of the Rue Saint-Denis.

But for their visits to Provins, whither they went thrice a year, at times when they could shut the store for two or three days, they would never have gotten any store assistants. But old Rogron packed off to his children every unhappy creature intended by its parents to go into trade; he carried on for them a business in apprentices in Provins, where he vaunted with much vanity his children's fortune. The parents, tempted by the remote hope of having their son or daughter well taught and well looked after, and the chance of seeing a child some day step into Rogron junior's business, sent the youth who was in the way to the house kept by the old bachelor and old maid. But as soon as the apprentices, man or maid, for whom the fee of a hundred crowns was always paid, saw any way of escaping from these galleys, they fled with a glee which added to the terrible notoriety of the Rogrons. The indefatigable innkeeper always supplied them with fresh victims.

From the age of fifteen Sylvie Rogron, accustomed to grimace over the counter, had two faces—the amiable mask of the saleswoman and the natural expression of a shriveled old maid. Her assumed countenance was a marvelous piece of mimicry; she smiled all over; her voice turned soft and insinuating, and held the customers under a commercial spell. Her real face was what she had shown between the two half-opened shutters. It would have scared the bravest of the Cossacks of 1815, though they dearly loved every variety of Frenchwomen.

When the letter came from the Lorrains, the Rogrons, in mourning for their father, had come into possession of the house they had almost stolen from Pierrette's grandmother, of the innkeeper's acquired land, and finally of certain sums derived from usurious loans in mortgages on land in the hands of peasant-owners whom the old drunkard hoped to dispossess. The charge on the business was paid off. The Rogrons had stock to the value of about sixty thousand francs in the shop, about forty thousand francs in their cash-box or in assets, and the value of their good-will. Seated on the bench, covered with striped-green worsted velvet, and fitted into a square recess behind· the cash-desk, with just such another desk opposite for the forewoman, the brother and sister held council as to their plans. Every tradesman hopes to retire. If they realized their whole stock and business, they ought to have about a hundred and fifty thousand francs, without counting their inheritance from old Rogron. Thus by investing in the funds the capital at their disposal, each of them would have three to four thousand francs a year, even if they devoted the price of the business—which would no doubt be paid in installments—to restoring their paternal home. So they might go to Provins and live there in a house of their own.

Their forewoman was the daughter of a rich farmer at Donnemarie, who was burthened with nine children; thus he was obliged to place them all in business, for his wealth, divided among nine, would be little enough for each. But in five years the farmer lost seven of his children, consequently the forewoman had become an interesting person; so much so, that Rogron had attempted, but vainly, to make her his wife. The young lady manifested an aversion for the master which nullified all his manœuvres. On the other hand, Mademoiselle Sylvie did not encourage the plan; she even opposed her brother's marriage, and wanted rather to have so clever a woman as their successor. Rogron's marriage she postponed till they should be settled at Provins.

No passer-by can understand the motive-power that underlies the cryptogamic lives of certain storekeepers; as we look at them we wonder, "On what, and why do they live? What becomes of them? Where did they come from?" We lose ourselves in vacancy as we try to account for them. To discover the little poetry that germinates in these brains and vivifies these existences, we must dig into them; but we soon reach the tufa on which everything rests. The Paris storekeeper feeds on hopes more or less likely to be realized, and without which he would evidently perish: one dreams of building or managing a theatre, another struggles for the honors of the Mairie; this one has a castle in the air three leagues from Paris, a so-called park, where he plants colored plaster statues and arranges fountains that look like an end of thread, and spends immense sums; that one longs for promotion to the higher grades of the National Guard. Provins, an earthly

paradise, excited in the two haberdashers the fanaticism which
the inhabitants of every pretty town in France feel for their
home. And to the glory of Champagne, it may be said that
this affection is amply justified. Provins, one of the most
charming spots in France, rivals Frangistan and the valley
of Cashmere; not only has it all the poetry of Saadi, the
Homer of Persia, but it also has pharmaceutical treasures for
medical science. The crusaders brought roses from Jericho
to this delightful valley, where, by some chance, the flowers
developed new qualities without losing anything of their color.
And Provins is not only the Persia of France; it might be
Baden, Aix, Bath; it has mineral waters.

This is the picture seen year after year, which now and
again appeared in a vision to the haberdashers on the muddy
pavement of the Rue Saint-Denis.

After crossing the gray flats that lie between La Ferté-
Gaucher and Provins—a desert, but a fertile one, a desert
of wheat—you mount a hill. Suddenly, at your feet, you
see a town watered by two rivers; at the bottom of the slope
spreads a green valley broken by graceful lines and retreating
distances. If you come from Paris you take Provins length-
ways; you see the everlasting French high-road running along
the foot of the hill and close under it, owning its blindman
and its beggars, who throw in an accompaniment of lamentable
voices when you pause to gaze at this unexpectedly picturesque
tract of land. If you arrive from Troyes you come in from
the plain. The castle and the old town, with its rampart,
climb the shelves of the hill. The new town lies below.

There are upper and lower Provins ; above, a town in the
air, with steep streets and fine points of view, surrounded
by hollow roads like ravines between rows of walnut trees,
furrowing the narrow hilltop with deep cuttings: a silent
town this, clean and solemn, overshadowed by the imposing
ruins of the stronghold ; then, below, a town of mills, watered
by the Voulzie and the Durtain, two rivers of Brie, narrow,

sluggish, and deep; a town of inns and trade, of retired tradespeople, traversed by diligences, chaises, and heavy carts. These two towns—or this town—with its historical associations, with the melancholy of its ruins, the gaiety of its valley, its delightful ravines full of unkempt hedgerows and wildflowers, its river terraced with gardens, has so sure a hold on the love of its children that they behave like the sons of Auvergne, of Savoy, of France. Though they leave Provins to seek their fortune, they always come back to it. The phrase, "To die in one's burrow," made for rabbits and faithful souls, might be taken by the natives of Provins as their motto.

And so the two Rogrons thought only of their beloved Provins. As he sold thread, the brother saw the old town. While packing cards covered with buttons, he was gazing at the valley. He rolled and unrolled tape, but he was following the gleaming course of the rivers. As he looked at his pigeon-holes he was climbing the sunk roads whither of old he fled to evade his father's rage, to eat walnuts, and to cram on blackberries. The little square at Provins above all filled his thoughts; he would beautify the house; he dreamed of the front he would rebuild, the bedrooms, the sitting-room, the billiard-room, the dining-room; then of the kitchen garden, which he would turn into an English garden with a lawn, grottoes, fountains, statues, and what not?

The rooms in which the brother and sister slept on the third floor of the house, three windows wide and six stories high—there are many such in the Rue Saint-Denis—had no furniture beyond what was strictly necessary; but not a soul in Paris had finer furniture than this haberdasher. As he walked in the streets he would stand in the attitude of an ecstatic, looking at the handsome pieces on show, and examining hangings with which he filled his house. On coming home he would say to his sister, "I saw a thing in such or such a store that would just do for us!" The next day

he would buy another, and invariably he gave up one month
the choice of the month before.   The revenue would not have
paid for his architectural projects; he wanted everything, and
always gave the preference to the newest thing.   When he
studied the balconies of a newly built house, and the doubtful
attempts at exterior decoration, he thought the mouldings,
sculpture, and ornament quite out of place.   "Ah!" he
would say to himself, "those fine things would look much
better at Provins than they do there."   As he digested his
breakfast on his doorstep, leaning his back against the store
side, with a hazy eye the haberdasher saw a fantastic dwelling,
golden in the sunshine of his dream; he walked in a garden,
listening to his fountain as it splashed in a shower of diamonds
on a round flag of limestone.   He played billiards on his own
table; he planted flowers.

When his sister sat, pen in hand, lost in thought, and for-
getting to scold the shopmen, she was seeing herself receiving
the townsfolk of Provins, gazing at herself in the tall mirrors
of her drawing-room, and wearing astounding caps.   Both
brother and sister were beginning to think that the atmosphere
of the Rue Saint-Denis was unwholesome, and the smell of
the mud in the market made them long for the scent of the
roses of Provins.   They suffered alike from home-sickness and
monomania, both thwarted by the necessity for selling their
last remnants of thread, reels of silk, and buttons.   The promised land of the valley of Provins attracted these Israelites all
the more strongly because they had for a long time really
suffered, and had crossed with gasping breath the sandy
deserts of haberdashery.

The letter from the Lorrains arrived in the middle of a
meditation on that beautiful future.   The haberdashers scarcely
knew their cousin Pierrette Lorrain.   The settlement of
Auffray's estate, long since, by the old innkeeper, had taken
place when they were going into business, and Rogron never
said much about his money matters.   Having been sent to

Paris so young, the brother and sister could hardly remember their aunt Lorrain. It took them an hour of genealogical discussion to recall their aunt, the daughter of their grandfather Auffray's second wife, and their mother's half-sister. They then remembered that Madame Lorrain's mother was the Madame Néraud who had died of grief. They concluded that their grandfather's second marriage had been a disastrous thing for them, the result being the division of Auffray's estate between two families. They had, indeed, heard sundry recriminations from their father, who was always somewhat of the grudging publican. The pair studied the Lorrains' letter through the medium of these reminiscences, which were not in Pierrette's favor. To take charge of an orphan, a girl, a cousin, who in any case would be their heiress in the event of neither of them marrying—this was matter for discussion. The question was regarded from every point of view. In the first place, they had never seen Pierrette. Then it would be very troublesome to have a young girl to look after. Would they not be binding themselves to provide for her? It would be impossible to send her away if they did not like her. Would they not have to find her a husband? And if, after all, Rogron could find "a shoe to fit him" among the heiresses of Provins, would it not be better to keep all they had for his children? The shoe that would fit her brother, according to Sylvie, was a rich girl, stupid and ugly, who would allow her sister-in-law to rule her. The couple decided that they would refuse.

Sylvie undertook to reply. Business was sufficiently pressing to retard this letter, which she did not deem urgent, and indeed the old maid thought no more about it when the forewoman consented to buy the business and stock-in-trade of the *Sœur de famille.*

Sylvie Rogron and her brother had gone to settle in Provins four years before the time when Brigaut's appearance brought so much interest into Pierrette's life. But the doings of these

two persons in the country require a description no less than
their life in Paris; for Provins was fated to be as evil an influence for Pierrette as her cousins' commercial antecedents.

When a small tradesman who has come to Paris from the
provinces returns to the country from Paris, he inevitably
brings with him some notions; presently he loses them in the
habits of the place where he settles down, and where his
fancies for innovation gradually sink.   Hence come those
slow, small, successive changes which are gradually scratched
by Paris on the surface of country-town life, and which are
the essential stamp of the change of a retired storekeeper into
a confirmed provincial.   This change is a real distemper.
No small tradesman can pass without a shock from perpetual
talk to utter silence, from the activity of his Paris life to the
stagnation of the country.   When the good folks have earned
a little money, they spend a certain amount on the passion
they have so long been hatching, and work off the last spasms
of an energy which cannot be stopped short at will.   Those
who have never cherished any definite plan, travel or throw
themselves into the political interests of the municipality.
Some go out shooting or fishing, and worry their farmers and
tenants.   Some turn usurers, like old father Rogron, or speculate, like many obscure persons.

The dream of this brother and sister is known to you; they
wanted to indulge their magnificent fancy for handling the
trowel, for building a delightful house.   This fixed idea had
graced the square of lower Provins with the frontage which
Brigaut had just been examining, the interior arrangements
of the house, and its luxurious furniture.   The builder drove
never a nail in without consulting the Rogrons, without
making them sign the plans and estimates, without explaining
in lengthy detail the structure of the object under discussion,
where it was made, and the various prices.   As to anything
unusual, it had always been introduced by Monsieur Tiphaine
or Madame Julliard the younger, or Monsieur Garceland, the

mayor. Such a resemblance with some wealthy citizen of Provins always carried the day in the builder's favor.

"Oh, if Monsieur Garceland has one we will have one, too!" said Mademoiselle Sylvie. "It must be right; he had good taste."

"Sylvie, he also suggests we should have ovolos in the cornice of the passage."

"You call that an ovolo?"

"Yes, mademoiselle."

"But why? What a queer name! I never heard it before."

"But you have seen them?"

"Yes."

"Do you know Latin?"

"No."

"Well, it means egg-shaped; the ovolo is egg-shaped," explained the builder.

"You are a queer crew, you architects!" cried Rogron. "That, no doubt, is the reason you charge so much; you don't throw away your egg-shells!"

"Shall we paint the passage?" asked the builder.

"Certainly not!" cried Sylvie. "Another five hundred francs!"

"But the drawing-room and the stairs are so nice, it is a pity not to decorate the passage," said the builder. "Little Madame Lesourd had hers painted last year."

"And yet her husband, being crown prosecutor, cannot stay at Provins——"

"Oh! he will be president of the courts here some day," said the builder.

"And what do you think is to become of Monsieur Tiphaine then?"

"Monsieur Tiphaine! He has a pretty wife; I am not uneasy about him. Monsieur Tiphaine will go to Paris."

"Shall we paint the corridor?"

"Yes; the Lesourds will, at any rate, see that we are as good as they are," said Rogron.

The first year of their residence in Provins was wholly given up to these discussions, to the pleasure of seeing the workmen busy, to the surprises and information of all kinds that they got by it, and to the attempts made by the brother and sister to scrape acquaintance with the most important families in the town.

The Rogrons had never had any kind of society; they had never gone out of their store; they knew literally no one in Paris, and they thirsted for the pleasures of visiting. On their return they found first Monsieur and Madame Julliard, of the *Ver chinois*, with their children and grandchildren; then the Guépin family, or, to be exact, the Guépin clan; the grandson still kept the shop of the *Trois Quenouilles;* and, finally, Madame Guénée, who had sold them the business of the *Sœur de famille;* her three daughters were married in Provins. These three great tribes—the Julliards, the Guépins, and the Guénées—spread over the town like couch-grass on a lawn. Monsieur Garceland, the mayor, was Monsieur Guépin's son-in-law. The curé, Monsieur l'Abbé Péroux, was own brother to Madame Julliard, who was a Péroux. The president of the court, Monsieur Tiphaine, was brother to Madame Guénée, who signed herself "*née* Tiphaine."

The queen of the town was Madame Tiphaine, *junior*, the handsome only daughter of Madame Roguin, who was the wealthy wife of a notary of Paris; but he was never mentioned. Delicate, pretty, and clever, married to a provincial husband by the express management of her mother, who would not have her with her, and had taken her from school only a few days before her marriage, Mélanie felt herself an exile at Provins, where she behaved admirably well. She was already rich, and had great expectations. As to Monsieur Tiphaine, his old father had advanced his eldest daughter, Madame Guénée, so much money on account of her share of the property, that an estate worth eight thousand francs a year, at about five leagues from Provins, would fall to the president. Thus the Tiphaines, who had married on twenty thousand francs a year, exclusive of the president's salary and residence, expected some day to have twenty thousand francs a year more. They were not out of luck, people said.

Madame Tiphaine's great and only object in life was to secure her husband's election as deputy. Once in Paris, the deputy would be made judge, and from the lower court she promised herself he should soon be promoted to the high court of justice. Hence she humored everybody's vanity, and strove to please; more difficult still, she succeeded. The young woman of two-and-twenty received twice a week, in her handsome house in the old town, all the citizen class of Provins. She had not yet taken a single awkward step on the slippery ground where she stood. She gratified every conceit, patted every hobby; grave with serious folks and a girl with girls, of all things a mother with the mothers, cheerful with the young wives, eager to oblige, polite to all; in short, a pearl, a gem, the pride of Provins. She had not yet said the word, but all the electors of the town awaited the day when their dear president should be old enough to nominate him at once. Every voter, sure of his talents, made him his man and his patron. Oh, yes, Monsieur Tiphaine would get on; he would be keeper of the seals, and he would promote the interests of Provins.

These were the means by which Madame Tiphaine had been so fortunate as to obtain her ascendency over the little town of Provins. Madame Guénée, Monsieur Tiphaine's sister, after seeing her three daughters married—the eldest to Monsieur Lesourd the public prosecutor, the second to Monsieur Martener the doctor, and the third to Monsieur Auffray the notary—had herself married again Monsieur Galardon, the collector of taxes. Mesdames Lesourd, Martener, and Auffray, and their mother Madame Galardon, regarded the president as the wealthiest and cleverest man in the family. The public prosecutor, Monsieur Tiphaine's nephew by marriage, had the greatest interest in getting his uncle to Paris, so as to be made president himself. Hence these four ladies —for Madame Galardon adored her brother—formed a little court about Madame Tiphaine, taking her opinion and advice on every subject.

Then Monsieur Julliard's eldest son, married to the only daughter of a rich farmer, was taken with a sudden passion, a *grande passion*, secret and disinterested, for the president's wife—that angel dropped from the sky of Paris. Mélanie, very wily, incapable of burdening herself with a Julliard, but perfectly capable of keeping him as an Amadis and making use of his folly, advised him to start a newspaper to which she was the Egeria. So for two years now Julliard, animated by his romantic passion, had managed a paper and run a diligence for Provins. The newspaper, entitled *La Ruche* (The Beehive), included literary, archæological, and medical papers concocted in the family. The advertisements of the district paid the expenses; the subscriptions—about two hundred—were all profit. Melancholy verses sometimes appeared in it, unintelligible to the country people, and addressed "To Her ! ! !" with the three points of exclamation. Thus the young Julliard couple, singing the merits of Madame Tiphaine, had allied the clan Julliard to that of the Guénées. Thenceforward the president's drawing-room, of course, led the society of the town. The very few aristocrats who lived at Provins met in a single house in the old town, that of the old Comtesse de Bréautey.

During the first six months after their transplanting, the Rogrons, by favor of their old-time connection with the Julliards, the Guépins, and the Guénées, and by emphasizing their relationship to Monsieur Auffray the notary—a great grand-nephew of their grandfather—were received at first by

Madame Julliard the elder and Madame Galardon ; then, not
without difficulty, they found admission to the beautiful
Madame Tiphaine's drawing-room. Everybody wished to
know something about the Rogrons before inviting them
to call. It was a little difficult to avoid receiving tradespeople of the Rue Saint-Denis, natives of Provins, who had
come back to spend their money there. Nevertheless, the
instinct of society is always to bring together persons of
similar fortune, education, manners, acquaintance, and character.

Now the Guépins, the Guénées, and the Julliards were
of a higher grade and of older family than the Rogrons
—the children of a money-lending innkeeper who could not
be held blameless in his private life, nor with regard to the
Auffray inheritance. Auffray the notary, Madame Galardon's
son-in-law, knew all about it ; the estate had been wound up
in his predecessor's office. Those older merchants, who had
retired twelve years since, had found themselves on the level
of education, breeding, and manners of the circle to which
Madame Tiphaine imparted a certain stamp of elegance, of
Paris varnish. Everything was homogeneous ; they all understood each other, and knew how to conduct themselves, and
talk so as to be agreeable to the rest. They knew each other's
characters, and were accustomed to agree. Having been once
received by Monsieur Garceland the mayor, the Rogrons flattered themselves that they should soon be on intimate terms
with the best society of the town. Sylvie learned to play
boston. Rogron, far too stupid to play any game, twirled his
thumbs and swallowed his words when once he had talked
about his house. But the words acted like medicine ; they
seemed to torture him cruelly ; he rose, he looked as if he
were about to speak ; he took fright and sat down again, his
lips comically convulsed. Sylvie unconsciously displayed
her nature at games. Fractious and complaining whenever
she lost, insolently triumphant when she won, contentious

and fretful, she irritated her adversaries and her partners, and was a nuisance to everybody.

Eaten up with silly and undisguised envy, Rogron and his sister tried to play a part in a town where a dozen families had formed a net of close meshes; all their interests, all their vanities made, as it were, a slippery floor on which newcomers had to tread very cautiously to avoid running up against something or getting a fall. Allowing that the rebuilding of their house might cost thirty thousand francs, the brother and sister between them would still have ten thousand francs a year. They fancied themselves very rich, bored their acquaintance to death with their talk of future splendor, and so gave the measure of their meanness, their crass ignorance, and their idiotic jealousy. The evening they were introduced to Madame Tiphaine the beauty — who had already watched them at Madame Garceland's, at her sister-in-law's, Madame Galardon's, and at the elder Madame Julliard's—the queen of Provins said in a confidential tone to Julliard, *junior*, who remained alone with her and the president a few minutes after every one was gone—

"You all seem to be much smitten with these Rogrons?"

"I!" said the Amadis of Provins; "they bore my mother; they overpower my wife; and when Mademoiselle Sylvie was sent, thirty years ago, as an apprentice to my father, even then he could not endure her."

"But I have a very great mind," said the pretty lady, putting a little foot on the bar of the fender, "to give them to understand that my drawing-room is not an inn-parlor."

Julliard cast up his eyes to the ceiling as much as to say—

"Dear heaven, what wit, what subtlety!"

"I wish my company to be select, and if I admit the Rogrons it will certainly not be that."

"They have no heart, no brain, no manners," said the president. "When after having sold thread for twenty years, as my sister did, for instance——"

"My dear, your sister would not be out of place in any drawing-room," said Madame Tiphaine, in a parenthesis.

"If people are so stupid as to remain haberdashers to the end," the president went on; "if they do not cast their skin; if they think that 'Comtes de Champagne' means 'accounts for wine,' as the Rogrons did this evening, they should stay at home."

"They are noisome!" said Julliard. "You might think there was only one house in Provins. They want to crush us, and, after all, they have hardly enough to live on."

"If it were only the brother," said Madame Tiphaine, "we might put up with him. He is not offensive. Give him a Chinese puzzle, and he would sit quietly in a corner. It would take him the whole winter to put up one pattern. But Mademoiselle Sylvie! What a voice—like a hyena with a cold! What lobster's claws! Do not repeat anything of this Julliard."

When Julliard was gone, the little lady said to her husband—

"My dear, there are enough of the natives that I am obliged to receive; these two more will be the death of me; and with your permission, we will deprive ourselves of the pleasure."

"You are the mistress in your own house," said the president, "but we shall make many enemies. The Rogrons will join the Opposition, which hitherto has had no solidity in Provins. That Rogron is already hanging on to Baron Gouraud and Vinet the lawyer."

"Heh!" said Mélanie, with a smile, "they will do you service then. Where there are no enemies, there is no triumph. A Liberal conspiracy, an illegal society, a fight of some kind, would bring you into the foreground."

The president looked at his young wife with a sort of alarmed admiration.

Next day every one at Madame Garceland's said in every one else's ear that the Rogrons had not had a success at

Madame Tiphaine's, and her remark about the inn-parlor was
much applauded.   Madame Tiphaine took a month before returning Mademoiselle Sylvie's visit.   This rudeness is much
remarked on in the country.   Then, at Madame Tiphaine's
when playing boston with the elder Madame Julliard, Sylvie
made a most unpleasant scene about a splendid *misère* hand,
on which her erewhile mistress caused her to lose—maliciously
and on purpose, she declared.   Sylvie, who loved to play
nasty tricks on others, could never accept a return in kind.
Madame Tiphaine, therefore, set the example of making up
the card-parties before the Rogrons arrived, so that Sylvie was
reduced to wandering from table to table, watching others
play, while they looked askance at her with meaning glances.
At old Madame Julliard's whist was now the game, and Sylvie
could not play it.   The old maid at last understood that she
was an outlaw, but without understanding the reason.   She
believed herself to be an object of jealousy to everybody.

Ere long the Rogrons were asked nowhere; but they persistently spent their evenings at various houses.   Clever people
made game of them, without venom, quite mildly, leading
them to talk utter nonsense about the *ovolos* in their house,
and about a certain cellaret for liqueurs, matchless in Provins.
Meanwhile they gave themselves the final blow.   Of course,
they gave a few sumptuous dinners, as much in return for the
civilities they had received as to show off their splendor.
The guests came solely out of curiosity.   The first dinner was
given to Monsieur and Madame Tiphaine, with whom the
Rogrons had not once dined; to Messieurs and Mesdames
Julliard, father and son, mother and daughter-in-law; to
Monsieur Lesourd, Monsieur the curé, Monsieur and Madame
Galardon.   It was one of those provincial spreads, where the
guests sit at table from five o'clock till nine.   Madame
Tiphaine had introduced the grand Paris style to Provins, the
well-bred guests going away as soon as coffee had been served.
She had some friends that evening at home, and tried to steal

away, but the Rogrons escorted the couple to the very street; and when they returned, bewildered at having failed to keep the president and his wife, the other guests explained Madame Tiphaine's good taste, and imitated it with a promptitude that was cruel in a country-town.

"They will not see our drawing-room lighted up!" cried Sylvie, "and candle-light is like rouge to it."

The Rogrons had hoped to give their guests a surprise. No one hitherto had been admitted to see this much-talked-of house. And all the frequenters of Madame Tiphaine's drawing-room impatiently awaited her verdict as to the marvels of the "*Palais* Rogron."

"Well," said little Madame Martener, "you have seen the Louvre? Tell us all about it."

"But all—like the dinner—will not amount to much."

"What is it like?"

"Well, the front door, of which we were, of course, required to admire the gilt-iron window-frames that you all know, opens into a long passage through the house, dividing it unequally, since there is but one window to the street on the right, and two on the left. At the garden end this passage has a glass door to steps leading down to the lawn, a lawn with a decorative pedestal supporting a plaster cast of the Spartacus, painted to imitate bronze. Behind the kitchen the architect has contrived a little pantry under the staircase, which we were not spared seeing. The stair, painted throughout like yellow-veined marble, is a hollow spiral, just like the stairs that in a café lead from the ground floor to the entresol. This trumpery structure of walnut-wood, really dangerously light, and with banisters picked out with brass, was displayed to us as one of the seven new wonders of the world. The way to the cellars is beneath.

"On the other side of the passage, looking on the street, is the dining-room, opening by folding doors into the drawing-room, of the same size, but looking on to the garden."

" So there is no hall?" said Madame Auffray.

"The hall, no doubt, is the long passage where you stand in a draught," replied Madame Tiphaine. " We have had the eminently national, liberal, constitutional, and patriotic notion," she went on, " of making use only of wood grown in France ! In the dining-room, the floor, laid in a neat pattern, is of walnut-wood. The sideboards, table, and chairs are also in walnut. The window-curtains are of white cotton with red borders, looped back with vulgar ropes over enormous pegs with elaborate dull-gilt rosettes, the mushroom-like object standing out against a reddish paper. These magnificent curtains run on rods ending in huge scrolls, and are held up by lions' claws in stamped brass, one at the top of each pleat.

" Over one of the sideboards is a regular café clock, draped, as it were, with a sort of napkin in bronze gilt, an idea that quite enchants the Rogrons. They tried to make me admire this device ; and I could find nothing better to say than that if it could ever be proper to hang a napkin round a clock face, it was, no doubt, in a dining-room. On this sideboard are two large lamps, like those which grace the counters of grand restaurants. Over the other is a highly decorative barometer, which seems to play an important part in their existence ; Rogron gazes at it as he might gaze at his bride-elect. Between the windows the builder has placed a white earthenware stove in a hideously ornate niche. The walls blaze with a splendid paper in red and gold, such as you will see in these same restaurants, and Rogron chose it there no doubt on the spot.

" Dinner was served in a set of white-and-gold china ; the dessert service is bright blue with green sprigs ; but they opened the china closet to show us that they had another service of stoneware for every-day use. The linen is in large cupboards facing the sideboards. Everything is varnished, shining, new, and harsh in color. Still, I could accept the dining-room; it has a character of its own which, though not pleasing, is fairly representative of that of the owners; but there is no enduring the five engravings—those black-and-white things against which the minister of the interior ought really to get a decree; they represent Poniatowski leaping into the Elster; the Defense of the Barrière de Clichy, Napoleon himself pointing a gun; and two prints of Mazeppa, all in gilt frames of a vulgar pattern suitable to the prints, which are enough to make one loathe popularity. Oh! how much I prefer Madame Julliard's pastels representing fruits, those capital pastels which were done in the time of Louis XV., and which harmonize with the nice old dining-room and its dark, rather worm-eaten panels, which are at least characteristic of the country, and suit the heavy family silver, the antique china, and all our habits. The country is provincial; it becomes ridiculous when it tries to ape Paris. You may perhaps retort, '*Vous êtes orfèvre, Monsieur Josse!*'—'You are to the manner born.' But I prefer this old room of my father-in-law Tiphaine's, with its heavy curtains of green-and-white damask, its Louis XV. chimney-piece, its scroll pattern pier glass, its old beaded mirrors and time-honored card-tables; my jars of old Sèvres, old blue, mounted in old gilding; my clock with its impossible flowers, my out-of-date chandelier, and my tapestried furniture, to all the splendor of their drawing-room."

"What is it like?" said Monsieur Martener, delighted with the praise of the country so ingeniously brought in by the pretty Parisienne.

"The drawing-room is a fine red—as red as Mademoiselle Sylvie when she is angry at losing a *misère.*"

"Sylvie-red," said the president, and the word took its place in the vocabulary of the district.

"The window-curtains — red! the furniture — red! the chimney-piece—red marble veined with yellow! the candelabra and clock—red marble veined with yellow, and mounted in a heavy vulgar style; Roman lamp-brackets supported on Greek foliage! From the top of the clock a lion stares down on you, stupidly, as the Rogrons stare; a great good-natured lion, the ornamental lion so-called, which will long continue to dethrone real lions; he spends his life clutching a black ball exactly like a deputy of the left. Perhaps it is a constitutional allegory. The dial of this clock is an extraordinary piece of work.

"The chimney glass is framed with appliqué ornaments, which look poor and cheap, though they are a novelty. But the upholsterer's genius shines most in a panel of red stuff of which the radiating folds all centre in a rosette in the middle of the chimney-board—a romantic poem composed expressly for the Rogrons, who display it with ecstasy. From the ceiling hangs a chandelier, carefully wrapped in a green cotton shroud, and with reason; it is in the very worst taste, raw-toned bronze, with even more detestable tendrils of brown gold. Under it a round tea-table of marble, with more yellow than ever in the red, displays a shining metal tray, on which glitter cups of painted china—such painting!—arranged round a cut-glass sugar-basin, so bold in style that our grandchildren will open their eyes in amazement at the gilt rings round the edge and the diamond pattern on the sides, like a mediæval quilted doublet, and at the tongs for taking the sugar, which probably no one will ever use.

"This room is papered with red flock-paper imitating velvet, divided into panels by a beading of gilt brass, finished at the corners with enormous palms. A chromo-lithograph hangs on each panel, framed most elaborately in plaster casting of garlands to imitate fine wood-carving. The furniture of elm-root, upholstered with satin-cloth, classically consists of two sofas, two large easy-chairs, six armchairs, and six light chairs. The console is graced by an alabaster vase, called *à la Medicis*, under a glass shade, and by the much-talked-of liqueur-case. We were told often enough that ' there is not such another in Provins.' In each window bay, hung with splendid red silk curtains and lace curtains besides, stands a card-table. The carpet is Aubusson; the Rogrons have not failed to get hold of the crimson ground with medallions of flowers, the vulgarest of all the common patterns.

"The room looks uninhabited; there are no books or prints—none of the little things that furnish a table," and she looked at her own table covered with fashionable trifles, albums, and the pretty toys that were given her. "There are no flowers, none of the little nothings that fade and are renewed. It is all as cold and dry as Mademoiselle Sylvie. Buffon is right in saying that the style is the man, and certainly drawing-rooms have a style!"

Pretty Madame Tiphaine went on with her description by epigrams; and from this specimen, it is easy to imagine the rooms in which the brother and sister really lived on the first-floor, which they also displayed to their guests. Still, no one could conceive of the foolish expenses into which the cunning builder had dragged the Rogrons; the moulding of the doors, the elaborate inside shutters, the plaster ornaments on the cornices, the fancy painting, the brass-gilt knobs and bells, the ingenious smoke-consuming fireplaces, the contrivance for the prevention of damp, the sham inlaid wood on the staircase, the elaborate glass and smith's work—in short, all the fancy-work which adds to the cost of building, and delights the common mind, had been lavished without stint.

No one would go to the Rogrons' evenings; their pretensions were still-born. There were abundant reasons for refusing; every day was taken up by Madame Garceland, Madame Galardon, the two Julliard ladies, Madame Tiphaine, the sous-préfet, etc. The Rogrons thought that giving dinners was all that was needed to get into society; they secured some young people who laughed at them, and some diners-out, such as are to be found in every part of the world; but serious people quite gave them up. Sylvie, alarmed at the clear loss of forty thousand francs swallowed up without any return in the house she called her dear house, wanted to recover the sum by economy. So she soon ceased to give dinners that cost from thirty to forty francs, without the wine, as they failed to realize her hope of forming a circle—a thing as difficult to create in the country as it is in Paris. Sylvie dismissed her cook, and hired a country girl for the coarser work. She herself cooked " to amuse herself."

Thus, fourteen months after their return home, the brother and sister had drifted into a life of isolation and idleness. Her banishment from "the world" had roused in Sylvie's soul an intense hatred of the Tiphaines, Julliards, Auffrays, and Garcelands—in short, of everybody in Provins society, which she stigmatized as a "clique," with which she was on the most distant terms. She would gladly have set up a rival circle ; but the second-rate citizen class was composed entirely of small trades-people, never free but on Sundays and holidays ; or of persons in ill-odor, like Vinet the lawyer and Doctor Néraud ; or of rank Bonapartists, like General Gouraud ; and Rogron very rashly made friends with these, though the upper set had vainly warned him against them. The brother and sister were obliged to sit together by the fire of their dining-room stove, talking over their business, the faces of their customers, and other equally amusing matters.

The second winter did not come to an end without their being almost crushed by its weight of dullness. They had the greatest difficulty in spending the hours of their day. As they went to bed at night, they thought, "One more over !" They spun out the morning by getting up late and dressing slowly. Rogron shaved himself every morning ; he examined his face and described to his sister the changes he fancied he noted in it ; he squabbled with the maid over the temperature of the hot water ; he wandered into the garden to see if the flowers were sprouting ; he ventured down to the river-bank, where

he had built a summer-house; he examined the woodwork of
the house. Had it warped? Had the settling split any of
the panels? Was the paint wearing well? Then he came in
to discuss his anxieties as to a sick hen, or some spot where
the damp had left stains, talking to his sister, who affected
hurry in laying the table while she scolded the maid. The
barometer was the most useful article in the house to Rogron;
he consulted it for no reason, tapped it familiarly like a friend,
and then said, "Vile weather!" to which his sister would
reply, "Pooh, the weather is quite seasonable." If anybody
called, he would boast of the excellence of this instrument.

Their breakfast took up some little time. How slowly did
these two beings masticate each mouthful. And their digestion was perfect: they had no cause to fear catarrh of the
stomach. By reading the *Ruche* and the *Constitutionnel* they
got on to noon. They paid a third of the subscription to
the Paris paper with Vinet and Colonel Gouraud. Rogron
himself carried the paper to the colonel, who lived in the
square, lodging with Monsieur Martener; the soldier's long
stories were an immense delight to him. Rogron could only
wonder why the colonel was considered dangerous. He was
such an idiot as to speak to him of the ostracism under which
he lived, and retail the sayings of the "clique." God only
knows what the colonel—who feared no one, and was as re-
doubtable with the pistol as with the sword—had to say of
"la Tiphaine" and "her Julliard," of the ministerial officials of the upper town—"men brought over by foreigners,
capable of anything to stick in their places, cooking the lists
of votes at the elections to suit themselves," and the like.

At about two o'clock Rogron sallied forth for a little walk.
He was quite happy when a storekeeper, standing at his door,
stopped him with a "How d'ye do, Père Rogron?" He
gossiped, and asked, "What news in the town?" heard and
repeated scandal, or the tittle-tattle of Provins. He walked
to the upper town, or in the sunk roads, according to the

weather.   Sometimes he met other old men airing themselves
in like manner.   Such meetings were happy events in the
course of such a retired life.

There were at Provins certain men who were out of conceit
with the life of Paris, learned and modest men, living with
their books.   Imagine Rogron's frame of mind when he listened to a supernumerary judge named Desfondrilles, more of an
archæologist than a lawyer, saying to a man of education, old
Monsieur Martener, the doctor's father, as he pointed to the
valley—

"Will you tell me why the idlers of all Europe flock to
Spa rather than to Provins, when the waters of Provins are
acknowledged to be superior by the whole French faculty of
medicine, and to have effects and an energy worthy of the
medicinal properties of our roses?"

"What do you expect?" replied the man of the world,
"it is one of the caprices of caprice, and just as inexplicable.
The wines of Bordeaux were unknown a hundred years ago.
Maréchal Richelieu, one of the grandest figures of the last
century, the Alcibiades of France, was made governor of
Guyenne.   His chest was delicate—the world knew why—
the wine of the country strengthened and restored him to
health.   Bordeaux at once made a hundred millions of francs
a year, and the Marshal extended the Bordeaux district as
far as Angoulême and as far as Cahors; in short, to forty
leagues in every direction!   Who knows where the vineyards
of Bordeaux end?   And there is no equestrian statue of the
Marshal at Bordeaux!"

"Ah! if such an event should take place at Provins in this
century or the next," Monsieur Desfondrilles went on, "I hope
that either on the little square in the lower town, or on the
castle, or somewhere in the upper town, some bas-relief would
be seen representing the head of Monsieur Opoix, the redis-
coverer of the mineral waters of Provins!"

"But, my dear sir, it would perhaps be impossible to rehabilitate Provins," said old Monsieur Martener. "The town is bankrupt."

At this Rogron opened his eyes wide, and exclaimed—"What!"

"Provins was formerly a capital which, in the twelfth century, held its own as a rival to Paris, when the counts of Champagne held their court here as King René held his in Provence," replied the man of learning. "In those days civilization, pleasure, poetry, elegance, women—in short, all the splendor of social life was not exclusively restricted to Paris. Towns find it as hard as houses of business to rise again from ruin. Nothing is left to Provins but the fragrance of its historic past and that of its roses—and a sous-préfecture."

"Oh! to think what France might be if she still had all her feudal capitals!" said Desfondrilles. "Can our sous-préfets fill the place of the poetic, gallant, and warlike race of Thibault, who made Provins what Ferrara was in Italy, what Weimar was in Germany, and Munich would like to be in our day?"

"Provins was a capital?" asked Rogron.

"Why, where have you dropped from?" said Desfondrilles the archæologist.

The lawyer struck the pavement of the upper town where they were standing with his stick: "Do you not know," he cried, "that all this part of Provins is built on crypts?"

"Crypts?"

"Yes, to be sure, crypts of unaccountable loftiness and extent. They are like cathedral aisles, full of pillars."

"Monsieur Desfondrilles is writing a great antiquarian work in which he intends to describe these singular structures," said old Martener, seeing the lawyer mount his hobby.

Rogron came home enchanted to think that his house stood in this valley. The crypts of Provins kept him occupied for

five or six days in exploring them, and for several evenings
afforded a subject of conversation to the old couple. Thus
Rogron generally picked up something about old Provins,
about the intermarriages of the families, or some stale political
news which he retailed to his sister. And a hundred times
over in the course of his walk—several times even of the
same person—he would ask, " Well, what is the news ? What
has happened lately ? " When he came in he threw himself
on a sofa in the drawing-room as if he were tired out, but
really he was only weary of his own weight.

He got on to dinner-time by going twenty times to and fro
between the drawing-room and the kitchen, looking at the
clock, opening and shutting doors. So long as the brother
and sister spent the evenings in other houses they got through
the hours till bedtime, but after they were reduced to staying
at home the evening was a desert to traverse. Sometimes
people on their way home, after spending the evening out, as
they crossed the little plazza, heard sounds in the Rogrons'
house as if the brother were murdering the sister ; they recognized them as the terrific yawns of a haberdasher driven to
bay. The two machines had nothing to grind with their
rusty wheels, so they creaked.

The brother talked of marrying, but with a sense of despair.
He felt himself old and worn ; a wife terrified him. Sylvie,
who understood the need for a third person in the house,
then remembered their poor cousin, for whom no one in
Provins had ever inquired, for everybody supposed that little
Madame Lorrain and her daughter were both dead. Sylvie
Rogron never lost anything ; she was too thoroughly an old
maid to mislay anything, whatever it might be. She affected
to have found the letter from the Lorrains so as to make it
natural that she should mention Pierrette to her brother, and
he was almost happy at the possibility of having a little girl
about the house. Sylvie wrote to the old Lorrains in a half-
business-like, half-affectionate tone, attributing the delay in

her answer to the winding up of their affairs, to their move back to Provins, and settling there. She affected to be anxious to have her little cousin with her, allowing it to be understood that if Monsieur Rogron should not marry, Pierrette would some day inherit twelve thousand francs a year. It would be needful to have been, like Nebuchadnezzar, to some extent a wild beast, shut up in a cage in a beast-garden with nothing to prey on but butcher's meat brought in by the keeper, or else a retired tradesman with no shop-clerks to nag, to imagine the impatience with which the brother and sister awaited their cousin Lorrain. Three days after the despatch of the letter they were already wondering when the child would arrive.

Sylvie discerned in her so-called generosity to her penniless cousin a means of changing the views of Provins society with regard to herself. She called on Madame Tiphaine, who had stricken them with her disapproval, and who aimed at creating an upper class at Provins, like that at Geneva, and blew the trumpet to announce the advent of her cousin Pierrette, the child of Colonel Lorrain, pitying her woes, and congratulating herself as a lucky woman on having a pretty young heiress to introduce in society.

"You have been a long time discovering her," remarked Madame Tiphaine, who sat enthroned on a sofa by her fireside.

Madame Garceland, in a few words spoken in an undertone during a deal, revived the story of the Auffray property. The notary related the innkeeper's iniquities.

"Where is the poor little thing?" asked the president politely.

"In Brittany," said Rogron.

"But Brittany is a wide word!" remarked Monsieur Lesourd, the public prosecutor.

"Her grandfather and grandmother wrote to us. When was it, my dear?" asked Rogron.

Sylvie, absorbed in asking Madame Garceland where she had bought the stuff for her dress, did not foresee the effect of her answer, and said, "Before we sold our business."

"And you answered three days ago, Mademoiselle Sylvie?" exclaimed the notary.

Sylvie turned as red as the hottest coals in the fire.

"We wrote to the Institution of Saint-Jacques," replied Rogron.

"There is a sort of asylum there for old people," said a lawyer, who had been supernumerary judge at Nantes. "But she cannot be there, for they only take in persons who are past sixty."

"She is there with her grandmother Lorrain," said Rogron.

"She had a little money, the eight thousand francs left her by your father—no, I mean your grandfather," said the notary, blundering intentionally.

"Indeed!" said Rogron, looking stupid, and not understanding this sarcasm.

"Then you knew nothing of your first cousin's fortune or position?" asked the president.

"If Monsieur Rogron had known it, he would not have left her in a place which is no more than a respectable workhouse," said the judge severely. "I remember now that a house belonging to Monsieur and Madame Lorrain was sold at Nantes under an execution; and Mademoiselle Lorrain lost her claims, for I was the commissioner in charge."

The notary spoke of Colonel Lorrain, who, if he were alive, would indeed be astonished to think of his child being in an institution like that of Saint-Jacques. The Rogrons presently withdrew, thinking the world very spiteful. Sylvie perceived that her news had had no success; she had ruined herself in everybody's opinion; henceforth she had no hope of making her way in the higher society of Provins.

From that day the Rogrons no longer dissembled their hatred of the great citizen-families of Provins, and of all their adherents. The brother now repeated all the Liberal fables which Lawyer Vinet and Colonel Gouraud had crammed him with about the Tiphaines, the Guénées, the Garcelands, the Guépins, and the Julliards.

"I tell you what, Sylvie, I don't see why Madame Tiphaine should turn a cold shoulder on the Rue Saint-Denis : the best of her beauty was made there. Madame Roguin, her mother, is a cousin of the Guillaumes of the *Cat and Racket*, who gave over their business to their son-in-law Joseph Lebas. Her father is that notary, that Roguin, who failed in 1819, and ruined the Birotteaus. So Madame Tiphaine's money is stolen wealth ; for what is a notary's wife who takes her own settlement out of the fire and allows her husband to become a fraudulent bankrupt ? A pretty thing indeed ! Ah ! I understand ! She got her daughter married to live here at Provins through her connection with the banker du Tillet. And these people are proud ! Well ! However, that is what the world is ! "

On the day when Denis Rogron and his sister Sylvie thus broke out in abuse of the clique, they had without knowing it become persons of importance, and were on the high-road to having some society ; their drawing-room was on the point of becoming a centre of interests which only needed a stage. The retired haberdasher assumed historical and political dignity, for, still without knowing it, he gave strength and unity to the hitherto unstable elements of the Liberal party at Provins. And this was the way of it : The early career of the Rogrons had been anxiously observed by Colonel Gouraud and the advocate Vinet, who had been thrown together by their isolation and their agreement of ideas. These two men professed equal patriotism, and for the same reasons they wanted to acquire importance. But though they were anxious to be leaders, they lacked followers. The Liberals of Provins comprised an old soldier who sold lemonade ; an innkeeper ; Monsieur Cournant, a notary, Monsieur Auffray's rival ; Monsieur Néraud, a physician, Doctor Martener's rival ; and some independent persons, farmers scattered about the neighborhood, and holders of national stock.   The colonel and the lawyer, glad to attract an idiot whose money might help them in their manœuvres, who would support their subscriptions, who, in some cases, would take the bull by the horns, and whose house would be useful as a town-hall for the party, took advantage of the Rogrons' hostility towards the aristocrats of the place.   The colonel, the lawyer, and Rogron had a slight bond in their joint subscription to the *Constitutionnel;* it would not be difficult for the colonel to make a Liberal of the ex-haberdasher, though Rogron knew so little of political history that he had not heard of the exploits of Sergeant Mercier ; he thought he was a friend and brother.

The impending arrival of Pierrette hastened the hatching of certain covetous dreams to which the ignorance and folly of the old bachelor and old maid had given rise.   The colonel, seeing that Sylvie had lost all chance of getting her foot into the circle of the Tiphaines, had an idea.   Old soldiers have seen so many horrors in so many lands, so many naked corpses grimacing hideously on so many battlefields, that an ugly face has no terror for them, so the colonel took steady aim at the old maid's fortune.   This officer, a short, fat man, wore rings in his ears, which were already graced by bushy tufts of hair.   His floating gray whiskers were such as in 1799 had been called "fins."   His large, good-natured, red face was somewhat frost-bitten, as were those of all who escaped at the Beresina.   His huge, prominent stomach had the flattened angle below, characteristic of an old cavalry officer; Gouraud had commanded the second regiment of Hussars.   His gray mustache covered a huge mouth—a perfect trap—the only word to describe that abyss ; he did not eat, he devoured !   A sword-cut had shortened his nose.   His speech was in consequence thick and deeply nasal, like that ascribed to Capuchin friars.   His hands, which were small,

short, and broad, were such as make a woman say, " You
have the hands of a thorough scamp." His legs, below such
a huge body, looked frail. Within this active but clumsy
body lay a cunning spirit, entire experience of life and things,
hidden under the apparent carelessness of a soldier, and utter
contempt for the conventionalities of society. Colonel Gouraud had the pension of the cross of the Legion of Honor,
and two thousand four hundred francs a year as half-pay—a
thousand crowns a year in all for his whole income.

The lawyer, tall and lean, had no talent but his political
opinions, and no income but the meagre profits of his business. At Provins attorneys plead their own cases. In view of
his opinions, the court listened with small favor to Maître
Vinet ; and the most Liberal farmers, when entangled in lawsuits, would rely on an attorney in favor with the bench
rather than employ Vinet. This man was said to have led
astray a rich girl living near Coulommiers, and to have compelled her parents to let her marry him. His wife was one
of the Chargebœufs, an old family of nobles in La Brie, who
took their name from the exploit of a squire in Saint Louis'
expedition to Egypt. She had incurred her parents' displeasure, and they, to Vinet's knowledge, had arranged to leave
their whole fortune to their eldest son, charged, no doubt,
with a reversion in favor of his sister's children. Thus this
man's first ambitious scheme came to nothing. The lawyer,
soon haunted by poverty, and ashamed of not having enough
to enable his wife to keep up appearances, had made vain
efforts to get his foot into a ministerial career ; but the rich
branch of the Chargebœufs refused to assist him. These
Royalists were strictly moral, and disapproved of a compul-
sory marriage ; besides, their would-be relation's name was
Vinet ; how could they favor any one so common ? So the
lawyer was handed on from one branch to another when he
tried to utilize his wife's interest with her relations. Madame
Vinet found no assistance but from one of the family, a

4

widowed Madame Chargebœuf, with a daughter, quite poor, who lived at Troyes. And a day came when Vinet remembered the kind reception his wife met with from this lady.

Rejected by the whole world, full of hatred of his wife's family, of the government which refused him an appointment, and of the society of Provins, which would have nothing to say to him, Vinet accepted his poverty. His venom fermented and gave him energy to endure. He became a Liberal on perceiving that his fortune was bound up with the triumph of the Opposition, and vegetated in a wretched little house in the upper town, which his wife seldom quitted. This girl, born to a better fate, lived absolutely alone in her home with her one child. There are cases of poverty nobly met and cheerfully endured; but Vinet, eaten up by ambition, and feeling that he had wronged a young creature, cherished a dark indignation; his conscience expanded to admit every means to success. His face, still young, changed for the worse. People were sometimes terrified in court at the sight of his flat viperine head, with its wide mouth, and eyes that glittered through his spectacles; at hearing his sharp, shrill, rasping voice, that wrung their nerves. His muddy complexion, patchy with sickly hues of yellow and green, revealed his suppressed ambitions, his perpetual mortifications and hidden penury. He could argue and harangue; he had no lack of point and imagery; he was learned and crafty. Accustomed to indulge his imagination for the sake of rising by hook or by crook, he might have made a politician. A man who hesitates at nothing so long as it is legal is a strong man, and in this lay Vinet's strength.

This coming athlete of parliamentary debate—one of the men who were to proclaim the supremacy of the House of Orleans—had a disastrous influence over Pierrette's fate. At present he wanted to provide himself with a weapon by founding a newspaper at Provins. After having studied the Rogrons from afar, with the assistance of the colonel, he ended by reckoning on the brother. And this time he reckoned with his host; his poverty was to come to an end after seven dolorous years, during which more than one day had come round without bread. On the day when Gouraud announced to Vinet, on the little square, that the Rogrons had broken with the citizen aristocracy and official circles of the old town, the lawyer nudged him significantly in the ribs.

"This wife or that, ugly or handsome, it must be all the same to you," said he. "You should marry Mademoiselle Rogron, and then we could get something done here——"

"I was thinking of it. But they have sent for the daughter of poor Colonel Lorrain—their heiress," said Gouraud.

"You could make them leave you their money by will. You would have a very nicely fitted house."

"And the child, after all! Well, we shall see," said the colonel, with a jocose and deeply villainous leer, which showed a man of Vinet's temper how small a thing a little girl was in the eyes of this old soldier.

Since her grandparents had gone into the asylum where they were forlornly ending their days, Pierrette, young and full of pride, was so dreadfully miserable at living there on charity, that she was happy to learn that she had some rich connections. On hearing that she was leaving, Brigaut, the major's son, the companion of her childhood, who was now a joiner's apprentice at Nantes, came to give her the money needful for her journey by coach—sixty francs, all the savings of his odd earnings painfully hoarded; Pierrette accepted it with the sublime indifference of true friendship, showing that she in similar circumstances would have been hurt by thanks. Brigaut had gone every Sunday to Saint-Jacques to play with Pierrette, and to comfort her. The sturdy young workman had already gone through his delightful apprenticeship to the perfect and devoted care that we give to the object of our involuntary choice and affection. More than once ere now,

Pierrette and he, on a Sunday, sitting in a corner of the garden, had sketched their childish dreams on the veil of the future; the young craftsman, mounted on his plane, traveled round the world, making a fortune for Pierrette, who waited for him.

So, in the month of October, 1824, when Pierrette had almost completed her eleventh year, she was placed in the care of the guard of the diligence from Nantes to Paris by the two old people and the young apprentice, all three dreadfully sad. The guard was requested to put her into the coach for Provins, and to take great care of her. Poor Brigaut! he ran after the diligence like a dog, looking at his dear Pierrette as long as he could. In spite of the child's signals, he ran on for a league beyond the town, and when he was exhausted his eyes sent a last tearful glance at Pierrette, who cried when she could see him no more. Pierrette put her head out of the window, and discerned her friend standing squarely and watching the heavy vehicle that left him behind.

The Lorrains and Brigaut had so little knowledge of life that the little Bretonne had not a sou left when she arrived in Paris. The guard, to whom the child prattled of rich relations, paid her expenses at an inn in Paris, made the guard of the Troyes coach repay him, and desired him to deliver Pierrette to her family and collect the debt, exactly as if she were a parcel by carrier.

Four days after leaving Nantes, at about nine o'clock one Monday evening, a kind, burly old guard of the Messageries Royales took Pierrette by the hand, and, while the coach was unloading in the High Street such passengers and parcels as were to be deposited at Provins, he led her, with no luggage but two frocks, two pairs of stockings, and two shifts, to the house pointed out to him by the office clerk as that of Mademoiselle Rogron.

"Good-morning, mademoiselle, and gents all," said the guard. "I have brought you a cousin of yours, and here she

"*I HAVE BROUGHT YOU A COUSIN OF YOURS, AND HERE SHE BE.*"

be, and a pretty dear, too. You have forty-seven francs to pay. Though your little girl has no weight of baggage, please to sign my way-book."

Mademoiselle Sylvie and her brother gave way to their delight and astonishment.

"Begging your pardon," said the guard, "my coach is waiting—sign my sheet and give me forty-seven francs and sixty centimes, and what you please for me and the guard from Nantes, for we have taken as much care of her as if she were our own. We have paid out for her bed and food, her place in the coach here, and other little things."

"Forty-seven francs and twelve sous?" exclaimed Sylvie.

"You're never going to beat me down?" cried the guard.

"But where is the invoice?" said Rogron.

"The invoice! Here is my way-bill."

"You can talk afterwards, pay now!" said Sylvie to her brother; "you see, you cannot help paying."

Rogron went to fetch forty-seven francs twelve sous.

"And nothing for us—for my pal and me?" said the guard.

Sylvia produced a two-franc piece from the depths of her old velvet bag, where her keys lurked in bunches.

"Thank you—keep it," said the man. "We would rather have looked after the little girl for her own sake." He took up his sheet and went out, saying to the servant-girl: "A nice place this is! There are crocodiles of that sort without going to Egypt for 'em."

"Those people are horribly coarse!" said Sylvie, who had heard his speech.

"Dame! they took care of the child," replied Adèle, with her hands on her hips.

"We are not obliged to live with him," said Rogron.

"Where is she to sleep?" asked the maid.

Such was the reception that met Pierrette Lorrain on her arrival at her cousins' house, while they looked at her with a bewildered air. She was flung on their hands like a parcel, with no transition between the wretched room in which she had lived with her grandparents and her cousins' dining-room, which struck her as palatial. She stood there mute and shy. To any one but these retired haberdashers the little Bretonne would have been adorable in her frock of coarse blue serge, a pink cotton apron, her blue stockings, thick shoes, and white kerchief; her little red hands were covered by ' knitted mittens of red wool edged with white that the guard had bought for her. Her little Brittany cap, which had been washed in Paris—it had gotten tumbled in the course of the journey from Nantes—really looked like a glory round her bright face. This native cap, made of fine cambric, with a stiff lace border ironed into flat pleats, deserves a description, it is so smart and so simple. The light, filtered through the muslin and lace, casts a half-shadow, a twilight softness, on the face; it gives it the virginal grace which painters try to find on their palettes, and which Léopold Robert has succeeded in lending to the Raphael-like face of the woman holding a child in his picture of "The Reapers." Within this setting of broken lights shone an artless rose and white face, beaming with vigorous health. The heat of the room brought the blood to her head, and it suffused the edge of her tiny ears with fire, tinging her lips and the tip of a finely cut nose, while by contrast it made her bright complexion look whiter than before.

"Well, have you nothing to say to us?" said Sylvie. "I am your cousin Sylvie, and that is your cousin Denis."

"Are you hungry?" asked Rogron.

"When did you leave Nantes?" asked Sylvie.

"She is dumb," said Rogron.

"Poor child, she has very few clothes to her back!" observed sturdy Adèle, as she untied the bundle wrapped in a handkerchief belonging to old Lorrain.

"Kiss your cousin," said Sylvie. Pierrette kissed Rogron.

"Yes, kiss your cousin," said Rogron. Pierrette kissed Sylvie.

"She is scared by the journey, poor little thing; perhaps she is sleepy," said Adèle.

Pierrette felt a sudden and invincible aversion for her two relations, a feeling she had never before known. Sylvie and the maid went to put the little girl to bed in the room on the second floor where Brigaut was to see the cotton curtain. There were in this attic a small bed with a pole painted blue, from which hung a cotton curtain, a chest of drawers of walnut-wood, with no marble top, a smaller table of the same wood, a looking-glass, a common bed-table, and three wretched chairs. The walls and sloping roof to the front were covered with a cheap blue paper flowered with black. The floor was painted and waxed, and struck cold to the feet. There was no carpet but a thin bedside rug made of selvages. The chimney-shelf, of cheap marble, was graced with a mirror, two candlesticks of copper gilt, and a vulgar alabaster vase with two pigeons drinking to serve as handles; this Sylvie had had in her room in Paris.

"Shall you be comfortable here, child?" asked Sylvie.

"Oh! it is beautiful?" replied the little girl in her silvery treble.

"She is not hard to please," muttered the sturdy peasant-woman to herself. "I had better warm the bed, I suppose?" she asked.

"Yes," said Sylvie, "the sheets may be damp."

Adèle brought a headkerchief of her own when she came up with the warming-pan; and Pierrette, who had hitherto slept in sheets of coarse Brittany linen, was amazed at the fine, soft cotton sheets. When the little girl was settled and in bed, Adèle, as she went downstairs, could not help exclaiming, "All her things put together are not worth three francs, mademoiselle!"

Since adopting her system of strict economy, Sylvie always

made the servant sit in the dining-room, so as to have but one
lamp and one fire. When Colonel Gouraud and Vinet came,
Adèle withdrew to her kitchen. Pierrette's arrival kept
them talking for the rest of the evening.

"We must get her some clothes to-morrow," said Sylvie.
"She has hardly a stitch."

"She has no shoes but those thick ones she had on, and
they weigh a pound," said Adèle.

"They wear them so in those parts," said Rogron.

"How she looked at the room, which is none too fine
either, for a cousin of yours, mademoiselle!"

"So much the better; hold your tongue. You see she is
delighted with it."

"Lord above us! what shifts! They must rub her skin
raw. But none of these things are of any use," said Adèle,
turning out the contents of Pierrette's bundle.

Till ten o'clock master, mistress, and maid were busy deciding of what stuff and at what price the shifts should be
made, how many pairs of stockings and of what quality, and
how many under-petticoats would be needed, and calculating
the cost of Pierrette's wardrobe.

"You will not get off for less than three hundred francs,"
said Rogron to his sister, as he carried the price of each
article in his head from long practice, and added up the
total from memory.

"Three hundred francs!" exclaimed Sylvie.

"Yes, three hundred; work it out yourself."

The brother and sister began again, and made it three hundred francs without the sewing.

"Three hundred francs at one cast of the net!" cried
Sylvie, who went to bed on the idea so ingeniously expressed
by this proverbial figure of speech.

Pierrette was one of those children of love whom love has
blessed with tenderness, cheerfulness, brightness, generosity,
and devotedness; nothing had as yet chilled or crushed her

heart; it was almost wildly sensitive, and the way she was received by her relations weighed on it painfully. Though Brittany had to her been a home of poverty, it had also been a home of affection. Though the old Lorrains were the most unskillful traders, they were the simplest, most loving, most caressing souls in the world, as all disinterested people are. At Pen-Hoël their little granddaughter had had no teaching but that of nature. Pierrette went as she would in a boat on the pools, she ran about the village or the fields with her companion Jacques Brigaut, exactly like Paul and Virginia. Both the children, spoiled and petted by every one, and as free as the air, ran after the thousand joys of childhood; in summer they went to watch the fishermen, they caught insects, plucked flowers, and gardened; in winter they made slides, built smart snow-palaces and snow-men, or made snowballs to pelt each other They were everywhere welcome; everybody smiled on them.

When it was time that they should learn something, misfortunes came. Jacques, left destitute by his father's death, was apprenticed by his relations to a cabinetmaker, and maintained by charity, as Pierrette was soon after in the asylum of Saint-Jacques. But even in this almshouse, pretty little Pierrette had been made much of, loved, and kindly treated by all. The child, thus accustomed to so much affection, no longer found, in the home of these longed-for and wealthy relations, the look, the tone, the words, the manner which she had hitherto met with in every one, even in the guards of the diligences. Thus her amazement, already great, was complicated by the changed moral atmosphere into which she had been plunged. The heart can turn suddenly cold and hot as the body can. The poor child longed to cry without knowing what for. She was tired, and she fell asleep.

Accustomed to rise very early, like all country-bred children, Pierrette awoke next morning two hours before the cook. She dressed, trotted about her room over her cousin's head, looked out on the little square, and was going downstairs; she was astonished at the splendor of the staircase; she examined every detail—the rosettes, the brass-work, the mouldings, the painting, etc. Then she went down; she could not open the garden door, so she came up again; went down once more when Adèle was about, and sprang into the garden. She took possession of it, ran to the river, was amazed by the summer-house, went into the summer-house; she had enough to see and wonder at in all she saw till her cousin Sylvie was up. During breakfast Sylvie said to her—

"So it was you, little bird, who was trotting up and downstairs at daybreak, and making such a noise? You woke me so completely that I could not get to sleep again. You must be very quiet, very good, and learn to play without making a sound. Your cousin does not like noise?"

"And you must take care about your feet," said Rogron. "You went into the summer-house with muddy shoes, and left your footsteps printed on the floor. Your cousin likes everything to be clean. A great girl like you ought to be cleanly. Were you not taught to be clean in Brittany? To be sure, when I went there to buy flax it was dreadful to see what savages they were! She has a fine appetite at any rate," said Rogron, turning to his sister; "you might think she had not seen food these three days."

And so, from the very first, Pierrette felt hurt by her cousins' remarks, hurt without knowing why. Her frank and upright nature, hitherto left to itself, had never been used to reflect; incapable, therefore, of understanding wherein her cousins were wrong, she was doomed to tardy enlightenment through suffering.

After breakfast, the couple, delighted by Pierrette's astonishment, and eager to enjoy it, showed her their fine drawing-room, to teach her to respect its splendor. Unmarried people, as a result of their isolation, and prompted by the craving for something to interest them, are led to supply the place of natural affections by artificial affections—the love of dogs, cats, or canary birds, or their servant or their spiritual director. Thus Rogron and Sylvie had an immoderate affection for the house and furniture that had cost them so much. Sylvie had taken to helping Adèle every morning, being of opinion that the woman did not know how to wipe furniture, to brush it, and make it look like new. This cleaning was soon her constant occupation. Thus, far from diminishing in value, the furniture was improved. Then the problem was to use it without wearing it out, without staining it, without scratching the wood or chilling the polish. This idea ere long became an old maid's monomania. Sylvie kept in a closet woolen rags, wax, varnish, and brushes; she learned to use them as skillfully as a polisher; she had feather brooms and dusters, and she could rub without fear of hurting herself, she was so strong! Her clear, blue eye, as cold and hard as steel, constantly peered under the furniture, and you were more likely to find a tender chord in her heart than a speck of flue under a chair.

After what had passed at Madame Tiphaine's, Sylvie could not possibly shirk the outlay of three hundred francs. During the first week Sylvie was wholly occupied, and Pierrette constantly amused, by the frocks to be ordered and tried on, the shifts and petticoats to be cut out and made by needle-women working by the day. Pierrette did not know how to sew.

"She has been nicely brought up!" cried Rogron. "Do you know nothing, child?"

Pierrette, who only knew how to love, answered but by a pretty childish shrug.

"What did you do all day long in Brittany?" asked her cousin Rogron.

"I played," she replied guilelessly. "Everybody played with me. Grandmamma and grandpapa—and everybody told me stories. Oh! they were very fond of me."

"Indeed!" replied Rogron, "and so you lived like a lady."

Pierrette did not understand this tradesman's wit. She opened her eyes wide.

"She is as stupid as a wooden stool," said Sylvie to Mademoiselle Borain, the best workwoman in Provins.

"So young!" said the needlewoman, looking at Pierrette, whose delicate little face looked up at her with a knowing expression.

Pierrette liked the workwomen better than her cousins; she put on pretty airs for them, watched them sewing, said quaint things—the flowers of childhood, such as Rogron and Sylvie had already silenced by fear, for they liked to impress all dependents with a wholesome alarm. The sewing-women were charmed with Pierrette. The outfit, however, was not achieved without some terrible interjections.

"That child will cost us the eyes in our heads!" said Sylvie to Rogron.

"Hold yourself up, child, do. The deuce is in it! the clothes are for you, not for me," said she to Pierrette, when she was being measured or fitted.

"Come, let Mademoiselle Borain do her work; you won't pay her day's wages!" she exclaimed, seeing the child ask the head needlewoman to do something for her.

"Mademoiselle," asked Mademoiselle Borain, "must this seam be back-stitched?"

"Yes; make everything strongly; I do not want to have such a piece of work again in a hurry."

But it was the same with the little cousin as with the house. Pierrette was to be as well dressed as Madame Garceland's little girl. She had fashionable little boots of bronze kid, like the little Tiphaine girl. She had very fine cotton stockings, stays by the best maker, a frock of blue reps, a pretty cape lined with white silk, all in rivalry with young Madame Julliard's little girl. And the underclothes were as good as the outside show, Sylvie was so much afraid of the keen and scrutinizing eye of the mothers of children. Pierrette had pretty shifts of fine calico. Mademoiselle Borain said that madame the sous-préfèt's little girls wore cambric drawers with embroidery and frilling—the latest thing, in short; Pierrette had frilled drawers. A charming drawn bonnet was ordered for her of blue velvet lined with white satin, like the little Martener girl's. Thus Pierrette was the smartest little person in Provins. On Sunday, on coming out from church, all the ladies kissed her. Mesdames Tiphaine, Garceland, Galardon, Auffray, Lesourd, Martener, Guépin, and Julliard doted on the sweet little Bretonne. This excitement flattered old Sylvie's vanity, and in her lavishness she thought less of Pierrette than of gratified pride.

However, Sylvie was fated to find offense in her little cousin's success, and this was how it came about: Pierrette was asked out, and, still to triumph over her neighbors, Sylvie allowed her to go. Pierrette was called for to play games and have dolls' dinner-parties with these ladies' children. Pierrette was a much greater success than the Rogrons; Mademoiselle Sylvie was aggrieved that Pierrette was in demand at other houses, but that no one came to see Pierrette at home. The artless child made no secret of her enjoyment at the houses of the Tiphaines, the Marteners, the Galardons, the Julliards, the Lesourds, the Auffrays, and the Garcelands, whose kindness contrasted strangely with the vexatiousness of her cousins. A mother would have been glad of her child's happiness; but the Rogrons had taken Pierrette to please themselves, not to please her; their feelings, far from being paternal, were tainted with egoism and a sort of commercial interest.

The beautiful outfit, the fine Sunday clothes, and the every-day frocks began Pierrette's misfortunes. Like all children free to amuse themselves and accustomed to follow the dictates of fancy, she wore out her shoes, boots, and frocks with frightful rapidity, and, above all, her frilled drawers. A mother when she scolds her child thinks of the child only; she is only hard when driven to extremities, and when the child is in the wrong; but in this great clothes question, the cousins' money was the first consideration; that was the real point, and not Pierrette. Children have a dog-like instinct for discerning injustice in those who rule them; they feel without fail whether they are tolerated or loved. Innocent hearts are more alive to shades than to contrasts; a child that does not yet understand evil knows when you offend the sense of beauty bestowed on it by nature. The lessons that Pierrette brought upon herself as to the behavior of a well-bred young lady, as to modesty and economy, were the corollary of this main idea—"Pierrette is ruining us."

These scoldings, which had a fatal issue for Pierrette, led the old couple back into the familiar commercial ruts from which their home-life at Provins had led them to wander, and in which their nature could expand and blossom. After being used to domineer, to make remarks, to give orders, to scold their clerks sharply, Rogron and his sister were perishing for lack of victims. Small natures require despotism to exercise their sinews, as great souls thirst for equality to give play to their heart. Now narrow minds can develop as well through persecution as through benevolence; they can assure themselves of their power by tyrannizing cruelly or beneficently over others; they go the way their nature guides them. Add to this the guidance of interest, and you will have the key to most social riddles. Pierrette now became very necessary to her cousins' existence. Since her arrival the Rogrons had been absorbed in her outfit, and then attracted by the novelty of companionship. Every new thing, a feeling, or even a tyranny, must form its set, its creases. Sylvie began by calling Pierrette "my child;" she gave up "my child" for "Pierrette" unqualified. Her reproofs, at first sourly gentle, became hard and sharp. As soon as they had started on this road, the brother and sister made rapid progress.

They were no longer dull. It was not a deliberate scheme of malice and cruelty; it was the instinct of unreasoning tyranny. They believed that they were doing good to Pierrette, as of old to their apprentices.

Pierrette, whose sensitiveness was genuine, noble, and overstrung, the very antipodes of the Rogrons' aridity, had a horror of being blamed; it struck her so cruelly that tears rose at once to her large, clear eyes. She had a hard struggle to suppress her engaging liveliness, which charmed every one out of the house. She might indulge it before the mothers of her little friends; but at her home, by the end of the first month, she began to sit silent, and Rogron asked her if she were ill. At this strange question she flew off to the bottom of the garden to cry by the river, into which her tears fell, as she was one day to fall in the torrent of society.

One day, in spite of her care, the little girl tore her best reps frock at Madame Tiphaine's where she had gone to play one fine day. She at once burst into tears, foreseeing the scolding that awaited her at home. On being questioned, she let fall a few words about her terrible cousin Sylvie in the midst of her tears. Pretty Madame Tiphaine had some stuff to match, and she herself put in a new front breadth. Mademoiselle Rogron heard of the trick, as she called it, played on her by that limb of a little girl. From that day she would never let Pierrette visit any of the ladies.

The new life which Pierrette was to lead at Provins was fated to fall into three very distinct phases. The first lasted three months, during which she enjoyed a kind of happiness, divided between the old people's cold caresses and the scoldings, which she found scorching. The prohibition that kept her from seeing her little friends, emphasizing the necessity for beginning to learn everything that a well-brought-up girl should know, put an end to the first phase of Pierrette's life at Provins, the only period when she found existence endurable.

The domestic changes produced at the Rogrons' house by Pierrette's residence there were studied by Vinet and the colonel with the cunning of a fox bent on getting into a fowl-house, and uneasy at discovering a new creature on the scene. They both paid calls at long intervals, so as not to scare Mademoiselle Sylvie; they found various excuses for chatting with Rogron, and made themselves masters of the situation with an air of reserve and dignity that the great Tartufe might have admired. The colonel and the lawyer spent at the Rogrons the evening of the very day when Sylvie had refused, in very harsh terms, to let Pierrette go to Madame Tiphaine's. On hearing of her refusal, the colonel and the lawyer looked at each other as folks who knew their Provins.

"She positively tried to make a fool of you?" said the lawyer. "We warned Rogron long ago of what has now happened. There is no good to be gotten out of those people."

"What can you expect of the anti-national party?" cried the colonel, curling up his mustache and interrupting Vinet. "If we had tried to get you away from them, you might have thought that we had some malicious motive for speaking to you so. But why, mademoiselle, if you are fond of a little game, should you not play boston in the evenings at home in your own house? Is it impossible to find any one in the place of such idiots as the Julliards? Vinet and I play boston; we will find a fourth. Vinet might introduce his wife to you; she is very nice, and she is one of the Chargebœufs. You will not be like those apes in the upper town; you will not expect a good little housewife, who is compelled by her family's disgraceful conduct to do all her own housework, to dress like a duchess—and she has the courage of a lion and the gentleness of a lamb."

Sylvie Rogron displayed her long yellow teeth in a smile at the colonel, who endured the horrible phenomenon very well, and even assumed a flattering air.

"If there are but four of us, we cannot play boston every evening," replied she.

"Why, where else have I to go—an old soldier like me who has nothing to do, and lives on his pensions? The lawyer is free every evening. Besides, you will have company, I promise you," he added, with a mysterious air.

"You have only to declare yourselves frankly opposed to the ministerial party in Provins, and hold your own against them," said Vinet. "You would see how popular you would be in Provins; you would have a great many people on your side. You would make the Tiphaines furious by having an opposition salon. Well, then, let us laugh at others, if others laugh at us. The 'clique' do not spare you, I can tell you."

"What do they say?" asked Sylvie.

In country towns there is always more than one safety-valve by which gossip finds a vent from one set into another. Vinet had heard all that had been said about the Rogrons in the drawing-rooms from which the haberdashers had been definitively banished. The supernumerary judge Desfondrilles, the archæologist, was of neither party. This man, like some other independent members of society, repeated everything he heard, out of provincial habit, and Vinet had had the benefit of his chit-chat. The malicious lawyer repeated Madame Tiphaine's pleasantries with added venom. As he revealed the practical jokes of which Sylvie and Rogron had been the unconscious victims, he stirred the rage and aroused the revengeful spirit of these two arid souls, craving some aliment for their mean passions.

A few days later Vinet brought his wife, a well-bred woman, shy, neither plain nor pretty, very meek, and very conscious of her misfortune. Madame Vinet was fair, rather worn by the cares of her penurious housekeeping, and very simply dressed. No woman could have better pleased Sylvie. Madame Vinet put up with Sylvie's airs, and gave way to her like a woman accustomed to give way. On her round fore-

5

head, her rose-pink cheeks, in her slow, gentle eyes, there were traces of those deep reflections, that clear-sighted thoughtfulness, which women who are used to suffering bury under perfect silence. The influence of the colonel, displaying for Sylvie's behoof *courtieresque* graces that seemed wrung from his soldierly roughness, with that of the wily Vinet, soon made itself felt by Pierrette. The child, the pretty squirrel, shut up in the house, or going out only with old Sylvie, was every instant checked by a " Don't touch that, Pierrette ! " and by incessant sermons on holding herself up. Pierrette stooped and held her shoulders high ; her cousin wanted her to be as straight as herself, and she was like a soldier presenting arms to his colonel ; she would sometimes give her little slaps on her back to make her hold herself up. The free and light-hearted child of the Marais learned to measure her movements and imitate an automaton.

One evening, which marked the beginning of the second period, Pierrette, whom the three visitors had not seen in the drawing-room during the evening, came to kiss her cousins and curtsey to the company before going to bed. Sylvie coldly offered her cheek to the pretty little thing, as if to be kissed and have done with it. The action was so cruelly significant that tears started from Pierrette's eyes.

" Have you pricked yourself, my little Pierrette," said the abominable Vinet.

" What is the matter with you ? " asked Sylvie severely.

" Nothing," said the poor child, going to kiss Rogron.

" Nothing ? " repeated Sylvie. " You cannot be crying for nothing ! "

" What is it, my little pet ? " asked Madame Vinet.

" My rich cousin Sylvie does not treat me so well as my poor grandmother ! "

" Your grandmother stole your money," said Sylvie, " and your cousin will leave you hers."

The colonel and Vinet exchanged covert glances.

"I would rather be robbed and loved," meekly replied Pierrette in return.

"Very well, you shall be sent back to the place you came from."

"But what has the dear child done?" asked Madame Vinet.

Vinet fixed his eye on his wife, with that terrible cold, fixed stare that belongs to those who rule despotically. The poor lonely woman, unceasingly punished for not having the one thing required of her—namely, a fortune—took up her cards again.

"What has she done?" cried Sylvie, raising her head with a jerk so sudden that the yellow wallflowers in her cap were shaken. "She does not know what to do next to annoy us. She opened my watch to examine the works, and touched the wheel, and broke the mainspring. Mademoiselle listens to nothing. All day long I am telling her to take care what she is about, and I might as well talk to the lamp."

Pierrette, ashamed of being reprimanded in the presence of strangers, went out of the room very gently.

"I cannot think how to quell that child's turbulence," said Rogron.

"Why, she is old enough to go to school," said Madame Vinet.

Another look from Vinet silenced his wife, to whom he had been careful not to confide his plans and the colonel's with regard to the bachelor couple.

"That is what comes of taking charge of other people's children," cried Gouraud. "You might have some of your own yet, you or your brother; why do you not both marry?"

Sylvie looked very sweetly at the colonel; for the first time in her life she beheld a man to whom the idea that she might marry did not seem absurd.

"Madame Vinet is right!" cried Rogron, "that would keep Pierrette quiet. A master would not cost much."

The colonel's speech so entirely occupied Sylvie that she did not answer her brother.

"If only you would stand the money for the opposition paper we were talking about, you might find a tutor for your little cousin in the responsible editor. We could get that poor schoolmaster who was victimized by the encroachments of the priests. My wife is right; Pierrette is a rough diamond that needs polishing," said Vinet to Rogron.

"I fancied that you were a baron," said Sylvie to the colonel, after a long pause, while each player seemed meditative.

"Yes. But having won the title in 1814, after the battle of Nangis, where my regiment did wonders, how could I find the money or the assistance needed to get it duly registered? The barony, like the rank of general, which I won in 1815, must wait for a revolution to secure them to me."

"If you could give a mortgage as your guarantee for the money," said Rogron presently, " I could do it."

"That could be arranged with Cournant," replied Vinet. "The newspaper would lead to the colonel's triumph, and make your drawing-room more powerful than those of Tiphaine and Co."

"How is that?" asked Sylvie.

At this moment, while Madame Vinet was dealing, and the lawyer explaining all the importance that the publication of an independent paper for the district of Provins must confer on Rogron, the colonel, and himself, Pierrette was bathed in tears. Her heart and brain were agreed; she thought Sylvie far more to blame than herself. The little Bretonne instinctively perceived how unfailing charity and benevolence should be. She hated her fine frocks and all that was done for her. She paid too dear for these benefits. She cried with rage at having given her cousins a hold over her, and determined to behave in such a way as to reduce them to silence, poor child! Then she saw how noble Brigaut had been to give her his savings. She thought her woes had reached a climax, not knowing that at that moment new misfortunes were being plotted in the drawing-room.

A few days later Pierrette had a writing-master. She was to learn to read, write, and do sums. Pierrette's education involved the house of Rogron in fearful disaster. There was ink on the tables, on the furniture. and on her clothes; writing-books and pens strewn everywhere, powder on the upholstery, books torn and dog's-eared while she was learning her lessons. They already spoke to her—and in what a way!—of the necessity for earning her living and being a burden on no one. As she heard these dreadful warnings, Pierrette felt a burning in her throat; she was choking, her heart beat painfully fast. She was obliged to swallow down her tears; for each one was reckoned with an offense against her magnanimous relations. Rogron had found the occupation that suited him. He scolded Pierrette as he had formerly scolded his shopmen; he would fetch her in from the midst of her play to compel her to study ; he heard her repeat her lessons; he was the poor child's fierce tutor. Sylvie, on her part, thought it her duty to teach Pierrette the little she knew of womanly accomplishments.

Neither Rogron nor his sister had any gentleness of nature. These narrow souls, finding a real pleasure in bullying the poor little thing, changed unconsciously from mildness to the greatest severity. This severity was, they said, the consequence of the child's obstinacy; she had begun too late to learn, and was dull of comprehension. Her teachers did not understand the art of giving lessons in a form suited to the pupil's intelligence, which is what should distinguish private from public education. The fault lay far less with Pierrette than with her cousins. It took her an immensely long time to learn the beginnings. For the merest trifle she was called stupid and silly, foolish and awkward. Incessantly ill used by hard words, Pierrette never met any but cold looks from

the two old people. She fell into the stolid dullness of a
sheep ; she dared do nothing when she found her actions mis-
judged, misunderstood, misinterpreted. In everything she
awaited Sylvie's orders and the expression of her cousin's
will, keeping her thoughts to herself and shutting herself up
in passive obedience. Her bright color began to fade.
Sometimes she complained of aches and pains. When Sylvie
asked her where? the poor child, who felt generally ailing,
replied, "All over."

"Was there ever such a thiug heard of as aching all over?
If you were ill all over, you would certainly be dead!" retorted Sylvie.

"You may have a pain in your chest," said Rogron the
expositor, "or in your teeth, or your head, or your feet, or
your stomach, but no one ever had pains everywhere. What
do you mean by ' all over?' Pain all over is pain nowhere.
Do you know what you are doing? You are talking for talking's sake."

Pierrette at last never spoke, finding that her artless girlish
remarks, the flowers of her opening mind, were met with
commonplace retorts which her good sense told her were
ridiculous.

"You are always complaining, and you eat like a fasting
friar ! " said Rogron.

The only person who never distressed this sweet fragile
flower was the sturdy servant Adèle. Adèle always warmed
the little girl's bed, but in secret, since one evening when,
being discovered in the act of thus "spoiling" her master's
heiress, she was scolded by Sylvie.

"Children must be hardened ; that is the way to give
them strong constitutions. Have we been any the worse for
it, my brother and I?" said Sylvie. "You will make Pierrette a peeky coddle ! "—*une picheline*, a word of the Rogron
vocabulary used by them to designate weakly and complaining
persons.

The little angel's caressing expressions were regarded as mere acting. The roses of affection that budded so fresh and lovely in this young soul, and longed to open to the day, were mercilessly crushed. Pierrette felt the hardest blows on the tenderest spots of her heart. If she tried to soften these two savage natures by her pretty ways, she was accused of expressing her tenderness out of self-interest. "Tell me plainly what you want," Rogron would exclaim roughly; "you are certainly not coaxing me for nothing."

Neither the sister nor the brother recognized affection, and Pierrette was all affection.

Colonel Gouraud, anxious to please Mademoiselle Rogron, declared her right in all that concerned Pierrette. Vinet no less supported the old cousins in their abuse of Pierrette; he ascribed all the reported misdeeds of this angel to the obstinacy of the Breton character, and said that no power, no strength of will, could ever conquer it. Rogron and his sister were flattered with the utmost skill by these two courtiers, who had at last succeeded in extracting from Rogron the surety money for the newspaper, the *Provins Courrier*, and from Sylvie five thousand francs, as a shareholder. The colonel and Vinet now took the field. They disposed of a hundred shares at five hundred francs each to the electors who held state securities, and whom the Liberal journals filled with alarms, to farmers, and to persons who were called independent. They even extended their ramifications over the whole department, and beyond it, to some adjacent townships. Each shareholder subscribed for the paper, of course. Then the legal and other advertisements were divided between the *Ruche* and the *Courrier*. The first number contained a grandiloquent column in praise of Rogron, who was represented as the Laffitte of Provins.

As soon as the public mind found a leader, it became easy to perceive that the coming elections would be hotly contested. Madame Tiphaine was in despair.

" Unfortunately," said she, as she read an article attacking her and Monsieur Julliard, " unfortunately, I forgot that there is always a rogue not very far away from a dupe, and that folly always attracts a clever man of the fox species."

As soon as the newspaper was to be seen for twenty leagues round, Vinet had a new coat and boots, and a decent waist-coat and trousers. He displayed the famous white hat affected by Liberals, and showed his collar and cuffs. His wife en-gaged a servant, and appeared dressed as became the wife of an influential man ; she wore pretty caps.

Vinet, out of self-interest, was grateful. He and his friend, Cournant, notary to the Liberal side, and Auffray's opponent, became the Rogrons' advisers, and did them two great ser-vices. The leases granted by old Rogron, their father, in 1815, under unfortunate circumstances, were about to fall in. Horticulture and market gardening had lately developed enormously in the Provins district. The pleader and the notary made it their business to effect an increase of fourteen hundred francs a year on granting the new leases. Vinet also won for them two lawsuits against two villages, relating to plantations of trees, in which the loss of five hundred poplars was involved. The money for the poplars, with the Rogrons' savings, which for the last three years had amounted to six thousand francs deposited at compound interest, was skillfully laid out in the purchase of several plots of land. Finally, Vinet proposed and carried out the eviction of certain peasant proprietors, to whom Rogron the elder had loaned money, and who had killed themselves with cultivating and manuring their land to enable them to repay it, but in vain.

Thus the damage done to the Rogrons' capital by the reconstruction of their house was to a great extent remedied. Their estates in the immediate neighborhood of the town, chosen by their father as innkeepers know how to choose, cut up into small holdings of which the largest was less than five acres, and let to perfectly solvent tenants, themselves owners of some plots of land mortgaged to secure the farm rents, brought in at Martinmas, in November, 1826, five thousand francs. The taxes were paid by the tenants, and there were no buildings to repair or insure against fire.

The brother and sister each possessed four thousand six hundred francs in the five per cents; and, as their selling value was above par, Vinet exhorted them to invest the money in land, promising them—seconded by the notary—that they should not lose a farthing of interest by the transfer.

By the end of this second period life was so intolerable to Pierrette—the indifference of all about her, the senseless fault-finding and lack of affection in her cousins became so virulent, she felt so plainly the cold chill of the tomb blowing upon her, that she entertained the daring project of going away, on foot, with no money, to Brittany to rejoin her grandfather and grandmother. Two events prevented this : Old Lorrain died, and Rogron was appointed Pierrette's guardian by a family council held at Provins. If her old grandmother had died first, it is probable that Rogron, advised by Vinet, would have called upon the grandfather to repay the child's eight thousand francs, and have reduced him to beggary.

" Why, you may inherit Pierrette's money," said Vinet with a hideous smile. "You never can tell who will live or who will die."

Enlightened by this speech, Rogron left the widow Lorrain no peace as Pierrette's debtor till he had made her secure to the little girl the capital of the eight thousand francs by a deed of gift, of which he paid the cost.

Pierrette was strangely affected by this loss. Just as the blow fell on her she was to be prepared for her first communion, the other event which by its obligations tied her to Provins. This necessary and simple ceremony was to bring about great changes for the Rogrons. Sylvie learned that the curé, Monsieur Péroux, was instructing the little Julliards,

the Lesourds, Garcelands, and others.   She made it therefore
a point of honor to put Pierrette under the guidance of the
Abbé Péroux's superior, Monsieur Habert, a man who was
said to belong to the Jesuit congregation—very zealous for
the interests of the church, much dreaded in Provins, and
hiding immense ambition under the strictest severity of principle.   This priest's sister, an unmarried woman of about
thirty, had a school for girls in the town.   The brother and
sister were much alike; both lean, sallow, atrabilious, with
black hair.

Pierrette, a Bretonne nurtured in the practice and poetry
of the Catholic faith, opened her heart and ears to the teaching of this imposing priest.   Suffering predisposes the mind
to devoutness; and most young girls, prompted by instinctive
tenderness, lean towards mysticism, the obscurer side of
religion.   So the priest sowed the seed of the gospel and the
dogmas of the church in good ground.   He completely
changed Pierrette's frame of mind.   Pierrette loved Jesus
Christ, as presented to girls in the sacrament, as a celestial
bridegroom; her moral and physical sufferings now had their
meaning; she was taught to see the hand of God in everything.   Her soul, so cruelly stricken in this house, while she
could not accuse her cousins, took refuge in the sphere
whither fly all who are wretched, borne on the wings of the
three Christian virtues.   She gave up the idea of flight.
Sylvie, amazed at the alteration produced in Pierrette by
Monsieur Habert, became curious.   And so, while preparing
the child for her first communion, Monsieur Habert won to
God the hitherto wandering soul of Mademoiselle Sylvie.
Sylvie became a bigot.

Denis Rogron, over whom the supposed Jesuit could get no
hold—for at that time the spirit of his late lamented majesty,
Constitution the First, was in some simpletons supreme above
that of the church—Denis remained faithful to Colonel
Gouraud, Vinet, and Liberalism.

Mademoiselle Rogron, of course, made acquaintance with Mademoiselle Habert, with whom she was in perfect sympathy. The two old maids loved each other like two loving sisters. Mademoiselle Habert proposed to take Pierrette under her care, and spare Sylvie the trouble and vexations of educating a child; but the brother and sister replied that Pierrette's absence would make the house feel too empty. The Rogrons' attachment to their little cousin seemed from this expression to be quite excessive.

On seeing Mademoiselle Habert in possession, Colonel Gouraud and Vinet ascribed to the ambitious priest, on his sister's behalf, the matrimonial scheme imagined by the colonel.

"Your sister wants to see you married," said the lawyer to the ex-haberdasher.

"And to whom?" said Rogron.

"To that old sibyl of a schoolmistress," cried the colonel, curling his mustache.

"She has said nothing to me about it," said Rogron blankly.

A woman so determined as Sylvie was sure to make great progress in the ways of salvation. The priest's influence soon grew in the house, supported as it was by Sylvie, who managed her brother. The two Liberals, very legitimately alarmed, understood that if the priest had determined to get Rogron for his sister's husband—a far more suitable match than that of Sylvie and the colonel—he would urge Sylvie to the excessive practice of religion, and make Pierrette go into a convent. They would thus lose the reward of eighteen months of efforts, meanness, and flattery. They took a terribly dumb hatred of the priest and his sister, and yet, if they were to keep up with them step for step, they felt the necessity of remaining on good terms with them.

Monsieur and Mademoiselle Habert, who played both whist and boston, came every evening. Their assiduity excited

that of the others. The lawyer and the soldier felt that they
were pitted against adversaries stronger than themselves, a
preconception which Monsieur Habert and his sister fully
shared. This situation was in itself a battle. Just as the
colonel gave to Sylvie a foretaste of the unhoped-for joys of
an offer of marriage—for she had brought herself to regard
Gouraud as a man worthy of her—so Mademoiselle Habert
wrapped the retired haberdasher in the cotton wool of her
attentions, her speeches, and her looks. Neither party could
say to itself the great word of great politicians, "Divide the
spoil!" each insisted on the whole prize.

Besides, the two wily foxes of the Opposition at Provins—
an opposition that was growing in strength—were rash enough
to believe themselves stronger than the priesthood ; they were
the first to fire. Vinet, whose gratitude was stirred up by
the claw-fingers of self-interest, went to fetch Mademoiselle
de Chargebœuf and her mother. The two women, who had
about two thousand francs a year, lived very narrowly at
Troyes. Mademoiselle Bathilde de Chargebœuf was one of
those splendid women who believe in marrying for love, and
change their minds towards their five-and-twentieth year on
finding themselves still unwedded. Vinet succeeded in per-
suading Madame de Chargebœuf to combine her two thousand francs with the thousand crowns he was making now that
the newspaper was started, and to come and live with him at
Provins, where Bathilde, he said, might marry a simpleton
named Rogron, and, so clever as she was, rival handsome
Madame Tiphaine.

The reinforcement of Vinet's household and ideas by the
arrival of Madame and Mademoiselle de Chargebœuf gave
the utmost cohesion to the Liberal party. This coalition
brought consternation to the aristocracy of Provins and the
Tiphaine party. Madame de Bréautey, in dismay at seeing
two women of family so misled, begged them to come to see
her. She bewailed the blunders committed by the Royalists,

and was furious with those of Troyes on learning the poverty
of this mother and daughter.

"What! was there no old country gentleman who would
marry that dear girl, born to rule a château?" cried she.
"They have let her run to seed, and now she will throw herself at the head of a Rogron!"

She hunted the department through, and failed to find one
gentleman who would marry a girl whose mother had but two
thousand francs a year. Then the "clique" of the Tiphaines
and the sous-préfet also set to work, but too late, to discover
such a man. Madame de Bréautey inveighed loudly against
the selfishness that was eating up France, the result of materi-
alism and of the power conferred on money by the laws; the
nobility was nothing in these days! Beauty was nothing!
Rogrons and Vinets were defying the King of France!

Bathilde had the indisputable advantage over her rival not
merely of beauty, but of dress. She was dazzlingly fair.
At five-and-twenty her fully-developed shoulders and splendid
modeling were exquisitely full. The roundness of her throat,
the slenderness of her articulations, the splendor of her fine
fair hair, the charm of her smile, the elegant shape of her
head, the dignity and outline of her face, her fine eyes under
a well-moulded brow, her calm and well-bred movements, and
her still girlish figure, all were in harmony. She had a fine
hand and a narrow foot. Her robust health gave her,
perhaps, the look of a handsome inn-servant; "but that
should be no fault in a Rogron's eyes," said pretty Madame
Tiphaine.

The first time Mademoiselle de Chargebœuf was seen she
was dressed simply enough. Her dress of brown merino,
edged with green embroidery, was cut low; but a kerchief of
tulle, neatly drawn down by invisible strings, covered her
shoulders, back, and bust, a little open at the throat, though
fastened by a brooch and chain. Under this fine network
Bathilde's beauty was even more attractive, more suggestive.

She took off her velvet bonnet and her shawl on entering,
and showed pretty ears with gold eardrops. She had a little
cross and heart on black velvet round her neck, which contrasted with its whiteness like the black that fantastic nature
sets round the tail of a white Angora cat. She was expert in
all the arts of girls on their promotion : twisting her fingers
to arrange curls that are not out of place, displaying her wrists
by begging Rogron to button her cuff, which the hapless man,
quite dazzled, bluntly refused to do, hiding his agitation under
assumed indifference. The bashfulness of the only passion
our haberdasher was ever to know in his life always gave it
the demeanor of hatred. Sylvie, as well as Céleste Habert,
misunderstood it ; not so the lawyer, the superior man of this
company of simpletons, whose only enemy was the priest, for
the colonel had long been his ally.

Gouraud, on his part, thenceforth behaved to Sylvie as
Bathilde did to Rogron. He appeared in clean linen every
evening ; he wore velvet collars, which gave effect to his mar-
tial countenance, set off by the corners of his white shirt
collars ; he adopted white drill waistcoats, and had a new frock-
coat made of blue cloth, on which his red rosette was conspicuous, and all under pretense of doing honor to the fair
Bathilde. He never smoked after two o'clock. His grizzled
hair was brushed down in a wave over his ochre-colored skull.
In short, he assumed the appearance and attitude of a party
chief, of a man who was prepared to rout the enemies of
France—in one word, the Bourbons—with tuck of drum.

The satanical pleader and the cunning colonel played a still
more cruel trick on Monsieur and Mademoiselle Habert than
that of introducing the beautiful Mademoiselle de Chargebœuf, who was pronounced by the Liberal party and by the
Bréauteys to be ten times handsomer than the beautiful
Madame Tiphaine. These two great country-town politicians had it rumored from one to another that Monsieur
Habert had agreed with them on all points. Provins before

long spoke of him as a "Liberal priest." Called up before the bishop, Monsieur Habert was obliged to give up his evenings with the Rogrons, but his sister still went there. Thenceforth the Rogron drawing-room was a fact and a power.

And so, by the middle of that year, political intrigues were not less eager than matrimonial intrigues in the Rogrons' rooms. While covert interests, buried out of sight, were fighting wildly for the upper hand, the public struggle won disastrous notoriety. Everybody knows that the Villèle ministry was overthrown by the elections of 1826. In the Provins constituency, Vinet, the Liberal candidate—for whom Monsieur Cournant had obtained his qualification by the purchase of some land of which the price remained unpaid— came very near beating Monsieur Tiphaine. The president had a majority of only two.

Mesdames Vinet and de Chargebœuf, Vinet and the colonel were sometimes joined by Monsieur Cournant and his wife; then by Néraud the doctor, a man whose youth had been very "stormy," but who now took serious views of life; he had devoted himself to science, it was said, and, if the Liberals were to be believed, was a far cleverer man than Monsieur Martener. To the Rogrons their triumph was as inexplicable as their ostracism had been.

The handsome Bathilde de Chargebœuf, to whom Vinet spoke of Pierrette as an enemy, was horribly disdainful to the child. The humiliation of this poor victim was necessary to the interest of all. Madame Vinet could do nothing for the little girl who was being brayed in the mortar of the pitiless egotisms which the lady at last understood. But for her husband's imperative desire she would never have come to the Rogrons; it grieved her too much to see their ill-usage of the pretty little thing who clung to her, understanding her secret good-will, and begged her to teach her such or such a stitch or embroidery pattern. Pierrette had shown that when she was thus treated she understood and succeeded to admiration. But Madame Vinet was no longer of any use, so she came no more.

Sylvie, who still cherished the notion of marriage, now regarded Pierrette as an obstacle. Pierrette was nearly fourteen; her sickly fairness, a symptom that was quite overlooked by the ignorant old maid, made her lovely. Then Sylvie had the bright idea of indemnifying herself for the expenses caused by Pierrette by making a servant of her. Vinet, as representing the interests of the Chargebœufs, Mademoiselle Habert, Gouraud, all the influential visitors, advised Sylvie by all means to dismiss Adèle. Could not Pierrette cook and keep the house in order? When there was too much to be done, she need only engage the colonel's housekeeper, a very accomplished person, and one of the best cooks in Provins. Pierrette ought to learn to cook and to polish the floors, said the baleful lawyer, to sweep, keep the house neat, go to market, and know the price of things. The poor little girl, whose unselfishness was as great as her generosity, offered it herself, glad to pay thus for the hard bread she ate under that roof.

Adèle went. Thus Pierrette lost the only person who might perhaps have protected her. Strong as she was, from that hour she was crushed body and soul. The old people had less mercy on her than on a servant; she was their property! She was scolded for mere nothings, for a little dust left on the corner of a chimney-shelf or a glass shade. These objects of luxury that she had so much admired became odious to her. In spite of her anxiety to do right, her relentless cousin Sylvie always found some fault with everything she did. In two years Pierrette never heard a word of praise or of affection. Her whole happiness consisted in not being scolded. She submitted with angelic patience to the dark moods of these two unmarried beings, to whom the gentler feelings were unknown, and who made her suffer every day for her dependency. This life in which the young girl was gripped, as it were, between the two haberdashers as in the jaws of a vise, increased her malady. She had such violent fits of inexplicable distress, such sudden bursts of secret grief, that her physical development was irremediably checked. And thus, by slow degrees, through terrible though concealed sufferings, Pierrette had come to the state in which the friend of her childhood had seen her as he stood on the little square and greeted her with his Breton ballad.

Before entering on the story of the domestic drama in the Rogrons' house, to which Brigaut's arrival gave rise, it will be necessary, to avoid digressions, to account for the lad's settling at Provins, since he is in some sort a silent personage on the stage.

Brigaut, as he fled, was alarmed not merely by Pierrette's signal, but also by the change in his little friend; hardly could he recognize her, but for the voice, eyes, and movements which recalled his lively little playfellow, at once so gay and so loving. When he had gotten far away from the house, his legs quaked under him, his spine felt on fire! He had seen the shadow of Pierrette, and not Pierrette herself. He made his way up to the old town, thoughtful and uneasy, till he found a spot whence he could see the place and the house where Pierrette lived; he gazed at it sadly, lost in thought as infinite as the troubles into which we plunge without knowing where they may end. Pierrette was ill; she was unhappy; she regretted Brittany! What ailed her? All these questions passed again and again through Brigaut's mind, and racked his breast, revealing to him the extent of his affection for his little adopted sister.

It is very rarely that a passion between two children of different sexes remains permanent. The charming romance of Paul and Virginia no more solves the problem of this strange moral fact than does that of Brigaut and Pierrette. Modern history offers the single illustrious exception of the sublime

6

Marchesa di Pescara and her husband, who, destined for each
other by their parents at the age of fourteen, adored each
other, and were married. Their union gave to the sixteenth
century the spectacle of boundless conjugal affection, never
clouded. The Marchesa, a widow at four-and-thirty, beautiful, witty, universally beloved, refused monarchs, and buried
herself in a convent, where she never saw, never heard, any
one but nuns.

Such perfect love as this blossomed suddenly in the heart
of the poor Breton artisan. Pierrette and he had so often
been each other's protectors, he had been so happy in giving
her the money for her journey, he had almost died of running
after the diligence, and Pierrette had not known it! The
memory of it had often warmed him during the chill hours of
his toilsome life these three years past. He had improved
himself for Pierrette; he had learned his craft for Pierrette;
he had come to Paris for Pierrette, intending to make a fortune for her. After being there a fortnight, he could no
longer control his longing to see her; he had walked from
Saturday evening till Monday morning. He had intended to
return to Paris, but the pathetic appearance of his little friend
held him fast to Provins. A wonderful magnetism—still disputed, it is true, in spite of so many instances—acted on him
without his knowing it; and tears filled his eyes, while they
also dimmed Pierrette's sight. If to her he was Brittany and
all her happy childhood, to him Pierrette was life! At sixteen Brigaut had not yet learned to draw or give the section
of a moulding; there were many things he did not know;
but at piecework he had earned from four to five francs a day.
So he could live at Provins; he would be within reach of
Pierrette; he would finish learning his business by working
under the best cabinetmaker in the town, and watch over the
little girl.

Brigaut made up his mind at once. He flew back to Paris,
settled his accounts, collected his pass, his luggage, and his

tools. Three days later he was working for Monsieur Frappier, the best carpenter in Provins. Energetic workmen, steady, and averse to turbulency and taverns, are rare enough to make a master glad to get a young fellow like Brigaut. To conclude his story on that score, by the end of a fortnight he was foreman, lodging and boarding with Frappier, who taught him arithmetic and linear drawing. The carpenter lived in the High Street, about a hundred yards from the little oblong plazza, at the end of which stood the Rogrons' house.

Brigaut buried his love in his heart, and was not guilty of the smallest indiscretion. He got Madame Frappier to tell him the history of the Rogrons; from her he learned how the old innkeeper had set to work to get the money left by old Auffray. Brigaut was fully informed as to the character of the haberdasher and his sister. One morning he met Pierrette at market with Mademoiselle Sylvie, and shuddered to see her with a basket on her arm full of provisions. He went to see Pierrette again at church on Sunday, where the girl appeared in all her best; there, for the first time, Brigaut understood that Pierrette was Mademoiselle Lorrain.

Pierrette saw her friend, but she made him a mysterious signal to keep himself out of sight. There was a world of meaning in this gesture, as in that by which, a fortnight since, she had bidden him vanish. What a fortune he would have to make in ten years to enable him to marry the companion of his childhood, to whom the Rogrons would leave a house, a hundred acres of land, and twelve thousand francs a year, not to mention their savings! The persevering Breton would not tempt fortune till he had acquired the knowledge he still lacked. So long as it was theory alone, it was all the same whether he learned in Paris or at Provins, and he preferred to remain near Pierrette, to whom he also proposed to explain his plans and the sort of help she might count on. Finally, he would certainly not leave her till he understood the secret of the pallor which had already dimmed the life of the feature which generally retains it longest—the eyes; till he knew what caused the sufferings that gave her the look of a girl bowing before the scythe of death, and about to be cut down.

Her two pathetic signals, which were not false to their . friendship, but which enjoined the greatest caution, struck terror into the lad's heart. Evidently Pierrette desired him to wait, and not to try to see her, or there would be danger and peril for her. As she came out of church she gave him a look, and Brigaut saw that her eyes were full of tears. The Breton would more easily have squared the circle than have guessed what had happened in the Rogrons' house since his arrival.

It was not without lively apprehensions that Pierrette came down from her room that day when Brigaut had plunged into her morning dream like another dream. Having risen and opened her window, Mademoiselle Rogron must have heard the song and its words—compromising, no doubt, in the ears of an old maid; but Pierrette knew nothing of the causes that made her cousin so alert. Sylvie had good reasons for getting up and running to the window. For about a week past strange secret events and cruel pangs of feeling had agitated the principal figures in the Rogron salon. These unknown events, carefully concealed by all concerned, were to fall on Pierrette like an icy avalanche.

The realm of mysteries, which ought perhaps to be called the foul places of the human heart, lies at the bottom of the greatest revolutions, political, social, or domestic; but in speaking of them it may be extremely useful to explain that their algebraical expression, though accurate, is not faithful so far as form is concerned. These deep calculations do not express themselves so brutally as history reports them. Any attempt to relate the circumlocutions, the rhetorical involutions, the long colloquies, in which the mind designedly darkens the light it casts, the honeyed words diluting the venom of certain insinuations, would mean writing a book as long as the noble poem called "Clarissa Harlowe."

Mademoiselle Habert and Mademoiselle Rogron were equally desirous of marrying; but one was ten years younger than the other, and probability allowed Céleste Habert to think that her children would inherit the Rogrons' whole fortune. Sylvie was almost forty-two, an age at which marriage has its risks. In confiding their ideas to each other to secure mutual approbation, Céleste Habert, on a hint from the vindictive abbé, had enlightened Sylvie as to the possibilities of the position. The colonel, a violent man, with the health of a soldier, a burly bachelor of forty-five, would no doubt act on the moral of all fairy tales: they lived happy, and had many children. This form of happiness alarmed Sylvie; she was afraid of dying—a fear which tortures unmarried women to the utmost.

But the Martignac ministry was now established — the second victory which upset the Villèle administration. Vinet's party held their head high in Provins. Vinet, now the leading advocate of La Brie, carried all before him, to use a colloquialism. Vinet was a personage; the Liberals prophesied his advancement; he would certainly be a deputy or public prosecutor. As to the colonel, he would be mayor of Provins. Oh! to reign as Madame Garceland reigned, to be the mayoress! Sylvie could not resist this hope; she determined to consult a doctor, though it might cover her with ridicule. The two women, one triumphant, and the other sure of having her in leading-strings, invented one of those stratagems which women advised by a priest are so clever in planning. To consult Monsieur Néraud, the Liberal physician, Monsieur Martener's rival, would be a blunder. Céleste Habert proposed to Sylvie to hide her in a dressing-closet while she, Mademoiselle Habert, consulted Monsieur Martener, who attended the school, on her own account. Whether he were Céleste's accomplice or not, Martener told his client that there was some, though very little, danger for a woman of thirty. "But with your constitution," he added, "you have nothing to fear."

"And if a woman is past forty?" asked Mademoiselle Céleste Habert.

"A woman of forty who has been married and had children need fear nothing."

"But an unmarried woman, perfectly well conducted—for example, Mademoiselle Rogron?"

"Well conducted! There can be no doubt," said Monsieur Martener. "In such a case the safe birth of a child is a miracle which God certainly works sometimes, but rarely."

"And why?" asked Céleste Habert.

Whereupon the doctor replied in a terrific pathological description, explaining that the elasticity bestowed by nature on the muscles and joints in youth ceased to exist at a certain age, particularly in women whose occupations had made them sedentary for some years, like Mademoiselle Rogron.

"And so, after forty, no respectable woman ought to marry?"

"Or she should wait," replied the doctor. "But then it is hardly a marriage; it is a partnership. What else could it be?"

In short, it was proved by this consultation, clearly, scientifically, seriously, and rationally, that after the age of forty a virtuous maiden should not rush into matrimony.

When Monsieur Martener had left, Mademoiselle Céleste Habert found Mademoiselle Rogron green and yellow, her eyes dilated—in fact, in a frightful state.

"Then you truly love the colonel?" said she.

"I still hoped," said the old maid.

"Well, then, wait," said Mademoiselle Habert, who knew that time would be avenged on the colonel.

The morality of this marriage was also doubtful. Sylvie went to sound her conscience in the confessional. The stern director expounded the views of the church, which regards marriage only as a means of propagating the race, reprobates second marriages, and scorns passions that have no social aim. Sylvie Rogron's perplexity was great. These mental struggles gave strange force to her passion, and lent it the unaccountable charm which forbidden joys have always had for women since the time of Eve.

Mademoiselle Rogron's disturbed state could not escape the lawyer's keen eye. One evening, after cards, Vinet went up to his dear friend Sylvie, took her hand, and led her to sit down with him on one of the sofas.

"Something ails you," he said in her ear.

She gloomily bent her head. The pleader let Rogron leave the room, sat alone with the old maid, and got her to make a clean breast of it.

"Well played, abbé! But you have played my game for me," he said to himself after hearing of all the private consultations Sylvie had held, of which the last was the most alarming.

This sly legal fox was even more terrible in his explanations than the doctor had been; he advised the marriage, but only ten years hence for greater safety. The lawyer vowed that all the Rogron fortune should be Bathilde's. He rubbed his hands and his very face grew sharper as he ran after Madame and Mademoiselle de Chargebœuf, whom he had left to start homewards with their servant armed with a lantern.

The influence exerted by Monsieur Habert, the physician of the soul, was entirely counteracted by Vinet, the physician of the purse. Rogron was by no means devout, so the man of the church and the man of the law, the two black gowns, pulled him opposite ways. When he heard of the victory carried off by Mademoiselle Habert, who hoped to marry Rogron, over Sylvie, hanging between the fear of death and the joy of becoming a baroness, Vinet perceived the possibility of removing the colonel from the scene of battle. He knew Rogron well enough to find some means of making him marry the fair Bathilde. Rogron had not been able to resist the blandishments of Mademoiselle de Chargebœuf; Vinet knew that the first time Rogron should be alone with Bathilde and himself their engagement would be settled. Rogron had come to the point of staring at Mademoiselle Habert, so shy was he of looking at Bathilde.

Vinet had just seen how much Sylvie was in love with the colonel. He understood the depth of such a passion in an old maid, no less eaten up by bigotry, and he soon hit on a plan for ruining at one blow both Pierrette and the colonel, getting rid of one by means of the other.

Next morning, on coming out of court, he met the colonel and Rogron walking together, their daily habit.

When these three men were seen together, their conjunction always made the town talk. This triumvirate, held in horror by the sous-préfet, the bench, and the Tiphaine partisans, made a triad of which the Liberals of Provins were proud. Vinet edited the *Courrier* single-handed; he was the head of the party; the colonel, the responsible manager of the paper, was its arm; Rogron, with his money, formed the sinews; he was considered as the link between the managing committee at Provins and the managing committee in Paris. To hear the Tiphaines, these three men were always plotting something against the government, while the Liberals admired them as defenders of the people. When the lawyer saw Rogron returning to the square, brought homewards by the dinner-hour, he took the colonel's arm and hindered him from accompanying the ex-haberdasher.

"Look here, colonel," said he, "I am going to take a great weight off your shoulders. You can do better than marry Sylvie; if you go to work the right way, in two years' time you may marry little Pierrette Lorrain."

And he told him the results of the Jesuit's skillful manœuvring in the interest of his sister Céleste.

"What a clever stroke—and reaching so far!" said the colonel.

"Colonel," said Vinet gravely, "Pierrette is a charming creature; you may be happy for the rest of your days. You have such splendid health, that such a match would not, for you, have the usual drawbacks of an ill-assorted marriage; still, do not imagine that this exchange of a terrible life for a pleasant one will be easy to effect. To convert your lady-love into your confidante is a manœuvre as dangerous as, in your profession, it is to cross a river under the enemy's fire. Keen as you are as a cavalry officer, you must study the position, and carry out your tactics with the superior skill which has won us our present position. If I should one day be public prosecutor, you may command the department. Ah! if only you had a vote, we should be farther on our way. I might have bought the votes of those two officials by indemnifying them for the loss of their places, and we should have had a majority. I should be sitting by Dupin, Casimir Périer, and——"

The colonel had for some time past been thinking of Pierrette, but he hid the thought with deep dissimulation; his roughness to Pierrette was only on the surface. The child could not imagine why the man who called himself her father's old comrade treated her so ill, when, if he met her alone, he put his hand under her chin and gave her a fatherly caress. Ever since Vinet had confided to him Mademoiselle Sylvie's terror of marriage, Gouraud had sought opportunities of seeing Pierrette alone, and then the rough officer was as mild as a cat; he would tell her how brave her father was, and say what a misfortune for her his death had been.

A few days before Brigaut's arrival, Sylvie had found Gouraud and Pierrette together. Jealousy had then entered into her soul with monastic vehemence. Jealousy, which is above all passions credulous and suspicious, is also that in which fancy has most power; but it does not lend wit, it takes it away; and in Sylvie jealousy gave birth to very strange ideas. She conceived that the man who had sung the words "Mistress Bride" to Pierrette must be the colonel; and Sylvie thought she had reason to ascribe this serenade to the colonel, because during the last week Gouraud's manner seemed to have undergone a change. This soldier was the only man who, in the solitude in which she had lived, had ever troubled himself about her; hence she watched him with all her eyes, all her understanding; and by dint of indulging in hopes alternately flourishing and blighted, she had given them so much scope that they produced the effect on her of a moral mirage. To use a fine but vulgar expression, by dint of looking she often saw nothing. By turns she rejected and struggled victoriously against the notion of this chimerical rivalry. She instituted comparisons between herself and Pierrette; she was forty and her hair was gray; Pierrette was a deliciously white little girl, with eyes tender enough to bring warmth to a dead heart. She had heard it said that men of fifty were fond of little girls like Pierrette.

Before the colonel had sown his wild oats and frequented the Rogrons' drawing-room, Sylvie had heard at the Tiphaines' parties strange reports of Gouraud and his doings. Old maids in love have the exaggerated Platonic notions which girls of twenty are apt to profess; they have never lost the hard-and-fast ideas which cling to all who have no experience of life, nor learned how social forces modify, erode, and coerce such fine and lofty notions. To Sylvie the idea of being deceived by her colonel was a thought that hammered at her brain.

So from the hour, that morning, which every celibate spends in bed between waking and rising, the old maid had thought of nothing but herself and Pierrette, and the song which had roused her by the words, "Mistress Bride." Like a simpleton, instead of peeping at the lover through the Venetian shutters, she had opened her window, without

reflecting that Pierrette would hear her. If she had but had
the common wit of a spy, she would have seen Brigaut, and
the fateful drama then begun would not have taken place.

Pierrette, weak as she was, removed the wooden bars
which fastened the kitchen shutters, opened the shutters, and
hooked them back, then she opened the passage door leading
into the garden. She took the various brooms needed for
sweeping the carpet, the dining-room floor, the passage, the
stairs, in short, for cleaning everything with such care and
exactitude as no servant, not even a Dutch one, would give to
her work; she hated the least reproof. To her, happiness
consisted in seeing Sylvie's little blue eyes, colorless and cold,
with a look—not indeed of satisfaction, that they never wore
—only calm when she had examined everything with the
owner's eye, the inscrutable glance which sees what escapes
the keenest observer.

By the time Pierrette returned to the kitchen her skin was
moist; then she put everything in order, lighted the stove so
as to have live charcoal, made the fire in her cousins' rooms,
and put hot water for their toilet, though she had none for
hers. She laid the table for breakfast and lighted the dining-
room stove. For all these various tasks she had to go to the
cellar to fetch brushwood, leaving a cool place to go to a hot
one, or a hot place to go into the cold and damp. These
sudden changes, made with the reckless haste of youth, merely
to avoid a hard word, or to obey some order, aggravated the
state of her health beyond remedy. Pierrette did not know
that she was ill. Still she felt the beginnings of sufferings;
she had strange longings, and hid them; a passion for raw
salad, which she devoured in secret. The innocent child had
no idea that this state meant serious disease, and needed the
greatest care. Before Brigaut's arrival, if Néraud, who might
accuse himself of her grandmother's death, had revealed this
mortal peril to the little girl, she would have smiled; she
found life too bitter not to smile at death. But within these

last few minutes, she, who added to her physical ailments the
Breton home-sickness—a moral sickness so well known, that
colonels of regiments reckon on it in the Bretons who serve
in their regiments—she loved Provins. The sight of that
gold-colored flower, that song, the presence of the friend of
her childhood, had revived her as a plant long deprived of
water recovers after hours of rain. She wanted to live; she
did not believe that she had suffered!

She timidly stole into Sylvie's room, lighted the fire, left
the hot-water pot, spoke a few words, went to awake her
guardian, and then ran downstairs to take in the milk, the
bread, and the other provisions supplied by the tradesmen.
She stood for some time on the doorstep, hoping that Brigaut
would have the wit to return; but Brigaut was already on the
road to Paris. She had dusted the drawing-room and was
busy in the kitchen, when she heard her cousin Sylvie coming downstairs. Mademoiselle Rogron made her appearance
in a Carmelite-gray silk dressing-gown; on her head a tulle
cap decorated with bows, her false curls put on askew, her
nightdress showing above the wrapper, her feet slipshod in her
slippers. She inspected everything, and came to her little
cousin, who was waiting to know what they would have for
breakfast.

"So there you are, Miss Ladylove!" said Sylvie to Pierrette, in a half-merry, half-mocking tone.

"I beg your pardon, cousin?"

"You crept into my room like a sneak and out again in the
same way; but you must have known that I should have
something to say to you."

"To me?"

"You have had a serenade this morning like a princess,
neither more nor less."

"A serenade?" exclaimed Pierrette.

"A serenade!" echoed Sylvie, mimicking her. "And
you have a lover."

"Cousin, what do you mean by a lover?" Sylvie evaded the question, and said—

"Do you dare to say, mademoiselle, that a man did not come under our windows and talk to you of marriage?"

Persecution had taught Pierrette the cunning indispensable to slaves; she boldly replied, "I do not know what you mean——"

"Dog——" added the old maid, in vinegar tones.

"Cousin," said Pierrette humbly.

"And you did not get up, I suppose, and did not go barefoot to your window? Enough to give you some bad illness. Well, catch it, and serve you right! And I suppose you did not talk to your lover?"

"No, cousin."

"I knew you had a great many faults, but I did not know you told lies. Think of what you are about, mademoiselle. You will have to tell your cousin Denis and me all about the scene of this morning, and explain it, too; otherwise your guardian will have to take strong measures."

The old maid, devoured by jealousy and curiosity, was trying intimidation. Pierrette did as all people must who are enduring beyond their strength—she kept silent. Silence is to all creatures thus attacked the only means of salvation; it fatigues the Cossack charges of the envious, the enemy's savage rushes; it results in a crushing and complete victory. What is more complete than silence? It is final. Is it not one of the modes of the Infinite?

Sylvie looked stealthily at Pierrette. The child colored; but instead of flushing all over, the red lay in patches on her cheeks, in burning spots of symptomatic hue. On seeing these signals of ill-health, a mother would at once have changed her note; she would have taken the child on her knee, have questioned her, have acquired long since a thousand proofs of Pierrette's perfect and beautiful innocence, have suspected her weakness, and understood that the blood and humors diverted from their course were thrown back on the lungs after disturbing the digestive functions. Those eloquent scarlet patches would have warned her of imminent and mortal danger. But an old maid to whom the feelings that guard the family, the needs of childhood, the care required in early womanhood were all unknown could have none of the indulgence and the pity that are inspired by the thousand incidents of married and maternal life. The sufferings of misery, instead of softening her heart, had made it callous.

"She blushes—she has done wrong!" thought Sylvie. So Pierrette's silence received the worst construction.

"Pierrette," said she, "before your cousin Denis comes down we will have a little talk. Come," she went on in a milder tone. "Shut the door to the street. If any one comes, they will ring; we shall hear."

In spite of the damp fog rising from the river, Sylvie led Pierrette along the graveled path that zigzagged between the grass-plots, to the edge of the terrace built in a so-called picturesque style of broken rock-work planted with flags and other water-plants. The old cousin now changed her tactics; she would try to catch Pierrette by gentleness. The hyena would play the cat.

"Pierrette," said she, "you are no longer a child; you will soon set foot in your fifteenth year, and it would not be at all astonishing if you had a lover."

"But, cousin," said Pierrette, raising her eyes of angelic sweetness to her cousin's cold, sour face, for Sylvie had put on her saleswoman expression, "what is a lover?"

It was impossible to Sylvie to define to her brother's ward with accuracy and decency what she meant by a lover; instead of regarding the question as the result of adorable innocence, she treated it as mendacious.

"A lover, Pierrette, is a man who loves you and wishes to marry you."

"Ah!" said Pierrette. "In Brittany when two persons are agreed, we call the young man a suitor."

"Well, understand that there is not the smallest harm in confessing your feeling for a man, my child. The harm is in secrecy. Have you, do you think, taken the fancy of any man who comes here?"

"I do not think so."

"You do not love one of them?"

"No one."

"Quite sure?"

"Quite sure."

"Look me in the face, Pierrette."

Pierrette looked at her cousin.

"And yet a man spoke to you from the square this morning?"

Pierrette looked down.

"You went to your window, you opened it, and spoke to him."

"No, cousin; I wanted to see what the weather was like, and I saw a countryman on the square."

"Pierrette, since your first communion you have improved greatly, you are obedient and pious, you love your relations and God; I am pleased with you, but I have never told you so for fear of inflaming your pride."

The horrible woman mistook the dejection, the submission, the silence of wretchedness for virtues! One of the sweetest things that brings comfort to the sufferer, to martyrs, to artists, in the midst of the Divine wrath roused in them by envy and hatred, is to meet with praise from some quarter whence they have always had blame and bad faith. So Pierrette looked up at her cousin with attentive eyes, and felt ready to forgive her all the pain she had caused her.

"But if it is all mere hypocrisy, if I am to find in you a serpent I have cherished in my bosom, you would be an in-famous, a horrible creature!"

"I do not think I have anything to blame myself for," said Pierrette, feeling a dreadful pang at her heart on this sudden transition from unexpected praise to the terrible accent of the hyena.

"You know that lying is a mortal sin?"

"Yes, cousin."

"Well, then, you stand before God!" said the old maid, pointing with a solemn gesture to the gardens and the sky. "Swear to me that you do not know that countryman."

"I will not swear," said Pierrette.

"Ah! he was not a countryman! Little viper!"

Pierrette fled across the garden like a startled fawn, appalled by this moral dilemma. Her cousin called to her in an awful voice.

"The bell," she replied.

"What a sly little wretch!" said Sylvie to herself. "She has a perverse nature, and I am sure now that the little serpent has twisted herself round the colonel. She has heard us say that he is a baron. A baroness, indeed! Little fool! Oh! I will be rid of her by placing her as an apprentice, and pretty soon too!"

Sylvie was so lost in thought that she did not see her brother coming down the walk and contemplating the mischief done by the frost to his dahlias.

"Well, Sylvie, what are you thinking about there? I thought you were looking at the fishes; sometimes they jump out of the water."

"No," said she.

"Well, how did you sleep?" and he proceeded to tell her his dreams of the past night. "Do you not think that my face looks patchy?" a favorite word with the Rogrons. Since Rogron had loved—nay, we will not profane the word—had desired Mademoiselle de Chargebœuf, he had been very anxious about his appearance and himself.

At this moment Pierrette came down the steps and called

to them that breakfast was ready. On seeing her little cousin, Sylvie's complexion turned green and yellow; all her bile rose. She examined the passage, and said that Pierrette ought to have polished it with foot-brushes.

"I will polish it if you wish," replied the angel, not knowing how injurious this form of labor is to a young girl.

The dining-room was above blame. Sylvie sat down, and all through breakfast affected to want things that she never would have thought of in a calmer frame of mind, seeking for them simply to make Pierrette rise to fetch them, and always just as the poor child was beginning to eat. But mere nagging was not enough; she sought some subject for fault-finding, and fumed with internal rage at finding none. If they had been eating eggs, she would certainly have complained of the boiling of hers. She hardly replied to her brother's silly talk, and yet she looked only at him; her eyes avoided Pierrette, who was keenly aware of this behavior.

Pierrette brought in the coffee for her cousins in a large silver cup, which served to heat the milk in, mixed with cream, in a saucepan of hot water. The brother and sister then added, to their taste, the black coffee which was made by Sylvie. When she had carefully prepared this dainty, Sylvie detected in it a faint cloud of coffee dust; she carefully skimmed it off the tawny mixture and looked at it, leaning over to examine it more minutely. Then the storm burst.

"What is the matter?" asked Rogron.

"The matter! Miss, here, has put ashes in my coffee. Ashes in coffee are so nice! Well, well! It is not astonishing; no one can do two things at once. Much she was thinking of the coffee! A blackbird might have flown through the kitchen, and she would not have heeded it this morning! How should she see the ashes flying? And then —only her cousin's! Much she cares about it!"

She went on in this way, while she elaborately laid on the edge of her plate some fine coffee that had passed through

7

the filter, mixed with some grains of sugar that had not melted.

" But, cousin, that is coffee," said Pierrette.

" So I am a liar now?" exclaimed Sylvie, looking at Pierrette, and scorching her by a fearful flash that her eyes could dart when she was angry.

These temperaments, which passion has never exhausted, have at command a great supply of the vital fluid. This phenomenon of extreme brightness in her eye under the influence of rage was all the more confirmed in Mademoiselle Rogron because formerly, in her shop, she had had occasion to try the power of her gaze by opening her eyes enormously wide, always to fill her dependents with salutary terror.

" I will teach you to give me the lie," she went on; " you, who deserve to be sent away from table to feed by yourself in the kitchen."

"What is the matter with you both?" cried Rogron. " You are as cross as two sticks this morning."

"Oh, my lady knows what I mean! I am giving her time to make up her mind before speaking to you about it, for I am much kinder to her than she deserves."

Pierrette looked through the window out on to the square, so as not to meet her cousin's eyes, which frightened her.

" She pays no more heed than if I were talking to this sugar-basin! And she has sharp ears, too; she can speak from the top of the house to answer some one below. She is that perverse! Your ward is aggravating beyond words, and you need look for nothing good from her; do you hear me, Rogron?"

" What has she done that is so wicked?" asked Rogron.

"At her age too! It is beginning young!" cried the old maid in a fury.

Pierrette rose to clear away, just to keep herself in countenance; she did not know which way to look. Though such language was nothing new to her, she never could get used to it. Her cousin's rage made her feel as though she had committed some crime. She wondered what her rage would be if she knew of Brigaut's escapade. Perhaps they would keep Brigaut away. All the thousand ideas of a slave crowded on her at once, thoughts swift and deep, and she resolved to resist by absolute silence as to an incident in which her conscience could see no evil.

She had to endure words so cruel, so harsh, insinuations so insulting, that on her return to the kitchen she was seized with cramp in the stomach and a violent attack of sickness. She dared not complain; she was not sure of getting any care. She turned pale and faint, said that she felt ill, and went up to bed, clinging to the banisters at every step, and believing that her last hour had come. "Poor Brigaut!" thought she.

"She is ill," said Rogron.

"She ill! It is all megrims," said Sylvie, loud enough to be overheard. "She was not ill this morning, I can tell you!"

This last shot was too much for Pierrette, who crept to bed in tears, praying to God to remove her from this world.

For a month past Rogron had no longer carried the *Constitutionnel* to Gouraud; the colonel obsequiously came to fetch the newspaper, to make talk, and take Rogron out when the weather was fine. Sylvie, sure of seeing the colonel, and being able to question him, dressed herself coquettishly. The old maid thought she achieved this by putting on a green gown, a little yellow cashmere shawl bordered with red, and a white bonnet with meagre gray feathers. At the hour when the colonel was due, she settled herself in the drawing-room with her brother, making him keep on his dressing-gown and slippers.

"It is a fine morning, colonel," said Rogron, hearing Gouraud's heavy step; "but I am not dressed, my sister perhaps wanted to go out, she left me to mind the house ; wait for me.''

Rogron went off, leaving Sylvie with the colonel.

"Where are you going ? you are dressed like a goddess,'' observed Gouraud, seeing a certain solemnity of expression on the old maid's battered face.

" Yes, I was going out ; but as the child is not well, I must stay at home.''

" What is the matter with her ? ''

" I do not know ; she asked to go to bed.''

Gouraud's cautiousness, not to say his distrust, was constantly on the alert as a result of his collusion with Vinet. The lawyer evidently had the best of it. He edited the paper, he ruled it as a master, and applied the profits to the editing ; whereas the colonel, the responsible stalking-horse, got little enough. Who was to be the député ? Vinet. Who the great electioneer ? Vinet. Who was always consulted ? Vinet.

Then he knew, at least as well as Vinet, the extent and depth of the passion consuming Rogron for the fair Bathilde de Chargebœuf. This passion was becoming a mania, as all the lowest passions of men do. Bathilde's voice made the old bachelor thrill. Rogron, thinking only of his desire, concealed it ; he dared not hope for such a match. The colonel, to sound him, had told Rogron that he was about to propose for Bathilde's hand ; Rogron had turned pale at the mere thought of such a formidable rival ; he had become cold to Gouraud, almost hostile. Thus Vinet in every way ruled the roost, while he, the colonel, was tied to the house only by the doubtful bond of a love which, on his part, was but feigned, and on Sylvie's as yet unconfessed. When the lawyer had divulged the priest's manœuvre and advised him to throw over Sylvie and pay his addresses to Pierrette, Vinet had humored his inclinations ; still, as the colonel analyzed the true purport of this suggestion, and examined the ground on which he stood, he fancied he could discern in his ally some hope of making mischief between him and Sylvie, and taking advantage of the old maid's fears to make the whole of Rogron's fortune fall into Mademoiselle de Chargebœuf's hands.

Hence, when Rogron left him alone with Sylvie, the colonel's acumen seized on the slight indications which betrayed some uneasiness in Sylvie. He saw that she had planned to be under arms and alone with him for a minute. Gouraud, who already vehemently suspected Vinet of playing him some malignant trick, ascribed this conference to a secret suggestion of this legal ape; he put himself on guard, as when he had been making a reconnoissance in the enemy's country, keeping an eye on the whole prospect, listening for the least sound, his mind alert, his hand on his weapon. It was the colonel's weakness never to believe a word said by a woman; and when the old maid spoke of Pierrette, and said she was in bed at midday, he concluded that Sylvie had simply put her in disgrace in her room out of jealousy.

"The child is growing very pretty," said he, in an indifferent tone.

"Yes, she will be pretty," replied Mademoiselle Rogron.

"You ought now to send her to a shop in Paris," added the colonel. "She would make a fortune. They look out for very pretty girls now in the milliners' shops."

"Is that really your advice?" asked Sylvie, in an anxious voice.

"Good! I have hit it!" thought the colonel. "Vinet's advice that Pierrette and I should marry by-and-by was only intended to place me in this old witch's black-books. Why," he said aloud, "what do you expect to do with her? Do you not see a perfectly lovely girl, Bathilde de Chargebœuf, of noble birth, well connected, and left to become an old maid. No one will have anything to say to her. Pierrette has nothing; she will never marry. Do you suppose that youth and beauty have any attraction for me, for instance?—for me, who, as captain of artillery in the Imperial Guard from the first day when the Emperor had a guard, have had my feet in every capital in Europe, and known the prettiest women in them all? Youth and beauty—they are deuced common and silly. Don't talk of them to me!

"At eight-and-forty," he went on, adding to his age, "when a man has gone through the retreat from Moscow and the dreadful campaign in France, his loins are a bit weary; I am an old fellow. Now, a wife like you would cosset me and take care of me; her fortune, added to my few thousand francs of pension, would secure me suitable comfort for my old age, and I should like her a thousand times better than a minx who would give me no end of trouble, who would be thirty and have her passions when I should be sixty and have the rheumatism. At my time of life we think of these things. And, between you and me, I may add that if I marry, I should hope to have no children."

Sylvie's face was transparent to the colonel all through this speech, and her reply was enough to assure him of Vinet's perfidy.

"So you are not in love with Pierrette?" she exclaimed.

"Bless me! Are you crazy, my dear Sylvie?" cried he. "When we have lost all our teeth, is it time to crack nuts? Thank God, I still have my wits, and know myself."

Sylvie would not then say more about herself; she thought herself very wily in using her brother's name.

"My brother," said she, "had thought of your marrying her."

"Your brother can never have had such a preposterous notion. A few days ago, to find out his secret, I told him that I was in love with Bathilde; he turned as white as your collar."

"Is he in love with Bathilde?" said Sylvie.

"Madly! And Bathilde certainly loves only his money."

("One for you, Vinet," thought Gouraud.) "What should have made him speak of Pierrette? No, Sylvie," he went on, taking her hand and pressing it with meaning, "since you have led to the subject "—he went close to her—" well " —he kissed her hand; he was a cavalry colonel, and had given proofs of courage—"know this: I want no wife but you. Though the marriage will look like a marriage for money, I feel true affection for you."

"But it was I who wished that you should marry Pierrette; and if I were to give her my money—what then, colonel?"

"But I do not want to have a wretched home, or to see, ten years hence, some young whippersnapper, such as Julliard, hovering around my wife, and writing verses to her in the newspaper. I am too much a man on that score; I will never marry a woman out of all proportion, too young."

"Well, colonel, we will talk that over seriously," said Sylvie, with a glance she thought amorous, and which was very like that of an ogress. Her cold, raw purple lips parted over her yellow teeth, and she fancied she was smiling.

"Here I am," said Rogron, and he led away the colonel, who bowed courteously to the old maid.

Gouraud was determined to hasten his marriage with Sylvie and so become master of the house; promising himself that, through the influence he would acquire over Sylvie during the honeymoon, he would get rid both of Bathilde and of Céleste Habert. So, as they walked, he told Rogron that he had been making fun of him the other day; that he had no intentions of winning Bathilde's heart, not being rich enough to take a wife who had no money. Then he confided his projects; he had long since chosen Sylvie for her admirable qualities; in short, he aspired to the honor of becoming his brother-in-law.

"Oh, colonel! Oh, Baron! If only my consent were needed, it would be done as soon as legal delays should allow!" cried Rogron, delighted to find himself relieved of this terrible rival.

Sylvie spent the whole morning examining her own rooms to see if there were accommodation for a couple. She determined on building another story for her brother, and having the second floor for herself and her husband; but she also promised herself, in accordance with the notions of every old maid, to put the colonel to some tests, so as to judge of his heart and habits before making up her mind. She still had doubts, and wanted to make sure that Pierrette had no intimacy with the colonel.

At dinner-time the girl came down to lay the cloth. Sylvie had been obliged to do the cooking, and had spotted her gown, exclaiming, "Curse Pierrette!" For it was evident, indeed, that if Pierrette had cooked the dinner, Sylvie would not have had a grease-stain on her silk dress.

"So here you are, you little coddle. You are like the blacksmith's dog that sleeps under the forge and wakes at the sound of a saucepan. So you want me to believe that you are ill, you little story-teller!"

The one idea, "You did not confess the truth as to what took place this morning, therefore everything you say is a lie," was like a hammer with which Sylvie was prepared to hit incessantly on Pierrette's head and heart.

To Pierrette's great astonishment, Sylvie sent her after dinner to dress for the evening. The liveliest imagination is no match for the energy which suspicion gives to the mind of an old maid. In such a case, the old maid beats politicians, attorneys, and notaries, bill-brokers and misers. Sylvie promised herself that she would consult Vinet after looking well about her. She meant to keep Pierrette in the room, so as to judge for herself by the child's face whether the colonel had told the truth.

The first to come were Madame de Chargebœuf and her daughter. By her cousin Vinet's advice, Bathilde had dressed with twice her usual elegance. She wore a most becoming blue cotton-velvet gown, the clear kerchief as before, bunches of grapes in garnets and gold for earrings, her hair in ringlets, the artful necklet, little black satin shoes, gray silk stockings, and Suède gloves, and then queenly airs and girlish coquettishness enough to catch every Rogron in the river. Her mother, calm and dignified, had preserved, as had Bathilde, a certain aristocratic impertinence by which these two women redeemed everything, betraying the spirit of their caste. Bathilde was gifted with superior intelligence, though Vinet alone had been able to discern it after the two months that these ladies had spent in his house. When he had sounded the depths of this girl, depressed by the useless-ness of her youth and beauty, but enlightened by the con-tempt she felt for the men of a period when money was their sole idol, Vinet exclaimed in surprise—

"If I had but married you, Bathilde, by this time I should have been keeper of the seals; I would have called myself Vinet de Chargebœuf, and have sat on the right."

Bathilde had no vulgar aims in her wish to be married; she would not marry for motherhood, nor for the sake of hav-ing a husband; she would marry to be free, to have a "re-sponsible publisher," as it were—to be called madame, and to act as men act. Rogron to her was a name; she thought she could make something of this imbecile creature—a député, who might vote while she pulled the wires; she wanted to be revenged on her family, who had paid little heed to a penni-less girl. Vinet, admiring and encouraging her ideas, had greatly extended and strengthened them.

"My dear cousin," said he, explaining to her the influence exerted by women, and pointing out the sphere of action proper to them, "do you suppose that Tiphaine, a profoundly mediocre man, can by his own merits rise to sit on the lower bench in Paris? It is Madame Tiphaine who got him returned as deputy; it is she who will carry him to Paris. Her mother, Madame Roguin, is a cunning body, who does what she pleases with du Tillet the banker, one of Nucingen's chief allies, both of them close friends of Keller's; and these three houses do great services to the government or its most devoted adherents; the offices are on the best possible terms with these lynxes of the financial world, and men like those know all Paris. There is nothing to hinder Tiphaine from rising to be the presiding judge of one of the higher courts. Marry Rogron; we will make him deputy for Provins as soon as I have secured for myself some other constituency in Seine-et-Marne. Then you will have a receivership—one of those places where Rogron will have nothing to do but sign his name. We will stick to the Opposition if it triumphs; but if the Bourbons remain in power, O how gently we will incline towards the centre! Besides, Rogron will not live for ever, and you can marry a title by-and-by. And then, if you are in a good position, the Chargebœufs will help us. Your poverty—like mine—has, no doubt, enabled you to estimate what men are worth; they are to be made use of only as post-horses. A man or a woman can take us from one stage to the next!"

Vinet had made a little Catherine de Medici of Bathilde. He left his wife at home, happy with her two children, and always attended Madame de Chargebœuf and Bathilde to the Rogrons. He appeared in all his glory as the tribune of Champagne. He wore neat gold spectacles, a silk waistcoat, a white cravat, black trousers, thin boots, a black coat made in Paris, a gold watch and chain. Instead of the Vinet of old—pale, lean, haggard, and gloomy—he exhibited the Vinet of the day, in all the bravery of a political personage; sure of his luck, he trod with the decision peculiar to a busy advocate familiar with the caverns of justice. His small,

MATHILDE——PUT HER PRETTY FOOT ON THE BAR OF
THE FENDER.

cunning head was so smartly brushed, and his clean-shaven chin gave him such a finished though cold appearance, that he looked quite pleasing, in the style of Robespierre. He might certainly become a delightful public prosecutor, with an elastic, dangerous, and deadly flow of eloquence, or an orator, with all the subtlety of Benjamin Constant. The acrimony and hatred which had formerly animated him had turned to perfidious softness. The poison had become medicine.

"Good-evening, my dear, how are you?" said Madame de Chargebœuf to Sylvie.

Bathilde went straight to the fireplace, took off her hat, looked at herself in the glass, and put her pretty foot on the bar of the fender to display it to Rogron.

"What ails you, monsieur?" said she, looking at him. "You give me no greeting? Well, indeed! I may put on a velvet frock for your benefit——"

She stopped Pierrette, bidding her put her hat on a chair, and the girl took it from her, Bathilde resigning it to her as though Pierrette had been the housemaid.

Men are thought very fierce, and so are tigers; but neither tigers, nor vipers, nor diplomats, nor men of law, nor executioners, nor kings, can in their utmost atrocities come near the gentle cruelty, the poisoned sweetness, the savage scorn of young ladies to each other when certain of them think themselves superior to others in birth, fortune, or grace, and when marriage is in question, or precedence, or, in short, any feminine rivalry. The "Thank you, mademoiselle," spoken by Bathilde to Pierrette, was a poem in twelve cantos.

Her name was Bathilde, the other's was Pierrette; she was a Chargebœuf, the other a Lorrain! Pierrette was undersized and fragile, Bathilde was tall and full of vitality! Pierrette was fed by charity, Bathilde and her mother lived on their own money! Pierrette wore a stuff frock with a deep tucker, Bathilde dragged the serpentine folds of her blue velvet ! Bathilde had the finest shoulders in the department and an arm like a queen's, Pierrette's shoulder-blades and arms were skinny; Pierrette was Cinderella, Bathilde the fairy; Bathilde would get married, Pierrette would die a maid! Bathilde was worshiped, Pierrette had no one to love her! Bathilde had her hair dressed—she had taste; Pierrette hid her hair under a little cap, and knew nothing of the fashions! *Epilogue*—Bathilde was everything, Pierrette was nothing. The proud little Bretonne perfectly understood this cruel poem.

"Good-evening, child," said Madame de Chargebœuf from the summit of her grandeur, and with an accent given by her narrow-pinched nose.

Vinet put the crowning touch to these insulting civilities by looking at Pierrette and saying, on three notes, "Oh, oh, oh! How fine we are this evening, Pierrette!"

"I!" said the poor child. "You should say that to your cousin, not to me. She is beautiful!"

"Oh, my cousin is always beautiful," replied the lawyer. "Do you not say so, Père Rogron?" he added, turning to the master of the house, and shaking hands with him.

"Yes," said Rogron.

"Why force him to say what he does not think? I never was to his taste," replied Bathilde, placing herself in front of Rogron. "Is not that the truth? Look at me."

Rogron looked at her from head to foot, and gently closed his eyes, like a cat when its poll is scratched.

"You are too beautiful," said he, "too dangerous to look at."

"Why?"

Rogron gazed at the fire-logs and said nothing.

At this moment Mademoiselle Habert came, followed by the colonel. Céleste Habert, everybody's enemy now, had none but Sylvie on her side; but each one showed her all the greater consideration, politeness, and amiable attention because all were undermining her, so that she doubted between this display of civil interest and the distrust which her brother

had implanted in her. The priest, though standing apart
from the theatre of war, guessed everything; and so, when
he perceived that his sister's hopes were at an end, he became
one of the Rogrons' most formidable antagonists.

The reader can at once imagine what Mademoiselle Habert
was like on being told that even if she had not been mistress
—arch-mistress—of a school, she would still always have
looked like a governess. Governesses have a particular way,
of putting on their caps. Just as elderly Englishwomen have
monopolized the fashion of turbans, so governesses have the
monopoly of these caps; the crown of the cap towers above
the flowers, the flowers are more than artificial; stored carefully in a wardrobe, this cap is always new and always old,
even on the first day. These old maids make it a point of
honor to be like a painter's lay-figure; they sit on their
haunches, not on their chairs. When they are spoken to they
turn their whole body; and when their gowns creak, we are
tempted to believe that the springs of the machinery are out
of order. Mademoiselle Habert, a type of her kind, had a
hard eye, a set mouth, and under her chin, furrowed with
wrinkles, the limp and crumpled cap-strings wagged and
frisked as she moved. She had an added charm in two
moles, rather large and rather brown, with hairs that she left
to grow like untied clematis. Finally, she took snuff, and
without grace.

They sat down to the toil of boston. Sylvie had opposite
to her Mademoiselle Habert, and the colonel sat on one side,
opposite Madame de Chargebœuf. Bathilde placed herself
near her mother and Rogron. Sylvie put Pierrette between
herself and the colonel. Rogron opened another card-table
in case Monsieur Néraud should come, and Monsieur Cournant and his wife. Vinet and Bathilde could both play
whist, which was Monsieur and Madame Cournant's game.
Ever since the Chargebœuf ladies—as they say in Provins—
had been in the habit of coming to the Rogrons, the two

lamps blazed on the chimney-piece between the candelabra
and the clock, and the tables were lighted by wax-lights at
two francs a pound, which, however, were paid for by win-
nings at cards.

" Now, Pierrette, my child, take your sewing," said Sylvie
with treacherous gentleness, seeing her watch the colonel's
play.

In public she always pretended to treat Pierrette very
kindly.   This mean deceit irritated the honest Bretonne,
and made her despise her cousin.   Pierrette fetched her
embrodiery ; but as she set the stitches, she looked now and
then at the colonel's game.   Gouraud seemed not to know
that there was a little girl at his side.   Sylvie began to think
this indifference extremely suspicious.   At a certain moment
in the game the old maid declared *misère* in hearts ; the pool
was full of counters, and there were twenty-seven sous in it
besides.   The Cournants and Néraud had come.   The old
supernumerary judge, Desfondrilles—a man in whom the
minister of justice had discerned the qualifications for a judge
when appointing him examining magistrate, but who was
never thought clever enough for a superior position—had for
the last two months forsaken the Tiphaines and shown a
leaning towards Vinet's party.   He was now standing in
front of the fire, holding up his coat-tails, and gazing at the
gorgeous drawing-room in which Mademoiselle de Chargebœuf shone ; for the setting of crimson looked as if it had
been contrived on purpose to show off the beauty of this
magnificent   young   woman.   Silence   reigned ;   Pierrette
watched the play, and Sylvie's attention was diverted by the
excitement of the game.

" Play that," said Pierrette to the colonel, pointing to a
heart.

The colonel led from a sequence in hearts ; the hearts lay
between him and Sylvie ; the colonel forced the ace, though
it was guarded in Sylvie's hand by five small cards.

"It is not fair play! Pierrette saw my hand, and the colonel allowed her to advise him!"

"But, mademoiselle," said Céleste, "it was the colonel's game to lead hearts since he found that you had one!"

The speech made Desfondrilles smile; he was a keen observer, who amused himself with watching all the interests at stake in Provins, where he played the part of "Rigaudin" in Picard's play of "La Maison en Loterie."

"It was the colonel's game," Cournant put in, without knowing anything about it.

Sylvie shot at Mademoise'le Habert a look of old maid against old maid, villainous but honeyed.

"Pierrette, you saw my hand," said Sylvie, fixing her eyes on the girl.

"No, cousin."

"I was watching you all," said the archæological judge; "I can bear witness that the little girl saw no one's hand but the colonel's."

"Pooh! these little girls know very well how to steal a glance with their sweet eyes," said Gouraud in alarm.

"Indeed!" said Sylvie.

"Yes," replied Gouraud; "she may have looked over your hand to play you a trick. Was it not so, my beauty?"

"No," said the honest Bretonne. "I am incapable of such a thing! In that case I should have followed my cousin's game."

"You know very well that you are a story-teller and a little fool into the bargain," said Sylvie. "Since what took place this morning, who can believe a word you may say? You are a——"

Pierrette did not wait to hear her cousin end the sentence in her presence. Anticipating a torrent of abuse, she rose, went out of the room without a light, and up to her room. Sylvie turned pale with rage, and muttered between her teeth, "I will pay her out!"

" Will you pay your losses ? " said Madame de Chargebœuf.

At this moment poor Pierrette hit her head against the passage door which the judge had left open.

" Good ! That serves her right ! " cried Sylvie.

" What has happened ? " asked Desfondrilles.

" Nothing that she does not deserve," replied Sylvie.

" She has given herself some severe blow," said Mademoiselle Habert.

Sylvie tried to evade paying her stakes by rising to see what Pierrette had done ; but Madame de Chargebœuf stopped her.

" Pay us first," said she, laughing ; " by the time you return you will have forgotten all about it."

This suggestion, based on the bad faith the ex-haberdasher showed in the matter of her gambling debts, met with general approval. Sylvie sat down and thought no more of Pierrette ; and no one was surprised at her indifference. All the evening Sylvie was absent-minded. When cards were over, at about half-past nine, she sank into an easy-chair by the fire, and only rose to take leave of her guests. The colonel tortured her ; she did not know what to think about him.

" Men are so false ! " said she to herself as she fell asleep.

Pierrette had given herself a frightful blow against the edge of the door, just over her ear, where girls part their hair to put the forepart into curl-papers. Next morning there was a bad purple-veined bruise.

" God has punished you," said Sylvie at breakfast; " you disobeyed me, you showed a great want of respect in not listening to me, and in going away in the middle of my sentence. You have received no more than you have justly deserved."

" Still," said Rogron, " you should put on a rag dipped in salt and water."

" Pooh ! It is nothing ! " said Sylvie.

7

The poor child had come to the point when she thought her guardian's remark a proof of interest.

The week ended as it had begun, in constant torment. Sylvie became ingenious, and carried her refinement of tyranny to an extreme pitch. The Iroquois, Cherokees, and Mohicans might have learned of her. Pierrette dared not complain of her misery and the intense pain she suffered in her head. At the bottom of Sylvie's displeasure lay the girl's refusal to tell anything about Brigaut; and Pierrette, with Breton obstinacy, was determined to keep a very natural silence. Every one can imagine what a glance she gave Brigaut, who, as she believed, would be lost to her if he were discovered, and whom she instinctively longed to keep near her, happy in knowing that he was at Provins. What a delight to her to see Brigaut again! The sight of the companion of her childhood was to her like the view an exile gets from afar of his native land; she looked on him as a martyr gazes at the sky when, during his torments, his eyes, blessed with double sight, see through to heaven.

Pierrette's parting glance had been so perfectly intelligible to the major's son that, while he planed his boards, opened his compasses, took his measurements, and fitted his pieces, he racked his brains for some means of corresponding with Pierrette. Brigaut at last hit on this extremely simple plan. At a certain hour at night Pierrette must let down a string, and he would tie a letter to the end of it. In the midst of her terrible sufferings from two maladies, an abscess which was forming in her head, and her general disorderment, Pierrette was sustained by the idea of corresponding with Brigaut. The same desire agitated both hearts; though apart, they understood each other! At every pang that made her heart flutter, at every pain that shot through her brain, Pierrette said to herself, "Brigaut is at hand!" and then she could suffer without complaining.

On the next market-day after their first meeting in the

church, Brigaut looked out for his little friend. Though he saw that she was pale, and trembling like a November leaf about to drop from the bough, without losing his head he went to bargain for some fruit at the stall where the terrible Sylvie was beating down the price of her purchases. Brigaut contrived to slip a note into Pierrette's hand, and he did it naturally, while jesting with the market-woman, and with all the dexterity of a rake, as if he had never done anything else, so coolly did he manage it, in spite of the hot blood that sang in his ears and surged boiling from his heart, almost bursting the veins and arteries. On the surface he had the determination of an old housebreaker, and within the quaking heart of innocence, like mothers sometimes in their mortal anguish, when they are gripped between two dangers, between two precipices. Pierrette felt Brigaut's dizziness; she crushed the paper into her apron pocket; the pallor of her cheeks changed to the cherry redness of a fierce fire. These two children each unconsciously went through sensations enough for ten commonplace love-affairs. That instant left in their souls a wellspring of emotions. Sylvie, who did not recognize the Breton accent, could not suspect a lover in Brigaut, and Pierrette came home with her treasure.

The letters of these two poor children were destined to serve as documents in a horrible legal squabble; for, but for that fatal circumstance, they never would have been seen. This is what Pierrette read that evening in the quiet seclusion of her attic room:

"My dear Pierrette:—At midnight, when everybody is asleep, but when I shall be awake for your sake, I will come every night under the kitchen window. You can let down out of your window a string long enough to reach me, which will make no noise, and tie to the end of it whatever you want to write to me. I will answer you in the same way. I knew that you had been taught to read and write by those wretched relations who were to do you so much good, and who are doing you so much harm! You, Pierrette, the daughter of a colonel who died for France, are compelled by these monsters to cook for them! That is how your pretty color and your fine health have vanished. What has become of my Pierrette? What have they done to her? I can see plainly that you are not happy.

"Oh! Pierrette, let us go back to Brittany. I can earn enough to give you everything you need; you may have three francs a day, for I earn from four to five, and thirty sous are plenty for me. Oh! Pierrette, how I have prayed to God for you since seeing you again. I have asked Him to give me all your pain, and to grant you all the pleasures.

"What have you to do with them that they keep you? Your grandmother is more to you than they are. These Rogrons are venomous; they have spoiled all your gaiety. You do not even walk at Provins as you used to move in Brittany. Let us go home to Brittany. In short, here I am to serve you, to do your bidding; and you must tell me what you wish. If you want money, I have sixty crowns of ours, and I shall have the grief of sending them to you by the string instead of kissing your dear hands respectfully when I give you the money. Ah! my dear Pierrette, the blue sky has now for a long time been dark to me. I have not had two hours of joy since I put you into that ill-starred diligence; and when I saw you again, like a shade, that witch of a cousin disturbed our happiness. However, we shall have the comfort of praying to God together every Sunday; He will perhaps hear us the better. Not good-by, dear Pierrette, only till to-night."

This letter agitated her so greatly that she sat for above an hour reading and re-reading it; but she reflected, not without pain, that she had nothing to write with. So she made up her mind to the difficult expedition from her attic to the dining-room, where she could find ink, pen, and paper; and she accomplished it without waking Sylvie. A few minutes before midnight she had finished this letter, which was also produced in court:

"My Friend:—Oh, yes, my friend! For there is no one but you, Jacques, and my grandmother, who loves me. God forgive me, but you are the only two persons I love, one as much as the other, neither more nor less. I was too little to remember my mother; but you, Jacques, and my grandmother, and my grandfather too, God rest his soul, for he suffered much from his ruin, which was mine too—in short, you are the only two remaining, and I love you as much as I am wretched! So to know how much I love you, you would have to know how much I suffer; but I do not wish that—it would make you too unhappy. I am spoken to as you would not speak to a dog; I am treated as if I were dirt; and in vain I examine myself as if I were before God, I cannot see that I am in fault towards them. Before you sang the bride's song to me I saw that God was good in my misery; for I prayed to Him to take me out of this world, and as I felt very ill, I said to myself, ' God has heard me ! '

"But since you have come, Brigaut, I want to go away with you to Brittany to see my grandmamma, who loves me, though they tell me she has robbed me of eight thousand francs. Brigaut, if they are really mine, can you get them? But it is all a lie; if we had eight thousand francs, grandmamma would not be at Saint-Jacques. I would not trouble that good saintly woman's last days by telling her of my miseries; it would be enough to kill her. Ah! if she could know that they make her grandchild wash the pots and pans —she who would say to me, ' Leave that alone, my darling,' when I tried to help her in her troubles; ' leave it, leave it, my pet; you will spoil your pretty little hands.' Well, my nails are clean at any rate! Many times I cannot carry the market basket, and the handle saws my arm as I come home from market.

"At the same time, I do not think that my cousins are cruel ; but it is their way always to be scolding, and it would seem that I can never get away from them. My cousin Rogron is my guardian. One day when I meant to run away, as I was too miserable, and I told them so, my cousin Sylvie answered that the police would go after me, that the law was on my guardian's side ; and I saw very clearly that cousins can no more take the place of our father and mother than the saints can take the place of God. My poor Jacques, what use could I make of your money? Keep it for our journey. Oh ! how I have thought of you and Pen-Hoël and the large pool. We ate our cake first, out there. I think that I am getting worse. I am very ill, Jacques. I have such pains in my head that I could scream, and in my back and my bones ; something round my loins that half kills me; and I have no appetite but for nasty things, leaves and roots, and I like the smell of printed paper. There are times when I should cry if I were alone, for I may not do anything as I wish; I am not even allowed to cry. I have to hide myself to offer up my tears to Him from whom we receive those mercies which we call our afflictions. Was it not He who inspired you with the good idea of coming to sing the bride's song under my window ? Oh ! Jacques, cousin Sylvie,.who heard you, told me I had a lover. If you will be my lover, love me very much ; I promise always to love you, as in the past, and to be your faithful servant,

"PIERRETTE LORRAIN.

"You will always love me, won't you ? "

The girl had taken a crust of bread from the kitchen, in which she made a hole to stick her letter in, so as to weight the thread. At midnight, after opening her window with excessive caution, she let down her note with the bread, which could make no noise by tapping against the wall or the shutters. She felt the thread pulled by Brigaut, who broke it, and then went stealthily away. When he was in the middle of the square she could see him, though indistinctly, in the starlight; but he could gaze at her in the luminous band projected by the candle. The two young things remained there for an hour, Pierrette signaling to him to go away, he going and she remaining, and he returning to his post, while Pierrette again waved to him to be gone. This was several times repeated, till the girl shut her window, got into bed, and blew out her light.

Once in bed, she went to sleep, happy though suffering; she had Brigaut's letter under her pillow. She slept the sleep of the persecuted, a sleep blessed by the angels, the sleep of golden and far-away glories full of the arabesques of heaven, which Raphael dreamed of and drew.

Her delicate physical nature was so responsive to her moral nature that Pierrette rose next morning as glad and light as a lark, beaming and gay. Such a change could not escape Sylvie's eye; this time, instead of scolding her, she proceeded to watch her with the cunning of a raven.

" What makes her so happy? " was suggested by jealousy, and not by tyranny. If Sylvie had not been possessed by the idea of the colonel, she would certainly have said as usual, " Pierrette, you are very turbulent, or very heedless of what is said to you." The old maid determined to spy on Pierrette, as only old maids can spy. The day passed in gloom and silence, like the hour before a storm.

" So you are no longer so ailing, miss? " said Sylvie at dinner. " Did I not tell you that she shams it all to worry us? " she exclaimed, turning to her brother, without waiting for Pierrette's reply.

" On the contrary, cousin, I have a sort of fever," said the distressed child.

"What sort of fever. You are as gay as a linnet. You have seen some one again, perhaps?"

Pierrette shuddered, and kept her eyes on her plate.

"*Tartufe!*" cried Sylvie. "At fourteen! Already! What a nature! Why, you will be a wretch indeed!"

"I do not know what you mean," replied Pierrette, raising her fine luminous hazel eyes to her cousin's face.

"This evening," said Sylvie, "you will remain in the dining-room to sew by a candle. You are in the way in the drawing-room, and I will not have you looking over my hand to advise your favorites."

Pierrette did not flinch.

"Hypocrite!" exclaimed Sylvie as she left the room.

Rogron, who could not understand what his sister was talking about, said to Pierrette, "What is the matter between you two? Try, Pierrette, to please your cousin; she is most indulgent, most kind; and if she is put out with you, certainly you must be wrong. Why do you squabble? For my part, I like a quiet life. Look at Mademoiselle Bathilde; you should try to copy her."

Pierrette could bear it all; Brigaut would come, beyond doubt, at midnight to bring his answer, and this hope was her viaticum for the day. But she was exhausting her last strength. She did not go to sleep; she sat up listening to the clocks strike the hours, and fearing to make a sound. At last twelve struck; she softly opened her window, and this time she used a string she had made long enough by tying several bits together. She heard Brigaut's step, and when she drew up the string she read the following letter, which filled her with joy:

"My dear Pierrette:—If you are in such pain, you must not tire yourself by sitting up for me. You will be sure to hear me call like a 'Chouan.' My father luckily taught me to imitate their cry. So I shall repeat it three times, and you will know that I have come, and that you must let down the string, but I shall not come again for some few days. I hope then to have good news for you. Oh! Pierrette, not death! What are you thinking of? All my heart quaked; I thought I was dead myself at the mere idea. No, my Pierrette, you shall not die; you shall live happy, and soon be rescued from your persecutors. If I should not succeed in what I am attempting, to save you, I would go to the lawyers and declare in the face of heaven and earth how you are treated by your cruel relations.

"I am certain that you have only to endure a few days more; have patience. Pierrette, Brigaut is watching over you, as he did in the days when we went to slide on the pond, and I pulled you out of the deep hole where we were so nearly lost together. Good-by, my dear Pierrette; in a few days we shall be happy, please God. Alas! I dare not tell you of the only thing that may hinder our meeting. But God loves us! So in a few days I shall be able to see my dear Pierrette in liberty, without a care, without any one hindering my looking at you, for I am very hungry to see you, Oh Pierrette! Pierrette, who condescends to love me and to tell me so. Yes, Pierrette, I will be your lover, but only when I have earned the grand fortune you deserve, and till then I will be no more to you than a devoted servant whom you may command. Adieu.

"JACQUES BRIGAUT."

This was what the young fellow did not tell Pierrette. He had written the following letter to Madame Lorrain at Nantes:

"MADAME LORRAIN:—Your granddaughter will die, killed by ill-usage, if you do not come to claim her back. I hardly knew her again; and to enable you to judge for yourself of the state of things, I enclose in this letter one from Pierrette to me. You are reported here to have your grandchild's fortune, and you ought to justify yourself on this point. In short, if you can, come quickly; we may yet be happy, or later you will find Pierrette dead.

"I remain, with respect, your humble servant,

"JACQUES BRIGAUT.

"At Monsieur Frappier's, master joiner, Grand' Rue, Provins."

Brigaut only feared lest Pierrette's grandmother might be dead.

Though this letter from him, whom in her innocence she called her lover, was almost inexplicable to Pierrette, she accepted it with virgin faith. Her heart experienced the feeling which travelers in the desert know when they see from afar the palm grove round a well. In a few days her miseries would be ended, Brigaut said it; she slept on the promise of her childhood's friend; and yet, as she laid this letter with the former one, a dreadful thought found dreadful expression—

"Poor Brigaut," said she to herself, "he does not know the hole I have my feet in!"

Sylvie had heard Pierrette; she had also heard Brigaut below the window; she sprang up, rushed to look out on the square through the shutter slats, and saw a man going away towards the house where the colonel lived. In front of that Brigaut stopped. The old maid gently opened her door, went upstairs, was amazed at seeing a light in Pierrette's room, peeped through the keyhole, and could see nothing.

"Pierrette," said she, "are you ill?"

"No, cousin," said Pierrette, startled.

"Then why have you a light in your room at midnight? Open your door. I must know what you are about."

Pierrette, barefoot, opened the door, and Sylvie saw the skein of twine which Pierrette, never dreaming of being caught, had neglected to put away. Sylvie pounced upon it.

"What do you use that for?"

"Nothing, cousin."

"Nothing!" said she. "Very good. Lies again! You will not find that the way to heaven. Go to bed; you are cold."

She asked no more, but disappeared, leaving Pierrette terror-stricken by such leniency. Instead of an outbreak, Sylvie had suddenly made up her mind to steal a march on the colonel and Pierrette, to possess herself of the letters, and confound the couple who were deceiving her. Pierrette, inspired by danger, put the two letters inside her stays and covered them with calico.

This was the end of the loves of Pierrette and Brigaut.

Pierrette was glad of her friend's decision, for Sylvie's suspicions would be disconcerted by having nothing to feed on. And, in fact, Sylvie spent three nights out of her bed and three evenings in watching the innocent colonel, without discovering anything in Pierrette's room, or in the house or out of it, that hinted at their having any understanding. She sent Pierrette to confession, and took advantage of her absence to hunt through everything in the child's room as dexterously and as keenly as the spies and searchers at the gates of Paris. She found nothing. Her rage rose to the climax of human passion. If Pierrette had been present, she would certainly have beaten her without ruth. To a woman of this temper, jealousy was not so much a feeling as a possession; she breathed, she felt her heart beat, she had emotions in a way hitherto completely unknown to her; at the least movement she was on the alert, she listened to the faintest sounds, she watched Pierrette with gloomy concentration.

"That little wretch will be the death of me!" she would say.

Sylvie's severity to the child became at last the most refined cruelty, and aggravated the miserable state in which Pierrette lived. The poor little thing was constantly in a fever, and the pain in her head became intolerable. By the end of a week she displayed to the frequenters of the Rogrons' house a face of suffering which must certainly have softened any less cruel egotism; but Doctor Néraud, advised perhaps by Vinet, did not call for more than a week. The colonel, suspected by Sylvie, was afraid she might break off their marriage if he showed the smallest anxiety about Pierrette; Bathilde accounted for her indisposition by simple causes, in no way dangerous.

At last, one Sunday evening, when the drawing-room was full of company, Pierrette could not endure the pain; she fainted completely away; and the colonel, who was the first to observe that she had lost consciousness, lifted her up and carried her to a sofa.

"She did it on purpose," said Sylvie, looking at Mademoiselle Habert and the other players.

"Your cousin is very ill, I assure you," said the colonel.

"She was very well in your arms," retorted Sylvie, with a hideous smile.

"The colonel is right," said Madame de Chargebœuf; "you ought to send for a doctor. This morning in church every one was talking of Mademoiselle Lorrain's state as they came out—it is obvious."

"I am dying," said Pierrette.

Desfondrilles called to Sylvie to unfasten the girl's frock. Sylvie complied, saying, "It is all a sham!"

She undid the dress, and was going to loosen the stays. Then Pierrette found superhuman strength; she sat up, and exclaimed, "No, no; I will go to bed."

Sylvie had touched her stays, and had felt the papers. She allowed Pierrette to escape, saying to everybody, "Well, do you think she is so very ill? It is all put on; you could never imagine the naughtiness of that child."

She detained Vinet at the end of the evening; she was

furious, she was bent on revenge; she was rough with the
colonel as he bid her good-night.   Gouraud shot a glance at
Vinet that seemed to pierce him to the very bowels, and
mark the spot for a bullet.   Sylvie begged Vinet to remain.
When they were alone, the old maid began—

"Never in my life, nor in all my days, will I marry the
colonel!"

"Now that you have made up your mind, I may speak.
The colonel is my friend; still, I am yours rather than his.
Rogron has done me services I can never forget.   I am as
firm a friend as I am an implacable enemy.   Certainly, when
once I am in the Chamber you will see how I shall rise, and
I will make Rogron a receiver-general.   Well, swear to me
never to repeat a word of our conversation!"   Sylvie nodded
assent.   "In the first place, our gallant colonel is an invet-
erate gambler."

"Indeed!" said Sylvie.

"But for the difficulties this passion has gotten him into,
he might perhaps have been a marshal of France," the lawyer
went on.   "So he might squander all your fortune.   But he
is a deep customer.   Do not believe that married people have
or have not children, and you know what will happen to you.
No.   If you wish to marry, wait till I am in the Chamber,
and then you can marry old Desfondrilles, who will be president of the court here.   To revenge yourself, make your
brother marry Mademoiselle de Chargebœuf; I will undertake
to get her consent; she will have two thousand francs a year,
and you will be as nearly connected with the Chargebœufs as
I am.   Take my word for it, the Chargebœufs will call us
cousins some day."

"Gouraud is in love with Pierrette," replied Sylvie.

"He is quite capable of it," said Vinet; "and quite capable of marrying her after your death."

"A pretty little scheme!" said she.

"I tell you, he is as cunning as the devil.   Make your

brother marry, and announce that you intend to remain unmarried and leave your money to your nephews or nieces;
you will thus hit Pierrette and Gouraud by the same blow,
and you will see how foolish he will look."

"To be sure," cried the old maid; "I can catch them.
She shall go into a store, and will have nothing. She has not
a penny. Let her do as we did, and work."

Vinet having got his idea into Sylvie's head, and knowing
her obstinacy, left the house. The old maid ended by thinking that the plan was her own.

Vinet found the colonel outside, smoking a cigar while he
waited for him.

"Hold hard!" said the colonel. "You have pulled me to
pieces, but there are stones enough in the ruins to bury you."

"Colonel!"

"There is no 'colonel' in the case. I am going to lead
you a dance. In the first place, you will never be deputy——"

"Colonel!"

"I can surely command ten votes, and the election depends
on——"

"Colonel, just listen to me. Is there no one in the world
but old Sylvie? I have just been trying to clear you. You
are accused and proved guilty of writing to Pierrette; she
has seen you coming out of your house at midnight to stand
below the girl's window——"

"Well imagined!"

"She means her brother to marry Bathilde, and will keep
her fortune for their children."

"Will Rogron have any?"

"Yes," said Vinet. "But I promise to find you a young
and agreeable woman with a hundred and fifty thousand francs.
Are you mad? Can you and I afford to quarrel? Things
have turned against you in spite of me; but you do not
know me."

"Well, we must learn to know each other," replied the

colonel. "Get me a wife with fifty thousand crowns before the elections—otherwise, your servant. I do not like awkward bed-fellows, and you have pulled all the blankets to your side. Good-night."

"You will see," said Vinet, shaking hands affectionately with the colonel.

At about one in the morning three clear, low hoots, like those of an owl, admirably mimicked, sounded in the plazza; Pierrette heard them in her fevered sleep. She got up, quite damp, opened her window, saw Brigaut, and threw out a ball of silk, to which he tied a letter.

Sylvie, excited by the events of the evening and her own deliberations, was not asleep; she was taken in by the owl's cry.

"Ah! what a bird of ill-omen. But, hark! Pierrette is out of bed. What does she want?"

On hearing the attic window open, Sylvie rushed to her own window and heard Brigaut's paper rustle against the shutters. She tied her jacket strings, and nimbly mounted the stairs to Pierrette's room; she found her untying the silk from round the letter.

"So I have caught you!" cried the old maid, going to the window, whence she saw Brigaut take to his heels. "Give me that letter."

"No, cousin," said the girl, who, by one of the stupendous inspirations of youth, and sustained by her spirit, rose to the dignity of resistance which we admire in the history of some nations reduced to desperation.

"What, you will not?" cried Sylvie, advancing on her cousin, and showing her a hideous face full of hatred and distorted by rage.

Pierrette drew back a step or two to have time to clutch her letter in her hand, which she kept shut with invincible strength. On seeing this, Sylvie seized Pierrette's delicate white hand in her lobster's claws, and tried to wrench it open. It was a fearful struggle, an infamous struggle, as everything is that dares to attack thought, the only treasure that God has set beyond the reach of power, and keeps as a secret bond between the wretched and Himself.

The two women, one dying, the other full of vigor, looked steadfastly at each other. Pierrette's eyes flashed at her torturer such a look as the Templar's who received on his breast the blows from a mace in the presence of Philippe le Bel. The King could not endure that fearful gleam, and retired appalled by it; Sylvie, a woman, and a jealous woman, answered that magnetic glance by an ominous glare. Awful silence reigned. The Bretonne's clenched fingers resisted her cousin's efforts with the tenacity of a steel vise. Sylvie wrung Pierrette's arm, and tried to open her hand; as this had no effect, she vainly set her nails in the flesh. Finally, madness reinforced her anger; she raised Pierrette's fist to her teeth to bite her fingers and subdue her by pain. Pierrette still defied her with the terrifying gaze of innocence. The old maid's fury was roused to such a pitch that she was blind to all else; gripping Pierrette's arm, she beat the girl's fist on the window-sill, and on the marble chimney-piece, as we beat a nut to crack it and get at the kernel.

"Help, help!" cried Pierrette; "I am being killed."

"So you scream, do you, when I find you with a lover in the middle of the night?"

And she hit again and again without mercy.

"Help, help!" cried Pierrette, whose fist was bleeding.

At this moment there were violent blows on the street-door. Both equally exhausted, the two women ceased.

Rogron, aroused and anxious, not knowing what was happening, had gotten out of bed, gone to his sister's room, and not finding her he was alarmed, went down and opened the door, and was almost upset by Brigaut, followed by what seemed a phantom.

At the same instant Sylvie's eyes fell on Pierrette's stays; she remembered having felt the papers in them; she threw herself on them like a tiger on his prey, twisted the stays round her hand, and held them up with a smile, as an Iroquois smiles at his foe before scalping him.

"I am dying——" said Pierrette, dropping on her knees. "Who will save me?"

"I will," cried a woman with white hair, turning on Pierrette an aged, parchment face in which a pair of gray eyes sparkled.

"Ah, grandmother, you have come too late!" cried the poor child, melting into tears.

Pierrette went to fall on her bed, bereft of all her strength, and half-killed by the reaction, which in a sick girl was inevitable after such a violent struggle. The tall, withered apparition took her in her arms as a nurse takes a child, and went out, followed by Brigaut, without saying a word to Sylvie, at whom, by a tragic glance, she hurled majestic accusation. The sight of this dignified old woman in her Breton costume, shrouded in her *coiffe*, which is a sort of long cloak made of black cloth, and accompanied by the terrible Brigaut, appalled Sylvie; she felt as if she had seen death.

She went downstairs, heard the door shut, and found herself face to face with her brother, who said to her. "They have not killed you then?"

"Go to bed," said Sylvie. "To-morrow morning we will see what is to be done."

She got into bed again, unpicked the stays, and read Brigaut's two letters, which utterly confounded her. She went to sleep in the strangest perplexity, never dreaming of the terrible legal action to which her conduct was to give rise.

Brigaut's letter to the widow Lorrain had found her in the greatest joy, which was checked when she read it. The poor old woman, now past seventy, had been dying of grief at having to live without Pierrette at her side; she only comforted herself for her loss by the belief that she had sacrificed herself to her grandchild's interests. She had one of those ever-young hearts to which self-sacrifice gives strength and vitality. Her old husband, whose only joy Pierrette had been, had grieved for the child ; day after day he had looked for her and missed her. It was an old man's sorrow; the sorrow old men live on, and die of at last.

Everybody can therefore imagine the joy felt by this poor woman, shut up in an almshouse, on hearing of one of those actions which, though rare, are still heard of in France.

After his failure François Joseph Collinet, the head of the house of Collinet, sailed for America with his children. He was a man of too much good feeling to sit down at Nantes, ruined and bereft of credit, in the midst of the disasters caused by his bankruptcy. From 1814 till 1824 this brave merchant, helped by his children and by his cashier, who remained faithful to him and loaned him the money to start again, valiantly worked to make a second fortune. After incredible efforts, that were crowned by success, by the eleventh year he was able to return to Nantes and rehabilitate himself, leaving his eldest son at the head of the American house. He found Madame Lorrain of Pen-Hoël at Saint-Jacques, and beheld the resignation with which the most hapless of his fellow-victims endured her penury.

"God forgive you ! " said the old woman, "since you give me on the brink of the grave the means of securing my grandchild's happiness. I, alas ! can never see my poor old man's credit re-established."

Monsieur Collinet had brought to his creditor her capital and interest at trade rates, altogether about forty-two thousand francs. His other creditors, active, wealthy, and capable men, had kept themselves above water, while the Lorrains' overthrow had seemed to old Collinet irremediable ; he had now promised the widow that he would rehabilitate her husband's good name, finding that it would involve an expenditure of only about forty thousand francs more. When this act of

9

generous restitution became known on 'change at Nantes, the authorities were eager to reopen its doors to Collinet before he had surrendered to the court at Rennes; but the merchant declined the honor, and submitted to all the rigor of the commercial code.

Madame Lorrain, then, had received forty-two thousand francs the day before the post brought her Brigaut's letters. As she signed her receipt, her first words were—

"Now I can live with my Pierrette, and let her marry poor Brigaut, who will then be able to make a fortune out of my money!"

She could not sit still; she fussed and fidgeted, and wanted to set out for Provins. And when she had read the fatal letters, she rushed out into the town like a mad thing, asking how she could get to Provins with the swiftness of lightning. She set out by mail when she heard of the governmental rapidity of that conveyance. From Paris she took the Troyes coach; she had arrived at eleven that evening at Frappier's, where Brigaut, seeing the old Bretonne's deep despair, at once promised to fetch her granddaughter, after describing Pierrette's state in a few words. Those few words so alarmed the old woman that she could not control her impatience; she ran out to the square. When Pierrette screamed, her grandmother's heart was pierced by the cry as keenly as was Brigaut's. The two together would no doubt have roused all the inhabitants, if Rogron, in sheer terror, had not opened the door. This cry of a girl in her extremity filled the old woman with strength as great as her horror; she carried her dear Pierrette all the way to Frappier's, where his wife had hastily arranged Brigaut's room for Pierrette's grandmother. So in this miserable lodging, on a bed scarcely made, they laid the poor child; she fainted away, still keeping her hand closed, bruised and bleeding as it was, her nails set in the flesh. Brigaut, Frappier, his wife, and the old woman contemplated Pierrette in silence, all lost in unutterable astonishment.

"Why is her hand covered with blood?" was the grandmother's first question.

Pierrette, overcome by the sleep which follows such an
extreme exertion of strength, and knowing that she was safe
from any violence, relaxed her fingers. Brigaut's letter fell
out as an answer.

"They wanted to get my letter," said Brigaut, falling on
his knees and picking up the note he had written, desiring his
little friend to steal softly out of the Rogrons' house. He
piously kissed the little martyr's hand.

Then there was a thing which made the joiners shudder:
it was the sight of old Madame Lorrain, a sublime spectre,
standing by the child's bedside. Horror and vengeance fired
with fierce expression the myriad wrinkles that furrowed her
skin of ivory yellow; on her brow, shaded by thin, gray
locks, sat divine wrath. With the powerful intuition granted
to the aged as they approach the tomb, she read all Pierrette's
life, of which indeed she had been thinking all the way she
had come.

She understood the malady that threatened the life of her
darling. Two large tears gathered painfully in her gray-and-
white eyes, which sorrow had robbed of lashes and eyebrows;
two beads of grief that gave a fearful moisture to those eyes,
and swelled and rolled over those withered cheeks without
wetting them.

"They have killed her!" she exclaimed at last, clasping
her hands.

She dropped on her knees, which hit two sharp blows on
the floor; she was making a vow, no doubt, to Sainte-Anne
d'Auray, the most powerful Madonna of Brittany.

"A doctor from Paris," she next said to Brigaut. "Fly
there, Brigaut. Go!"

She took the artisan by the shoulders and turned him round
with a despotic gesture.

"I was coming at any rate, my good Brigaut," she said,

calling him back. "I am rich. Here!" She untied the ribbon that fastened her bodice across her bosom, took out a paper, in which were wrapped forty-two bank-notes, and said, "Take as much as you need; bring back the greatest doctor in Paris."

"Keep that," said Frappier; "he could not change a bank-note at this hour. I have money; the diligence will pass presently, he will be sure to find a place in it. But would it not be better first to consult Monsieur Martener, who will give us the name of a Paris physician? The diligence is not due for an hour; we have plenty of time."

Brigaut went off to rouse Monsieur Martener. He brought the doctor back with him, not a little surprised to find Mademoiselle Lorrain at Frappier's. Brigaut described to him the scene that had just taken place at the Rogrons. The loquacity of a despairing lover threw light on this domestic drama, though the doctor could not suspect its horrors or its extent. Martener gave Brigaut the address of the famous Horace Bianchon, and Jacques and his master left the room on hearing the approach of the diligence.

Monsieur Martener sat down, and began by examining the bruises and wounds on the girl's hand, which hung out of bed.

"She did not hurt herself in such a way," said he.

"No, the dreadful creature I was so unhappy as to trust her with was torturing her," said the grandmother. "My poor Pierrette was crying out, 'Help! Murder!' It was enough to touch the heart of an executioner."

"But why?" said the doctor, feeling Pierrette's pulse. "She is very ill," he went on, bringing the light close to the bed. "We shall hardly save her," said he, after looking at her face. "She must have suffered terribly, and I cannot understand their having left her without care."

"It is my intention," said the old woman, "to appeal to justice. Had these people, who wrote to ask me for my granddaughter, saying that they had twelve thousand francs a

year, any right to make her their cook and give her work far
beyond her strength?"

"They did not choose to see that she was obviously suffering from one of the ailments to which young girls are sometimes subject, and needed the greatest care!" cried Monsieur
Martener.

Pierrette was roused, partly by the light held by Madame
Frappier so as to show her face more clearly, and partly by
the dreadful pain in her head, caused by reactionary collapse
after her struggle.

"Oh, Monsieur Martener, I am very ill," said she, in her
pretty voice.

"Where is the pain, my child?" said the doctor.

"There," she replied, pointing to a spot on her head
above the left ear.

"There is an abscess!" cried the doctor, after feeling
Pierrette's head for some time, and questioning her as to the
pain. "You must tell us everything, my dear, to enable us
to cure you. Why is your hand in this state? You did not
injure it like this yourself."

Pierrette artlessly told the tale of her struggle with her
cousin Sylvie.

"Make her talk to you," said the doctor to her grandmother, "and learn all about it. I will wait till the surgeon
arrives from Paris, and we will call in the head surgeon of the
hospital for a consultation. It seems to me very serious. I
will send a soothing draught to give mademoiselle some
sleep. She needs rest."

The old Bretonne, left alone with her grandchild, made
her tell everything, by exerting her influence over her, and
explaining to her that she was rich enough for all three, so
that Brigaut need never leave them. The poor child confessed all her sufferings, never dreaming of the lawsuit she
was leading up to. The monstrous conduct of these two
loveless beings, who knew nothing of family affection,

revealed to the old woman worlds of torment, as far from her conception as the manners of the savage tribes must have been to the first travelers who penetrated the savannahs of America.

Her grandmother's presence, and the certainty of living with her for the future in perfect ease, lulled Pierrette's mind as the draught lulled her body. The old woman watched by her, kissing her brow, hair, and hands, as the holy women may have kissed Jesus while laying Him in the sepulchre.

By nine in the morning Monsieur Martener went to the president of the courts, and related to him the scene of the past night between Sylvie and Pierrette, the moral and physical torture, the cruelty of every kind inflicted by the Rogrons on their ward, and the two fatal maladies which had been developed by this ill-usage. The president sent for the notary, Monsieur Auffray, a connection of Pierrette's on her mother's side.

At this moment the war between the Vinet party and the Tiphaine party was at its height. The gossip circulated in Provins by the Rogrons and their adherents as to the well-known *liaison* between Madame Roguin and du Tillet the banker, and the circumstances of Monsieur Roguin's bankruptcy—Madame Tiphaine's father was said to have committed forgery—hit all the more surely because, though it was scandal, it was not calumny. Such wounds pierced to the bottom of things; they attacked self-interest in its most vital part. These statements, repeated to the partisans of Tiphaine by the same speakers who also reported to the Rogrons all the sarcasms uttered by the "beautiful Madame Tiphaine" and her friends, added fuel to their hatred, complicated as it was with political feeling.

The irritation caused in France at that time by party spirit, which had waxed excessively violent, was everywhere bound up, as it was at Provins, with imperiled interests and offended and antagonistic private feelings. Each coterie eagerly pounced on anything that might damage its rival. Party animosity was not less implicated than personal conceit in even trivial questions, which were often carried to great lengths. A whole town threw itself into some dispute, raising it to the dignity of a political contest. And so the president discerned, in the action between Pierrette and the Rogrons, a means of confuting, discrediting, and humiliating the owners of that drawing-room where plots were hatched against the monarchy, and where the opposition newspaper had had its birth.

He sent for the public prosecutor. Then Monsieur Lesourd, Monsieur Auffray the notary—appointed the legal guardian of Pierrette—and the president of the court discussed in the greatest privacy, with Monsieur Martener, what steps could be taken. The legal guardian was to call a family council (a formality of French law), and, armed with the evidence of the three medical men, would demand the dismissal of Rogron from his guardianship. The case thus formulated would be brought before the tribunal, and then Monsieur Lesourd would get it carried into the criminal court by demanding an inquiry.

By mid-day all Provins was in a stir over the strange reports of what had taken place at the Rogrons in the course of the past night. Pierrette's screams had been remotely heard in the square, but they had not lasted long; no one had gotten up; but everybody had asked in the morning, "Did you hear the noise and screaming at about one o'clock? What was it?" Gossip and comment had given such magnitude to the horrible drama that a crowd collected in front of Frappier's shop, everybody cross-questioning the honest joiner, who described the girl's arrival at his house with her hand bleeding and her fingers mangled.

At about one in the afternoon a post-chaise, containing Doctor Bianchon, by whom sat Brigaut, stopped at Frappier's door, and Madame Frappier went off to the hospital to fetch Monsieur Martener and the head surgeon. Thus the reports heard in the town received confirmation.

The Rogrons were accused of having intentionally mal-treated their young cousin, and endangered her life. The news reached Vinet at the law courts; he left his business and hurried to the Rogrons. Rogron and his sister had just finished breakfast. Sylvie had avoided telling her brother of her defeat during the night; she allowed him to question her, making no reply but: "It does not concern you." And she bustled to and fro between the kitchen and dining-room to avoid all discussion.

She was alone when Vinet walked in.

"Do you know nothing of what is going on?" asked the lawyer.

"No," said Sylvie.

"You are going to have a criminal action brought against you for the way in which matters stand with Pierrette," the lawyer informed her.

"A criminal action!" said Rogron, coming in. "Why? What for?"

"In the first place," said Vinet, looking at Sylvie, "tell me exactly, without subterfuge, all that took place last night, as though you were before God, for there is some talk of cut-ting off Pierrette's hand."

Sylvie turned ashy pale and shivered.

"Then there was something?" said the lawyer.

Mademoiselle Rogron told the story, trying to justify her-self; but, on being cross-questioned, related all the details of the horrible conflict.

"If you have only broken her fingers, you will only appear in the police court; but if her hand has to be amputated, you will find yourself brought up at the assizes. The Tiphaines will do anything to get you there."

Sylvie, more dead than alive, confessed her jealousy, and,

which was even harder to bring out, how her suspicions had
blundered.

"What a case for trial!" exclaimed Vinet. "You and
your brother may be ruined by it; you will be thrown over
by many of your friends even if you gain it. If you do not
come out clear, you will have to leave Provins."

"Oh! my dear Monsieur Vinet—you who are such an able
lawyer," cried Rogron, horrified, "advise us, save us!"

Vinet dexterously fomented the fears of these two fools to
the utmost, and declared positively that Madame and Mademoiselle de Chargebœuf would hesitate to go to their house
again. To be forsaken by these two ladies would be a fatal
condemnation. In short, after an hour of magnificent manœuvring, it was agreed that in order to induce Vinet to save
the Rogrons he must have an interest at stake in defending
them in the eyes of all Provins. In the course of the evening
Rogron's engagement to marry Mademoiselle de Chargebœuf
was to be announced. The banns were to be published on
Sunday. The marriage-contract would at once be drawn up
by Cournant, and Mademoiselle Rogron would figure in it as
abandoning, in consideration of this alliance, the capital of
her share of the estate by a deed of gift to her brother, reserv-
ing only a life-interest. Vinet impressed on Rogron and his
sister the necessity of having a draft of this deed drawn up
two or three days before that event, so as to put Madame and
Mademoiselle de Chargebœuf under the necessity, in public
opinion, of continuing their visits to the Rogrons.

"Sign that contract, and I will undertake to get you out of
the scrape," said the lawyer. "It will no doubt be a hard
fight, but I will go into it body and soul, and you will owe
me a very handsome taper."

"Yes, indeed," said Rogron.

By half-past eleven the lawyer was empowered to act for
them, alike as to the contract and as to the management of
the case. At noon the president was informed that a sum-

mons was applied for by Vinet against Brigaut and the widow
Lorrain for abducting Pierrette Lorrain, a minor, from the
domicile of her guardian.   Thus the audacious Vinet took up
the offensive, putting Rogron in the position of a man having
the law on his side.   This, indeed, was the tone in which the
matter was commented on in the law courts.   The president
postponed hearing the parties till four o'clock.   The excitement of the town over all these events need not be described.
The president knew that the medical consultation would be
ended by three o'clock; he wished that the legal guardian
should appear armed with the physician's verdict.

The announcement of Rogron's engagement to the fair
Bathilde de Chargebœuf, and of the deed of gift added by
Sylvie to the contract, promptly made the Rogrons two
enemies—Mademoiselle Habert and the colonel, who thus
saw all their hopes dashed.   Céleste Habert and the colonel
remained ostensibly friends to the Rogrons, but only to
damage them more effectually.   So, as soon as Monsieur
Martener spoke of the existence of an abscess on the brain in
the haberdashers' hapless victim, Céleste and the colonel
mentioned the blow Pierrette had given herself that evening
when Sylvie had driven her out of the room, and remembered
Mademoiselle Rogron's cruel and barbarous remarks.   They
related various instances of the old maid's utter indifference
to her ward's sufferings.   Thus these friends of the couple
admitted serious wrong, while affecting to defend Sylvie and
her brother.

Vinet had foreseen this storm ; but Mademoiselle de Chargebœuf was about to acquire the whole of the Rogrons' fortune,
and he promised himself that in a few weeks he should see her
living in the nice house on the plazza, and reign conjointly
with her over Provins; for he was already scheming for a
coalition with the Bréauteys to serve his own ambitions.

From twelve o'clock till four all the ladies of the Tiphaine
faction—the Garcelands, the Guépins, the Julliards, Mesdames

Galardon, Guénée, and the sous-préfet's wife—all sent to inquire after Mademoiselle Lorrain. Pierrette knew nothing whatever of this commotion in the town on her behalf. In the midst of acute suffering she felt ineffably happy at finding herself between her grandmother and Brigaut, the objects of her affection. Brigaut's eyes were constantly full of tears, and the old woman petted her beloved grandchild.

God knows the grandmother spared the three men of science none of the details she had heard from Pierrette about her life with the Rogrons! Horace Bianchon expressed his indignation in unmeasured terms. Horrified by such barbarity, he insisted that the other doctors of the town should be called in ; so Monsieur Néraud was present, and was requested, as being Rogron's friend, to contradict if he could the terrible inferences derived from the consultation, which, unfortunately for Rogron, were unanimously subscribed to. Néraud, who was already credited with having made Pierrette's maternal grandmother die of grief, was in a false position, of which Martener adroitly took advantage, delighted to overwhelm the Rogrons, and also to compromise Monsieur Néraud, his antagonist. It is needless to give the text of this document, which also was produced at the trial. If the medical terms of Molière's age were barbarous, those of modern medicine have the advantage of such extreme plain speaking that an account of Pierrette's maladies, though natural, and unfortunately common, would shock the ear. The verdict was indisputably final, attested by so famous a name as that of Horace Bianchon.

After the court sitting was over, the president remained in his place, while Pierrette's grandmother came in with Monsieur Auffray, Brigaut, and a considerable crowd. Vinet appeared alone. This contrast struck the spectators, including a vast number of merely inquisitive persons. Vinet, who had kept his gown on, raised his hard face to the president, settling his spectacles as he began in his harsh, sawing tones to set forth that certain strangers had made their way into the house of Monsieur and Mademoiselle Rogron by night, and had carried away the girl Lorrain, a minor. Her guardian claimed the protection of the court to recover his ward.

Monsieur Auffray, as the guardian appointed by the court, rose to speak.

"If Monsieur le Président," said he, "will take into his consideration this consultation, signed by one of the most eminent Paris physicians, and by all the doctors and surgeons of Provins, he will perceive how unreasonable is Monsieur Rogron's claim, and that sufficient reasons induced the minor's grandmother to release her at once from her tormentors. The facts are these : A deliberate consultation, signed unanimously by a celebrated Paris doctor, sent for in great haste, and by all the medical authorities of the town, ascribe the almost dying state of the ward to the ill-treatment she had received at the hands of the said Rogron and his sister. As a legal formality a family council will he held, with the least possible delay, and consulted on the question whether the guardian ought not to be held disqualified for his office. We petition that the minor shall not be sent back to her guardian's house, but shall be placed in the hands of any other member of the family whom Monsieur le Président may see fit to designate."

Vinet wanted to reply, saying that the document of the consultation ought to be communicated to him that he might contravene it.

"Certainly not to Vinet's side," said the president severely, "but perhaps to the public prosecutor. The case is closed."

At the foot of the petition the president wrote the following injunction :

"Inasmuch as that by a consultation unanimously signed by the medical faculty of this town and by Doctor Bianchon of the medical faculty of Paris, it is proved that the girl Lorrain, a minor, claimed by her guardian Rogron, is in a very serious state of sickness brought on by the ill-usage and cruelty inflicted on her in the house of her guardian and his sister.

"We, president of the lower court of justice at Provins,

"Decree on the petition and enjoin that until the family council shall have been held, which, as the provisional guardian appointed by the law declares, is at once to be convened, the said minor shall not re-enter her guardian's residence, but shall be transferred to that of the guardian appointed by the law.

"And in the second place, in consideration of the minor's present state of health, and the traces of violence which, in the opinion of the medical men, are to be seen on her person, we commission the chief physician and chief surgeon of the hospital of Provins to attend her ; and in the event of the cruelty being proved to have been constant, we reserve all the rights and powers of the law, without prejudice to the civil action taken by Auffray, the legalized temporary guardian."

This terrible injunction was pronounced by Monsieur le Président Tiphaine with a loud voice and distinct utterance.

"Why not the hulks at once ?" said Vinet. "And all this fuss about a little girl who carried on an intrigue with a carpenter's apprentice ! If this is the way the case is conducted," he added insolently, "we shall apply for other judgment on the plea of legitimate suspicions."

Vinet left the court, and went to the chief leaders of his party to explain the position of Rogron, who had never given his little cousin a finger-flip and whom the tribunal had treated, he declared, less as Pierrette's guardian than as the chief voter in Provins.

To hear him, the Tiphaines were making much ado about nothing. The mountain would bring forth a mouse. Sylvie, an eminently religious and well-conducted person, had detected an intrigue between her brother's ward and a carpenter's boy, a Breton named Brigaut. The young rascal knew very well that the girl would have a fortune from her grandmother, and wanted to tamper with her—— Vinet to talk of tampering! —— Mademoiselle Rogron, who had kept the letters in which this little wench's wickedness was made clear, was not so much to blame as the Tiphaines tried to make her seem. Even if she had been betrayed into violence to obtain a letter, which could easily be accounted for by the irritation produced in her by Breton obstinacy, in what was Rogron to blame?

The lawyer thus made the action a party matter, and contrived to give it political color. And so, from that evening, there were differences of opinion on the question.

"If you hear but one bell, you hear but one note," said the wise-heads. "Have you heard what Vinet has to say? He explains the case very well."

Frappier's house was regarded as unsuitable for Pierrette on account of the noise, which would cause her much pain in the head. Her removal from there to her appointed guardian's house was as desirable from a medical as from a legal point of view. This business was effected with the utmost care, and calculated to make a great sensation. Pierrette was placed on a stretcher with many mattresses, carried by two men, escorted by a gray sister holding in her hand a bottle of ether, followed by her grandmother, Brigaut, Madame Auffray, and her maid. The people stood at the windows and in the doors to see the little procession pass. No doubt the state in which Pierrette was seen and her death-like pallor gave immense support to the party adverse to the Rogrons. The Auffrays were bent on showing to all the town how right the president had been in pronouncing his injunction. Pierrette and her grandmother were established on the second floor of Monsieur Auffray's house. The notary and his wife lavished on them the generosity of the amplest hospitality; they made a display of it. Pierrette was nursed by her grandmother,

and Monsieur Martener came to see her again the same even‑
ing, with the surgeon.

From that evening dated much exaggeration on both sides.
The Rogrons' room was crowded. Vinet had worked up the
Liberal faction in the matter. The two Chargebœuf ladies
dined with the Rogrons, for the marriage contract was to be
signed forthwith. Vinet had had the banns put up at the
Mairie that morning. He treated the business of Pierrette as
a mere trifle. If the court of Provins could not judge it dis‑
passionately, the superior court would judge of the facts,
said he, and the Auffrays would think twice before rushing
into such an action. Then the connection between the Ro‑
grons and the Chargebœufs was of immense weight with cer‑
tain people. To them the Rogrons were as white as snow,
and Pierrette an excessively wicked little girl whom they
had cherished in their bosom.

In Madame Tiphaine's drawing-room vengeance was taken
on the horrible scandals the Vinet party had promulgated for
the last two years. The Rogrons were monsters, and the
guardian would find himself in the criminal court. In the
square, Pierrette was perfectly well; in the upper town, she
must infallibly die; at the Rogrons, she had a few scratches
on her hand; at Madame Tiphaine's, she had her fingers
smashed; one would have to be cut off.

Next day the *Courrier de Provins* had an extremely clever
article, well written, a masterpiece of innuendo mixed up
with legal demurs, which placed the Rogrons above suspicion.
The *Ruche*, which came out two days later, could not reply
without risk of libel; but it said that in a case like the pres‑
sent, the best thing was to leave justice to take its course.

The family council was constituted by the justice of the
peace of the Provins district, as the legal president, in the
first place, of Rogron and the two Auffrays, Pierrette's next‑
of-kin; then of Monsieur Ciprey, a nephew of Pierrette's
maternal grandmother. He added to these Monsieur Habert,

the young girl's director, and Colonel Gouraud, who had always given himself out to be a comrade of her father, Colonel Lorrain. The justice's impartiality was highly applauded in including in this family council Monsieur Habert and the colonel, whom all the town regarded as great friends of the Rogrons. In the difficult position in which he found himself, Rogron begged to be allowed the support of Maître Vinet on the occasion. By this manœuvre, evidently suggested by Vinet, he succeeded in postponing the meeting of the family council till the end of December.

At that date the president and his wife were in Paris, living with Madame Roguin, in consequence of the sitting of the Chambers. Thus the ministerial party at Provins was bereft of its head. Vinet had already quietly made friends with the worthy examining judge, Monsieur Desfondrilles, in case the business should assume the penal or criminal aspect that Tiphaine had endeavored to give it.

For three hours Vinet addressed the family council; he proved an intrigue between Brigaut and Pierrette, to justify Mademoiselle Rogron's severity; he pointed out how natural it was that the guardian should have left his ward under the control of a woman; he dwelt on his client's non-interference in the mode of Pierrette's education as conducted by Sylvie. But in spite of Vinet's efforts, the meeting unanimously decided on abolishing Rogron's guardianship. Monsieur Auffray was appointed Pierrette's guardian, and Monsieur Ciprey her legal guardian.

They heard the evidence given by Adèle the maid, who incriminated her former master and mistress; by Mademoiselle Habert, who repeated Sylvie's cruel remarks the evening when Pierrette had given herself the dreadful blow that everybody had heard; and the comments on Pierrette's health made by Madame de Chargebœuf. Brigaut produced the letter he had received from Pierrette, which established their innocence. It was proved that the deplorable state in which the minor now was resulted from the neglect of her guardian, who was responsible in all that related to his ward. Pierrette's illness had struck everybody, even persons in the town who did not know the family. Thus the charge of cruelty against Rogron was fully sustained. The matter would be made public.

By Vinet's advice Rogron put in a protest against the confirmation by the court of the decision of the family council. The minister of justice now intervened, in consequence of the increasingly critical condition of Pierrette Lorrain. This singular case, though put on the lists forthwith, did not come up for trial till near the month of March, 1828.

By that time the marriage of Rogron to Mademoiselle de Chargebœuf was an accomplished fact. Sylvie was living on the second floor of the house, which had been arranged to accommodate her and Madame de Chargebœuf; for the first floor was entirely given up to Madame Rogron. The beautiful Madame Rogron now succeeded to the beautiful Madame Tiphaine. The effect of this marriage was enormous. The town no longer came to Mademoiselle Sylvie's salon, but to the beautiful Madame Rogron's.

Monsieur Tiphaine, the president of the Provins court, pushed by his mother-in-law and supported by du Tillet and by Nucingen, the Royalist bankers, found an opportunity of being useful to the ministry. He was one of the most highly respected speakers of the Centre, was made a judge of the lower court in the Seine district, and got his nephew, Lesourd, nominated president in his place at Provins. This appointment greatly annoyed Monsieur Desfondrilles, still an archæologist, and more supernumerary than ever. The keeper of the seals sent a protégé of his own to fill Lesourd's place. Thus Monsieur Tiphaine's promotion did not lead to any advancement in the legal forces at Provins.

Vinet took advantage of these circumstances very cleverly. He had always told the good folks of Provins that they were

10

only serving as a step-ladder to Madame Tiphaine's cunning and ambition. The president laughed in his sleeve at his friends. Madame Tiphaine secretly disdained the town of Provins ; she would never come back to it.

Monsieur Tiphaine *père* presently died ; his son inherited the estate of Le Fay, and sold his handsome house in the upper town to Monsieur Julliard. This sale showed how little he intended to come back to Provins. Vinet was right! Vinet had been a true prophet! These facts had no little influence on the action relating to Rogron's guardianship.

The horrible martyrdom so brutally inflicted on Pierrette by two imbecile tyrants—which led, medically speaking, to her being subjected by Monsieur Martener, with Bianchon's approval, to the terrible operation of trepanning ; the whole dreadful drama, reduced to judicial statements, was left among the foul medley known to lawyers as outstanding cases. The action dragged on through the delays and inextricable intricacies of "proceedings," constantly checked by the quibbles of a contemptible lawyer, while the calumniated Pierrette languished in suffering from the most terrible pains known to medical science. We could not avoid these details as to the strange variations in public opinion and the slow march of justice before returning to the room where she was living— where she was dying.

Monsieur Martener and the whole of the Auffray family were in a very few days completely won by Pierrette's adorable temper, and by the old Bretonne, whose, feelings, ideas, and manners bore the stamp of an antique Roman type. This matron of the Marais was like one of Plutarch's women.

The doctor desired to contend with death, at least, for his prey ; for from the first the Paris and the provincial physicians had agreed in regarding Pierrette as past saving. Then began between the disease and the doctor, aided by Pierrette's youth, one of those struggles which medical men alone know ;

the reward, in the event of success, is neither in the pecuniary profit nor even in the rescued sufferer; it lies in sweet
satisfaction of conscience, and in a sort of ideal and invisible
palm of victory gathered by every true artist from the joyful
certainty of having achieved a fine work.   The physician
makes for healing as the artist makes for the beautiful, urged
on by a noble sentiment which we call virtue.   This daily
recurring battle had extinguished in this man, though a provincial, the squalid irritation of the warfare going on between
the Vinet party and that of the Tiphaines, as happens with
men who have to fight it out with great suffering.

Monsieur Martener had at first wished to practice his profession in Paris; but the activity of the great city, the callous-
ness produced at last in a doctor's mind by the terrific number
of sick people and a multitude of serious cases, had appalled
his gentle soul, which was made for a country life.   He was
in bondage, too, to his pretty birthplace.   So he had come
back to Provins to marry and settle there, and take almost
tender care of a population he could think of as a large family.
All the time Pierrette was ill he could not bear to speak of
her illness.   His aversion to reply when any one asked for
news of the poor child was so evident, that at last nobody
questioned him about her.   Pierrette was to him what she
could not help being—one of those deep, mysterious poems,
immense in its misery, such as occur in the terrible life of a
physician.   He had for this frail girl an admiration of which
he would betray the secret to no one.

This feeling for his patient was infectious, as all true sentiments are; Monsieur and Madame Auffray's house, so long as
Pierrette lived in it, was peaceful and still.   Even the children, who of old had such famous games with Pierrette, understood, with childlike grace, that they were not to be noisy
or troublesome.   They made it a point of honor to be good
because Pierrette was ill.

Monsieur Auffray's house is in the upper town, below the

ruined castle; built, indeed, on one of the cliff-like knolls formed by the overthrow of the old ramparts. From there the residents have a view over the valley as they walk in a little orchard supported by the thick walls rising straight up from the lower town. The roofs of the houses rise to the level of the wall that upholds this garden. Along this terrace is a walk ending at the glass-door of Monsieur Auffray's study. At the other end are a vine-covered arbor and a fig-tree sheltering a round table, a bench, and some chairs, all painted green.

Pierrette had a room over that of her new guardian. Madame Lorrain slept there on a camp-bed by her grandchild's side. From her window Pierrette could see the beautiful valley of Provins, which she hardly knew—she had so rarely been out of the Rogrons' sinister dwelling. Whenever it was fine, she liked to drag herself, on her grandmother's arm, as far as this arbor. Brigaut, who now did no work, came three times a day to see his little friend; he was absorbed in grief, which made him indifferent to life; he watched for Monsieur Martener with the eagerness of a spaniel, always went in with him and came out with him.

It would be difficult to imagine all the follies every one was ready to commit for the dear little invalid. Her grandmother, drunk with grief, hid her despair; she showed the child the same smiling face as at Pen-Hoël. In her wish to delude herself, she made her a Breton cap such as Pierrette had worn when she came to Provins, and put it on her; the girl then looked to her more like herself; she was sweet to behold, with her face framed in the aureola of cambric edged with starched lace. Her face, as white as fine white porcelain, her forehead on which suffering set a semblance of deep thoughtfulness, the purity of outline refined by sickness, the slowness and occasional fixity of her gaze, all made Pierrette a master-work of melancholy.

The child was waited on with fanatical devotion; she was

so tender, so loving. Madame Martener had sent her piano to Madame Auffray, her sister, thinking it might amuse Pierrette, to whom music was rapture. It was a poem to watch her listening to a piece by Weber, Beethoven, or Hérold, her eyes raised to heaven in silence, regretting, no doubt, the life she felt slipping from her. Monsieur Péroux the curé and Monsieur Habert, her two priestly comforters, admired her pious resignation.

Is it not a strange fact, worthy of the attention alike of philosophers and of mere observers, that a sort of seraphic perfection is characteristic of youths and maidens marked amid the crowd with the red cross of death, like saplings in a forest ? He who has witnessed such a death can never remain or become an infidel. These beings exhale, as it were, a heavenly fragrance, their looks speak of God, their voice is eloquent in the most trivial speech, and often sounds like a divine instrument, expressing the secrets of futurity. When Monsieur Martener congratulated Pierrette on having carried out some disagreeable prescription, this angel would say in the presence of all, and with what a look !—

"I wish to live, dear Monsieur Martener, less for my own sake than for my grandmother's, for my poor Brigaut's, and for you all, who will be sorry when I die."

The first time she took a walk, in the month of November, under a bright Martinmas sun, escorted by all the family, Madame Auffray asked her if she were tired.

"Now that I have nothing to bear but the pain God sends me, I can endure it. I find strength to bear suffering in the joy of being loved."

This was the only time she ever alluded, even so remotely, to her horrible martyrdom at the Rogrons; she never spoke of them ; and as the remembrance could not fail to be painful, no one mentioned their name.

"Dear Madame Auffray," said she one day at noon on the terrace, while gazing at the valley lighted up by brilliant sun-

shine and dressed in the russet tints of autumn, "my dying
days in your house will have brought me more happiness than
all the three years before."

Madame Auffray looked at her sister, Madame Martener,
and said to her in a whisper :

" How she would have loved ! "

And, indeed, Pierrette's tone and look gave her words
unutterable meaning.

Monsieur Martener kept up a correspondence with Doctor
Bianchon, and tried no serious treatment without his approbation. He hoped first to restore the girl to normal health,
and then to enable the abscess to discharge itself through the
ear. The more acute her pain was, the more hopeful he felt.
With regard to the first point he had some success, and that
was a great triumph. For some days Pierrette recovered her
appetite, and could satisfy it with substantial food, for which
her unhealthy state had hitherto given her great aversion ; her
color improved, but the pain in her head was terrible. The
doctor now begged the great physician, his consultee, to come
to Provins. Bianchon came, stayed two days, and advised
an operation ; he threw himself into all poor Martener's
anxiety, and went himself to fetch the famous Desplein. So
the operation was performed by the greatest surgeon of ancient or modern times ; but this terrible augur said to Martener as he went away with Bianchon, his best-beloved pupil :

" You can save her only by a miracle. As Horace has told
you, necrosis has set in. At that age the bones are still so
tender."

The operation was performed early in March, 1828. All
that month Monsieur Martener, alarmed by the fearful torments Pierrette endured, made several journeys to Paris ; he
consulted Desplein and Bianchon, to whom he even suggested
a treatment resembling that known as lithotrity—the insertion
of a tubular instrument into the skull, by which a heroic
remedy might be introduced to arrest the progress of decay.

The daring Desplein dared not attempt this surgical feat, which only despair had suggested to Martener as a last resort to save Pierrette.

When the doctor returned from his last journey to Paris, his friends thought him crestfallen and gloomy. One fatal evening he was compelled to announce to the Auffray family, to Madame Lorrain, to the confessor, and to Brigaut, who were all present, that science could do no more for Pierrette, that her life was in the hands of God alone. Her grandmother took a vow and begged the curé to say, every morning at daybreak, before Pierrette rose, a mass which she and Brigaut would attend.

The case came up for trial. While the Rogrons' victim lay dying, Vinet was calumniating her to the court. The court ratified the decision of the family council, and the lawyer immediately appealed. The newly appointed public prosecutor delivered an address which led to an inquiry. Rogron and his sister were obliged to find sureties to avoid being sent to prison. The inquiry necessitated the examination of Pierrette herself. When Monsieur Desfondrilles went to the Auffrays' house, Pierrette, was actually dying; the priest was at her bedside, and she was about to take the last sacrament. At that moment she was entreating all the assembled family to forgive her cousins as she herself forgave them, saying, with excellent good-sense, that judgment in such cases belonged to God alone.

"Grandmother," said she, "leave all you possess to Brigaut"—Brigaut melted into tears—"and," Pierrette went on, "give a thousand francs to good Adèle, who used to warm my bed on the sly. If she had stayed with my cousins, I should be alive——"

It was at three o'clock on Easter Tuesday, on a beautiful day, that this little angel ceased to suffer. Her heroical grandmother insisted on sitting by her all night with the priests and on sewing the winding-sheet on her with her old hands.   Towards evening Brigaut left the house and went back to Frappier's.

"I need not ask you the news, my poor boy," said the carpenter.

"Père Frappier—yes ; it is all over with her, and not with me ! "

The apprentice looked round the workshop at all the wood store with gloomy but keen eyes.

"I understand, Brigaut," said the worthy Frappier. "There, that is what you want," and he pointed to some two-inch oak planks.

"Do not help me, Monsieur Frappier," said the Breton. "I will do it all myself."

Brigaut spent the night in planing and joining Pierrette's coffin, and more than once he ripped off with one stroke a long shaving wet with his tears.   His friend Frappier smoked and watched him.   He said nothing to him but these few words when his man put the four sides together—

"Make the lid to slide in a groove, then her poor friends will not hear you nail it down."

At daybreak Brigaut went for lead to line the coffin.   By a singular coincidence the sheets of lead cost exactly the sum he had given to Pierrette for her journey from Nantes to Provins.   The brave Breton, who had borne up under the dreadful pain of making a coffin for the beloved companion of his childhood, overlaying each funereal board with all his memories, could not endure this coincidence ; he turned faint and could not carry the lead ; the plumber accompanied him, and offered to go with him and solder down the top sheet as soon as the body should be laid in the coffin.

The Breton burned his plane and all the tools he had used for the work, he wound up his accounts with Frappier, and bade him good-by.

The heroism which enabled the poor fellow, like the grandmother, to busy himself with doing the last services to the dead, led to his intervening in the crowning scene which put a climax to the Rogrons' tyranny.

Brigaut and the plumber arrived at Monsieur Auffray's just in time to decide by brute force a horrible and shameful legal question. The chamber of the dead was full of people, and presented a strange scene to the two workmen. The Rogrons stood hideous by the victim's corpse to torture it even in death. The body of the poor girl, sublime in its beauty, lay on her grandmother's camp-bed. Pierrette's eyes were closed, her hair smoothly braided, her body sewn into a winding-sheet of coarse cotton.

By this bed, her hair in disorder, on her knees, with out-stretched hands and a flaming face, old Madame Lorrain was crying out—

"No, no; it shall never be!"

At the foot of the bed were the guardian Monsieur Auffray, the Curé Monsieur Péroux, and Monsieur Habert. Tapers were still burning. Opposite the grandmother stood the hospital surgeon, and Monsieur Néraud, supported by the smooth-tongued and formidable Vinet. A registrar was present. The surgeon had on his dissecting apron; one of his assistants had opened his roll of instruments and was handing him a scalpel.

This scene was disturbed by the noise made by the fall of the coffin, which Brigaut and the plumber dropped; and by Brigaut himself, who, entering first, was seized with horror on seeing old Madame Lorrain in tears and the significant actions of the intruders.

"What is the matter?" asked Brigaut, placing himself by her side, and convulsively clutching a chisel he had brought with him.

"The matter!" said the old woman. "They want to open my grandchild's body, to split her skull—to rend her heart after her death as they did in her lifetime!"

"Who?" said Brigaut, in a voice to crack the drum of the lawyer's ears.

"The Rogrons."

"By the God above us!——"

"One moment, Brigaut," said Monsieur Auffray, seeing the Breton brandish his chisel.

"Monsieur Auffray," said Brigaut, as pale as the dead girl, "I listen to you because you are Monsieur Auffray. But at this moment I would not listen to——"

"Justice!" Auffray put in.

"Is there such a thing as justice?" cried Brigaut in a quick and excited tone.

"That—that is justice!" he went on, threatening the lawyer, the surgeon, and the clerk with his chisel that flashed in the sunlight.

"My good fellow," said the curé, "Monsieur Rogron's lawyer has appealed to justice. His client lies under a serious accusation, and it is impossible to refuse a suspected person the means of clearing himself. According to Monsieur Rogron's advocate, if this poor child died of the abscess on the brain, her former guardian must be regarded as guiltless; for it is proved that Pierrette for a long time concealed the blow she had given herself——"

"That will do!" said Brigaut.

"My client——" Vinet began.

"Your client," cried the Breton, "shall go to hell, and I to the scaffold; for if one of you makes an attempt to touch her whom your client killed—if that sawbones does not put his knife away, I will strike him dead."

"This is overt resistance," said Vinet; "we shall lay it before the court."

The five strangers withdrew.

"Oh, my son!" said the old woman, starting up and throwing her arms round Brigaut's neck, "let us bury her at once; they will come back."

"When once the lead is soldered," said the plumber, "perhaps they will not dare."

Monsieur Auffray hurried off to his brother-in-law, Monsieur Lesourd, to try to get this matter settled. Vinet wished for nothing better. Pierrette once dead, the action as to the guardianship, which was not yet decided, must die a natural death, without any possibility of argument either for or against the Rogrons; the question remained an open one. So the shrewd lawyer had perfectly foreseen the effect his demand would produce.

At noon Monsieur Desfondrilles reported to the bench on the inquiry relating to the Rogrons, and the court pronounced a verdict of no case, on self-evident grounds.

Rogron dared not show his face at Pierrette's funeral, though all the town was present. Vinet tried to drag him there; but the ex-haberdasher feared the excitement of universal reprobation.

Brigaut, after seeing the grave filled up in which Pierrette was laid, left Provins and went on foot to Paris. He addressed a petition to the Dauphiness to be allowed, in consideration of his father's name, to enlist in the Royal Guard, and was soon afterwards enrolled. When an expedition was fitted out for Algiers, he again wrote to the Dauphiness, begging to be ordered on active service. He was then sergeant; Marshal Bourmount made him sub-lieutenant of the line. The major's son behaved like a man seeking death. But death has hitherto respected Jacques Brigaut, who has distinguished himself in all the recent expeditions without being once wounded. He is now at the head of a battalion in the line. There is not a more taciturn or a better officer. Off duty he is speechless, walks alone, and lives like a machine. Every one understands and respects some secret sorrow. He has forty-six thousand francs, left him by old Madame Lorrain, who died in Paris in 1829.

Vinet was elected deputy in 1830, and the services he has

rendered to the new government have earned him the place
of prosecutor-general.   His influence is now so great that he
will always be returned as deputy.   Rogron is receiver-general
in the town where Vinet exercises his high functions, and by
a singular coincidence Monsieur Tiphaine is the chief president of the supreme court there ; for the judge unhesitatingly
attached himself to the new dynasty of July.   The ex-beau-
tiful Madame Tiphaine lives on very good terms with the
beautiful Madame Rogron.   Vinet and President Tiphaine
agree perfectly.

As to Rogron, utterly stupid, he says such things as this :

" Louis Philippe will never be really king till he can create
nobles."

This speech is obviously not his own.

His failing health allows Madame Rogron to hope that ere
long she may be free to marry General the Marquis de Mon-
triveau, a peer of France, who is governor of the department, and attentive to her.   Vinet is always in a hurry to
condemn a man to death ; he never believes in the innocence
of the accused.   This man, born to be a public prosecutor,
is considered one of the most amiable men of his district,
and is not less successful in Paris and in the Chamber ; at
court he is the exquisite courtier.

General Baron Gouraud, that noble relic of our glorious
armies, has married—as Vinet promised that he should—a
Demoiselle Matifat, five-and-twenty years of age, the daughter of a druggist in the Rue des Lombards, who had a fortune of fifty thousand crowns.   He is governor—as Vinet
prophesied—of a department close to Paris.   He was made
a peer of France as the reward of his conduct in the riots
under Casimir Périer's ministry.   Baron Gouraud was one of
the generals who took the church of Saint-Merry, delighted
to " rap the knuckles " of the civilians who had bullied them
for fifteen years ; and his zeal won him the grand cordon of
the Legion of Honor.

None of those who were implicated in Pierrette's death have any remorse. Monsieur Desfondrilles is still an archæologist; but, to promote his own election, Attorney-General Vinet took care to have him appointed president of the court. Sylvie holds a little court and manages her brother's affairs; she lends at high interest, and does not spend more than twelve hundred francs a year.

From time to time, in the little square, when some son of Provins comes home from Paris to settle there, and is seen coming out of Mademoiselle Rogron's house, some former partisan of the Tiphaines will say, " The Rogrons had a very sad affair once about a ward——"

" A mere party question," President Desfondrilles replies. "Monstrous tales were given out. Out of kindness of heart they took this little Pierrette to live with them, a nice child enough, without a penny; just as she was growing up she had some intrigue with a joiner's apprentice, and would come to her window barefoot to talk to the lad, who used to stand just there, do you see? The lovers sent each other notes by means of a string. As you may suppose, in her state, and in the months of October and November, that was quite enough to upset a little pale-faced girl. The Rogrons behaved admirably; they never claimed their share of the child's inheritance; they gave everything to the grandmother. The moral of it all, my friends, is that the devil always punishes us for a good action."

" Oh ! this is quite another story; old Frappier told it in a very different way ! "

" Old Frappier consults his cellar more than his memory," remarked a frequenter of Mademoiselle Rogron's drawing-room.

" But then old Monsieur Habert——"

" Oh ! you know about his share in the matter ? " rejoined Desfondrilles.

" No."

"Why, he wanted to get his sister married to Monsieur Rogron, the receiver-general."

Two men daily think of Pierrette—Doctor Martener and Major Brigaut, who alone know the terrible truth.

To give that truth immense proportions, it is enough to recall the fact that if we change the scene to the middle ages, and to the vast theatre of Rome, a sublime girl, Beatrice Cenci, was dragged to the scaffold for reasons and by intrigues almost the same as those which brought Pierrette to the tomb. Beatrice Cenci found none to defend her but an artist—a painter. And to-day history and living people, on the evidence of Guido Reni's portrait, condemn the pope, and regard Beatrice as one of the most pathetic victims of infamous passions and factions.

And we may agree that the law would be a fine thing for social roguery, if there were no God.

November, 1830.

THE ABBÉ BIROTTEAU.

(*Le Curé de Tours.*)

To David, Sculptor.

The duration of the work on which I write your name—doubly illustrious in our age—is most uncertain, while you inscribe mine on bronze, which outlives nations even when stamped only by the vulgar die of the coiner. Will not numismatists be puzzled by the many crowned heads in your studio, when they find among the ashes of Paris these lives, prolonged by you beyond the life of nations, in which they will fancy they discover dynasties? Yours is this divine prerogative—mine be the gratitude.

DE BALZAC.

In the early autumn of 1826 the Abbé Birotteau, the principal personage of this story, was caught in a shower on his way home from the house where he had spent the evening. He was just crossing, as fast as his burly weight permitted, a little deserted square known as the Close, lying behind the apse of Saint-Gatien at Tours.

The Abbé Birotteau, a short man of apoplectic build, and now sixty years of age, had already had several attacks of gout. Hence, of all the minor miseries of human life, that which the worthy man held in most horror was the sudden wetting of his shoes with their large silver buckles, and the immersion of their soles. In fact, notwithstanding the flannel lining in which he packed his feet in all weathers, with the care a priest always takes of himself, they often got a little damp; then, next day, the gout unfailingly gave him proof of its constancy.

However, as the cobbles in the Close are always dry, and as the abbé had won three francs and ten sous at whist from Madame de Listomère, he submitted to the rain with resignation from the middle of the Place de l'Archevêché, where it had begun to fall heavily. Moreover, at this moment he was brooding over his chimera, a longing already twelve years old, a priest's day-dream! A dream which, recurring every evening, now seemed likely to find fulfillment; in short, he was too well wrapped in the fur sleeves of a canon's robes to be sensitive to the severities of the weather. In the course of this evening the accustomed guests who met at Madame de Listomère's had as good as promised him a nomination to the canon's stall at present vacant in the metropolitan chapter of Saint-Gatien, by proving to him that no one better deserved it than he, whose claims were indisputable, though so long ignored. If he had lost at cards, if he had heard that the canonry was given to the Abbé Poirel, his rival, the good man would have found the rain very cold; he might have abused life. But he was in one of those rare moments when delightful sensations make us forget everything. Though he hastened his pace, it was in obedience to a mechanical impulse, and truth—so indispensable in a tale of domestic life—requires us to say that he was thinking neither of the shower nor of the gout.

There were formerly round this Close, on the side by the Grand' Rue, a number of houses standing within a wall, and belonging to the cathedral, inhabited by certain dignitaries of the chapter. Since the sequestration of ecclesiastical property, the town has taken the alley dividing these houses as a public way, by the name of Rue de la Psalette, leading from the Close to the High Street. The name itself shows that here formerly dwelt the precentor with his schools and those who were within his jurisdiction. The left side of the street is formed of one large house, its garden walls being bridged by the flying buttresses of Saint-Gatien, which spring from the ground of its strip of garden, making it doubtful whether the cathedral was built before or after that ancient dwelling. But by examining the mouldings and the shape of the windows, the arch of the doorway, and the external architecture of the house, darkened by time, an archæologist detects that it had always been part and parcel of the magnificent church to which it is wedded. An antiquarian—if there were one at Tours, one of the least literary towns of France—might even discern at the entrance to the passage from the Close some traces of the covered archway which of old served as an entry to these priestly dwellings, and which must have harmonized in character with the main edifice.

This house, being to the north of Saint-Gatien, lies always in the shadow of this vast cathedral, on which time has cast its gloomy mantle, stamped wrinkles, and set its damp chill, its mosses, and straggling weeds. And it is perennially wrapped in the deepest silence, broken only by the tolling of the bells, the chanted service heard through the cathedral walls, or the cawing of jackdaws nesting at the top of the belfries. The spot is a desert of masonry, a solitude full of individuality, in which none could dwell but beings absolutely mindless, or gifted with immense strength of soul.

The house in question had always been the home of abbés, and belonged to an old maid named Mademoiselle Gamard. Although during the Terror the property had been bought from the nation by Mademoiselle Gamard's father, as the worthy maiden had for twenty years past let the rooms to priests, no one, at the Restoration, could take it ill that a bigot should not surrender a piece of national property; religious persons may have supposed that she meant to bequeath it to the chapter, and the worldly saw no change in its uses.

11

It was to this house, then, that the Abbé Birotteau was
making his way; he had lived in it for two years. His rooms
there had been till then, as the canonry was now, the object
of his desires, and his *hoc erat in votis* for a dozen years before.
To board with Mademoiselle Gamard and to be made a canon
were the two great aims of his life; and perhaps they completely sum up the ambitions of a priest who, regarding himself as a pilgrim to eternity, can in this world wish for no
more than a good room, a good table, clean clothes, shoes
with silver buckles—all-sufficient for his animal needs—and a
canonry to satisfy his pride, the indefinable feeling which
will accompany us, no doubt, into the presence of God, since
there are grades of rank among the saints in the heavenly
mansions.

But the Abbé Birotteau's desire for the rooms he now
occupied, so trivial a feeling in the eyes of the worldly wise,
had been to him a perfect passion, a passion full of obstacles,
and, like the most criminal passions, full of hopes, joys, and
remorse.

The arrangements and space in her house did not allow
Mademoiselle Gamard to take more than two resident boarders. Now, about twelve years before the day when Birotteau
went to lodge with this maiden lady, she had undertaken to
preserve in health and contentment Monsieur l'Abbé Troubert
and Monsieur l'Abbé Chapeloud. The Abbé Troubert still
lived, the Abbé Chapeloud was dead, and Birotteau had been
his immediate successor.

The late Abbé Chapeloud, in his lifetime canon of Saint-
Gatien, had been the Abbé Birotteau's intimate friend.
Every time the priest had gone into the canon's rooms he
had unfailingly admired them, the furniture, and the books.
This admiration one day gave birth to a desire to possess
these fine things. The Abbé Birotteau had found it impossible to smother this desire, which often made him dreadfully
unhappy when he reflected that only the death of his best

friend could satisfy this hidden covetousness, which nevertheless constantly increased.

The Abbé Chapeloud and his friend Birotteau were not
rich. Both sons of peasants, they had nothing but the poor
emolument doled out to priests, and their small savings had
been spent in tiding over the evil days of the Revolution.
When Napoleon re-established Catholic worship, the Abbé
Chapeloud was made canon of Saint-Gatien, and the Abbé
Birotteau became vicar, or mass-priest, of the cathedral.
It was then that Chapeloud went to board with Mademoiselle
Gamard. When Birotteau first called on the canon in his
new residence, he thought the rooms delightfully arranged,
but that was all. The beginnings of this concupiscence for
furniture were like those of a real passion in a young man,
which often at first is no more than cold admiration of the
woman he subsequently loves for ever.

These rooms, reached by a stone staircase, were on the side
of the house looking south. The Abbé Troubert inhabited
the first floor, and Mademoiselle Gamard the second floor of
the main front to the street. When Chapeloud went in, the
rooms were bare and the ceilings blackened by smoke. The
chimney fronts, clumsily carved in stone, had never been
painted. All the furniture the poor canon could at first put
in consisted of a bed, a table, some chairs, and his few books.
The apartment was like a fine woman in rags.

But two or three years later, an old lady having left the
Abbé Chapeloud two thousand francs, he laid out the money
in the purchase of an oak bookcase, saved from the destruction of an old château pulled down by the Black Band (a
company who bought old buildings to demolish), and remarkable for carvings worthy of the admiration of artists.
The abbé made the purchase, fascinated less by its cheapness
than by its exact correspondence in size with the dimensions
of his corridor. His savings then allowed him completely to
restore this corridor, until now abandoned to neglect. The

floor was carefully waxed, the ceiling white-washed, the wood-work painted and grained to imitate the tone and knots of oak. A marble chimney-shelf replaced the old one. The canon had taste enough to hunt up and find some old arm-chairs of carved walnut-wood. Then a long ebony table and two little Boulle cabinets gave this library a finish full of character.

Within two years, the liberality of various devout persons, and the bequests of pious penitents, though small, had filled the shelves of the bookcase hitherto vacant. Finally, an uncle of Chapeloud's, an old oratorian, left him his collection in folio of the "Fathers of the Church," and several other large works of value to an ecclesiastic.

Birotteau, more and more surprised by the successive trans-formations in this formerly bare corridor, by degrees became involuntarily covetous. He longed to possess this study, so perfectly adapted to the gravity of priestly habits. This passion grew day by day. Spending whole days, as he often did, in working in this snuggery, he could appreciate the silence and peace of it, after having at first admired its com-fortable arrangement. For the next few years the Abbé Chapeloud used this retreat as an oratory which his lady friends delighted to embellish. Later, again, a lady pre-sented to the canon a piece of furniture in worsted-work for his bedroom, at which she had long been stitching under the amiable priest's eyes without his suspecting its purpose. Then Birotteau was as much dazzled by the bedroom as by the library.

Finally, three years before his death, the Abbé Chapeloud had completed the comfort of his rooms by decorating the drawing-room. Though simply furnished with red Utrecht velvet, this had been too much for Birotteau. From the day when the canon's friend first saw the red silk curtains, the mahogany furniture, the Aubusson carpet that graced this large room, freshly painted, Chapeloud's apartment became to him the object of a secret monomania. To live there, to sleep in the great bed with silk curtains in which the canon slept, and have all his comforts about him as Chapeloud had, seemed to Birotteau perfect happiness; he looked for nothing beyond. Every feeling which envy and ambition arouse in the souls of other men was, in that of the Abbé Birotteau, centred in the deep and secret longing with which he wished for a home like that created for himself by the Abbé Chapeloud. When his friend fell ill, it was no doubt sincere affection that brought Birotteau to see him; but on first hearing of the canon's sickness, and while sitting with him, there rose from the depths of his soul a thousand thoughts, of which the simplest formula was always this, "If Chapeloud dies, I can have his rooms." Still, as Birotteau had a good heart, strict principles, and a narrow intellect, he never went so far as to conceive of means for getting his friend to leave him his library and furniture.

The Abbé Chapeloud, an amiable and indulgent egoist, guessed his friend's mania—which it was not difficult to do, and forgave it—which for a priest would seem less easy. Still, Birotteau, whose friendship remained unaltered, never ceased to walk day after day with the canon up and down the same path in the mall at Tours without curtailing by a single minute the time devoted to this exercise for the last twenty years. Birotteau thought of his involuntary wishes as sins, and would have been capable, in sheer contrition, of the utmost devotion for Chapeloud's sake.

The canon paid his debt to this sincere and artless brotherliness by saying, a few days before his death, to the priest, who was reading to him from the *Quotidienne*, "You will get the rooms this time. I feel that it is all over with me."

In fact, by his will, the Abbé Chapeloud left his library and furniture to Birotteau. The possession of these much-longed-for things, and the prospect of being taken as a boarder by Mademoiselle Gamard, greatly softened Birotteau's grief

at the loss of his friend the canon. He would not perhaps
have called him to life again, but he wept for him. For several days he was like Gargantua, whose wife died in giving
birth to Pantagruel, and who knew not whether to rejoice
over his son's birth or to lament at having buried his good
Badebec, and made the mistake of rejoicing at his wife's death
and deploring the birth of Pantagruel.

The Abbé Birotteau spent the first days of his grief in veri-
fying the volumes of *his* library and enjoying the use of *his*
furniture, examining them, and saying in a tone which, unfortunately, could not be recorded, "Poor Chapeloud!" In
short, his joy and his grief were so absorbing that he felt no
distress at seeing the canonry bestowed on another, though
the lamented Chapeloud had always hoped that Birotteau
might be his successor. Mademoiselle Gamard received the
abbé with pleasure as a boarder, and he thus enjoyed thenceforth all the delights of material existence that the deceased
canon had so highly praised.

Incalculable advantages! For, to hear the late departed
Canon Chapeloud, not one of the priests who dwelt in the
town of Tours, not even the archbishop himself, could be the
object of care so delicate or so precise as that lavished by
Mademoiselle Gamard on her two boarders. The first words
spoken by the canon to his friend as they walked in the mall
had almost always referred to the excellent dinner he had just
eaten; and it was a rare thing if, in the course of the seven
walks they took in the week, he did not happen to say at least
fourteen times, "That good woman has certainly a vocation
for taking charge of the priesthood."

"Only think," said the canon to Birotteau, "for twelve
successive years clean linen, albs, surplices, bands—nothing
has ever been missing. I always find everything in its place
and in sufficient numbers, all smelling of orris-root. My
furniture is constantly polished and so well wiped that for a
long time past I have not known what dust means. Did you

ever see a speck in my rooms? Then the fire-logs are well chosen, the smallest things are all good ; in short, it is as if Mademoiselle Gamard always had an eye on my room. I cannot recollect in ten years ever having had to ring twice for anything whatever. That I call living ! never to have to look for a thing, not even for one's slippers ; always to find a good fire and a good table. Once my bellows put me out, the nozzle had gotten burnt ; I had not to complain twice. The very next day mademoiselle had bought me a nice pair of bellows and the pair of tongs you see me use to put the fire together."

Birotteau's only reply was, " Smelling of orris-root ! " That smelling of orris-root always struck him. The canon's words painted a really ideal state of happiness to the poor priest whose bands and albs nearly turned his brain ; for he had no sense of order, and not unfrequently forgot to bespeak his dinner. And so, whenever he caught sight of Mademoiselle Gamard at Saint-Gatien, either while going round for the offertory or while reading mass, he never failed to give her a gentle and kindly glance such as Saint Theresa may have raised to heaven.

Though the comfort which every creature desires, and of which he had so often dreamed, had now fallen to his lot, as it is difficult for any man, even for a priest, to live without a hobby, for the last eighteen months the Abbé Birotteau had substituted for his two gratified passions a craving for a canonry. The title of canon had become to him what that of a peer must be to a plebeian minister. And the probability of a nomination, the hopes he had just been encouraged in at Madame de Listomère's, had so effectually turned his brain that it was only on reaching home that he discovered that he had left his umbrella at her house. Perhaps, indeed, but for the rain that fell in torrents, he would not have remembered it then, so completely was he absorbed in repeating to himself all that had been said on the subject of his preferment by the members of the party at Madame de Listomère's—an old lady with whom he spent every Wednesday evening.

The abbé rang sharply as a hint to the maid not to keep him waiting. Then he shrank into the corner by the door so as to be splashed as little as possible; but the water from the roof ran off precisely on the toes of his shoes, and the gusts of wind blew on to him squalls of rain not unlike a repeated shower-bath. After calculating the time necessary for coming from the kitchen to pull the latch-string under the door, he rang again, a very significant peal. "They cannot have gone out," thought he, hearing not a sound within. And for the third time he rang, again and again, a peal that sounded so sharply through the house, and was so loudly repeated by every echo in the cathedral, that it was impossible not to be roused by this assertive jangle. And a few moments after it was not without satisfaction, mingled with annoyance, that he heard the maid's wooden shoes clattering over the pebbly stone floor. Still, the gouty priest's troubles were not over so soon as he thought. Instead of pulling the latch, Marianne was obliged to unlock the door with the huge key, and draw back the bolts.

"How can you leave me to ring three times in such weather?" said he to Marianne.

" Why, sir, as you see, the house was locked up. Everybody has been in bed a long time; it has struck a quarter to ten. Mademoiselle must have thought you had not gone out."

"But you yourself saw me go out. Besides, mademoiselle knows very well that I go to Madame de Listomère's every Wednesday."

" Well, sir, I only did as mademoiselle told me," replied Marianne, locking the door again.

These words were a blow to the abbé, which he felt all the more keenly for the intense bliss of his day-dream. He said nothing, but followed Marianne to the kitchen, to fetch his bedroom candle, which he supposed would have been brought down there. But instead of going to the kitchen, Marianne lighted the abbé up to his rooms, where he found the candle-stick on a table outside the door of the red drawing-room, in a sort of anteroom, formed of the stair-landing, which the canon had shut in for the purpose by a large glass partition. Dumb with surprise, he hurried into his bedroom, found no fire on the hearth, and called Marianne, who had not yet had time to go downstairs.

"You have not lighted my fire?" said he.

"I beg your pardon, sir; it must have gone out again."

Birotteau looked again at the hearth, and saw plainly that the ashes had been piled there since the morning.

"I want to dry my feet," he went on; "make up the fire."

Marianne obeyed with the haste of a woman who wants to go to sleep, while the abbé himself hunted for his slippers; failing to see them in the middle of his bed-rug, as usual, he made certain observations as to the way Marianne was dressed, which proved to a demonstration that she had not just gotten out of bed, as she had asserted. And he then remembered that for about a fortnight past he had been weaned from all the little attentions that had made life so endurable for the last eighteen months. Now, as it is in the nature of narrow minds to argue from minute things, he at once gave himself up to deep reflections on these four incidents, imperceptible to anybody else, but to him nothing less than four catastrophes. The oversight as to his slippers, Marianne's falsehood with regard to the fire, the unaccustomed removal of his candle-stick to the table in the anteroom, and the long waiting so ingeniously inflicted on him, on the threshold in the rain, were ominous of a complete wreck of his happiness.

When the fire was blazing on the dogs, when his night-lamp was lighted, and Marianne had left him without inquir-ing as usual, "Does monsieur need anything further?" the

abbé sank gently into his departed friend's roomy and handsome easy-chair; still his action as he dropped into it was
somewhat melancholy. The worthy man was oppressed by
the presentiment of terrible disaster. His eyes fell in succession on the handsome timepiece, the chest of drawers, the
chairs, curtains, and rugs, the four-post bed, the holy-water
shell and the crucifix, on a Virgin by Le Valentin, on a Christ
by Lebrun—in short, on all the details of the room; the expression of his face betrayed the pangs of the tenderest farewell that a lover ever looked at his first mistress, or an old
man at his latest plantation. The abbé had just detected—a
little late, it is true—the symptoms of a covert persecution to
which he had for about three months been subjected by Mademoiselle Gamard, whose ill-will would no doubt have been
suspected sooner by a man of keener intelligence.

Have not all old maids a certain talent for emphasizing the
acts and words suggested to them by hatred? They scratch
as cats do. And not only do they hurt, but they take pleasure in hurting, and in making their victim see that they can
hurt. While a man of the world would not have allowed himself to be clawed a second time, the worthy Birotteau had
taken several scratches in the face before he had conceived of
malignant purpose.

Immediately, with the inquisitorial shrewdness acquired by
priests, accustomed as they are to direct consciences and to
investigate trifles from the shades of the confessional, the Abbé
Birotteau set to work to formulate the following proposition—
as though it were the basis of a religious controversy. Granting that Mademoiselle Gamard may have forgotten Madame
de Listomère's evening—that Marianne had neglected to light
my fire—that they thought I was at home; as it is certain that
I, *myself*, must have taken my candlestick downstairs this
morning ! ! !—it is impossible that Mademoiselle Gamard,
seeing it in her sitting-room, could have supposed I had gone
to bed. *Ergo*, Mademoiselle Gamard left me at the door in

the rain on purpose; and by having the candlestick carried
up to my rooms she meant me to know it. "What does it
mean?" he said aloud, carried away by the gravity of the
case, as he rose to take off his wet clothes and put on his
dressing-gown and his nightcap. Then he went from the bed
to the fire, gesticulating and jerking out such comments as
these, in various tones of voice, all ended in a falsetto pitch
as though to represent points of interrogation:

"What the deuce have I done? Why does she owe me a
grudge? Marianne cannot have forgotten my fire; mademoiselle must have told her not to light it! I should be
childish not to see from the tone and manner she assumes
towards me that I have been so unfortunate as to displease
her. Nothing of the kind ever happened to Chapeloud! It
will be impossible for me to live in the midst of the annoyances that—— At my age too!"

He went to bed, hoping to clear up on the morrow the
cause of the hatred which was destroying for ever the happiness he had enjoyed for two years after wishing for it so long.
Alas! the secret motives of Mademoiselle Gamard's feeling
against him were destined to remain for ever unknown to him;
not because they were difficult to guess, but because the poor
man had not the simple candor which enables great minds
and thorough scoundrels to recognize and judge themselves.
Only a man of genius or a master of intrigue ever says to himself, "I was to blame." Interest and talent are the only con-
scientious and lucid counselors.

Now, the Abbé Birotteau, whose kindliness went to the
pitch of silliness, whose knowledge was a sort of veneer laid
on by patient work, who had no experience whatever of the
world and its ways, and who lived between the altar and the
confessional, chiefly engaged in deciding trivial cases of conscience in his capacity of confessor to the schools of the
town, and to some noble souls who appreciated him—the
Abbé Birotteau was, in short, to be regarded as a big baby to

whom the greater part of social customs were absolutely unknown. At the same time, the selfishness natural to all human
beings, reinforced by the egoism peculiar to a priest, and by
that of the narrow life of a provincial town, had insensibly
grown strong in him without his suspecting it. If any one
had taken enough interest in searching the good man's soul to
show him that, in the infinitely small details of his existence
and the trivial duties of his private life, he failed essentially
in the self-sacrifice he professed, he would have punished and
mortified himself in all sincerity.

But those whom we offend, even unwittingly, reck not of
our innocence ; they desire and achieve revenge. Thus Birotteau, weak as he was, was doomed to suffer under the hand
of that great distributive justice which always trusts the world
to carry out its sentences, known to many simpletons as the
misfortunes of life.

There was this difference between Canon Chapeloud and
the abbé : one was a witty and ingenious egoist, the other an
honest and clumsy one.   When Monsieur Chapeloud had
come to board with Mademoiselle Gamard, he could perfectly
well gauge his landlady's character.   The confessional had
enlightened him as to the bitterness infused into an old
maid's heart by the misfortune of finding herself outside
society ; his behavior to Mademoiselle Gamard was shrewdly
calculated.   The lady being no more than eight-and-thirty,
still had those little pretensions which, in such discreet
persons, turn in later years into a high opinion of themselves.

The canon understood that, to live comfortably with Mademoiselle Gamard, he must always show her the same respect
and attention, and be more infallible than the pope. To
obtain this end he established no points of contact between
himself and her beyond what the strictest politeness required,
and those necessarily subsisting between two persons living
under the same roof. Thus, though he and the Abbé Trou-

bert regularly took their three meals a day, he had never appeared at breakfast, but had accustomed Mademoiselle Gamard to send up to him, in his bed, a cup of coffee with milk. Then he had avoided the boredom of supper by always taking tea at some house where he spent the evening. Thus he rarely saw his landlady at any time of the day excepting at dinner, but he always came into the room a few minutes before the hour. During this polite little visit, every day of the twelve years he had spent under her roof he had asked her the same questions and received the same answers. How Mademoiselle Gamard had slept during the night, the breakfast, little domestic events, the appearance of her face, the health of her person, the weather, the length of the church services, the incidents of the morning's mass, the health of this or that priest, constituted the themes of this daily dialogue.

During dinner he always indulged her with indirect flattery, going on from the quality of the fish, the excellence of some seasoning, or the merits of a sauce, to those of Mademoiselle Gamard and her virtues as a housekeeper. He was sure of soothing all the old maid's conceits when he praised the art with which her preserves were made, her gherkins pickled, and the excellence of her jam, her pies, and other gastronomical inventions. Finally, the wily canon never quitted her yellow drawing-room without remarking that there was not another house in Tours where the coffee was so good as that he had just been drinking.

Thanks to this perfect comprehension of Mademoiselle Gamard's character, and this science of life as practiced by the canon for those twelve years, no grounds had ever occurred for a discussion on any matter of domestic discipline. The Abbé Chapeloud had from the first discerned every angle, every rasping edge, every asperity in this old maid, and had so regulated the effect of the tangents where they inevitably met as to secure from her every concession needed for peace

and happiness in life. And Mademoiselle Gamard would
always say that Canon Chapeloud was a most amiable man,
very easy to live with, and full of wit.

As to the Abbé Troubert, the bigot never by any chance
spoke of him. Troubert had so completely fallen into the
routine of her life, like a satellite in the orbit of its planet,
that he had become to her a sort of mongrel creature between
those of the human and those of the canine species; he filled
a place in her mind exactly below that occupied by her friends
and that filled by a fat asthmatic pug-dog to which she was
tenderly devoted; she managed him completely, and their
interests became so inextricably knit that many persons of
Mademoiselle Gamard's circle supposed that the Abbé Troubert
had an eye to the old maid's fortune, and was attaching her
to him by his constant patience, guiding her all the more
effectually because he affected to obey her, never allowing her
to see in him the faintest wish to rule her.

When the canon died, the old maid, anxious to have
a boarder of quiet habits, naturally thought of this priest.
The canon's will had not yet been opened when Mademoiselle Gamard was already meditating giving the departed canon's upper rooms to her worthy Abbé Troubert,
whom she thought but poorly lodged on the ground floor.
But when the Abbé Birotteau came to discuss with her the
written conditions of her terms, she found that he was so
much in love with the lodgings for which he had long
cherished a passion he might now avow, that she did not
venture to propose an exchange, and affection gave way
before the pressure of interest. To console her favorite
abbé, mademoiselle substituted a parquet flooring in a neat
pattern for the white Château-Renaud tiles in the ground-
floor rooms, and rebuilt a chimney that smoked.

The Abbé Birotteau had seen his friend Chapeloud constantly for twelve years without it ever having occurred to
him to wonder why he was so excessively circumspect in his

intercourse with the old maid. When he came to live under this saintly damsel's roof he felt like a lover on the verge of happiness. Even if he had not been blinded by natural stupidity, his eyes were too much dazzled by contentment for him to be capable of gauging Mademoiselle Gamard or of considering the due measure of his daily relations with her. Mademoiselle Gamard, seen from afar, through the prism of the material enjoyment the abbé dreamed of finding with her, appeared to him an admirable creature, a perfect Christian, an essentially charitable soul, the woman of the gospel, the wise virgin graced with the humble and modest virtues which shed celestial fragrance over life. And thus, with all the enthusiasm of a man who has reached a long-wished-for goal, with the simplicity of a child and the silly heedlessness of an old man devoid of worldly experience, he came into Mademoiselle Gamard's life as a fly is caught in a spider's web.

So the first day he was to dine and sleep in the old maid's house he lingered in her drawing-room, as much in the wish to make acquaintance with her as in the inexplicable embarrassment that often troubles shy people and makes them fear lest they should be rude if they break off a conversation to leave the room. So there he remained all the evening. Another old maid, a friend of Birotteau's, Mademoiselle Salomon de Villenoix, came in the evening. Then Mademoiselle Gamard had the joy of arranging a game of boston. The abbé, as he went to bed, thought he had had a very pleasant evening.

As yet he knew Mademoiselle Gamard and the Abbé Troubert but very little, and saw only the surface. Few persons show their faults unveiled at first. Generally everybody tries to assume an attractive exterior. So Birotteau conceived the delightful purpose of devoting his evenings to Mademoiselle Gamard instead of spending them elsewhere. The lady had some few years since conceived a desire which revived more strongly every day. This desire, common to

old men, and even to pretty women, had become in her a
passion like that of Birotteau for his friend Chapeloud's
rooms, and was rooted in the old maid's heart by the feelings
of pride, egoism, envy, and vanity which are innate in the
worldly-minded.   This story repeats itself in every age.   You
have but slightly to enlarge the circle at the bottom of which
these personages are about to move to find the coefficient
motive of events which happen in the highest ranks of society.

Mademoiselle Gamard spent her evenings at six or eight
different houses by turns.   Whether it was that she was annoyed at having to seek company, and thought that at her
age she had a right to expect some return ; whether her conceit was affronted by her having no circle of her own ; or
whether it was that her vanity craved the compliments and
amusements she saw her friends enjoying—all her ambition
was to make her salon a centre of union towards which a
certain number of persons would tend every evening with
pleasure.   When Birotteau and his friend Mademoiselle
Salomon had spent a few evenings in her room with the
faithful and patient Abbé Troubert, one night, as she came
out of Saint-Gatien, Mademoiselle Gamard said to the kind
friends of whom she had hitherto considered herself the slave,
that those who cared to see her might very well come once
a week to her house, where a sufficient party met already to
make up a game of boston ; that she could not leave her new
boarder, the Abbé Birotteau, alone ; that Mademoiselle Salomon had not yet missed a single evening of the week ; that
she belonged to her boarders ; and that, etc., etc.

Her speech was all the more humbly haughty and volubly
sweet because Mademoiselle Salomon de Villenoix belonged
to the most aristocratic circle in Tours.   Though Mademoiselle Salomon came solely for the abbé's sake, Mademoiselle
Gamard triumphed in having her in her drawing-room.
Thanks to the Abbé Birotteau, she found herself on the eve
of succeeding in her great scheme of forming a circle which

might become as numerous and as agreeable as were those of Madame de Listomère, of Mademoiselle Merlin de la Blottière, and other devout persons in a position to receive the pious society of Tours. But, alas! the Abbé Birotteau brought Mademoiselle Gamard's hopes to an overthrow.

Now, if any persons, who have attained in life the enjoyment of a long-wished-for happiness, have entered into the gladness the abbé must have felt in lying down to rest in Chapeloud's bed, they must also form a slight notion of Mademoiselle Gamard's chagrin at the ruin of her cherished scheme. After accepting his good fortune patiently enough for six months, Birotteau deserted his home, carrying with him Mademoiselle Salomon.

In spite of unheard-of efforts, the ambitious Gamard had secured no more than five or six recruits, whose fidelity was very problematical, and at least four unfailing visitors were needed for regular boston. She was consequently obliged to make honorable amends and return to her old friends, for old maids are too poor company to themselves not to crave the doubtful pleasures of society.

The causes of this defection are easily imagined. Though the abbé was one of those to whom paradise shall one day be opened in virtue of the words, "Blessed are the poor in spirit," he, like many fools, could not endure the weariness inflicted on him by other fools. Unintelligent persons are like weeds that thrive in good ground; they love to be amused in proportion to the degree in which they weary themselves. Being the incarnation of the dullness they suffer from, the craving they perpetually feel to be divorced from themselves produces the mania for excitement, the need to be where they are not, which characterizes them as it does other creatures who lack feeling, or whose lot is a failure, or who suffer by their own fault. Without understanding too clearly the vacuity and nullity of Mademoiselle Gamard, or discerning the smallness of her mind, poor Birotteau discovered, too

12

late for happiness, the faults she had in common with all old maids, as well as those personal to herself.

What is evil, in other people, contrasts so strongly with what is good, that it generally strikes the eye before inflicting a wound. This moral phenomenon might at need justify the tendency that leads us all more or less to evil speaking. Socially speaking, it is so natural to satirize the faults of others that we ought to forgive the severe gossip to which our own absurdities give rise, and wonder at nothing but calumny.

But the good abbé's eyes were never at the precise focus which enables the worldly wise to see and at once evade their neighbors' sharp tongues; to discover his landlady's fault, he was obliged to endure the warning given by nature to all its creatures, that of suffering.

Old maids, having never bent their temper or their lives to other lives and other tempers, as woman's destiny requires, have for the most part a mania for making everything about them bend to them. In Mademoiselle Gamard this feeling had degenerated into despotism, but this despotism could only be exerted in small things. For instance—out of a thousand cases—the basket of counters and fish placed on the boston table for the Abbé Birotteau must be left on the spot where she had put it, and the abbé irritated her extremely by moving it, as he did almost every evening. What was the cause of this touchiness foolishly provoked by mere trifles, and what was its object? No one could say; Mademoiselle Gamard herself did not know.

Though very lamblike by nature, the new boarder did not like to feel the crook too often, any more than a sheep, especially a crook set with nails. Without understanding Canon Troubert's amazing patience, Birotteau was anxious to escape the bliss which Mademoiselle Gamard was bent on seasoning to her own taste, for she thought she could compound happiness as she could preserves; but the luckless priest set to work very clumsily, as a result of his perfectly artless nature. So the separation was not effected without some clawing and pricking, to which the Abbé Birotteau tried to seem insensible.

By the end of the first year of his life under Mademoiselle Gamard's roof the abbé had fallen into his old habits, spending two evenings a week at Madame de Listomère's, three with Mademoiselle Salomon, and the other two with Mademoiselle Merlin de la Blottière. These ladies moved in the aristocratic sphere of Tours society, to which Mademoiselle Gamard was not admitted. So the landlady was excessively indignant at the abbé's defection, which made her aware of her small importance : any kind of selection implying some contempt for the rejected object.

"Monsieur Birotteau did not find us good enough company," the Abbé Troubert would say to Mademoiselle Gamard's friends when she was obliged to give up her "evenings." "He is a wit, a *gourmet!* He must have fashion, luxury, brilliant conversation, the tittle-tattle of the town."

And such words always prompted Mademoiselle Gamard to praise the canon's excellent temper at the expense of Birotteau's.

"He is not so clever when all is said," she remarked. "But for Canon Chapeloud he would never have been received by Madame de Listomère. Oh, I lost a great deal when the Abbé Chapeloud died. What an amiable man ! and so easy to live with ! Indeed, in twelve years we never had the smallest difficulty or disagreement."

Mademoiselle Gamard painted so unflattering a portrait of Monsieur Birotteau that her innocent boarder was regarded by this citizen circle, secretly hostile to the aristocratic class, as an essentially fractious man, very difficult to get on with. Then for a few weeks the old maid had the satisfaction of hearing herself pitied by her female friends, who, without believing a word of what they said, repeated again and again, " How can you, who are so gentle and so kind, have inspired him with such dislike?——" or, "Be comforted, dear Mademoiselle Gamard, every one knows you too well——" and so forth.

Delighted, nevertheless, to escape spending an evening each week in the Close—the most deserted and gloomy spot in all Tours, and the most remote from the centre of life—they all blessed the abbé.

Love or hatred must constantly increase between two persons who are always together; every moment fresh reasons are found for loving or hating better. Thus to Mademoiselle Gamard the Abbé Birotteau became unendurable. Eighteen months after taking him as a boarder, just when the good man believed he had found the peace of contentment in the silence of aversion, and prided himself on having come so comfortably to terms with the old woman, to use his expression, he was to her the object of covert persecution and calmly planned animosity.

The four capital facts of the closed door, the forgotten slippers, the lack of fire, the candlestick taken to his rooms, alone could betray the terrible enmity of which the last effects were not to fall on him till the moment when they would be irremediable. As he went to sleep, the good abbé racked his brain, but vainly—and, indeed, he must soon have come to the bottom of it—to account for Mademoiselle Gamard's singularly uncivil behavior. In point of fact, as he had originally acted very logically, obeying the natural law of his egoism, he could not possibly form a guess as to how he had offended his landlady. While great things are simple to understand and easy to express, the mean things of life need much detail. The incidents which constitute the prologue, as it were, to this parochial drama, in which the passions will be seen not less violent than if they had been excited by important interests, necessitated this long introduction, and any exact historian would have found it difficult to abridge the trivial tale.

When he awoke next morning, the abbé's thoughts were so much set on the canonry that he forgot the four circumstances, which, the evening before, had appeared to him to be sinister prognostics of a future full of disaster. Birotteau was not the man to get up without a fire; he rang to announce to Marianne that he was awake, and wanted her; then, as he was wont, he lay lost in a somnolent, half-dreamy state, during which, as a rule, the woman made the fire, and dragged him gently from his last doze by a hum of inquiry and quiet bustle—a sort of music that he liked.

Half an hour went by, and Marianne had not appeared. The abbé, already half a canon, was about to ring again, when he stayed his hand on hearing a man's step on the stairs. In fact, the Abbé Troubert, after discreetly tapping at the door, at Birotteau's bidding came in. This call did not surprise him; the priests were in the habit of paying each other a visit once a month. The canon was at once amazed that Marianne should not yet have lighted his quasi-colleague's fire. He opened a window, called Marianne in a rough tone, and bid her come up at once; then, turning to his brother priest, he said, "If mademoiselle should hear that you have no fire, she would give Marianne a good scolding."

After this speech he inquired for Birotteau's health, and asked him, in an insinuating voice, whether he had any recent news that could encourage his hope of being made a canon. The abbé explained to him what was being done, and guilelessly told him who the personages were that Madame de Listomère was canvassing, not knowing that Troubert had never forgiven that lady for not inviting him to her house—him—Canon Troubert, twice designated to be made vicar-general of the diocese.

It would be impossible to meet with two figures offering so many points of contrast as those of these two priests. Troubert, tall and lean, had a bilious-yellow hue, while Birotteau was what is familiarly called crummy. His face, round and florid, spoke of good-nature devoid of ideas; while Troubert's, long and furrowed by deep wrinkles, wore at times an expression of irony and scorn; still, attentive examination was needed to discover these feelings. The canon was habitually and absolutely placid, his eyelids almost always lowered over a pair of orange-hazel eyes, whose glance was at will very clear and piercing. Red hair completed this countenance, which was constantly clouded under the shroud cast over his features by serious meditations. Several persons had at first supposed him to be absorbed in high and rooted ambition; but those who thought they knew him best had ended by demolishing this opinion, representing him as stultified by Mademoiselle Gamard's tyranny, or worn by long fasting. He rarely spoke, and never laughed. When he happened to be pleasurably moved, a faint smile appeared and lost itself in the furrows on his cheeks.

Birotteau, on the other hand, was all expansiveness, all openness; he liked titbits, and could be amused by a trifle with the artlessness of a man free from gall and malice. The Abbé Troubert at first sight inspired an involuntary feeling of dread, while the vicar made every one who looked at him smile kindly. When the tall canon stalked solemnly along the cloisters and aisles of Saint-Gatien, his brow bent, his eye stern, he commanded respect; his bowed figure harmonized with the yellow vaulting of the cathedral; there was something monumental in the folds of his gown, and worthy of the sculptor's art. But the good little abbé moved without dignity, trotted and pattered, looking as if he rolled along.

And yet the two men had one point of resemblance. While Troubert's ambitious looks, by making the world afraid of him, had perhaps contributed to condemn him to the modest dignity of a mere canon, Birotteau's character and appearance seemed to stamp him forever as no more than a vicar of the cathedral. The Abbé Troubert meanwhile, at the age of fifty, by the moderation of his conduct, by the apparently total absence of any ambition in his aims, and by his saintly life, had dispelled the fears his superiors had conceived of his supposed cleverness and his alarming exterior. Indeed, for a year past, his health had been seriously impaired, so that his early promotion to the dignity of vicargeneral by the archbishop seemed probable. His rivals even hoped for his appointment, to enable them the more effectually to prepare for their own, during the short span of life that might yet be granted him by a malady that had become chronic. Birotteau's triple chin, far from suggesting the same hopes, displayed to the candidates who were struggling for the canonry all the symptoms of vigorous health, and his gout seemed to them the proverbial assurance of a long life.

The Abbé Chapeloud, a man of great good sense, whose amiability had secured him the friendship of persons in good society and of the various heads of the diocese, had always opposed the elevation of the Abbé Troubert, secretly and with much address; he had even hindered his admission to any of the salons where the best set in Tours were wont to meet, though during his lifetime Troubert always treated him with great respect, and on all occasions showed him the utmost deference. This persistent submissiveness had not availed to change the deceased canon's opinion ; during his last walk with Birotteau, he had said to him once more—

"Do not trust that dry pole Troubert! He is Sixtus V. reduced to the scale of a bishopric."

This was Mademoiselle Gamard's friend and messmate, who, the very day after that on which she had, so to speak, declared war with poor Birotteau, had come to call on him with every mark of friendliness.

"You must excuse Marianne," said Troubert, as she came in. "I fancy she did my room first. My place is very damp, and I coughed a great deal during the night. You are very healthily situated here," he added, looking up at the mouldings.

"Oh, I am lodged like a canon!" replied Birotteau with a smile.

"And I like a curate," replied Abbé Troubert the humble priest.

"Yes, but before very long you will be lodged in the archbishop's palace," said the good abbé, who only wanted that everybody should be happy.

"Oh! or in the graveyard. God's will be done!" and Troubert looked up to heaven with a resigned air. "I came," he went on, "to beg you to lend me the 'General Clergy List.' No one but you has the book at Tours."

"Take it out of the bookcase," replied Birotteau, reminded by the canon's last words of all the joys of his life.

The tall priest went into the library, and remained there all the time the abbé was dressing. Presently the breakfast-bell rang, and Birotteau, reflecting that but for Troubert's visit here he would have had no fire to get up by, said to himself, "He is a good man!"

The two priests went down together, each armed with an enormous folio, which they laid on one of the consoles in the dining-room.

"What in the world is that?" asked Mademoiselle Gamard in sharp tones, addressing Birotteau. "You are not going to lumber up my dining-room with old books I hope!"

"They are some books I wanted," said the Abbé Troubert. "Monsieur is kind enough to lend them to me."

"I might have guessed that," said she with a scornful smile. "Monsieur Birotteau does not often study such big books."

"And how are you, mademoiselle?" asked the abbé in a piping voice.

"Why, not at all well," she replied curtly. "You were the cause of my being roused from my first sleep, and I felt the effects all night." And as she seated herself, Mademoiselle Gamard added, "Gentlemen, the milk will get cold."

Astounded at being so sourly received by his hostess when he expected her to apologize, but frightened, as timid people are, by the prospect of a discussion, especially when they themselves are the subject of it, the poor abbé took his place in silence. Then, recognizing in Mademoiselle Gamard's face the obvious symptoms of a bad temper, he sat warring with his common sense, which advised him not to submit to her want of manners, while his nature prompted him to avoid a quarrel. Birotteau, a prey to this internal struggle, began by seriously studying the broad-green stripes painted on the oilcloth cover, which, from immemorial habit, Mademoiselle Gamard always left on the table during breakfast, heedless of the frayed edges and scars innumerable that covered this cloth. The two boarders were seated opposite each other, in cane armchairs at each end of the table, a royal square ; the place between them being occupied by the landlady, who towered above the table from a chair mounted on runners, padded with cushions, and backing on the dining-room stove. This room and the common sitting-room were on the ground floor, under the Abbé Birotteau's bedroom and drawing-room. When the abbé had received from Mademoiselle Gamard his cup of sweetened coffee, he felt chilled by the utter silence in which he was doomed to perform the usually cheerful function of breakfast. He dared not look either at Troubert's expressionless face or at the old maid's threatening countenance ; so, to do something, he turned to the pug-dog, overburdened with fat, lying near the stove on a cushion whence it never stirred, finding always on the left a little plate of dainties, and on the right a saucer of clean water.

"Well, my pet," said he, "so you want your coffee ! "

This personage, one of the most important members of the household, but not a troublesome one, since he never barked

now, and left the conversation to his mistress, looked up at
Birotteau with little eyes buried in the folds of fat that
wrinkled his face.   Then he cunningly shut them again.

.To give the measure of the priest's discomfiture, it must
be explained that, being gifted with a voice and volubility as
resonant and meaningless as the sound of an India-rubber ball,
he asserted, without being able to give the faculty any reason
for his opinion, that speech favored digestion.   Mademoiselle
Gamard, who shared this theory of hygiene, had never
hitherto failed to converse during meals, notwithstanding
their misunderstanding ; but now for some few days the abbé
had racked his wits in vain to ask her insidious questions
which might loosen her tongue.   If the narrow limits to which
this story is restricted would allow of a report in full of one
of these conversations which always provoked the Abbé
Troubert's bitter and sardonic smiles, it would give a perfect
picture of the Bœotian existence of provincials.   Some clever
men might perhaps be even pleased to know the extraordinary
amplitude given by the Abbé Birotteau and Mademoiselle
Gamard to their personal opinions on politics, religion, and
literature.   There would certainly be some very funny things
to tell : such as their reasons, in 1820, for doubting the death
of Napoleon, or the conjectures which led them to believe in
the survival of Louis XVII., smuggled away in a hollow log
of wood.   Who would not have laughed to hear them assert-
ing, with arguments peculiarly their own, that the King of
France alone spent the money collected in taxes ; that the
Chambers met to destroy the clergy ; that more than thirteen
hundred thousand persons had perished on the scaffold during
the Revolution ?   Then they discussed the press, knowing
nothing of how many newspapers were issued, having not the
smallest idea of what this modern power is.   Finally, Monsieur Birotteau listened respectfully to Mademoiselle Gamard
when she asserted that a man fed on an egg every morning
would infallibly die at the end of a year, and that it had

been known that a soft roll eaten without drinking for a few days would cure sciatica; that all the workmen who had been employed in the destruction of the Abbey of Saint-Martin had died within six months; that a certain préfet had done his utmost in Bonaparte's time to ruin the towers of Saint-Gatien, and a thousand other absurd stories.

But at the present juncture Birotteau felt his tongue dead within him; so he resigned himself to eating without trying to converse. He soon thought that such silence was perilous to his digestion, and boldly said, " This is excellent coffee! " But the courageous act fell flat.

After looking at the narrow strip of sky above the garden, between the two black buttresses of Saint-Gatien, the abbé again was brave enough to remark, " It will be finer to-day than it was yesterday."

At this Mademoiselle Gamard did no more than cast one of her most ingratiating glances at Monsieur Troubert, and then turn her eyes full of terrible severity on Birotteau, who was happily looking down.

No being of the female sex was better able to assume the elegiac attitude of an old maid than Mademoiselle Sophie Gamard; but to do justice in describing a person whose character will give the greatest interest to the trivial events of this drama, and to the antecedent lives of the figures playing a part in it, it will be well here to epitomize the ideas of which the old maid is the outcome. The habits of life form the soul, and the soul forms the countenance. If in society, as in the universe, everything must have a purpose, there yet are on this earth some existences of which the use and purpose are undiscoverable; morality and political economy alike reject the individual that consumes without producing, that fills a place on earth without diffusing either good or evil—for evil, no doubt, is a form of good of which the results are not immediately manifest. Very rarely does an old maid fail to place herself by her own act in this class of unproductive creatures. Now if the consciousness of work done gives productive beings a sense of satisfaction which helps them to endure life, the knowledge that they are a burthen on others, or even merely useless, must produce the contrary effect, and give to the inert a contempt for themselves as great as that they provoke in others. This stern social reprobation is one of the causes which, unknown to themselves, contribute to implant in their soul the grievance which is stamped on their faces.

A prejudice, not perhaps without a basis of truth, everywhere gives rise—and in France more than elsewhere—to marked disfavor being felt towards a woman with whom no man has chosen to share his fortunes or to endure the woes of life. And an age comes to unmarried women when the world, rightly or wrongly, condemns them on the strength of the disdain to which they are victims. If ugly, the amiability of their nature ought to have redeemed the imperfections of their persons; if pretty, their loneliness must have its cause in serious reasons. It is hard to decide which of the two classes is most to be contemned. If their single life is deliberately chosen, if it is a determination to be independent, neither men nor mothers can forgive them for having shirked the sacrifice of woman by refusing to know the passions that make her sex pathetic. To reject its sufferings is to forego its poetry, to cease to deserve the sweet consolations to which a mother has always uncontested rights. Then the generous feelings, the exquisite qualities of woman, can only be developed by constant exercise. When she remains unmarried, a creature of the female sex is a self-contradiction : egoistical and cold, she fills us with horror.

This pitiless verdict is unfortunately too just for old maids to misinterpret its motives. These ideas germinate in their heart as naturally as the effects of their desolate life are imprinted on their features. Thus they wither, because the constant expansion, or the happiness that blooms in a woman's face and lends softness to her movements, has never existed in them. Then they grow harsh and discontented, because a creature that fails of its purpose is unhappy, it suffers, and suffering brings forth viciousness. In fact, before an unmarried woman spites herself for her loneliness, she accuses the whole world, and from accusation there is but one step to the desire for revenge.

Again, the ill grace that disfigures their persons is an inevitable outcome of their life. Never having felt the necessity to please, elegance and good taste are unknown to them. This feeling gradually leads them to choose everything to suit their own convenience at the cost of what might be agreeable to others. Without quite understanding their dissimilarity to other women, at last they observe it and suffer from it. Jealousy is an indelible passion in the female heart. Old maids are jealous for nothing, and know only the woes of the single passion which men can forgive in women because it flatters them. Thus tormented on every side, and compelled to reject the development of their nature, old maids are always conscious of a moral uneasiness to which they never become accustomed. Is it not hard at any age, especially for a woman, to read a feeling of repugnance on every face, when it ought to have been her fate to inspire none but sensations of kindliness in the hearts of those about her? Hence an old maid's glance is always askance, not so much from modesty as from fear and shame.

Now, it is impossible that a person perpetually at war with herself, or at loggerheads with life, should leave others in peace and never envy their happiness. This world of gloomy ideas lay complete in Mademoiselle Gamard's dull gray eyes; and the broad, dark circle in which they were set spoke of the long struggle of her solitary life. All the wrinkles on her face were straight lines. The form of her brow, head, and cheeks was characterized by rigidity and hardness. Without heeding them, she left the hairs, once brown, of two or three moles on her chin to grow as they would. Her thin lips scarcely covered her long but sufficiently white teeth. She was dark, and her hair had once been black, but terrible headaches had turned it white. This disaster led her to wear a front; but not knowing how to put it on so as to conceal the junction, there often was a small gap between her cap-border and the black ribbon that fastened this half-wig, very carelessly curled. Her gown, of thin silk in summer, of merinos in winter, and always of Carmelite brown, fitted her ungraceful figure and thin arms rather too closely. Her collar, always limp, betrayed a throat whose reddish skin was as finely lined as an oak leaf looked at in the light.

Her parentage accounted for the faults of her figure. She was the daughter of a dealer in fire-logs, a peasant who had risen in the world. At eighteen she might have been fresh and plump, but not a trace was now left either of the white skin or the fine color she boasted of having then had. The hues of her complexion had acquired the dull pallor common enough in very devout persons. An aquiline nose was of all her features that which most strongly expressed the despotism of her ideas, just as the flatness of her forehead revealed her narrowness of mind. Her movements had an odd abruptness bereft of all grace; and only to see her pull her handkerchief out of her bag and loudly blow her nose would have told you what her character and habits were. Fairly tall, she held herself very upright, justifying the remark of a naturalist, who explains the stiffness of old maids physiologically by declaring that all their joints anchylose. She walked so that the motion did not distribute itself equally over her whole person, or produce the graceful undulations that are so attractive in a woman; she moved all of a piece, so to speak, seeming to lift herself at every step, like the statue of the Commendatore.

In her few moments of good-humor she would give it out, as all old maids do, that she could have been married, but that, happily, she had found out her lover's faithlessness in

time, and she thus, without knowing it, passed judgment on
her heart in favor of her sense of self-interest.

This typical figure of an old maid was suitably set against
a background of the grotesque pattern, representing Turkish
landscapes, of a satin wall-paper with which the dining-room
was hung. Mademoiselle Gamard habitually occupied this
room, ornamented by two consoles and a barometer. In the
place occupied by each priest was a little footstool in worsted
work of faded hues.

The public sitting-room, where she received company, was
worthy of her. The room will be at once familiar when it is
known that it went by the name of the yellow drawing-room;
the hangings were yellow, the furniture and wall-paper yellow;
on the chimney-shelf, in front of a mirror with a gilt frame,
candlesticks and a clock in cut-glass reflected a hard glitter to
the eye. As to Mademoiselle Gamard's private sanctum, no
one had ever been allowed to enter it. It could only be con-
jectured that it was full of the odds and ends, the shabby
furniture, the rags and tatters, so to speak, which all old maids
collect and cling to so fondly.

This was the woman who was destined to exert the greatest
influence over the Abbé Birotteau's latter days. Having failed
to exercise the energies bestowed on woman in the way intended by nature, and urged by the need of expending them,
this old maid had thrown them into the sordid intrigue, the
petty tittle-tattle of provincial life, and the selfish scheming
which at last exclusively absorbs all old maids.

Birotteau, for his woe, had developed in Sophie Gamard
the only feelings this unhappy creature could possibly know,
those of hatred; these, till now latent, as a result of the calm
monotony of a country-town life, whose horizon was to her
more especially narrow, were presently to become all the more
intense for being wreaked on small things, and in a narrow
sphere of activity. Birotteau was one of those men who are
predestined to suffer everything, because, as they never foresee

anything, they can avoid nothing ; everything seems to fall on them.

"Yes, it will be fine," the canon replied after a pause, seeming to come out of his meditations and to wish to fulfill the laws of good manners.

Birotteau, frightened at the time that had elapsed between the remark and the reply, since he, for the first time in his life, had swallowed his coffee without speaking, left the dining-room, where his heart was held as in a vise. Feeling his cup of coffee lie heavy on his stomach, he went to walk, sadly enough, up and down the narrow box-edged paths which marked out a star in the garden. But as he turned after his first round, he saw the Abbé Troubert and Mademoiselle Gamard standing at the glass door of the drawing-room ; he with his arms crossed, as motionless as the statue on a tomb, she leaning against the shutter-door. Both, as they watched him, seemed to be counting the number of his steps.

To a timid person there is nothing so distressing as being the object of inquisitive inspection ; when it is made by the eyes of hatred, the sort of suffering it inflicts becomes an intolerable martyrdom. Presently the abbé fancied that he was hindering Mademoiselle Gamard and the canon from taking their walk. This notion, inspired alike by fear and by good-nature, acquired such proportions, that he abandoned the place. He went away, already thinking no more of his canonry, so greatly was he worried by the woman's maddening tyranny.

By chance, and happily for him, he was kept very busy at Saint-Gatien, where there were several funerals, a marriage, and two baptisms. This enabled him to forget his troubles. When his appetite warned him of the dinner hour, he took out his watch in some alarm, seeing that it was some minutes past four. He knew Mademoiselle Gamard's punctuality, so he hurried home.

He saw the first course brought down again as he passed the

kitchen. Then on going into the dining-room, the old maid said to him in a tone of voice which betrayed alike the harshness of a reproof and the glee of finding her boarder in fault, "It is half-past four, Monsieur Birotteau; you knew we should not wait for you."

The priest looked at the dining-room clock, and the arrangement of the gauze wrapper, intended to protect it from dust, showed him that his landlady had wound it in the course of the morning, and had allowed herself the pleasure of setting it faster than the clock of Saint-Gatien's. There was nothing to be said. The least word of the suspicion he had conceived would have sprung the most terrible and plausible of those explosions of eloquence which Mademoiselle Gamard, like all women of her class, could give vent to in such cases.

The thousand-and-one vexations that a maidservant can inflict on her master, or a wife on her husband, in the daily course of private life, were imagined by Mademoiselle Gamard, who heaped them on her boarder. The way in which she plotted her conspiracies against the poor abbé's domestic comfort bore the stamp of deeply malignant genius. She contrived never to be in the wrong.

By the end of a week after the opening of this tale, his life in the house, and his position towards Mademoiselle Gamard, revealed to him a plot, hatching for six months past. So long as the old maid had been covert in her revenge, and the priest could voluntarily keep up his self-deceit, refusing to believe in her malevolent purpose, the moral effects had made no great progress in him. But since the incidents of the displacement of the candlestick and the clock put too fast, Birotteau could no longer doubt that he was living under the rule of an aversion that kept an ever-watchful eye on him. From this he rapidly sank into despair, forever seeing Mademoiselle Gamard's lean and talon-like fingers ready to claw his heart.

The old maid, happy in living on a sentiment so teeming with excitement as revenge is, delighted in hovering and

13

wheeling above the abbé as a bird of prey hovers and circles over a field-mouse before seizing it.   She had long plotted a scheme which the bewildered priest could not possibly guess, and which she soon began to unfold, showing the genius that can be displayed in small things by isolated beings whose soul, incapable of apprehending the grandeur of true piety, has lost itself in the trivialities of devotion.   The last and most frightful aggravation of his torments was that the nature of them pro-hibited Birotteau, an effusive man who loved to be pitied and comforted, from enjoying the little solace of relating them to his friends.   The small amount of tact he owed to his shyness made him dread appearing ridiculous by troubling himself about such silly trifles.   At the same time, these silly trifles made up his whole life, the life he loved, full of busy vacuity and vacuous business, a dull, gray life, in which too strong a feeling was a misfortune, and the absence of all excitement is happiness.   Thus the poor abbé's paradise had suddenly be-come a hell.   In short, his torments were intolerable.

The terror with which he contemplated an explanation with Mademoiselle Gamard grew daily, and the secret misfortunes which blighted every hour of his old age injured his health. One morning, as he put on his speckled blue stockings, he observed that the circumference of his calf had shrunk by eight lines.   Appalled at such a terribly unmistakable symp-tom, he determined to make an effort to persuade the Abbé Troubert to intervene officially between himself and Made-moiselle Gamard.

When he found himself in the presence of the imposing canon, who came out of a study crammed with papers, where he was always at work, admitting nobody, to receive him in a bare room, the abbé was almost ashamed to speak of Made-moiselle Gamard's petty aggravations to a man who seemed so seriously occupied.   But after having suffered all the misery of mental deliberation which humble, weak, or irresolute per-sons go through, even with regard to trifles, he made up his mind to explain the position to the canon, not without feeling his heart swollen by extraordinary throbs. Troubert listened with a cold, grave air, trying, but in vain, to control some smiles, which, to intelligent eyes, might have betrayed the satisfaction of a secret desire. A flash sparkled in his eye when Birotteau described to him, with the eloquence inspired by true emotion, the bitterness that was incessantly poured out for him; but Troubert at once covered his eyes with his hand, a gesture common to great thinkers, and preserved his habitually dignified attitude.

When the abbé ceased speaking, he would have been puzzled indeed if he had tried to read any sign of the feelings he imagined he should excite in this mysterious priest, on his face, mottled now with yellow patches—yellower than even his usual bilious complexion. After a moment's silence, the canon made one of those replies of which every word must have been carefully studied to give them their full bearing, but which subsequently showed to capable persons the amazing depth of his mind and the power of his intellect.

He finally crushed Birotteau by saying that all these things surprised him the more, because, but for his brother's explanation, he would never have discerned them. He ascribed this dullness of perception to his important occupations, to his work, and to the supremacy of certain lofty thoughts, which did not allow of his heeding the trivialities of life. He pointed out, but without assuming the airs of wishing to censure the conduct of a man whose years and learning commanded his respect, that "the hermits of old rarely thought about their food, or their dwelling in the deserts, where they gave themselves up to holy contemplation," and that "in our days the priest could, in mind, make a desert for himself in every place." Then, returning to Birotteau, he remarked that such squabbles were quite a new thing to him. During twelve years nothing of the kind had ever arisen between Mademoiselle Gamard and the venerated Abbé Chapeloud.

As for himself he could, no doubt, act as moderator between
the priest and their landlady, since his friendship for her did
not overstep the limits imposed by the laws of the church on
its faithful ministers ; but then justice would require that he
should also hear Mademoiselle Gamard. At the same time,
he discerned no change in her; he had always seen her thus;
he had willingly yielded to some of her vagaries, knowing
that the excellent woman was kindness and sweetness itself;
these little caprices of temper were to be ascribed to the sufferings caused by a pulmonary trouble, of which she never
spoke, resigning herself to it as a true Christian.'' He ended
by saying that '' when he should have lived a few years longer
with mademoiselle, he would appreciate her better and recognize the beauties of her admirable character.''

The Abbé Birotteau came away bewildered. Under the
absolute necessity of taking counsel with himself alone, he
gauged Mademoiselle Gamard by himself. The poor man
thought that by absenting himself for a few days this woman's
hatred would burn itself out for lack of fuel. So he determined to go, as he had done before now, to spend some time
at a country place where Madame de Listomère always went
at the end of the autumn, a season when, in Touraine, the
sky is usually clear and mild. Poor man ! He was thus
carrying out the secret wishes of his terrible enemy, whose
schemes could not be thwarted by anything short of monk-
like endurance ; while he, guessing nothing and not knowing
his own business even, was doomed to fall like a lamb under
the first blow from the butcher.

Lying on the slope between the town of Tours and the
heights of Saint-Georges, facing the south, and sheltered by
cliffs, Madame de Listomère's estate combined all the charms
of the country with the pleasures of the town. It was not
more than a ten-minutes' drive from the Bridge of Tours to
the gate of this house, known as '' L'Alouette '' (The Lark)—

an immense convenience in a place where no one will disturb himself for any earthly thing, not even in quest of pleasure.

The poor Abbé Birotteau had been about ten days at "L'Alouette," when one morning, at the breakfast hour, the lodgekeeper came to tell him that Monsieur Caron wished to speak with him. Monsieur Caron was a lawyer employed by Mademoiselle Gamard. Birotteau, not remembering this, and conscious of no litigious difficulty to be settled with anybody in the world, left the table, not without some anxiety, to meet the lawyer; he found him sitting modestly on the parapet of a terrace.

"Your intention of remaining no longer as a resident under Mademoiselle Gamard's roof being now quite evident she——" the man of business began.

"Dear me, monsieur!" cried Birotteau, interrupting him, "I never thought of leaving her."

"And yet, monsieur," the lawyer went on, "you must certainly have expressed yourself to that effect to mademoiselle, since she has sent me to inquire whether you intend remaining long in the country. The event of a prolonged absence not having been provided for in your agreement might give rise to some discussion. Now, as Mademoiselle Gamard understands it, your board——"

"Monsieur," said Birotteau in surprise, and again interrupting the lawyer, "I did not think it could be necessary to take steps, almost legal in their nature, to——"

"Mademoiselle Gamard, wishing to preclude any difficulty," said Monsieur Caron, "has sent me to come to an understanding with you."

. "Very well, if you will be so obliging as to call again to-morrow, I, on my part, will have taken advice."

"So be it," said Caron with a bow.

The scrivener withdrew. The hapless priest, appalled by the pertinacity of Mademoiselle Gamard's persecution, went back to Madame de Listomère's dining-room looking quite upset.   At his mere appearance every one asked him, "Why, Monsieur Birotteau, what is the matter?"

The abbé, greatly distressed, sat down without answering, so overwhelmed was he by the vague vision of his misfortune. But after breakfast, when several of his friends had gathered round a good fire in the drawing-room, Birotteau artlessly told them the tale of his catastrophe.   The hearers, who were just beginning to be bored by their stay in the country, were deeply interested in an intrigue so completely in keeping with provincial life.   Everybody took the abbé's part against the old maid.

"Why!" cried Madame de Listomère, "do you not plainly see that the Abbé Troubert wants your rooms?"

In this place the historian would have a right to sketch this lady's portrait; but it occurs to him that even those persons to whom Sterne's cognomology is unknown could surely not utter the three words MADAME DE LISTOMÈRE without seeing her—noble and dignified, tempering the austerity of piety by the antique elegance of monarchical and classic manners and polite distinction; kind, but a little formal; speaking slightly through her nose; allowing herself to read "La Nouvelle Héloïse," and to go to the play; still wearing her own hair.

"The Abbé Birotteau must certainly not yield to that nagging old woman!" cried Monsieur de Listomère, a lieutenant in the navy, spending a holiday with his aunt.   "If the abbé has any courage, and will follow my advice, he will soon have recovered his peace of mind."

In short, everybody began to analyze Mademoiselle Gamard's proceedings with the acumen peculiar to provincials, who, it certainly cannot be denied, possess the talent of laying bare the most secret human actions.

"You have not hit the mark," said an old landowner who knew the country.   "There is something very serious under this which I have not yet mastered.   The Abbé Troubert is far too deep to be so easily seen through. Our good friend Birotteau is only at the beginning of his troubles. In the first place, would he be happy and left in peace even if he gave up his rooms to Troubert? I doubt it. If Caron came to tell you," he went on, turning to the puzzled abbé, "that you had intended to leave Mademoiselle Gamard, with the object of getting you out of her house—— Well, you will have to go, willy nilly. That kind of man never risks a chance; they only play when they hold the trumps."

This old gentleman, a certain Monsieur de Bourbonne, epitomized provincial ideas as completely as Voltaire epitomized the spirit of his time. This withered, little old man professed in matters of dress all the indifference of a proprietor whose estate has a quotable value in the department. His countenance, tanned by the sun of Touraine, was shrewd rather than clever. He was accustomed to weigh his words, to consider his actions, and he concealed his deep caution under a delusive bluntness. The very least observation was enough to discover that, like a Norman peasant, he would get the advantage in every stroke of business. He was great in œnology—the favorite science of the Tourangeaux. He had managed to extend the circle of one of his estates by taking in the alluvial land of the Loire without getting into a lawsuit with the state. This achievement had established his reputation as a clever man. If, charmed by Monsieur de Bourbonne's conversation, you had asked his biography of one of his fellow-provincials, "Oh! he is a cunning old fox," would have been the proverbial reply of all who envied him, and they were many. In Touraine, as in most provinces, jealousy lies at the base of the tongue.

Monsieur de Bourbonne's remark caused a brief silence, during which the members of this little committee seemed lost in thought.

At this juncture Mademoiselle Salomon de Villenoix was announced. She had just come from Tours, prompted by her wish to be of service to Birotteau, and the news she brought completely changed the aspect of affairs. At the moment when she came in, every one but the landowner was advising Birotteau to hold his own against Troubert and Gamard, under the auspices of the aristocratic party, who would support him.

"The vicar-general," said Mademoiselle Salomon, "who has all the promotions in his hands, has just been taken ill, and the archbishop has commissioned Canon Troubert to act in his place. The nomination to the canonry now depends entirely on him. Now yesterday, at Mademoiselle de la Blottière's, the Abbé Poirel was speaking of the annoyances Monsieur Birotteau occasioned to Mademoiselle Gamard, in such a way as to seem to justify the neglect which will certainly fall on our good abbé. 'The Abbé Birotteau is a man who badly needed the Abbé Chapeloud,' said he, 'and since that virtuous canon's death it has been proved that——' Then came a series of suppositions and calumnies. You understand?"

"Troubert will be made vicar-general," said Monsieur de Bourbonne solemnly.

"Come now," cried Madame de Listomère, looking at Birotteau, "which would you prefer—to be made canon or to remain with Mademoiselle Gamard?"

"To be made canon," was the general outcry.

"Well, then," Madame de Listomère went on, "the Abbé Troubert and Mademoiselle Gamard must be allowed to have their way. Have they not conveyed to you indirectly by Caron's visit that, provided you consented to leave your rooms, you shall be made canon. One good turn for another."

Every one exclaimed at Madame de Listomère's acumen and sagacity; but her nephew, the Baron de Listomère, said in a comical tone to Monsieur de Bourbonne—

"I should have liked to see the battle between the *Gamard* and the *Birotteau.*"

But, for the abbé's worse luck, the forces were not equal, with the worldly-wise on one side, and the old maid upheld by the Abbé Troubert on the other. The time was at hand when the struggle would become more decisive and assume a greater scope and immense proportions.

By the advice of Madame de Listomère and most of her adherents, who were beginning to take a passionate interest in this intrigue flung into the vacuity of their country life, a footman was despatched for Monsieur Caron. The lawyer returned with amazing promptitude, a fact that alarmed no one but Monsieur de Bourbonne.

"Let us adjourn any decision till we have fuller information," was the advice of this Fabius in a dressing-gown, whose deep reflections revealed to him some abstruse plan of battle on the Tours chessboard.

He tried to enlighten Birotteau as to the perils of his position. But the "old fox's" shrewdness did not subserve the frenzy of the moment; he was scarcely listened to.

The meeting between the lawyer and Birotteau was brief. The abbé came in looking quite scared, and saying, "He requires me to sign a paper declaring my decession."

"What barbarous word is that?" said the navy lieutenant.

"And what does it mean?" cried Madame de Listomère.

"It simply means that the abbé is to declare his readiness to leave Mademoiselle Gamard's house," replied Monsieur de Bourbonne, taking a pinch of snuff.

"Is that all? Sign it!" said Madame de Listomère to Birotteau. "If you have really made up your mind to quit her house, there can be no harm done by declaring your will. The *will* of Birotteau!"

"That is true," said Monsieur de Bourbonne, shutting his snuff-box with a dry snap, of which it is impossible to render the full meaning, for it was a language by itself. "But writing is always dangerous," he added, placing the snuff-box on the chimney-shelf with a look that terrified the abbé.

Birotteau was so bewildered by the upheaval of all his ideas, by the swiftness of events which had come on him and found him defenseless, and by the lightness with which his friends treated the most cherished circumstances of his lonely life, that he remained motionless, as if lost in the moon, not thinking of anything, but listening and trying to catch the sense of the hasty words everybody else was so ready with. He took up Monsieur Caron's document, and read it as though the lawyer's deed was in fact the object of his attention ; but it was merely mechanical, and he signed the paper by which he declared himself ready and willing to give up his residence with Mademoiselle Gamard as well as his board, as provided by the agreement between them. When Birotteau had signed the deed Caron took it, and asked him where his client was to bestow the goods and chattels belonging to him. Birotteau mentioned Madame de Listomère's house, and the lady by a nod consented to receive the abbé for some days, never doubting but that he would ere long be a canon. The old landowner wished to see this sort of act of renunciation, and Monsieur Caron handed it to him.

"Why," said he to the abbé, after having read it, "is there any written agreement between you and Mademoiselle Gamard? Where is it? What are the conditions?"

"The paper is in my rooms," said Birotteau.

"Do you know its contents?" the old gentleman asked the lawyer.

"No, monsieur," said Monsieur Caron, holding out his hand for the ominous document.

"Ah, ha!" said Monsieur de Bourbonne to himself, "you, master lawyer, are no doubt informed of what that agreement contains, but you are not paid to tell us." And he returned the deed of "decession" to the lawyer.

"Where am I to put all my furniture?" cried Birotteau, "and my books, my beautiful library, my nice pictures, my red drawing-room—all my things, in short!"

And the poor man's despair at finding himself thus uprooted was so guileless, it so perfectly showed the purity of his life, and his ignorance of the world, that Madame de Listomère and Mademoiselle Salomon said, to comfort him, and in the tone that mothers use when they promise a child a plaything:

"There, there, do not worry yourself about such silly trifles. We shall easily find you a home less cold and gloomy than Mademoiselle Gamard's house. If no lodging is to be found to suit you—well, one of us will take you as a boarder. Come, play a hit at backgammon. You can call on the Abbé Troubert to-morrow to ask his support, and you will see how well he will receive you."

Weak-minded persons are reassured as easily as they are frightened. So poor Birotteau, dazzled by the prospect of living with Madame de Listomère, forgot the ruin, now irremediably complete, of the happiness he had so long sighed for and so thoroughly reveled in. Still, at night, before falling asleep, with the anguish of a man to whom a removal and the formation of new habits were as the end of the world, he tortured his mind to imagine where he could find as convenient a home for his library as that corridor. As he pictured his books astray, his furniture dispersed, and his home broken up, he wondered a thousand times why his first year at Mademoiselle Gamard's had been so delightful, and the second so wretched. And again and again this disaster was a bottomless pit in which his mind was lost.

The canonry no longer seemed to him a sufficient compensation for so many misfortunes; he compared his life to a stocking in which one dropped stitch leads to a ladder all the way down the web. Mademoiselle Salomon was left to him. But, losing all his old illusions, the poor priest no longer dared believe in a new friend.

In the doleful city of old maids there are several, especially in France, whose life is a sacrifice nobly renewed day by day to

noble feeling. Some remain proudly faithful to a heart which
death untimely snatched from them ; martyrs to love, they
learn the secret of womanliness of soul. Others succumb to
a family pride which, to our shame, is daily waxing less ;
they have devoted themselves to make the fortune of a
brother, or to the care of orphan nephews ; such women are
mothers though remaining maids. These old maids rise to
the highest heroism of their sex, by consecrating every
womanly feeling to the worship of misfortune. They idealize
the concept of woman by renouncing all the rewards of her
natural destiny and accepting only its penalties. They live
enshrined in the beauty of their self-sacrifice, and men rever-
ently bow their heads before their faded forms. Mademoiselle
de Sombreuil is neither wife nor maid ; she was, and always
will be, an embodied poem.

Mademoiselle Salomon was one of these heroic creatures.
Her sacrifice was religiously sublime, inasmuch as it would
remain inglorious after having been a daily anguish. Young
and handsome, she was loved ; her lover lost his reason.
For five years she had devoted herself with the courage of
love to the mechanical joys of the unhappy man ; she was
so fully wedded to his madness that she did not think
him mad.

She was a woman of simple manners, frank in speech, with
a pale face not devoid of character, though the features were
regular. She never spoke of the experiences of her life.
Only, now and then, the sudden shudder with which she
heard the narrative of some dreadful or melancholy incident
betrayed in her the fine qualities evolved by great sorrows.
She had come to live at Tours after the death of her companion in life. There she could not be appreciated at her
true value ; she was regarded as a "good creature." She
was very charitable, and attached herself by preference to the
weak and helpless. For this reason she had, of course, the
deepest interest in the unhappy priest.

Mademoiselle Salomon de Villenoix, driving into town early next morning, took Birotteau with her, set him down on the cathedral quay, and left him making his way towards the Close, where he was in great haste to arrive, to save the canonry, at any rate, from the shipwreck, and to superintend the removal of his furniture. He rang, not without violent palpitations, at the door of the house, whither for fourteen years he had been in the habit of coming, in which he had dwelt, and whence he was now to be forever exiled after dreaming that he might die there in peace like his friend Chapeloud.

Marianne was surprised to see him. He told her he had come to speak to Monsieur Troubert, and turned towards the ground-floor rooms in which the canon lodged; but Marianne called out to him—

"The Abbé Troubert is not there, Monsieur le Vicaire; he is in your old rooms."

These words were a fearful shock to Birotteau, who at last understood Troubert's character, and the unfathomable depth of revenge so slowly worked out, when he saw him quite at home in Chapeloud's library, seated in Chapeloud's fine Gothic chair—sleeping, no doubt, in Chapeloud's bed, using Chapeloud's furniture, contravening Chapeloud's will, in short, disinheriting Chapeloud's friend;—that very Chapeloud who had for so long penned him in at Mademoiselle Gamard's, hindered his advancement, and kept him out of the drawing-rooms at Tours. By what magic wand had this transformation been effected? Were these things no longer Birotteau's?

Indeed, as he noted the sardonic expression with which Troubert looked round on this library, Birotteau inferred that the future vicar-general was secure of possessing for ever the plunder of the two men he had so bitterly hated—Chapeloud as an enemy, and Birotteau because in him he still saw Chapeloud. At the sight a thousand ideas surged up in the worthy man's heart and wrapped him in a sort of trance. He stood motionless, and, as it were, fascinated by Troubert's eye, which was fixed on him.

"I cannot suppose, monsieur," said Birotteau at last, "that you would wish to deprive me of the things that are mine. Though Mademoiselle Gamard may have been impatient to move you, she must surely be just enough to allow me time to identify my books and remove my furniture."

"Monsieur," said the canon coldly, and betraying no sort of feeling in his face, "Mademoiselle Gamard told me yesterday that you were leaving; of the cause of it I know nothing. If she moved me up here, it was because she was obliged to do so. Monsieur l'Abbé Poirel has taken my rooms. Whether the furniture in these rooms belongs to mademoiselle, I know not. If it is yours, you know her perfect honesty; the saintliness of her life is a guarantee for it.

"As to myself, you know how plainly I live. For fifteen years I slept in a bare room, never heeding the damp, which is killing me by inches. At the same time, if you wish to return to these rooms, I am ready to give them up to you."

As he listened to this terrible speech, Birotteau forgot the matter of the canonry; he went downstairs as briskly as a young man to find Mademoiselle Gamard, and met her at the bottom of the stairs in the large paved passage which joined the two parts of the house.

"Mademoiselle," said he, bowing, and not heeding the sour, sardonic smile that curled her lips, or the extraordinary fire that gave her eyes a glare like a tiger's, "I cannot understand why you did not wait till I had removed my furniture before——"

"What!" she exclaimed, interrupting him, "have not all your things been taken to Madame de Listomère's?"

"But my furniture?"

"Did you never read your agreement?" cried she, in tones which ought to be expressed in musical notation to show how many shades hatred could infuse into the accentuation of every word.

And Mademoiselle Gamard seemed to swell, her eyes flashed once more, and her face beamed; her whole person thrilled with satisfaction.

The Abbé Troubert opened a window to see better to read a folio volume.

Birotteau stood as if thunder-stricken.

Mademoiselle Gamard trumpeted at him, in a voice as shrill as a clarion, the following words:

"Was it not agreed that, in the event of your leaving my house, your furniture was to become mine to indemnify me for the difference between what you paid me for your board and what I received from the late respectable Abbé Chapeloud? Now, as Monsieur l'Abbé Poirel has been made canon——"

At these last words Birotteau bowed slightly as if to take leave; then he rushed out of the house. He was afraid lest, if he stayed any longer, he should faint, and so give his relentless foes too great a triumph. Walking like a drunken man, he got back to Madame de Listomère's town house, where, in a lower room, he found his linen, clothes, and papers all packed into a trunk. At the sight of those relics of his property, the unhappy priest sat down and hid his face in his hands to hide his tears from the sight of men. The Abbé Poirel was canon! He, Birotteau, found himself homeless, bereft of fortune and furniture.

Happily, Mademoiselle Salomon happened to drive past. The doorkeeper, understanding the poor man's despair, signaled to the coachman. After a few words of explanation between the lady and the porter, the abbé allowed himself to be led to his faithful friend, though he could only answer her in incoherent words. Mademoiselle Salomon, alarmed by the temporary derangement of a brain already so feeble, carried him at once to "L'Alouette," ascribing these symptoms of mental disturbance to the effect naturally produced on him by the Abbé Poirel's promotion. She knew nothing of the hapless priest's agreement with Mademoiselle Gamard, for the excellent reason that he himself did not know its full bearing. And as it is in the nature of things that comedy is often mixed up with the most pathetic incidents, Birotteau's bewildered answers almost made Mademoiselle Salomon laugh.

"Chapeloud was right," said he; "he is a monster."

"Who?" said she.

"Chapeloud. He has robbed me of everything."

"Then you mean Poirel?"

"No, Troubert."

At length they reached "L'Alouette," where the priest's friends lavished on him such effusive kindness, that by the evening he grew calmer, and they could extract from him an account of all that had occurred that morning.

Monsieur de Bourbonne, always phlegmatic, naturally asked to see the agreement which ever since the day before had seemed to him to contain the key to the riddle. Birotteau brought the fatal document out of his pocket, and held it out to the landowner, who read it hastily, presently coming to a sentence in these terms:

"Whereas there is a difference of eight hundred francs a year between the price paid by the late Monsieur Chapeloud and the sum for which the aforenamed Sophie Gamard agrees to lodge and board, on the terms hereinbefore stated, the said François Birotteau; whereas the said François Birotteau fully acknowledges that it is out of his power for some years to come to pay the full price paid by Mademoiselle Gamard's boarders, and more especially by the Abbé Troubert; and, finally, whereas the said Sophie Gamard has advanced certain sums of money, the said Birotteau hereby pledges himself to bequeath to her, as an indemnity, the furniture of which he may be possessed at the time of his decease; or in the event of his voluntarily departing, for whatever cause or reason, and quitting the premises at present let to him, and no longer availing himself of the benefits contracted for in the agreement made by Mademoiselle Gamard hereinbefore——"

"Heaven above us! What impudence!" exclaimed Monsieur de Bourbonne. "And what claws the said Sophie Gamard has!"

Poor Birotteau, never conceiving in his childish brain of any cause which could ever separate him from Mademoiselle Gamard, had counted on dying under her roof. He had not the least recollection of this clause, of which the terms had not even been discussed at the time when, in his eagerness to lodge with the old maid, he would have signed all the documents she might have chosen to lay before him. His innocence was so creditable, and Mademoiselle Gamard's conduct so atrocious; there was something so deplorable in the fate of this hapless sexagenarian, and his weakness made him so pitiable, that in a first impulse of indignation Madame de Listomère exclaimed, "I am the cause of your having signed the act that has ruined you; I ought to make up to you for the comfort you have lost."

"But," said Monsieur de Bourbonne, "such proceedings constitute a fraud; there are grounds for an action——"

"Good, Birotteau shall bring an action. If he loses it at Tours, he will win it at Orleans; if he loses it at Orleans, he will win it at Paris!" cried the Baron de Listomère.

"If he means to bring an action, I should advise him first to resign his benefice in the cathedral," said Monsieur de Bourbonne calmly.

"We will take legal advice," replied Madame de Listomère; "and we will bring an action if we ought. But this business is so disgraceful for Mademoiselle Gamard, and may prove so damaging to the Abbé Troubert, that we can surely effect a compromise."

After mature deliberation, everybody promised to assist the

14

Abbé Birotteau in the struggle that must ensue between him, his enemies, and their allies. A confident presentiment, an indescribable provincial instinct prompted every one to combine the names of Troubert and Gamard. But not a soul of those then assembled at Madame de Listomère's, excepting the " old fox," had any accurate notion of the importance of such a conflict.

Monsieur de Bourbonne took the poor priest into a corner.

" Of all the fourteen persons present," said he in a low voice, " not one will be still on your side within a fortnight. If you then want to call in help, you will perhaps find no one but myself bold enough to undertake your defense, because I know the country, men, and things, and, better still, their interests. All your friends here, though full of good intentions, are starting on the wrong road, which you can never get out of. Listen to my advice. If you want to live in peace, give up your office in Saint-Gatien and leave Tours. Tell no one where you go, but seek a cure of souls far from here, where this man Troubert can never again come across you."

" Leave Tours ! " cried the abbé, with unspeakable dismay.

It was to him a form of death. Was it not tearing up all the roots by which he held to the world? Celibates make habits take the place of feelings. And when to this system of ideas, by which they go through life rather than live, they add a weak nature, external things have an astonishing dominion over them. Birotteau had really become a sort of vegetable ; to transplant it was to endanger its guileless functions. Just as a tree, in order to live, must always find the same juices at hand, and always send its filaments into the same soil, so Birotteau must always patter round Saint-Gatien, always trot up and down the spot on the mall where he was wont to walk, always go through the same familiar streets, and constantly frequent the three drawing-rooms where evening after evening he played whist or backgammon.

"To be sure—I was not thinking," replied Monsieur de Bourbonne, looking compassionately at the priest.

Before long all Tours knew that Madame la Baronne de Listomère, widow of a lieutenant-general, had given a home to the Abbé Birotteau, vicar of Saint-Gatien. This fact, on which several persons threw doubts, cut short all questions and gave definiteness to party divisions, especially when Mademoiselle Salomon was the first to dare speak of fraud and an action at law.

Mademoiselle Gamard, with the subtle vanity and the fanatical sense of personal importance that are characteristic of old maids, considered herself greatly aggrieved by the line of conduct taken by Madame de Listomère. The Baroness was a woman of high rank, elegant in her habits, whose good taste, polished manners, and genuine piety were beyond dispute. By sheltering Birotteau she formally gave the lie to all Mademoiselle Gamard's asseverations, indirectly censured her conduct, and seemed to sanction the abbé's complaints of his former landlady.

For the better comprehension of this story, it is necessary here to explain how much power Mademoiselle Gamard derived from the discernment and analytical spirit with which old women can account to themselves for the actions of others, and to set forth the resources of her faction. Escorted by the always taciturn Abbé Troubert, she spent her evenings in four or five houses where a dozen persons were wont to meet, allied by common tastes and analogous circumstances. There were two or three old men, wedded to the whims and tittle-tattle of their cooks; five or six old maids, who spent their days in sifting the words and scrutinizing the proceedings of their neighbors and those a little below them in the social scale; and, finally, several old women wholly occupied in distilling scandal, in keeping an exact register of everybody's fortune, and a check on everybody's actions. They foretold marriages, and blamed their friends' conduct quite as harshly as their enemies'. These persons, filling in the town a position analogous to the capillary vessels of a plant, imbibed news with the thirst of a leaf for the dew, picked up the secrets of every household, discharged them and transmitted them mechanically to Monsieur Troubert, as leaves communicate to the plant the moisture they have absorbed. Thus, every evening of the week, these worthy bigots, prompted by the craving for excitement which exists in every one, struck an accurate balance of the position of the town with a sagacity worthy of the council of ten, and made an armed police out of the unerring espionage to which our passions give rise. Then, as soon as they had found the secret motive of any event, their conceit led them to appropriate, severally, the wisdom of their Sanhedrim, and to give importance to their gossip in their respective circles.

This idle and busybody assembly, invisible though omniscient, speechless but for ever talking, had at that time an influence which was apparently harmless in view of its contemptibility, but which nevertheless could be terrible when it was animated by a strong motive. Now it was a very long time since any event had occurred within range of their lives to compare in general importance to each and all with the contest between Birotteau, supported by Madame de Listomère, and the Abbé Troubert with Mademoiselle Gamard. In fact, the three drawing-rooms of Madame de Listomère, Mademoiselle Merlin de la Blottière, and Mademoiselle de Villenoix, being regarded as a hostile camp by those where Mademoiselle Gamard visited, there lay behind this quarrel a strong party spirit with all its vanities. It was the struggle of the Roman senate and people in a molehill, or a tempest in a glass of water, as Montesquieu said in speaking of the republic of San Marino, where public officials held their places but a day, so easy was it to seize despotic power.

But this storm in a teacup evolved as many passions in the

actors as would have sufficed to direct the largest social interests. Is it not a mistake to suppose that time flies swiftly
only to those whose hearts are a prey to such vast projects as
trouble life and make it boil? The Abbé Troubert's hours
were spent as busily, flew loaded with thoughts as anxious,
and marked by despair and hopes as deep as could the rack-
ing hours of the man of ambition, the gamester, or the lover.
God alone knows the secret of the energy we put forth to
win the occult triumphs we achieve over men, or things, or
ourselves. Though we do not always know whither we are
going, we know full well the fatigues of the voyage. Still, if
the historian may be allowed to digress from the drama he is
narrating, to assume for a moment the functions of the critic
—if he may invite you to glance at the lives of these old
maids and of these two priests, to investigate the causes of the
misfortune which vitiated their inmost core—you will perhaps
find it proved to a demonstration that man must necessarily
experience certain passions if he is to evolve those qualities
which give nobleness to life, which expand its limits and
silence the selfishness natural to all beings.

Madame de Listomère returned to town, not knowing that
for five or six days past several of her friends had been obliged
to dispute a rumor concerning herself, and accepted by some,
though she would have laughed at it had she heard of it,
which attributed her affection for her nephew to almost criminal causes.

She took the abbé to see her lawyer, who did not think
an action an easy matter. The abbé's friends, confident in
the feeling that comes of the justice of a good case, or else
dilatory about proceedings which did not concern them
personally, had postponed the preliminary inquiry till the
day when they should return to Tours. Thus Mademoiselle
Gamard's allies had been able to make the first move, and
had told the story in a way unfavorable to the Abbé Birotteau.
Hence the man of law, whose clients consisted exclusively of

the pious folks of the town, very much astonished Madame
de Listomère by urging her on no account to be mixed up in
such proceedings ; and he closed the interview by saying that
"he, at any rate, would not undertake the case, because, by
the terms of the agreement, Mademoiselle Gamard was right
in the eye of the law; that in equity, that is to say, out of
the jurisdiction of the court, Monsieur Birotteau would appear
in the eyes of the bench and of all honest folks to have fallen
away from the meek, peace-loving, and conciliatory character
he had hitherto enjoyed ; that Mademoiselle Gamard, regarded
as a gentle person and easy to live with, had accommodated
Birotteau by lending the money needed to pay the succession
duties arising from Chapeloud's bequest, without demanding
any receipt; that Birotteau was not of an age, nor of a nature, to sign a document without knowing what it contained
and recognizing its importance ; and that as he had ceased to
live at Mademoiselle Gamard's after only two years' residence,
whereas his friend Chapeloud had been with her for twelve
years and Troubert for fifteen, it would only be in accordance
with some plan best known to himself. That, consequently,
the action would be generally considered as an act of ingrati-
tude," etc.

After seeing Birotteau to the head of the stairs, the lawyer
detained Madame de Listomère a moment as he showed her
out, and besought her, as she loved her peace of mind, to
have nothing to do with the affair.

In the evening, however, the hapless abbé, as miserable as
a criminal in the condemned cell at Bicêtre while awaiting
the result of his petition to the court of appeal, could not
keep himself from telling his friends of the result of his visit
to the lawyer, at the hour before the card-parties were made
up, when the little circle was assembling round Madame de
Listomère's fire.

"I know no lawyer in Tours, excepting the solicitor for
the Liberal party, who would undertake the case, unless he

meant to lose it," exclaimed Monsieur de Bourbonne, "and I do not advise you to embark on it."

"Well, it is a rascally shame!" said the navy lieutenant. "I myself will take the abbé to see that lawyer!"

"Then go after dark," said Monsieur de Bourbonne, interrupting him.

"Why?"

"I have just heard that the Abbé Troubert is appointed vicar-general in the place of him who died the day before yesterday."

"Much I care for the Abbé Troubert!"

Unluckily, the Baron de Listomère, a man of six-and-thirty, did not see the sign made to him by Monsieur de Bourbonne warning him to weigh his words, and pointing significantly at a town councilor who was known to be a friend of Troubert's. So the officer went on with his denunciations of the abbé's treatment:

"If Monsieur Troubert is a rogue——"

"Dear me," said Monsieur de Bourbonne, "why bring the Abbé Troubert's name into a matter with which he has no concern whatever?"

"Nay," said the lieutenant, "is he not in the enjoyment of the Abbé Birotteau's furniture? I remember having called on Monsieur Chapeloud and seeing two valuable pictures. Suppose they are worth ten thousand francs? Can you believe that Monsieur Birotteau ever intended to give, in return for two years' board with this Gamard woman, ten thousand francs, when the library and furniture are worth almost as much more?"

The abbé opened his eyes very wide on hearing that he had ever owned such an enormous fortune. And the Baron went on vehemently to the end.

"By Jove! Monsieur Salmon, an expert from the Paris gallery, happens to be here on a visit to his mother-in-law. I will go to him this very evening with Monsieur l'Abbé, and beg him to value the pictures. From there I will take him to that lawyer.''

Two days after this conversation the action had taken shape. The solicitor to the Liberal party, now Birotteau's attorney, cast some obloquy on the abbé's case. The opposition to the government, and some persons known to love neither priests nor religion—two things which many people fail to distinguish—took up the matter, and the whole town was talking of it. The expert from Paris had valued "The Virgin," by Le Valentin, and "The Christ," by Lebrun, at eleven thousand francs; they were both choice examples. As to the bookcase and the Gothic furniture, the fashionable taste, daily growing in Paris, for that style of work gave them an immediate value of twelve thousand francs. In short, the expert, on examination, estimated the contents of the rooms at ten thousand crowns.

Now, it was obvious that as Birotteau had never intended to give Mademoiselle Gamard this immense sum in payment of the little money he might owe her in virtue of the stipulated indemnity, there were grounds, legally speaking, for a new contract, otherwise the old maid would be guilty of unintentional fraud. So the lawyer on Birotteau's behalf began by serving a writ on Mademoiselle Gamard, formulating the abbé's case. This statement, though exceedingly severe, and supported by quotations from leading judgments, and confirmed by certain articles of the code, was at the same time a masterpiece of legal logic, and so evidently condemned the old maid, that thirty or forty copies were maliciously circulated in the town by the opposite party.

A few days after this commencement of hostilities between the old maid and Birotteau, the Baron de Listomère, who, as commander of a corvette, hoped to be included in the next list of promotions, which had been expected for some time at the navy board, received a letter, in which a friend informed him that there was, on the contrary, some idea in the office of placing him on the retired list. Greatly amazed by this news, he at once set out for Paris, and appeared at the minister's next reception. This official himself seemed no less surprised, and even laughed at the fears expressed by the Baron de Listomère.

Next day, in spite of the minister's words, the Baron inquired at the office. With an indiscretion, such as is not unfrequently committed by heads of departments for their friends, a secretary showed him a minute confirming the fatal news, ready drawn up, but which had not yet been submitted to the minister, in consequence of the illness of a head clerk. The Baron at once went to call on an uncle, who, being a deputy, could without delay meet the minister at the chamber, and begged him to sound his excellency as to his views, since to him this meant the sacrifice of his whole career. He awaited the closing of the sitting in his uncle's carriage in the greatest anxiety.

Long before the end his uncle came out, and as they drove home to his house he asked the Baron—

"What the devil led you to make war against the priesthood? The minister told me at once that you had put yourself at the head of the Liberal party at Tours. Your opinions are detestable, you do not follow the line laid down by the government, and what not! His phrases were as confused as if he were still addressing the chamber. So then I said to him, 'Come, let us understand each other.' And his excellency ended by confessing that you were in a scrape with the lord high almoner. In short, by making some inquiries among my colleagues, I learned that you had spoken with much levity of a certain Abbé Troubert, who, though but a vicar-general, is the most important personage of the province, where he represents the ecclesiastical power. I answered for you to the minister in person. My noble nephew, if you want to get on in the world, make no enemies in the church.

"Now, go back to Tours, and make your peace with this devil of a vicar-general. Remember that vicars-general are men with whom you must always live in peace. Deuce take it! When we are all trying to re-establish the church, to cast discredit on the priests is a blunder in a ship's lieutenant who wants his promotion. If you do not make it up with this Abbé Troubert, you need not look to me; I shall cast you off. The minister for church affairs spoke to me of the man just now as certain to be a bishop. If Troubert took an aversion for our family, he might hinder my name from appearing in the next batch of peers. Do you understand?"

This speech explained to the navy lieutenant what Troubert's secret occupations were, when Birotteau so stupidly remarked, "I cannot think what good he gains by sitting up all night!"

The canon's position, in the midst of the feminine senate which so craftily kept a surveillance over the province, as well as his personal capabilities, had led to his being chosen by the church authorities from among all the priests in the town to be the unacknowledged proconsul of Touraine. Archbishop, general, préfet—high and low were under his occult domain.

The Baron de Listomère had soon made up his mind.

"I have no notion," said he to his uncle, "of receiving another ecclesiastical broadside below the water-line."

Three days after this diplomatic interview between the uncle and nephew, the sailor, who had suddenly returned to Tours by the mail-coach, explained to his aunt, the very evening of his arrival, all the danger that would be incurred by the Listomère family if they persisted in defending that idiot Birotteau. The Baron had caught Monsieur de Bourbonne at the moment when the old gentleman was taking up his stick and hat to leave after his rubber. The "old fox's" intelligence was indispensable to throw a light on the reefs among which the Listomères had been entangled; he rose so early to seek his hat and stick, only to be stopped by a word in his ear—

"Wait; we want to talk."

The young Baron's prompt return, and his air of satisfaction, though contrasting with the gravity his face assumed now and then, had vaguely hinted to Monsieur de Bourbonne of some checks the lieutenant might have received in his cruise against Gamard and Troubert. He manifested no surprise on hearing the Baron proclaim the secret power possessed by the vicar-general.

"I knew that," said he.

"Well, then," exclaimed the Baroness, "why did you not warn us?"

"Madame," he hastily replied, "if you will forget that I guessed this priest's occult influence, I will forget that you know it as well as I. If we should fail to keep the secret, we might be taken for his accomplices; we should be feared and hated. Do as I do. Pretend to be a dupe; but look carefully where you set your feet. I said quite enough; you did not understand me. I could not compromise myself."

"What must we do now?" said the Baron.

The desertion of Birotteau was not a matter of question; it was the primary condition, and so understood by this council of three.

"To effect a retreat with all the honors of war has always been the greatest achievement of the most skillful generals," said Monsieur de Bourbonne. "Yield to Troubert; if his hatred is less than his vanity, you will gain an ally; but if you yield too much, he will trample on your body, for, as Boileau says, 'Destruction is by choice the spirit of the church.' Make as though you were quitting the service, and you will escape him, Monsieur le Baron. Dismiss Birotteau, madame, and you will gain Gamard her lawsuit. When you meet the Abbé Troubert at the archbishop's, ask him if he plays whist; he will answer 'Yes.' Invite him to play a rubber in this drawing-room, where he longs to be admitted; he will certainly come. You are a woman; try to enlist this priest in your interest. When the Baron is a ship's captain, his uncle a peer of France, and Troubert a bishop, you can make Birotteau a canon at your leisure. Till then yield; but yield gracefully, and with a threat. Your family can give Troubert quite as much assistance as he can give you; you will meet half-way to admiration. And take soundings constantly as you go, sailor!"

"Poor Birotteau!" said the Baroness.

"Oh! begin at once," said the old man as he took leave. "If some clever Liberal should get hold of that vacuous brain, he would get you into trouble. After all, the law would pronounce in his favor, and Troubert must be afraid of the verdict. As yet he may forgive you for having begun the action, but after a defeat he would be implacable. I have spoken."

He snapped his snuff-box lid, went to put on his thick shoes, and departed.

The next morning, after breakfast, the Baroness remained alone with Birotteau, and said to him, not without visible embarrassment—

"My dear Monsieur Birotteau, I am going to make a request that you will think very unjust and inconsistent; but both for your sake and for ours you must, in the first place, put an end to your action against Mademoiselle Gamard by renouncing your claims, and also quit my house."

As he heard these words the poor priest turned pale.

"I am the innocent cause of your misfortunes," she went on; "and I know that but for my nephew you would never have begun the proceedings which now are working woe for you and for us. Listen to me."

And she briefly set forth the immense scope of this affair, explaining the seriousness of its consequences. Her meditations during the night had enabled her to form an idea of what the Abbé Troubert's former life had been. Thus she could unerringly point out to Birotteau the web in which he had been involved by this skillfully-plotted vengeance, could show him the superior cleverness and power of the enemy, revealing his hatred and explaining its causes; she pictured him as crouching for twelve years to Chapeloud, and now devouring and persecuting Chapeloud in the person of his friend.

The guileless Birotteau clasped his hands as if to pray, and wept with grief at this vision of human wickedness which his innocent soul had never conceived of. Terrified, as though he was standing on the verge of an abyss, he listened to his benefactress with moist and staring eyes, but without expressing a single idea. She said in conclusion—

" I know how vile it is to desert you; but, my dear abbé, family duties must supersede those of friendship. Bend before this storm, as I must, and I will prove my gratitude. I say nothing of your personal concerns; I undertake them; you shall be released from money difficulties for the rest of your life. By the intervention of Monsieur de Bourbonne, who will know how to save appearances, I will see that you lack nothing. My friend, give me the right to throw you over. I shall remain your friend while conforming to the requirements of the world. Decide."

The hapless abbé, quite bewildered, exclaimed—

" Ah! then Chapeloud was right when he said that if Troubert could drag him out of his grave by the heels, he would do it! He sleeps in Chapeloud's bed!"

"It is no time for lamentations," said Madame de Listomère. "We have no time to spare. Come——"

Birotteau was too kind-hearted not to submit in any great crisis to the impulsive self-sacrifice of the first moment. But, in any case, his life already was but one long martyrdom.

He answered with a heart-broken look at his protectress, which wrung her soul—

"I am in your hands.   I am no more than a straw in the street!"

The local word he used, *bourrier*, is peculiar to Touraine, and its only literal rendering is a straw.   But there are pretty little straws, yellow, shiny, and smart, the delight of children; while a *bourrier* is a dirty, colorless, miry straw, left in the gutter, driven by the wind, crushed by the foot of every passer-by.

"But, madame," he went on, "I should not wish to leave the portrait of Chapeloud for the Abbé Troubert.   It was done for me, and belongs to me; get that back for me, and I will give up everything else."

"Well," said Madame de Listomère, "I will go to Mademoiselle Gamard."   She spoke in a tone which showed what extraordinary effort the Baroness de Listomère was making in stooping to flatter the old maid's conceit.   "And I will try to settle everything," she went on.   "I hardly dare hope it. Go and see Monsieur de Bourbonne.   Get him to draw up your act of renunciation in due form, and bring it to me signed and witnessed.   With the help of the archbishop, I may perhaps get the thing settled."

Birotteau went away overpowered.   Troubert had assumed in his eyes the proportions of an Egyptian pyramid.   The man's hands were in Paris, and his elbows in the Close of Saint-Gatien.

"He," said he to himself, "to hinder Monsieur le Marquis de Listomère being made a peer of France!   And then, 'With the help of the archbishop, perhaps get the thing settled!'"

In comparison with such high interests, Birotteau felt himself a grasshopper; he was honest to himself.

The news of Birotteau's removal was all the more astounding because the reason was undiscoverable.   Madame de Listomère gave out that as her nephew wished to marry and retire from the service, she needed the abbé's room to add to her own. No one as yet had heard that Birotteau had withdrawn the action. Monsieur de Bourbonne's instructions were thus judiciously carried out.

These two pieces of news, when they should reach the ears of the vicar-general, must certainly flatter his vanity, by showing him that, though the Listomère family would not capitulate, it would at least remain neutral, tacitly recognizing the secret power of the church council; and was not recognition submission? Still, the action remained *sub judice.* Was not this to yield and to threaten?

Thus the Listomères had assumed an attitude precisely similar to that of the Abbé Troubert in this contest; they stood aside and could direct their forces as circumstances might dictate.

But a serious event now occurred, and added to their difficulties, hindering the success of the means by which Monsieur de Bourbonne and the Listomères hoped to mollify the Gamard and Troubert faction. On the previous day Mademoiselle Gamard had taken a chill on coming out of the cathedral, had gone to bed, and was reported to be seriously ill. The whole town rang with lamentations, excited by spurious commiseration. "Mademoiselle Gamard's highly strung sensibilities had succumbed to the scandal of this lawsuit. Though she was undoubtedly in the right, she was dying of grief. Birotteau had killed his benefactress." This was the sum and substance of the phrases fired off through the capillary ducts of the great feminine synod, and readily repeated by the town of Tours.

Madame de Listomère suffered the humiliation of calling on the old woman without gaining anything by her visit. She very politely requested to be allowed to speak to the vicar-general. Flattered, perhaps, at receiving a woman who had slighted him, in Chapeloud's library, by the fireplace over which the two famous pictures in dispute were hanging,

Troubert kept the Baroness waiting a minute, then he consented to see her.

No courtier, no diplomat, ever threw into the discussion of private interests or national negotiations greater skill, dissimulation, and depth of purpose than the Baroness and the abbé displayed when they found themselves face to face.

Old Bourbonne, like the sponsor, in the middle ages, who armed the champion, and fortified his courage by good counsel as he entered the lists, had instructed the Baroness—

"Do not forget your part; you are a peacemaker, and not an interested party. Troubert likewise is a mediator. Weigh your words. Study the tones of the vicar-general's voice. If he strokes his chin, you have won him."

Some caricaturists have amused themselves by representing the contrast that so frequently exists between what we say and what we think. In this place, to represent fully the interesting points of the duel of words that took place between the priest and the fine lady, it is necessary to disclose the thoughts they each kept concealed under apparently trivial speech.

Madame de Listomère began by expressing the regret she felt about this lawsuit of Birotteau's, and she went on to speak of her desire of seeing the affair settled to the satisfaction of both parties.

"The mischief is done, madame," said the abbé. "The admirable Mademoiselle Gamard is dying." ("*I care no more for that stupid creature than for Prester John,*" thought he, "*but I should like to lay her death at your door, and burthen your conscience, if you are silly enough to care.*")

"On hearing of her illness," said the Baroness, "I desired the abbé to sign a withdrawal, which I have brought to that saintly person." ("*I see through you,*" thought she, "*you old rascal; but we are no longer at the mercy of your vagaries. As for you, if you accept the deed, you will have put your foot in it; it will be a confession of complicity.*")

There was a brief silence.

"THE MISCHIEF IS DONE, MADAME," SAID THE ABBÉ.

"Mademoiselle Gamard's temporal affairs are no concern of mine," said the priest at length, closing the deep lids over his eagle eyes to conceal his excitement. (*"Ah, ha, you will not catch me tripping! But God be praised, those cursed lawyers will not fight out a case that might bespatter me! But what on earth can the Listomères want that they are so humble?"*)

"Monsieur," replied the Baroness, "the concerns of Monsieur l'Abbé Birotteau interest me no more than those of Mademoiselle Gamard do you. But, unluckily, religion might suffer from their quarrels, and in you I see but a mediator, while I myself come forward as a peacemaker——" (*"We can neither of us throw dust in the other's eyes, Monsieur Troubert,"* thought she. *"Do you appreciate the epigram in that reply?"*)

"Religion!" said the vicar-general. "Madame, religion stands too high for man to touch it." (*"Religion means me,"* thought he.) "God will judge us unerringly, madame," he coolly added, "and I can recognize no other tribunal."

"Well, then, monsieur," replied she, "let us try to make man's judgments agree with God's." (*"Yes, religion means you."*)

The Abbé Troubert changed his tone.

"Has not monsieur your nephew just been to Paris?" (*"You heard of me there, I fancy,"* thought he; *"I can crush you—you who scorned me! You have come to surrender."*)

"Yes, monsieur, thank you for taking so much interest in him. He is returning to Paris to-night, ordered there by the minister, who is kindness itself to us, and does not wish him to retire from the service." (*"No, Jesuit, you will not crush us,"* thought she; *"we understand your little game."*) A pause. "I have not approved of his conduct in this affair," she went on, "but a sailor may be forgiven for not under-

15

standing the law." (*"Come, let us be allies,"* thought she; *"we shall gain nothing by squabbling."*)

A faint smile dawned, and was lost, in the furrows of the abbé's face.

"He has done us some service by informing us of the value of those two pictures," said he, looking at them; "they will be a worthy ornament to the lady chapel." (*"You fired an epigram at me, madame,"* thought he; *"there are two for you and we are quits."*)

"If you present them to Saint-Gatien, I would beg you to allow me to offer to the church two frames worthy of the place and of the gift." (*"I should like to make you confess that you coveted Birotteau's property,"* thought she.)

"They do not belong to me," said the priest, well on his guard.

"Well, here is the deed that puts an end to all dispute," said Madame de Listomère, "and restores them to Mademoiselle Gamard." She laid the document on the table. (*"You see, monsieur, how much I trust you,"* thought she.) "It is worthy of you, monsieur, worthy of your fine character, to reconcile two Christians, though I have ceased to take much interest in Monsieur Birotteau."

"But he is your pensioner," said he, interrupting her.

"No, monsieur, he is no longer under my roof." (*"My brother-in-law's peerage and my nephew's promotion are leading me into very mean actions,"* thought she.)

The abbé remained unmoved, but his calm aspect was a symptom of violent agitation. Only Monsieur de Bourbonne had divined the secret of that superficial calm. The priest was triumphant.

"Why, then, did you take charge of his act of renunciation?" he asked, moved by a feeling similar to that which makes a woman fish for compliments.

"I could not help feeling some pity for him. Birotteau, whose feeble character must be well known to you, entreated me to see Mademoiselle Gamard in order to obtain from her, as the price of the surrender of"—the abbé frowned—"of his *rights*, as recognized by many distinguished lawyers, the portrait "—the priest looked hard at Madame de Listomère— "of Chapeloud," she said. "I leave it to you to judge of his claim to it——" (*"You would lose if you fought the case,"* thought she.)

The tone in which the Baroness uttered the words "distinguished lawyers" showed the priest that she knew the enemy's strength and weakness. Madame de Listomère displayed so much skill to this experienced connoisseur that at the end of this conversation, which was carried on for some time in the same key, he went down to see Mademoiselle Gamard to bring her answer as to the proposed bargain.

Troubert soon returned.

"Madame," said he, "I can but repeat the poor dying woman's words, 'Monsieur l'Abbé Chapeloud showed me too much kindness,' said she, 'for me to part from his portrait.' As for myself, if it were mine, I would not give it up to any one. I was too faithfully attached to my poor dead friend not to feel that I have a right to claim his likeness against anybody in the world."

"Well, monsieur, do not let us fall out over a bad picture." (*"I care for it no more than you do,"* thought she.) "Keep it; we will have it copied. I am proud to have brought this sad and deplorable lawsuit to an end, and I have personally gained the pleasure of making your acquaintance. I have heard that you are a fine whist player. You will forgive a woman for being curious," she added with a smile. "If you will come and play occasionally at my house, you cannot doubt that you will be heartily welcomed."

The Abbé Troubert stroked his chin. (*"He is caught; Bourbonne was right,"* thought she, *"he has his share of vanity."*)

In fact, the vicar-general was at this moment enjoying the

delicious sensation which Mirabeau found irresistible when, in the day of his power, he saw the gates of some mansion which formerly had been closed against him opened to admit his carriage.

" Madame," replied he, " my occupations are too important to allow of my going into society; but for you what would not a man do?" ("*It is all over with the old girl; I will make up to the Listomères, and do them a good turn if they do me one,*" thought he. "*It is better to have them for friends than for enemies.*")

Madame de Listomère went home, hoping that the archbishop would complete a pacification so happily begun. But Birotteau was to gain nothing even by his renunciation. Madame de Listomère heard next day that Mademoiselle Gamard was dead. The old maid's will being opened, no one was surprised to learn that she had constituted the Abbé Troubert her universal legatee. Her property was estimated at a hundred thousand crowns. The vicar-general sent two invitations to the service and burial to Madame de Listomère's house—one for herself and the other for her nephew.

" We must go," said she.

" That is just what it means!" exclaimed Monsieur de Bourbonne. " It is a test by which Monseigneur Troubert meant to try you. Baron, you must go all the way to the grave," he added to the navy lieutenant, who, for his sins, had not yet left Tours.

The service was held, and was marked by ecclesiastical magnificence. One person only shed tears. That was Birotteau, who, alone in a side chapel where he was not seen, believed himself guilty of this death, and prayed fervently for the soul of the departed, bitterly bewailing himself because he had not obtained her forgiveness for having wronged her.

The Abbé Troubert followed his friend's body to the grave in which she was to be laid. Standing on its brink, he delivered an address, and, thanks to his eloquence, gave monu-

mental dignity to his picture of the narrow life led by the
testatrix. The bystanders particularly noted these words in
the peroration :

"This life, full of days devoted to God and to religion—
this life, adorned by so many beautiful actions performed in
silence, so many modest and unrecognized virtues, was
blighted by a sorrow which we would call unmerited if, here,
on the verge of eternity, we could forget that all our afflictions are sent us by God. This holy woman's many friends,
knowing how noble was her guileless soul, foresaw that she
could endure anything excepting only such detraction as
would affect her whole existence. And so perhaps Providence
has taken her to rest in God only to rescue her from our petty
griefs. Happy are they who here on earth can live at peace
with themselves, as Sophie now reposes in the realms of the
blest, in her robe of innocence ! "

"And when he had ended this grandiloquent discourse,"
said Monsieur de Bourbonne, who reported all the details of
the funeral to Madame de Listomère that evening when, the
rubbers ended and the doors closed, they were left alone with
the Baron, "imagine, if you can, that Louis XI. in a priest's
gown giving the holy-water sprinkler a final flourish in this
style "—and Monsieur de Bourbonne took up the tongs and
imitated the Abbé Troubert's movement so exactly that the
Baron and his aunt could not help smiling. "In this alone,"
added the old man, "did he betray himself. Till then his
reserve had been perfect ; but now, when he had packed away
for ever the old maid he so utterly despised and hated, almost
as much perhaps as he had detested Chapeloud, he, no doubt,
found it impossible to hinder his satisfaction from betraying
itself in a gesture."

Next morning Mademoiselle Salomon came to breakfast
with Madame de Listomère, and as soon as she came in she
said quite sadly—

"Our poor Abbé Birotteau has just been dealt a dreadful blow which reveals the most elaborately studied hatred. He is made curé of Saint-Symphorien."

Saint-Symphorien is a suburb of Tours lying beyond the bridge. This bridge, one of the finest works of French architecture, is nearly two thousand feet long, and the open squares at each end are exactly alike.

"Do you understand?" she added, after a pause, amazed at the coolness with which Madame de Listomère heard this news. "The Abbé Birotteau will there be a hundred leagues from Tours, from his friends, from everything. Is it not exile, and all the more terrible because he will be torn from the town that his eyes will behold every day, while he can hardly ever come to it? He who, since his troubles, has hardly been able to walk, will be obliged to come a league to see us. At the present moment the poor man is in bed with a feverish attack. The priest's residence at Saint-Symphorien is cold and damp, and the parish is too poor to restore it. The poor old man will be buried alive in a real tomb. What a villainous plot!"

It will now, perhaps, suffice in conclusion of this story to report briefly a few subsequent events, and to sketch a last picture.

Five months later the vicar-general was a bishop; Madame de Listomère was dead, leaving fifteen hundred francs a year to the Abbé Birotteau. On the day when the Baroness' will was read, Monseigneur Hyacinthe, bishop of Troyes, was about to leave Tours and take up his residence in his diocese; but he postponed his departure. Furious at having been deceived by a woman to whom he had offered a hand, while she was secretly holding out hers to the man whom he chose to regard as an enemy, Troubert again threatened to mar the Baron's career and hinder the Marquis de Listomère from receiving his peerage. In full council, at the archbishop's palace, he uttered one of those priestly speeches, big with revenge, though smooth with honeyed mildness.

The ambitious lieutenant came to see this ruthless prelate, who dictated hard terms no doubt, for the Baron's conduct showed absolute subservience to the terrible Jesuit's will.

The new bishop, by a deed of gift, bestowed Mademoiselle Gamard's house on the cathedral chapter; he gave Chapeloud's bookcase and books to the little seminary; he dedicated the two disputed pictures to the lady chapel; but he kept the portrait of Chapeloud. No one could understand this almost complete surrender of all Mademoiselle Gamard's property. Monsieur de Bourbonne imagined that he secretly kept all the actual money to enable him to maintain his rank in Paris, if he should be called to sit on the bench of bishops in the upper chamber.

At last, on the very day before Monseigneur Troubert left Tours, the "old fox" detected the last plot which these gifts had covered, a *coup de grâce* dealt by the most relentless vengeance to the most helpless of victims. The Baron de Listomère disputed Madame de Listomère's bequest to Birotteau on the ground of undue influence! Within a few days of the first steps being taken in this action, the Baron was appointed to a ship with the rank of captain; the curé of Saint-Symphorien was, by an act of discipline, placed under an interdict. His ecclesiastical superiors condemned him by anticipation; so the assassin of the late Sophie Gamard was a rogue as well! Now, if Monseigneur Troubert had kept the old maid's property, he could hardly have secured Birotteau's disgrace.

At the moment, when Monseigneur Hyacinthe, bishop of Troyes, was passing in a post-chaise, along the quay of Saint-Symphorien, on his way to Paris, poor Birotteau had just been brought out in an armchair to sit in the sun on a terrace. The unhappy priest, stricken by his archbishop, was pale and haggard. Grief, stamped on every feature, had completely altered the face, which of old had been so blandly cheerful. Ill-health had cast a dimness that simulated thought over his eyes, which had been bright once with the pleasures of good living, and devoid of any weight of ideas. This was but the skeleton of that Birotteau who, only a year ago, vacuous but happy, had waddled across the Close. The bishop shot a glance of contempt and pity at his victim; then he vouchsafed to forget him, and passed on.

In other times Troubert would certainly have been a Hildebrand or an Alexander VI. Nowadays the church is no longer a political force, and does not absorb all the powers of isolated men. Hence celibacy has this crying evil, that by concentrating the powers of a man on one single passion, namely, egoism, it makes the unwedded soul mischievous or useless.

We live in a time when the fault of most governments is that they make man for society rather than society for man. A perpetual struggle is going on between the individual and the system that tries to turn him to account, while he tries to turn it to account for his own advantage; formerly, man having really more liberty, showed greater generosity for the public weal. The circle in which men move has insensibly widened; the soul that can apprehend it synthetically will never be anything but a grand exception, since, constantly, in moral as in physical force, what is gained in extent is lost in intensity. Society cannot be based on exceptions.

Originally, man was simply and solely a father; his heart beat warmly, concentrated within the radius of the family. Later on he lived for the clan or for a small republic; hence the grand historical heroism of Greece and Rome. Next, he became the member of a caste, or of a religion, and often was truly sublime in his devotion to its greatness; but then the field of his interests was increased by the addition of every intellectual realm. In these days his life is bound up with that of a vast fatherland; ere long his family will be the whole human race.

Will not this moral cosmopolitanism, the thing the Roman church hopes for, be a sublime mistake? It is so natural to believe in that noble chimera—the brotherhood of men. But, alas! the human machine has not such godlike proportions. The souls that are vast enough to wed a sentiment that is the prerogative of a great man will never be those of plain citizens, of fathers of families.

Certain physiologists opine that if the brain expands, the heart must necessarily shrink. That is a mistake. Is not what looks like egoism in the men who bear in their breast a science, a nation, or its laws, the noblest of passions? Is it not, in a way, a motherhood of the people? To bring forth new races or new ideas, must they not combine in their powerful brain the breast of the mother with the force of God? The history of an Innocent III., of a Peter the Great, of all who have guided an epoch or a nation, would at need prove to be, in the highest order of minds, the immense idea represented by Troubert in the depths of the Close of Saint-Gatien.

SAINT-FIRMIN, *April,* 1832.

COLONEL CHABERT.

*To Madame la Comtesse Ida de Bocarmé née
du Chasteler.*

"HULLO! There is that old box-coat again!"

This exclamation was made by a lawyer's clerk of the class called in French offices a gutter-jumper—a messenger in fact —who at this moment was eating a piece of dry bread with a hearty appetite. He pulled off a morsel of crumb to make into a bullet, and fired it gleefully through the open pane of the window against which he was leaning. The pellet, well aimed, rebounded almost as high as the window, after hitting the hat of a stranger who was crossing the courtyard of a house in the Rue Vivienne, where dwelt Maître Derville, attorney-at-law.

"Come, Simonnin, don't play tricks on people, or I will turn you out of doors. However poor a client may be, he is still a man, hang it all!" said the head clerk, pausing in the addition of a bill of costs.

The lawyer's messenger is commonly, as was Simonnin, a lad of thirteen or fourteen, who, in every office, is under the special jurisdiction of the managing clerk, whose errands and *billets-doux* keep him employed on his way to carry writs to the bailiffs and petitions to the courts. He is akin to the street boy in his habits and to the pettifogger by fate. The boy is almost always ruthless, unbroken, unmanageable, a ribald rhymester, impudent, greedy, and idle. And yet almost all these clerklings have an old mother lodging on some fifth floor with whom they share their pittance of thirty or forty francs a month.

"If he is a man, why do you call him old box-coat?"

asked Simonnin, with the air of a schoolboy who has caught out his master.

And he went on eating his bread and cheese, leaning his shoulder against the window jamb ; for he rested standing like a cab-horse, one of his legs raised and propped against the other, on the toe of his shoe.

"What trick can we play that chap?" said the third clerk, whose name was Godeschal, in a low voice, pausing in the middle of a discourse he was extemporizing in an appeal engrossed by the fourth clerk, of which copies were being made by two neophytes from the provinces.

Then he went on improvising :

"*But, in his noble and beneficent wisdom, his majesty, Louis the Eighteenth*—(write it at full length, heh ! Desroches the learned—you, as you engross it)—*when he resumed the reins of government, understood*—(what did that old nincompoop ever understand ?)—*the high mission to which he had been called by Divine Providence !*—(a note of exclamation and six stops. They are pious enough at the courts to let us put six) —*and his first thought, as is proved by the date of the order hereinafter designated, was to repair the misfortunes caused by the terrible and sad disasters of the revolutionary times, by restoring to his numerous and faithful adherents*—('numerous' is flattering, and ought to please the bench)—*all their unsold estates, whether within our realm or in conquered or acquired territory, or in the endowments of public institutions, for we are, and proclaim ourselves competent to declare, that this is the spirit and meaning of the famous, truly loyal order given in*—Stop," said Godeschal to the three copying clerks, "that rascally sentence brings me to the end of my page. Well," he went on, wetting the back fold of the sheet with his tongue, so as to be able to fold back the page of thick stamped paper, "well, if you want to play him a trick, tell him that the master can only see his clients between two and three in the morning ; we shall see if he comes, the old ruffian !"

And Godeschal took up the sentence he was dictating—
"*given in*—Are you ready?"

"Yes," cried the three writers.

It all went on together, the appeal, the gossip, and the conspiracy.

"*Given in*—Here, Daddy Boucard, what is the date of the order? We must dot our *i*'s and cross our *t*'s, by Jingo! It helps to fill the pages."

"By Jingo!" repeated one of the copying clerks before Boucard, the head clerk, could reply.

"What! have you written *by Jingo?*" cried Godeschal, looking at one of the novices, with an expression at once stern and humorous.

"Why, yes," said Desroches, the fourth clerk, leaning across his neighbor's copy, "he has written '*We must dot our i's and cross our t's, by Gingo,*' and spells it *G-i-n-g-o!*"

All the clerks shouted with laughter.

"Why! Monsieur Huré, you take 'By Jingo' for a law term, and you say you come from Mortagne!" exclaimed Simonnin.

"Scratch it cleanly out," said the head clerk. "If the judge, whose business it is to tax the bill, were to see such things, he would say you were laughing at the whole boiling. You would hear of it from the chief! Come, no more of this nonsense, Monsieur Huré! A Norman ought not to write out an appeal without thought. It is the 'Shoulder arms!' of the law."

"*Given in—in?*" asked Godeschal. "Tell me when, Boucard."

"June, 1814," replied the head clerk, without looking up from his work.

A knock at the office door interrupted the circumlocutions of the prolix document. Five clerks with rows of hungry teeth, bright, mocking eyes, and curly heads, lifted their noses towards the door, after crying all together in a singing tone, " Come in ! "

Boucard kept his face buried in a pile of papers—*broutilles* (odds and ends) in French law jargon—and went on drawing out the bill of costs on which he was busy.

The office was a large room furnished with the traditional stool which is to be seen in all these dens of law-quibbling. The stovepipe crossed the room diagonally to the chimney of a bricked-up fireplace ; on the marble chimney-piece were several chunks of bread, triangles of Brie cheese, pork cutlets, glasses, bottles, and the head-clerk's cup of chocolate. The smell of these dainties blended so completely with that of the immoderately overheated stove and the odor peculiar to offices and old papers, that the trail of a fox would not have been perceptible. The floor was covered with mud and snow, brought in by the clerks. Near the window stood the desk with a revolving lid, where the head clerk worked, and against the back of it was the second clerk's table. The second clerk was at this moment in court. It was between eight and nine in the morning.

The only decoration of the office consisted in huge yellow posters, announcing seizures of real estate, sales, settlements under trust, final or interim judgments—all the glory of a lawyer's office. Behind the head clerk was an enormous stack of pigeon-holes from the top to the bottom of the room, of which each division was crammed with bundles of papers with an infinite number of tickets hanging from them at the ends of red tape, which give a peculiar physiognomy to law-papers. The lower rows were filled with cardboard boxes, yellow with use, on which might be read the names of the more important clients whose cases were juicily stewing at this present time. The dirty window-panes admitted but little daylight. Indeed, there are very few offices in Paris where it is possible to write without lamplight before ten in the morning in the month of February, for they are all left to very natural neglect; every one comes and no one stays; no one has any personal interest in a scene of mere routine— neither the attorney, nor the counsel, nor the clerks trouble themselves about the appearance of a place which, to the youths, is a schoolroom; to the clients, a passage; to the chief, a laboratory. The greasy furniture is handed down to successive owners with such scrupulous care that in some offices may still be seen boxes of *remainders*, machines for twisting parchment gut, and bags left by the prosecuting parties of the châtelet (abbreviated to *chlet*)—a court which, under the old order of things, represented the present court of first instance (or county court).

So in this dark office, thick with dust, there was, as in all its fellows, something repulsive to the clients—something which made it one of the most hideous monstrosities of Paris. Nay, were it not for the mouldy sacristies where prayers are weighed out and paid for like groceries and for the old-clothes shops, where flutter the rags that blight all the illusions of life by showing us the last end of all our festivities—an attorney's office would be, of all social marts, the most loathsome. But we might say the same of the gambling-hell, of the law court, of the lottery office, of the brothel.

But why? In these places, perhaps, the drama being played in a man's soul makes him indifferent to accessories, which would also account for the single-mindedness of great thinkers and men of great ambitions.

"Where is my penknife?"

"I am eating my breakfast."

"You go and be hanged! here is a blot on the copy."

"Silence, gentlemen!"

These various exclamations were uttered simultaneously at the moment when the old client shut the door with the sort of humility which disfigures the movements of a man down on his luck. The stranger tried to smile, but the muscles of his face relaxed as he vainly looked for some symptoms of amenity on the inexorably indifferent faces of the six clerks. Accustomed, no doubt, to gauge men, he very politely addressed the gutter-jumper, hoping to get a civil answer from this boy of all work.

"Monsieur, is your master at home?"

The pert messenger made no reply, but patted his ear with the fingers of his left hand, as much as to say, "I am deaf."

"What do you want, sir?" asked Godeschal, swallowing as he spoke a mouthful of bread big enough to charge a fourpounder, flourishing his knife and crossing his legs, throwing up one foot in the air to the level of his eyes.

"This is the fifth time I have called," replied the victim. "I wish to speak to Monsieur Derville."

"On business?"

"Yes, but I can explain it to no one but——"

"M. Derville is in bed; if you want to consult him on some difficulty, he does no serious work till midnight. But if you will lay the case before us, we could help you just as well as he can to——"

The stranger was unmoved; he looked timidly about him, like a dog who has gotten into a strange kitchen and expects a kick. By grace of their profession, lawyers' clerks have no fear of thieves; they did not suspect the owner of the boxcoat, and left him to study the place, where he looked in vain for a chair to sit on, for he was evidently tired. Attorneys, on principle, do not have many chairs in their offices. The inferior client, being kept waiting on his feet, goes away grumbling, but then he does not waste time, which, as an old lawyer once said, is not allowed for when the bill is taxed.

"Monsieur," said the old man, "as I have already told you, I cannot explain my business to any one but M. Derville. I will wait till he is up."

Boucard had finished his bill. He smelt the fragrance of his chocolate, rose from his cane armchair, went to the chimney-piece, looked the old man from head to foot, stared at his coat, and made an indescribable grimace. He probably reflected that whichever way this client might be wrung, it would be impossible to squeeze out a centime, so he put in a few brief words to rid the office of a bad customer.

"It is the truth, monsieur. The chief only works at night. If your business is important, I recommend you to return at one in the morning." The stranger looked at the head clerk with a bewildered expression, and remained motionless for a moment. The clerks, accustomed to every change of countenance, and the odd whimsicalities to which indecision or absence of mind gives rise in "parties," went on eating, making as much noise with their jaws as horses over a manger, and paying no further heed to the old man.

"I will come again to-night," said the stranger at length, with the tenacious desire, peculiar to the unfortunate, to catch humanity at fault.

The only irony allowed to poverty is to drive justice and benevolence to unjust denials. When a poor wretch has once convicted society of falsehood, he throws himself more eagerly on the mercy of God.

"What do you think of that for a cracked pot?" said Simonnin, without waiting till the old man had shut the door.

"He looks as if he had been buried and dug up again," said a clerk.

"He is some colonel who wants his arrears of pay," said the head clerk.

"No, he is a retired concierge," said Godeschal.

"I bet you he is a nobleman," cried Boucard.

"I bet you he has been a porter," retorted Godeschal. "Only porters are gifted by nature with shabby box-coats, as worn and greasy and frayed as that old body's. And did you see his trodden-down boots that let the water in, and his stock which serves for a shirt? He has slept in a dry arch."

"He may be of noble birth, and yet have pulled the door-latch," cried Desroches. "It has been known!"

16

"No," Boucard insisted, in the midst of laughter, "I maintain that he was a brewer in 1789 and a colonel in the time of the Republic."

"I bet theatre tickets round that he never was a soldier," said Godeschal.

"Done with you," answered Boucard.

"Monsieur! monsieur!" shouted the little messenger, opening the window.

"What are you at now, Simonnin?" asked Boucard.

"I am calling him that you may ask him whether he is a colonel or a porter; he must know."

All the clerks laughed. As to the old man, he was already coming upstairs again.

"What can we say to him!" cried Godeschal.

"Leave it to me," replied Boucard.

The poor man came in nervously, his eyes cast down, perhaps not to betray how hungry he was by looking too greedily at the eatables.

"Monsieur," said Boucard, "will you have the kindness to leave your name, so that M. Derville may know——"

"Chabert."

"The colonel who was killed at Eylau?" asked Huré, who, having so far said nothing, was jealous of adding a jest to all the others.

"The same, monsieur," replied the good man, with antique simplicity. And he went away.

"Whew!"

"Done brown!"

"Poof!"

"Oh!"

"Ah!"

"Boum!"

"The old rogue!"

"Ting-a-ring-ting!"

"Sold again!"

"Monsieur Desroches, you are going to the play without paying," said Huré to the fourth clerk, giving him a slap on the shoulder that might have killed a rhinoceros.

There was a storm of cat-calls, cries, and exclamations, which all the onomatopeia of the language would fail to represent.

"Which theatre shall we go to?"

"To the opera," cried the head clerk.

"In the first place," said Godeschal, "I never mentioned which theatre. I might, if I chose, take you to see Madame Saqui."

"Madame Saqui is not the play."

"What is a play?" replied Godeschal. "First, we must define the point of fact. What did I bet, gentlemen? A play. What is a play? A spectacle. What is a spectacle? Something to be seen——"

"But on that principle you would pay your bet by taking us to see the water run under the Pont Neuf!" cried Simonnin, interrupting him.

"To be seen for money," Godeschal added.

"But a great many things are to be seen for money that are not plays. The definition is defective," said Desroches.

"But do listen to me!"

"You are talking nonsense, my dear boy," said Boucard.

"Is 'Curtius' a play?" asked Godeschal.

"No," said the head clerk, "it is a collection of figures—but it is a spectacle."

"I bet you a hundred francs to a sou," Godeschal resumed, "that Curtius' Waxworks form such a show as might be called a play or theatre. It contains a thing to be seen at various prices, according to the place you choose to occupy."

"And so on, and so forth!" said Simonnin.

"You mind I don't box your ears!" said Godeschal.

The clerks shrugged their shoulders.

"Besides, it is not proved that that old ape was not making

game of us," he said, dropping his argument, which was drowned in the laughter of the other clerks. "On my honor, Colonel Chabert is really and truly dead. His wife is married again to Comte Ferraud, councilor of state. Madame Ferraud is one of our clients."

"Come, the case is remanded till to-morrow," said Boucard. "To work, gentlemen. The deuce is in it; we get nothing done here. Finish copying that appeal; it must be handed in before the sitting of the fourth chamber, judgment is to be given to-day. Come, on you go!"

"If he really were Colonel Chabert, would not that impudent rascal Simonnin have felt the leather of his boot in the right place when he pretended to be deaf?" said Desroches, regarding this timely remark as certainly more conclusive than Godeschal's.

"Since nothing is settled," said Boucard, "let us all agree to go to the upper boxes of the Français and see Talma in 'Nero.' Simonnin may go to the pit."

And thereupon the head clerk sat down at his table, and the others followed his example.

"*Given in June eighteen hundred and fourteen* (in words)," said Godeschal. "Ready?"

"Yes," replied the two copying clerks and the engrosser, whose pens forthwith began to creak over the stamped paper, making as much noise in the office as a hundred cockchafers imprisoned by schoolboys in paper cages.

"*And we hope that my lords on the bench*," the extemporizing clerk went on. "Stop! I must read my sentence through again. I do not understand it myself."

"Forty-six (that must often happen) and three forty-nines," said Boucard.

"*We hope*," Godeschal began again, after reading all through the document, "*that my lords on the bench will not be less magnanimous than the august author of the decree, and that they will do justice against the miserable claims of the acting*

*committee of the chief board of the Legion of Honor by inter-
preting the law in the wide sense we have here set forth——"*

"Monsieur Godeschal, wouldn't you like a glass of water?"
said the little messenger.

"That imp of a boy!" said Boucard. "Here, get on
your double-soled shanks-mare, take this packet, and spin off
to the Invalides."

"*Here set forth,*" Godeschal went on. "Add *in the interest
of Madame la Vicomtesse* (at full length) *de Grandlieu.*"

"What!" cried the chief, "are you thinking of drawing
up an appeal in the case of Vicomtesse de Grandlieu against
the Legion of Honor—a case for the office to stand or fall
by? You are something like an ass! Have the goodness to
put aside your copies and your notes; you may keep all that
for the case of Navarreins against the Hospitals. It is late;
I will draw up a little petition myself, with a due allowance
of 'inasmuch,' and go to the courts myself."

This scene is typical of the thousand delights which, when
we look back on our youth, make us say, "Those were good
times."

At about one in the morning Colonel Chabert, self-styled,
knocked at the door of Maître Derville, attorney to the court
of first instance in the department of the Seine. The porter
told him that Monsieur Derville had not yet come in. The
old man said he had an appointment, and was shown upstairs
to the rooms occupied by the famous lawyer, who, notwithstanding his youth, was considered to have one of the longest
heads in Paris.

Having rung, the distrustful applicant was not a little
astonished at finding the head clerk busily arranging in convenient order on his master's dining-room table the papers
relating to the cases to be tried on the morrow. The clerk,
not less astonished, bowed to the colonel and begged him to
take a seat, which the client did.

"On my word, monsieur, I thought you were joking yesterday when you named such an hour for an interview," said the old man, with the forced mirth of a ruined man, who does his best to smile.

"The clerks were joking, but they were speaking the truth too," replied the man, going on with his work. "M. Derville chooses this hour for studying his cases, taking stock of their possibilities, arranging how to conduct them, deciding on the line of defense. His prodigious intellect is freer at this hour—the only time when he can have the silence and quiet needed for the conception of good ideas. Since he entered the profession, you are the third person to come to him for a consultation at this midnight hour. After coming in, the chief will discuss each case, read everything, spend four or five hours perhaps over the business, then he will ring for me and explain to me his intentions. In the morning, from ten till two, he hears what his clients have to say, then he spends the rest of his day in appointments. In the evening he goes into society to keep up his connections. So he has only the night for undermining his cases, ransacking the arsenal of the code, and laying his plan of battle. He is determined never to lose a case; he loves his art. He will not undertake every case, as his brethren do. That is his life, an exceptionally active one. And he makes a great deal of money."

As he listened to this explanation the old man sat silent, and his strange face assumed an expression so bereft of intelligence that the clerk, after looking at him, thought no more about him.

A few minutes later Derville came in, in evening dress; his head clerk opened the door to him, and went back to finish arranging the papers. The young lawyer paused for a moment in amazement on seeing in the dim light the strange client who awaited him. Colonel Chabert was as absolutely immovable as one of the wax figures in Curtius' collection to which Godeschal had proposed to treat his fellow-clerks. This quiescence would not have been a subject for astonishment if it had not completed the supernatural aspect of the man's whole person. The old soldier was dry and lean. His forehead, intentionally hidden under a smoothly combed wig, gave him a look of mystery. His eyes seemed shrouded in a transparent film; you would have compared them to dingy mother-of-pearl with a blue iridescence changing in the gleam of the wax-lights. His face, pale, livid, and as thin as a knife, if I may use such a vulgar expression, was the face of the dead. Round his neck was a tight black silk stock.

Below the dark line of this rag the body was so completely hidden in shadow that a man of imagination might have supposed the old head was due to some chance play of light and shade, or have taken it for a portrait by Rembrandt, without a frame. The brim of the hat which covered the old man's brow cast a black line of shadow on the upper part of the face. This grotesque effect, though natural, threw into relief by contrast the white furrows, the cold wrinkles, the colorless tone of the corpse-like countenance. And the absence of all movement in the figure, of all fire in the eye, were in harmony with a certain look of melancholy madness and the deteriorating symptoms characteristic of senility, giving the face an indescribably ill-starred look which no human words could render.

But an observer, especially a lawyer, could also have read in this stricken man the signs of deep sorrow, the traces of grief which had worn into this face, as drops of water from the sky falling on fine marble at last destroy its beauty. A physician, an author, or a judge might have discerned a whole drama at the sight of its sublime horror, while the least charm was its resemblance to the grotesques which artists amuse themselves by sketching on a corner of the lithographic stone while chatting with a friend.

On seeing the attorney, the stranger started, with the convulsive thrill that comes over a poet when a sudden noise rouses him from a fruitful reverie in silence and at night. The old man hastily removed his hat and rose to bow to the young man ; the leather lining of his hat was doubtless very greasy ; his wig stuck to it without his noticing it, and left his head bare, showing his skull horribly disfigured by a scar beginning at the nape of the neck and ending over the right eye, a prominent seam all across his head. The sudden removal of the dirty wig which the poor man wore to hide this gash gave the two lawyers no inclination to laugh, so horrible to behold was this riven skull. The first idea suggested by the sight of this old wound was, " His intelligence must have escaped through that cut."

" If this is not Colonel Chabert, he is some thorough-going trooper !" thought Boucard.

" Monsieur," said Derville, " to whom have I the honor of speaking ? "

" To Colonel Chabert."

" Which ? "

" He who was killed at Eylau," replied the old man.

On hearing this strange speech, the lawyer and his clerk glanced at each other, as much as to say, " He is mad."

" Monsieur," the colonel went on, " I wish to confide to you the secret of my position."

A thing well worthy of note is the natural intrepidity of lawyers. Whether from the habit of receiving a great many persons, or from the deep sense of the protection conferred on them by the law, or from confidence in their mission, they enter everywhere, fearing nothing, like priests and physicians. Derville signed to Boucard, who vanished.

" During the day, sir," said the attorney, " I am not so miserly of my time, but at night every minute is precious. So be brief and concise. Go to the facts without digression. I will ask for any explanations I may consider necessary. Speak."

Having bid his strange client to be seated, the young man sat down at the table ; but while he gave his attention to the deceased colonel, he turned over the bundles of papers.

" You know, perhaps," said the dead man, " that I commanded a cavalry regiment at Eylau. I was of important service to the success of Murat's famous charge which decided the victory. Unhappily for me, my death is a historical fact, recorded in *Victoires et Conquêtes*, where it is related in full detail. We cut through the three Russian lines, which at once closed up and formed again, so that we had to repeat the movement back again. At the moment when we were nearing the Emperor, after having scattered the Russians, I came against a squadron of the enemy's cavalry. I rushed at the obstinate brutes. Two Russian officers, perfect giants, attacked me both at once. One of them gave me a cut across the head that crashed through everything, even a black silk cap I wore next my head, and cut deep into the skull. I fell from my horse. Murat came up to support me ; he rode over my body, he and all his men, fifteen hundred of them—there might have been more ! My death was announced to the Emperor, who as a precaution—for he was fond of me, was the master—wished to know if there were no hope of saving the man he had to thank for such a vigorous attack. He sent two surgeons to identify me and bring me into the hospital, saying, perhaps too carelessly, for he was very busy, 'Go and see whether by any chance poor Chabert is still alive.' These rascally saw-bones, who had just seen me lying under the hoofs of the horses of two regiments, no doubt did not trouble themselves to feel my pulse, and reported that I was quite dead. The certificate of death was probably made out in accordance with the rules of military jurisprudence."

As he heard his visitor express himself with complete lucidity, and relate a story so probable though so strange, the young lawyer ceased fingering the papers, rested his left elbow on the table, and with his head on his hand looked steadily at the colonel.

"Do you know, monsieur, that I am lawyer to the Comtesse Ferraud," he said, interrupting the speaker, "Colonel Chabert's widow?"

"My wife—yes, monsieur. Therefore, after a hundred fruitless attempts to interest lawyers, who have all thought me mad, I made up my mind to come to you. I will tell you of my misfortunes afterwards; for the present, allow me to prove the facts, explaining rather how things must have fallen out rather than how they did occur. Certain circumstances, known, I suppose, to no one but the Almighty, compel me to speak of some things as hypothetical. The wounds I had received must presumably have produced tetanus, or have thrown me into a state analogous to that of a disease called, I believe, catalepsy. Otherwise how is it conceivable that I should have been stripped, as is the custom in time of war, and thrown into the common grave by the men ordered to bury the dead?

"Allow me here to refer to a detail of which I could know nothing till after the event, which, after all, I must speak of as my death. At Stuttgart, in 1814, I met an old quartermaster of my regiment. This dear fellow, the only man who chose to recognize me, and of whom I will tell you more later, explained the marvel of my preservation, by telling me that my horse was shot in the flank at the moment when I was wounded. Man and beast went down together, like a monk cut out of card-paper. As I fell, to the right or to the left, I was no doubt covered by the body of my horse, which protected me from being trampled to death or hit by a ball.

"When I came to myself, monsieur, I was in a position and an atmosphere of which I could give you no idea if I talked till to-morrow. The little air there was to breathe was foul. I wanted to move, and found no room. I opened my eyes, and saw nothing. The most alarming circumstance was the lack of air, and this enlightened me as to my situation. I understood that no fresh air could penetrate to me, and that I must die. This thought took off the sense of intolerable pain which had aroused me. There was a violent singing in my ears. I heard—or I thought I heard, I will assert nothing—groans from the world of dead among whom I was lying. Some nights I still think I hear those stifled moans; though the remembrance of that time is very obscure, and my memory very indistinct, in spite of my impressions of far more acute suffering I was fated to go through, and which have confused my ideas.

"But there was something more awful than cries; there was a silence such as I have never known elsewhere—literally, the silence of the grave. At last, by raising my hands and feeling the dead, I discerned a vacant space between my head and the human carrion above. I could thus measure the space, granted by a chance of which I knew not the cause. It would seem that, thanks to the carelessness and the haste with which we had been pitched into the trench, two dead bodies had leaned across and against each other, forming an angle like that made by two cards when a child is building a card castle. Feeling about me at once, for there was no time for play, I happily felt an arm lying detached, the arm of a Hercules! A stout bone, to which I owed my rescue. But for this unhoped-for help, I must have perished. But, with a fury you may imagine, I began to work my way through the bodies which separated me from the layer of earth which had no doubt been thrown over us—I say us, as if there had been others living! I worked with a will, monsieur, for here I am! But to this day I do not know how I succeeded in getting through the pile of flesh which formed a barrier between me and life. You will say I had three arms. This crowbar, which I used cleverly enough, opened out a little air between the bodies I moved, and I economized my breath. At last I saw daylight, but through snow!

"At that moment I perceived that my head was cut open. Happily my blood, or that of my comrades, or perhaps the torn skin of my horse, who knows, had in coagulating formed a sort of natural plaster. But, in spite of it, I fainted away when my head came into contact with the snow. However, the little warmth left in me melted the snow about me ; and when I recovered consciousness, I found myself in the middle of a round hole, where I stood shouting as long as I could. But the sun was rising, so I had very little chance of being heard. Was there any one in the fields yet ? I pulled myself up, using my feet as a spring, resting on one of the dead, whose ribs were firm. You may suppose that this was not the moment for saying, ' Respect courage in misfortune !' In short, monsieur, after enduring the anguish, if the word is strong enough for my frenzy of seeing for a long time, yes, quite a long time, those cursed Germans flying from a voice they heard where they could see no one, I was dug out by a woman, who was brave or curious enough to come close to my head, which must have looked as though it had sprouted from the ground like a mushroom. This woman went to fetch her husband, and between them they got me to their poor hovel.

"It would seem that I must have again fallen into a cata-lepsy—allow me to use the word to describe a state of which I have no idea, but which, from the account given by my hosts, I suppose to have been the effect of that malady. I remained for six months between life and death ; not speak-ing, or, if I spoke, talking in delirium. At last, my hosts got me admitted to the hospital at Heilsberg. You will understand, monsieur, that I came out of the womb of the grave as naked as I came from my mother's ; so that six months afterwards, when I remembered, one fine morning, that I had been Colonel Chabert, and when, on recovering my wits, I tried to exact from my nurse rather more respect than she paid to any poor devil, all my companions in the ward began to laugh. Luckily for me, the surgeon, out of professional pride, had answered for my cure, and was naturally interested in his patient. When I told him coherently about my former life, this good man, named Sparchmann, signed a deposition, drawn up in the legal form of his country, giving an account of the miraculous way in which I had escaped from the trench dug for the dead, the day and hour when I had been found by my benefactress and her husband, the nature and exact spot of my injuries, adding to these documents a description of my person.

"Well, monsieur, I have neither these important pieces of evidence nor the declaration I made before a notary at Heilsberg, with a view of establishing my identity. From the day when I was turned out of that town by the events of war, I have wandered about like a vagabond, begging my bread, treated as a madman when I have told my story, without ever having found or earned a sou to enable me to recover the deeds which would prove my statements and restore me to society. My sufferings have often kept me for six months at a time in some little town, where every care was taken of the invalid Frenchman, but where he was laughed at to his face as soon as he said he was Colonel Chabert. For a long time that laughter, those doubts, used to put me into rages which did me harm, and which even led to my being locked up at Stuttgart as a madman. And, indeed, as you may judge from my story, there was ample reason for shutting such a man up.

"At the end of two years' detention, which I was compelled to submit to, after hearing my keepers say a thousand times, 'Here is a poor man who thinks he is Colonel Chabert' to people who would reply, 'Poor fellow!' I became convinced of the impossibility of my own adventure. I grew melancholy, resigned and quiet, and gave up calling myself Colonel Chabert, in order to get out of my prison, and see France once more. Oh, monsieur! To see Paris again was a delirium which I——"

Without finishing his sentence, Colonel Chabert fell into a deep study, which Derville respected.

"One fine day," his visitor resumed, "one spring day, they gave me the key of the fields, as we say, and ten thalers, admitting that I talked quite sensibly on all subjects, and no longer called myself Colonel Chabert. On my honor, at that time, and even to this day, sometimes I hate my name. I wish I were not myself. The sense of my rights kills me. If my illness had but deprived me of all memory of my past life, I could be happy. I should have entered the service again under any name, no matter what, and should, perhaps, have been made a field-marshal in Austria or Russia. Who knows?"

"Monsieur," said the attorney, "you have upset all my ideas. I feel as if I heard you in a dream. Pause for a moment, I beg of you."

"You are the only person," said the colonel, with a melancholy look, "who ever listened to me so patiently. No lawyer has been willing to lend me ten napoleons to enable me to procure from Germany the necessary documents to begin my lawsuit——"

"What lawsuit?" said the attorney, who had forgotten his client's painful position in listening to the narrative of his past sufferings.

"Why, monsieur, is not the Comtesse Ferraud my wife? She has thirty thousand francs a year, which belong to me, and she will not give me a sou. When I tell lawyers these things — men of sense; when I propose—I, a beggar—to bring an action against a count and countess; when I—a dead man—bring up as against a certificate of death a certificate of marriage and registers of births, they show me out, either with the air of cold politeness, which you all know how to assume to rid yourselves of a hapless wretch, or brutally, like men who think they have to deal with a swindler or a madman —it depends on their nature. I have been buried under the dead; but now I am buried under the living, under papers, under facts, under the whole of society, which wants to shove me underground again ! "

" Pray resume your narrative," said Derville.

" ' Pray resume it ! ' " cried the hapless old man, taking the young lawyer's hand. " That is the first polite word I have heard since——"

The colonel wept. Gratitude choked his voice. The appealing and unutterable eloquence that lies in the eyes, in a gesture, even in silence, entirely convinced Derville, and touched him deeply.

" Listen, monsieur," said he ; " I have this evening won three hundred francs at cards. I may very well lay out half that sum in making a man happy. I will begin the inquiries and researches necessary to obtain the documents of which you speak, and until they arrive I will give you five francs a day. If you are Colonel Chabert, you will pardon the smallness of the loan as coming from a young man who has his fortune to make. Proceed."

The colonel, as he called himself, sat for a moment motionless and bewildered ; the depth of his woes had no doubt destroyed his powers of belief. Though he was eager in pursuit of his military distinction, of his fortune, of himself, perhaps it was in obedience to the inexplicable feeling, the latent germ in every man's heart, to which we owe the experiments of alchemists, the passion for glory, the discoveries of astronomy and of physics, everything which prompts man to expand his being by multiplying himself through deeds or ideas. In his mind the *Ego* was now but a secondary object, just as the vanity of success or the pleasure of winning become dearer to the gambler than the object he has at stake. The young lawyer's words were as a miracle to this man, for ten years repudiated by his wife, by justice, by the whole social creation. To find in a lawyer's office the ten gold-pieces which had so long been refused him by so many people, and in so many ways ! The colonel was like the lady who, having been ill of a fever for fifteen years, fancied she had some fresh complaint when she was cured. There are joys in which we have ceased to believe ; they fall on us, it is like a thunderbolt; they burn us. The poor man's gratitude was too great to find utterance. To superficial observers he seemed cold, but Derville saw complete honesty under this amazement. A swindler would have found his voice.

"Where was I?" said the colonel, with the simplicity of a child or of a soldier, for there is often something of the child in a true soldier, and almost always something of the soldier in a child, especially in France.

"At Stuttgart. You were just out of prison," said M. Derville, the attorney.

"You know my wife?" asked the colonel.

"Yes," said Derville, with a bow.

"What is she like?"

"Still quite charming."

The old man held up his hand, and seemed to be swallowing down some secret anguish with the grave and solemn resignation that is so characteristic of men who have stood the ordeal of blood and fire on the battlefield.

"Monsieur," said he, with a sort of cheerfulness—for he breathed again, the poor colonel; he had again risen from the grave; he had just melted a covering of snow less easily thawed than that which had once before frozen his head ; and he drew a deep breath, as if he had just escaped from a dungeon—"Monsieur, if I had been a handsome young fellow, none of my misfortunes would have befallen me. Women believe in men when they flavor their speeches with the word love. They hurry then, they come, they go, they are everywhere at once ; they intrigue, they assert facts, they play the very devil for a man who takes their fancy. But how could I interest a woman? I had a face like a requiem. I was dressed like a *sans-culotte*. I was more like an Esquimaux than a Frenchman—I, who had formerly been considered one of the smartest of fops in 1799!—I, Chabert, Count of the Empire.

"Well, on the very day when I was turned out into the streets like a dog, I met the quartermaster of whom I just now spoke. This old soldier's name was Boutin. The poor devil and I made the queerest pair of broken-down hacks I ever set eyes on. I met him out walking; but though I recognized him, he could not possibly guess who I was. We went into a tavern together. In there, when I told him my name, Boutin's mouth opened from ear to ear in a roar of laughter, like the bursting of a mortar. That mirth, monsieur, was one of the keenest pangs I have known. It told me without diguise how great were the changes in me! I was, then, unrecognizable even to the humblest and most grateful of my former friends!

"I had once saved Boutin's life, but it was only the repayment of a debt I owed him. I need not tell you how he did me this service; it was at Ravenna, in Italy. The house where Boutin prevented my being stabbed was not extremely respectable. At that time I was not a colonel, but, like Boutin himself, a common trooper. Happily there were certain details of this adventure which could be known only to us two, and when I recalled them to his mind his incredulity diminished. I then told him the story of my singular experiences. Although my eyes and my voice, he told me, were strangely altered, although I had neither hair, teeth, nor eyebrows, and was as colorless as an Albino, he at last recognized his colonel in the beggar, after a thousand questions, which I answered triumphantly.

"He related his adventures; they were not less extraordinary than my own; he had lately come back from the frontiers of China, which he had tried to cross after escaping from Siberia. He told me of the catastrophe of the Russian campaign, and of Napoleon's first abdication. That news was one of the things which caused me most anguish!

17

"We were two curious derelicts, having been rolled over the globe as pebbles are rolled by the ocean when storms bear them from shore to shore. Between us we had seen Egypt, Syria, Spain, Russia, Holland, Germany, Italy and Dalmatia, England, China, Tartary, Siberia; the only thing wanting was that neither of us had been to America or the Indies. Finally Boutin, who still was more locomotive than I, undertook to go to Paris as quickly as might be to inform my wife of the predicament in which I was. I wrote a long letter full of details to Madame Chabert. That, monsieur, was the fourth! If I had had any relations, perhaps nothing of all this might have happened; but, to be frank with you, I am but a workhouse child, a soldier, whose sole fortune was his courage, whose sole family is mankind at large, whose country is France, whose only protector is the Almighty. Nay, I am wrong! I had a father—the Emperor. Ah! if he were but here, the dear man! If he could see *his Chabert*, as he used to call me, in the state in which I am now, he would be in a rage! What is to be done? Our sun is set, and we are all out in the cold now. After all, political events might account for my wife's silence!

"Boutin set out. He was a lucky fellow! He had two bears, admirably trained, which brought him in a living. I could not go with him; the pain I suffered forbade my walking long stages. I wept, monsieur, when we parted, after I had gone as far as my state allowed in company with him and his bears. At Carlsruhe I had an attack of neuralgia in the head, and lay for six weeks on straw in an inn. I should never have ended if I were to tell you all the distresses of my life as a beggar. Moral suffering, before which physical suffering pales, nevertheless excites less pity, because it is not seen. I remember shedding tears, as I stood in front of a fine house in Strassburg where I once had given an entertainment, and where nothing was given me, not even a piece of bread. Having agreed with Boutin on the road I was to take, I went to every postoffice to ask if there were a letter or some money for me. I arrived at Paris without having found either. What despair I had been forced to endure! 'Boutin must be dead!' I told myself, and in fact the poor fellow was killed at Water-loo. I heard of his death later, and by mere chance. His errand to my wife had, of course, been fruitless.

"At last I entered Paris—with the Cossacks. To me this was grief on grief. On seeing the Russians in France, I quite forgot that I had no shoes on my feet nor money in my pocket. Yes, monsieur, my clothes were in tatters. The evening before I reached Paris I was obliged to bivouac in the woods of Claye. The chill of the night air no doubt brought on an attack of some nameless complaint which seized me as I was crossing the Faubourg Saint-Martin. I dropped almost senseless at the door of an ironmonger's shop. When I recovered I was in a bed in the Hôtel-Dieu. There I stayed very contentedly for about a month. I was then turned out; I had no money, but I was well, and my feet were on the good stones of Paris. With what delight and haste did I make my way to the Rue du Mont-Blanc, where my wife should be living in a house belonging to me! Bah! the Rue du Mont-Blanc was now the Rue de la Chaussée d'Antin; I could not find my house; it had been sold and pulled down. Speculators had built several houses over my gardens. Not knowing that my wife had married M. Ferraud, I could obtain no information.

"At last I went to the house of an old lawyer who had been in charge of my affairs. This worthy man was dead, after selling his connections to a younger man. This gentle-man informed me, to my great surprise, of the administration of my estate, the settlement of the moneys, of my wife's marriage, and the birth of her two children. When I told him that I was Colonel Chabert, he laughed so heartily that I left him without saying another word. My detention at Stuttgart had suggested possibilities of Charenton, and I de-

termined to act with caution. Then, monsieur, knowing
where my wife lived, I went to her house, my heart high with
hope. Well," said the colonel, with a gesture of concentrated fury, "when I called under an assumed name I was not
admitted, and on the day when I used my own I was turned
out of doors.

"To see the Countess come home from a ball or the play
in the early morning, I have sat whole nights through, crouching close to the wall of her gateway. My eyes pierced the
depths of the carriage, which flashed past me with the swiftness of lightning, and I caught a glimpse of the woman who
is my wife and no longer mine. Oh, from that day I have
lived for vengeance!" cried the old man in a hollow voice,
and suddenly standing up in front of Derville. "She knows
that I am alive; since my return she has had two letters written with my own hand. She loves me no more!—I—I know
not whether I love or hate her. I long for her and curse her
by turns. To me she owes all her fortune, all her happiness;
well, she has not sent me the very smallest pittance. Sometimes I do not know what will become of me!"

With these words the veteran dropped on to his chair again
and remained motionless. Derville sat in silence, studying
his client.

"It is a serious business," he said at length, mechanically.
"Even granting the genuineness of the documents to be pro-
cured from Heilsberg, it is not proved to me that we can at
once win our case. It must go before three tribunals in succession. I must think such a matter over with a clear head;
it is quite exceptional."

"Oh," said the colonel, coldly, with a haughty jerk of his
head, "if I fail, I can die—but not alone."

The feeble old man had vanished. The eyes now were those
of a man of energy, lighted up with the spark of desire and
revenge.

"We must perhaps compromise," said the lawyer.

"Compromise!" echoed Colonel Chabert. "Am I dead, or am I alive?"

"I hope, monsieur," the attorney went on, "that you will follow my advice. Your cause is mine. You will soon perceive the interest I take in your situation, almost unexampled in judicial records. For the moment I will give you a letter to my notary, who will pay you to your order fifty francs every ten days. It would be unbecoming for you to come here to receive alms. If you are Colonel Chabert, you ought to be at no man's mercy. I shall regard these advances as a loan; you have estates to recover; you are rich."

This delicate compassion brought tears to the old man's eyes. Derville rose hastily, for it was perhaps not correct for a lawyer to show emotion; he went into the adjoining room, and came back with an unsealed letter, which he gave to the colonel. When the poor man held it in his hand he felt through the paper two gold-pieces.

"Will you be good enough to describe the documents, and tell me the name of the town, and in what kingdom?" said the lawyer.

The colonel dictated the information, and verified the spelling of the names of places; then he took his hat in one hand, looked at Derville, and held out the other—a horny hand, saying with much simplicity—

"On my honor, sir, after the Emperor, you are the man to whom I shall owe the most. You are, indeed, a splendid fellow!"

The attorney clapped his hand into the colonel's, saw him to the stairs, and held a light for him.

"Boucard," said Derville to his head clerk, "I have just listened to a tale that may cost me five-and-twenty louis. If I am robbed, I shall not regret the money, for I shall have seen the most consummate actor of the day."

When the colonel was in the street and close to a lamp, he took the two twenty-franc pieces out of the letter and looked at them for a moment under the light. It was the first gold he had seen for nine years.

"I may smoke cigars!" he said to himself.

About three months after this interview, at night, in Derville's room, the notary commissioned to advance the half-pay on Derville's account to his eccentric client came to consult the attorney on a serious matter, and began by begging him to refund the six hundred francs that the old soldier had received.

"Are you amusing yourself with pensioning the old army?" said the notary, laughing—a young man named Crottat, who had just bought up the office in which he had been head clerk, his chief having fled in consequence of a disastrous bankruptcy.

"I have to thank you, my dear sir, for reminding me of that affair," replied Derville. "My philanthropy will not carry me beyond twenty-five louis; I have, I fear, already been the dupe of my patriotism."

As Derville finished the sentence, he saw on his desk the papers his head clerk had laid out for him. His eye was struck by the appearance of the stamps—long, square, and triangular, in red and blue ink, which distinguished a letter that had come through the Prussian, Austrian, Bavarian, and French postoffices.

"Ah, ha!" said he with a laugh, "here is the last act of the comedy; now we shall see if I have been taken in!"

He took up the letter and opened it; but he could not read it; it was written in German.

"Boucard, go yourself and have this letter translated, and bring it back immediately," said Derville, half opening his study door, and giving the letter to the head clerk.

The notary at Berlin, to whom the lawyer had written, informed him that the documents he had been requested to forward would arrive within a few days of this note announcing them. They were, he said, all perfectly regular and duly witnessed, and legally stamped to serve as evidence in law. He also informed him that almost all the witnesses to the facts recorded under these affidavits were still to be found at Eylau, in Prussia, and that the woman to whom M. le Comte Chabert owed his life was still living in a suburb of Heilsberg.

"This looks like business," cried Derville, when Boucard had given him the substance of the letter. "But look here, my boy," he went on, addressing the notary, "I shall want some information which ought to exist in your office. Was it not that old rascal Roguin——?"

"We will say that unfortunate, that ill-used Roguin," interrupted Alexandre Crottat with a laugh.

"Well, was it not that ill-used man who has just carried off eight hundred thousand francs of his clients' money, and reduced several families to despair, who effected the settlement of Chabert's estate? I fancy I have seen that in the documents in our case of Ferraud."

"Yes," said Crottat. "It was when I was third clerk; I copied the papers and studied them thoroughly. Rose Chapotel, wife and widow of Hyacinthe, called Chabert, Count of the Empire, grand officer of the Legion of Honor. They had married without settlement; thus they held all the property in common. To the best of my recollection, the personalty was about six hundred thousand francs. Before his marriage, Comte Chabert had made a will in favor of the hospitals of Paris, by which he left them one-quarter of the fortune he might possess at the time of his decease, the state to take the other quarter. The will was contested, there was a forced sale, and then a division, for the attorneys went at a pace. At the time of the settlement the monster who was then governing France handed over to the widow, by special decree, the portion bequeathed to the treasury."

"So that Comte Chabert's personal fortune was no more than three hundred thousand francs?"

"Consequently so it was, old fellow!" said Crottat. "You lawyers sometimes are very clear-headed, though you are accused of false practices in pleading for one side or the other."

Colonel Chabert, whose address was written at the bottom of the first receipt he had given the notary, was lodging in the Faubourg Saint-Marceau, Rue du Petit-Banquier, with an old quartermaster of the Imperial Guard, now a cow-keeper, named Vergniaud. Having reached the spot, Derville was obliged to go on foot in search of his client, for his coachman declined to drive along an unpaved street, where the ruts were rather too deep for cab-wheels. Looking about him on all sides, the lawyer at last discovered at the end of the street nearest to the boulevard, between two walls built of stones and mud, two shabby stone gate-posts, much knocked about by carts, in spite of two wooden stumps that served as blocks. These posts supported a cross-beam with a penthouse coping of tiles, and on the beam, in red letters, were the words, "Vergniaud, dairyman." To the right of this inscription were some eggs, to the left a cow, all painted in white. The gate was open, and no doubt remained open all day. Beyond a good-sized yard there was a house facing the gate, if indeed the name of house may be applied to one of the hovels built in the neighborhood of Paris, which are like nothing else, not even the most wretched dwellings in the country, of which they have all the poverty without their poetry.

Indeed, in the midst of fields, even a hovel may have a certain grace derived from the pure air, the verdure, the open country—a hill, a serpentine road, vineyards, quick-set hedges, moss-grown thatch and rural implements; but poverty in Paris gains dignity only by horror. Though recently built, this house seemed ready to fall into ruins. None of its materials had found a legitimate use; they had been collected from the various demolitions which are going on every day in

Paris. On a shutter made of the boards of a shop-sign Derville read the words, "Fancy Goods." The windows were all mismatched and grotesquely placed. The ground floor, which seemed to be the habitable part, was on one side raised above the soil, and on the other sunk in the rising ground. Between the gate and the house lay a puddle full of stable litter, into which flowed the rain-water and house-waste. The back wall of this frail construction, which seemed rather more solidly built than the rest, supported a row of barred hutches, where rabbits bred their numerous families. To the right of the gate was the cow-house, with a loft above for fodder; it communicated with the house through the dairy. To the left was a poultry-yard, with a stable and pig-styes, the roofs finished, like that of the house, with rough deal boards nailed so as to overlap, and shabbily thatched with rushes.

Like most of the places where the elements of the huge meal daily devoured by Paris are every day prepared, the yard Derville now entered showed traces of the hurry that comes of the necessity for being ready at a fixed hour. The large pot-bellied tin cans in which milk is carrried, and the little pots for cream, were flung pell-mell at the dairy door, with their linen-covered stoppers. The rags that were used to clean them fluttered in the sunshine, riddled with holes, hanging to strings fastened to poles. The placid horse, of a breed known only to milk-women, had gone a few steps from the cart, and was standing in front of the stable, the door being shut. A goat was munching the shoots of a starved and dusty vine that clung to the cracked yellow wall of the house. A cat, squatting on the cream jars, was licking them over. The fowls, scared by Derville's approach, scuttered away screaming, and the watch-dog barked.

"And the man who decided the victory at Eylau is to be found here!" said Derville to himself, as his eyes took in at a glance the general effect of the squalid scene.

The house had been left in charge of three little boys.

One, who had climbed to the top of a cart loaded with hay, was pitching stones into the chimney of a neighboring house, in the hope that they might fall into a saucepan; another was trying to get a pig into a cart by the back board, which rested on the ground; while the third, hanging on in front, was waiting till the pig had gotten into the cart, to hoist it by making the whole thing tilt. When Derville asked them if M. Chabert lived there, neither of them replied, but all three looked at him with a sort of bright stupidity, if I may combine these two words. Derville repeated his questions, but without success. Provoked by the saucy cunning of these three imps, he abused them with the sort of pleasantry which young men think they have a right to address to little boys, and they broke the silence with a horse-laugh. Then Derville was angry.

The colonel, hearing him, now came out of a little low room, close to the dairy, and stood on the threshold of his doorway with indescribable military coolness. He had in his mouth a very finely colored pipe—a technical phrase to a smoker—a humble, short clay pipe of the kind called "*brûle-gueule.*" He lifted the peak of a dreadfully greasy cloth cap, saw Derville, and came straight across the midden to join his benefactor the sooner, calling out in friendly tones to the boys—

"Silence in the ranks!"

The children at once kept a respectful silence, which showed the power the old soldier had over them.

"Why did you not write me?" he said to Derville. "Go along by the cow-house! There—the path is paved there," he exclaimed, seeing the lawyer's hesitancy, for he did not wish to wet his feet in the manure heap.

Jumping from one dry spot to another, Derville reached the door by which the colonel had come out. Chabert seemed but ill pleased at having to receive him in the bedroom he occupied; and, in fact, Derville found but one chair there.

The colonel's bed consisted of some trusses of straw, over which his hostess had spread two or three of those old fragments of carpet, picked up heaven knows where, which milkwomen use to cover the seats of their carts. The floor was simply the trodden earth. The walls, sweating saltpetre, green with mold, and full of cracks, were so excessively damp that on the side where the colonel's bed was a reed mat had been nailed. The famous box-coat hung on a nail. Two pairs of old boots lay in a corner. There was not a sign of linen. On the worm-eaten table the *Bulletins de la Grande Armée*, reprinted by Plancher, lay open, and seemed to be the colonel's reading ; his countenance was calm and serene in the midst of this squalor. His visit to Derville seemed to have altered his features ; the lawyer perceived in them traces of a happy feeling, a particular gleam set there by hope.

"Does the smell of a pipe annoy you?" he said, placing the dilapidated straw-bottom chair for his lawyer.

"But, colonel, you are dreadfully uncomfortable here!" remarked Derville.

The speech was wrung from Derville by the distrust natural to lawyers, and the deplorable experience which they derive early in life from the appalling and obscure tragedies at which they look on.

"Here," said he to himself, "is a man who has of course spent my money in satisfying a trooper's three theological virtues—play, wine, and women!"

"To be sure, monsieur, we are not distinguished for luxury here. It is a camp lodging, tempered by friendship, but——" And the soldier shot a deep glance at the man of law—"I have done no one wrong, I have never turned my back on anybody, and I sleep in peace."

Derville reflected that there would be some want of delicacy in asking his client to account for the sums of money he had advanced, so he merely said—

"But why would you not come to Paris, where you might

have lived as cheaply as you do here, but where you would have been better lodged?''

"Why," replied the colonel, "the good folks with whom I am living had taken me in and fed me *gratis* for a year. How could I leave them just when I had a little money. Besides, the father of those three pickles is an old *Egyptian*——''

"An Egyptian!"

"We give that name to the troopers who came back from the expedition into Egypt, of which I was one. Not merely are all who get back brothers; Vergniaud was in my regiment. We have shared a draught of water in the desert; and, besides, I have not yet finished teaching his brats to read.''

"He might have lodged you better for your money," said Derville.

"Bah!" said the colonel, "his children sleep on the straw as I do. He and his wife have no better bed; they are very poor, you see. They have taken a bigger business than they can manage. But if I recover my fortune—— However, it does very well.''

"Colonel, to-morrow or next day I shall receive your papers from Heilsberg. The woman who dug you out is still alive!"

"Curse the money! To think I haven't got any!" he cried, flinging his pipe on the ground.

Now, a well-colored pipe is to a smoker a precious possession; but the impulse was so natural, the emotion so generous, that every smoker, and the excise office itself, would have pardoned this crime of treason to tobacco. Perhaps the angels may have picked up the pieces.

"Colonel, it is an exceedingly complicated business," said Derville as they left the room to walk up and down in the sunshine.

"To me," said the soldier, "it appears exceedingly simple. I was thought to be dead, and here I am! Give me back my wife and my fortune ; give me the rank of general, to which I have a right, for I was made colonel of the Imperial Guard the day before the battle of Eylau.''

" Things are not done so in the legal world,'' said Derville. "Listen to me. You are Colonel Chabert, I am glad to think it ; but it has to be proved judicially to persons whose interest it will be to deny it. Hence, your papers will be disputed. That contention will give rise to ten or twelve preliminary inquiries. Every question will be sent under contradiction up to the supreme court, and give rise to so many costly suits, which will hang on for a long time, however eagerly I may push them. Your opponents will demand an inquiry, which we cannot refuse, and which may necessitate the sending of a commission of investigation to Prussia. But even if we hope for the best ; supposing that justice should at once recognize you as Colonel Chabert—can we know how the questions will be settled that will arise out of the very innocent bigamy committed by the Comtesse Ferraud ?

" In your case, the point of law is unknown to the code, and can only be decided as a point in equity, as a jury decides in the delicate cases presented by the social eccentricities of some criminal prosecutions. Now, you had no children by your marriage ; M. le Comte Ferraud has two. The judges might pronounce against the marriage where the family ties are weakest, to the confirmation of that where they are stronger, since it was contracted in perfect good faith. Would you be in a very becoming moral position if you insisted, at your age and in your present circumstances, in resuming your rights over a woman who no longer loves you ? You will have both your wife and her husband against you, two important persons who might influence the bench. Thus there are many elements which would prolong the case ; you will have time to grow old in the bitterest regrets.''

" And my fortune ? ''

" Do you suppose you had a fine fortune ? ''

" Had I not thirty thousand francs a year ? "

" My dear colonel, in 1799 you made a will before your marriage, leaving one quarter of your property to hospitals."

" That is true."

" Well, when you were reported dead, it was necessary to make a valuation, and have a sale, to give this quarter away. Your wife was not particular about honesty to the poor. The valuation, in which she no doubt took care not to include the ready money or jewelry, or too much of the plate, and in which the furniture would be estimated at two-thirds of its actual cost, either to benefit her or to lighten the succession duty, and also because a valuer can be held responsible for the declared value—the valuation thus made stood at six hundred thousand francs. Your wife had a right to half for her share. Everything was sold and bought in by her ; she got something out of it all, and the hospitals got their seventy-five thousand francs. Then, as the remainder went to the state, since you had made no mention of your wife in your will, the Emperor restored to your widow by decree the residue which would have reverted to the exchequer. So, now, what can you claim ? Three hundred thousand francs, no more, and minus the costs."

" And you call that justice ! " said the colonel, in dismay.

" Why, certainly——"

" A pretty kind of justice ! "

" So it is, my dear colonel. You see that what you thought so easy is not so. Madame Ferraud might even choose to keep the sum given to her by the Emperor."

" But she was not a widow. The decree is utterly void——"

" I agree with you. But every case can get a hearing. Listen to me. I think that under these circumstances a compromise would be both for her and for you the best solution of the question. You will gain by it a more considerable sum than you can prove a right to."

" That would be to sell my wife ! "

" With twenty-four thousand francs a year you could find a woman who, in the position in which you are, would suit you better than your own wife, and make you happier. I propose going this very day to see the Comtesse Ferraud and sounding the ground; but I would not take such a step without giving you due notice."

"Let us go together."

"What, just as you are?" said the lawyer. " No, my dear colonel, no. You might lose your case on the spot."

"Can I possibly gain it?"

"On every count," replied Derville. " But, my dear Colonel Chabert, you overlook one thing. I am not rich; the price of my connection is not wholly paid up. If the bench should allow you a maintenance, that is to say, a sum advanced on your prospects, they will not do so till you have proved that you are Comte Chabert, grand officer of the Legion of Honor."

" To be sure, I am a grand officer of the Legion of Honor; I had forgotten that," said he simply.

" Well, until then," Derville went on, " will you not have to engage pleaders, to have documents copied, to keep the underlings of the law going, and to support yourself? The expenses of the preliminary inquiries will, at a rough guess, amount to ten or twelve thousand francs. I have not so much to lend you—I am crushed as it is by the enormous interest I have to pay on the money I borrowed to buy my business; and you? Where can you find it?"

Large tears gathered in the poor veteran's faded eyes, and rolled down his withered cheeks. This outlook of difficulties discouraged him. The social and the legal world weighed on his breast like a nightmare.

" I will go to the foot of the Vendôme column!" he cried. "I will call out: ' I am Colonel Chabert who rode through the Russian square at Eylau!' The statue—he—he will know me."

"And you will find yourself in Charenton."

At this terrible name the soldier's transports collapsed.

"And will there be no hope for me at the ministry of war?"

"The war office!" said Derville. "Well, go there; but take a formal legal opinion with you, nullifying the certificate of your death. The government offices would be only too glad if they could annihilate the men of the Empire."

The colonel stood for a while speechless, motionless, his eyes fixed, but seeing nothing, sunk in bottomless despair. Military justice is ready and swift; it decides with Turk-like finality, and almost always rightly. This was the only justice known to Chabert. As he saw the labyrinth of difficulties into which he must plunge, and how much money would be required for the journey, the poor old soldier was mortally hit in that power peculiar to man, and called the will. He thought it would be impossible to live as party to a lawsuit; it seemed a thousand times simpler to remain poor and a beggar, or to enlist as a trooper if any regiment would pass him.

His physical and mental sufferings had already impaired his bodily health in some of the most important organs. He was on the verge of one of those maladies for which medicine has no name, and of which the seat is in some degree variable, like the nervous system itself, the part most frequently attacked of the whole human machine—a malady which may be designated as the heart-sickness of the unfortunate. However serious this invisible but real disorder might already be, it could still be cured by a happy issue. But a fresh obstacle, an unexpected incident, would be enough to wreck this vigorous constitution, to break the weakened springs, and produce the hesitancy, the aimless, unfinished movements, which physiologists know well in men undermined by grief.

Derville, detecting in his client the symptoms of extreme dejection, said to him:

"Take courage; the end of the business cannot fail to be in your favor. Only consider whether you can give me your whole confidence and blindly accept the result I may think best for your interests."

"Do what you will," said Chabert.

"Yes, but you surrender yourself to me like a man marching to his death."

"Must I not be left to live without a position, without a name? Is that endurable?"

"That is not my view of it," said the lawyer. "We will try a friendly suit, to annul both your death certificate and your marriage, so as to put you in possession of your rights. You may even, by Comte Ferraud's intervention, have your name replaced on the army-list as general, and no doubt you will get a pension."

"Well, proceed then," said Chabert. "I put myself entirely in your hands."

"I will send you a power of attorney to sign," said Derville. "Good-by. Keep up your courage. If you want money, rely on me."

Chabert warmly wrung the lawyer's hand, and remained standing with his back against the wall, not having the energy to follow him excepting with his eyes. Like all men who know but little of legal matters, he was frightened by this unforeseen struggle.

During their interview, several times, the figure of a man posted in the street had come forward from behind one of the gate-pillars, watching for Derville to depart, and he now accosted the lawyer. He was an old man, wearing a blue waistcoat and a white-pleated kilt, like a brewer's; on his head was an otter-skin cap. His face was tanned, hollow-cheeked, and wrinkled, but ruddy on the cheek-bones by hard work and exposure to the open air.

"Asking your pardon, sir," said he, taking Derville by the arm, "if I take the liberty of speaking to you. But I fancied, from the look of you, that you were a friend of our general."

18

"And what then?" replied Derville. "What concern have you with him? But who are you?" said the cautious lawyer.

"I am Louis Vergniaud," he at once replied. "I have two words to say to you."

"So you are the man who has lodged Comte Chabert as I have found him?"

"Asking your pardon, sir, he has the best room. I would have given him mine if I had had but one; I could have slept in the stable. A man who has suffered as he has, who teaches my kids to read, a general, an Egyptian, the first lieutenant I ever served under—What do you think? Of us all, he is best served. I shared what I had with him. Unfortunately, it is not much to boast of—bread, milk, eggs. Well, well; it's neighbors' fare, sir. And he is heartily welcome. But he has hurt our feelings."

"He?"

"Yes, sir, hurt our feelings. To be plain with you, I have taken a larger business than I can manage, and he saw it. Well, it worried him; he must needs mind the horse! I says to him, 'Really, general——' 'Bah!' says he, 'I am not going to eat my head off doing nothing. I learned to rub a horse down many a year ago.' I had some bills out for the purchase money of my dairy—a fellow named Grados—Do you know him, sir?"

"But, my good man, I have not time to listen to your story. Only tell me how the colonel offended you."

"He hurt our feelings, sir, as sure as my name is Louis Vergniaud, and my wife cried about it. He heard from our neighbors that we had not a sou to begin to meet the bills with. The old soldier, as he is, he saved up all you gave him, he watched for the bill to come in, and he paid it. Such a trick! While my wife and me, we knew he had no tobacco, poor old boy, and went without. Oh! now—yes, he has his cigar every morning! I would sell my soul for it

—No, we are hurt. Well, so I wanted to ask you—for he said you were a good sort—to lend us a hundred crowns on the stock, so that we may get him some clothes, and furnish his room. He thought he was getting us out of debt, you see. Well, it's just the other way; the old man is running us into debt—and hurt our feelings! He ought not to have stolen a march on us like that. And we his friends, too! On my word as an honest man, as sure as my name is Louis Vergniaud, I would sooner sell out and enlist than fail to pay you back your money——''

Derville looked at the dairyman, and stepped back a few paces to glance at the house, the yard, the manure-pool, the cow-house, the rabbits, the children.

"On my honor, I believe it is characteristic of virtue to have nothing to do with riches!'' thought he.

"All right, you shall have your hundred crowns, and more. But I shall not give them to you; the colonel will be rich enough to help, and I will not deprive him of the pleasure.''

"And will that be soon?''

"Why, yes.''

"Ah, dear God! how glad my wife will be!'' and the cow-keeper's tanned face seemed to expand.

"Now,'' said Derville to himself, as he got into his cab again, "let us call on our opponent. We must not show our hand, but try to see hers, and win the game at one stroke. She must be frightened. She is a woman. Now what frightens women most? A woman is afraid of nothing but——''

And he set to work to study the Countess' position, falling into one of those brown studies to which great politicians give themselves up when concocting their own plans and trying to guess the secrets of a hostile cabinet. Are not attorneys, in a way, statesmen in charge of private affairs?

But a brief survey of the situation in which the Comte

Ferraud and his wife now found themselves is necessary for a comprehension of the lawyer's cleverness.

Monsieur le Comte Ferraud was the only son of a former councilor in the old *Parlement* of Paris, who had emigrated during the Reign of Terror, and so, though he saved his head, lost his fortune. He came back under the Consulate, and remained persistently faithful to the cause of Louis XVIII., in whose circle his father had moved before the Revolution. He thus was one of the party in the Faubourg Saint-Germain which nobly stood out against Napoleon's blandishments. The reputation for capacity gained by the young Count—then simply called Monsieur Ferraud—made him the object of the Emperor's advances, for he was often as well pleased at his conquests among the aristocracy as at gaining a battle. The Count was promised the restitution of his title, of such of his estates as had not been sold, and he was shown in perspective a place in the ministry or as senator.

The Emperor fell.

At the time of Comte Chabert's death M. Ferraud was a young man of six-and-twenty, without fortune, of pleasing appearance, who had had his successes, and whom the Faubourg Saint-Germain had adopted as doing it credit; but Madame la Comtesse Chabert had managed to turn her share of her husband's fortune to such good account that, after eighteen months of widowhood, she had about forty thousand francs a year. Her marriage to the young Count was not regarded as news in the circles of the Faubourg Saint-Germain. Napoleon, approving of this union, which carried out his idea of fusion, restored to Madame Chabert the money falling to the exchequer under her husband's will; but Napoleon's hopes were again disappointed. Madame Ferraud was not only in love with her lover; she had also been fascinated by the notion of getting into the haughty society which, in spite of its humiliation, was still predominant at the imperial court. By this marriage all her vanities were as much grat-

ified as her passions. She was to become a real fine lady.
When the Faubourg Saint-Germain understood that the young
Count's marriage did not mean desertion, its drawing-rooms
were thrown open to his wife.

Then came the Restoration. The Count's political advancement was not rapid. He understood the exigencies of
the situation in which Louis XVIII. found himself; he was
one of the inner circle, who waited till the " Gulf of Revolution should be closed "—for this phrase of the King's, at
which the Liberals laughed so heartily, had a political sense.
The order quoted in the lawyer's long preamble at the beginning of this story had, however, put him in possession of two
tracts of forest, and of an estate which had considerably increased in value during its sequestration. At the present
moment, though Comte Ferraud was a councilor of state and
a director-general, he regarded his position as merely the first
step of his political career.

Wholly occupied as he was by the anxieties of consuming
ambition, he had attached to himself, as secretary, a ruined
attorney named Delbecq, a more than clever man, versed in
all the resources of the law, to whom he left the conduct of
his private affairs. This shrewd practitioner had so well understood his position with the Count as to be honest in his
own interest. He hoped to get some place by his master's
influence, and he made the Count's fortune his first care.
His conduct so effectually gave the lie to his former life that
he was regarded as a slandered man. The Countess, with the
tact and shrewdness of which most women have a share more
or less, understood the man's motives, watched him quietly,
and managed him so well, that she had made good use of
him for the augmentation of her private fortune. She had
contrived to make Delbecq believe that she ruled her husband, and had promised to get him appointed president of
an inferior court in some important provincial town, if he
devoted himself entirely to her interests.

The promise of a place, not dependent on changes of ministry, which would allow of his marrying advantageously, and rising subsequently to a high political position, by being chosen deputy, made Delbecq the Countess' abject slave. He had never allowed her to miss one of those favorable chances which the fluctuations of the Bourse and the increased value of property afforded to clever financiers in Paris during the first three years after the Restoration. He had trebled his protectress' capital, and all the more easily because the Countess had no scruples as to the means which might make her an enormous fortune as quickly as possible. The emoluments derived by the Count from the places he held she spent on the housekeeping, so as to reinvest her dividends; and Delbecq lent himself to these calculations of avarice without trying to account for her motives. People of that sort never trouble themselves about any secrets of which the discovery is not necessary to their own interests. And, indeed, he naturally found the reason in the thirst for money, which taints almost every Parisian woman; and as a fine fortune was needed to support the pretensions of Comte Ferraud, the secretary sometimes fancied that he saw in the Countess' greed a consequence of her devotion to a husband with whom she still was in love. The Countess buried the secrets of her conduct at the bottom of her heart. There lay the secrets of life and death to her, there lay the turning-point of this history.

At the beginning of the year 1818 the Restoration was settled on an apparently immovable foundation; its doctrines of government, as understood by lofty minds, seemed calculated to bring to France an era of renewed prosperity, and Parisian society changed its aspect. Madame la Comtessee Ferraud found that by chance she had achieved for love a marriage that had brought her fortune and gratified ambition. Still young and handsome, Madame Ferraud played the part of a woman of fashion, and lived in the atmosphere of the court.

Rich herself, with a rich husband who was cried up as one of the ablest men of the Royalist party, and, as a friend of the King, certain to be made minister, she belonged to the aristocracy, and shared its magnificence. In the midst of this triumph she was attacked by a moral canker. There are feelings which women guess in spite of the care men take to bury them. On the first return of the King, Comte Ferraud had begun to regret his marriage. Colonel Chabert's widow had not been the means of allying him to anybody; he was alone and unsupported in steering his way in a course full of shoals and beset by enemies. Also, perhaps, when he came to judge his wife coolly, he may have discerned in her certain vices of education which made her unfit to second him in his schemes.

A speech he made, *à propos* of Talleyrand's marriage, enlightened the Countess, to whom it proved that if he had still been a free man she would never have been Madame Ferraud. What woman could forgive this repentance? Does it not include the germs of every insult, every crime, every form of repudiation? But what a wound must it have left in the Countess' heart, supposing that she lived in the dread of her first husband's return? She had known that he still lived, and she had ignored him. Then during the time when she had heard no more of him, she had chosen to believe that he had fallen at Waterloo with the Imperial Eagle, at the same time as Boutin. She resolved, nevertheless, to bind the Count to her by the strongest of all ties, by a chain of gold, and vowed to be so rich that her fortune might make her second marriage indissoluble, if by chance Colonel Chabert should ever reappear. And he had reappeared ; and she could not explain to herself why the struggle she dreaded had not already begun. Suffering, sickness, had perhaps delivered her from that man. Perhaps he was half-mad, and Charenton might yet do her justice. She had not chosen to take either Delbecq or the police into her confidnce, for fear of putting herself in their power, or of hastening the catastrophe. There are in Paris many women who, like the Countess Ferraud, live with an unknown moral monster, or on the brink of an abyss; a callus forms over the spot that tortures them, and they can still laugh and enjoy themselves.

"There is something very strange in Comte Ferraud's position," said Derville to himself, on emerging from his long reverie, as his cab stopped at the door of the Hôtel Ferraud in the Rue de Varennes. "How is it that he, so rich as he is, and such a favorite with the King, is not yet a peer of France? It may, to be sure, be true that the King, as Mme. de Grandlieu was telling me, desires to keep up the value of the peerage by not bestowing it right and left. And, after all, the son of a councilor of the *Parlement* is not a Crillon nor a Rohan. A Comte Ferraud can only get into the Upper Chamber surreptitiously. But if his marriage were annulled, could he not get the dignity of some old peer who has only daughters transferred to himself, to the King's great satisfaction? At any rate this will be a good bogey to put forward and frighten the Countess," thought he as he went up the steps.

Derville had without knowing it laid his finger on the hidden wound, put his hand on the canker that consumed Madame Ferraud.

She received him in a pretty, winter dining-room, where she was at breakfast, while playing with a monkey tethered by a chain to a little pole with climbing-bars of iron. The Countess was in an elegant wrapper; the curls of her hair, carelessly pinned up, escaped from a cap, giving her an arch look. She was fresh and smiling. Silver, gilding, and mother-of-pearl shone on the table, and all about the room were rare plants growing in magnificent china jars. As he saw Colonel Chabert's wife, rich with his spoil, in the lap of luxury and the height of fashion, while he, poor wretch, was living with a poor dairymen among the beasts, the lawyer said to himself—

"The moral of all this is that a pretty woman will never

acknowledge as her husband, nor even as a lover, a man in an old box-coat, a tow wig, and boots with holes in them."

A mischievous and bitter smile expressed the feelings, half-philosophical and half-satirical, which such a man was certain to experience—a man well situated to know the truth of things in spite of the lies behind which most families in Paris hide their mode of life.

" Good-morning, Monsieur Derville," said she, giving the monkey some coffee to drink.

" Madame," said he, a little sharply, for the light tone in which she spoke jarred on him, " I have come to speak to you on a very serious matter."

" I am so *grieved*, M. le Comte is away——"

" I, madame, am delighted. It would be grievous if he could be present at our interview. Besides, I am informed through M. Delbecq that you like to manage your own business without troubling the Count."

" Then I will send for Delbecq," said she.

" He would be of no use to you, clever as he is," replied Derville. " Listen to me, madame ; one word will be enough to make you grave. Colonel Chabert is alive ! "

" Is it by telling me such nonsense as that that you think you can make me grave ? " said she with a shout of laughter. But she was suddenly quelled by the singular penetration of the fixed gaze which Derville turned on her, seeming to read to the bottom of her soul.

" Madame," he said, with cold and piercing solemnity, " you know not the extent of the danger which threatens you. I need say nothing of the indisputable authenticity of the evidence nor of the fullness of proof which testifies to the identity of Comte Chabert. I am not, as you know, the man to take up a bad cause. If you resist our proceedings to show that the certificate of death was false, you will lose that first case, and that matter once settled, we shall gain every point."

" What, then, do you wish to discuss with me ? "

"Neither the colonel nor yourself. Nor need I allude to the briefs which clever advocates may draw up when armed with the curious facts of this case, or the advantage they may derive from the letters you received from your first husband before your marriage to your second."

"It is false," she cried, with the violence of a spoilt woman. "I never had a letter from Comte Chabert; and if some one is pretending to be the colonel, it is some swindler, some returned convict, like Coignard perhaps. It makes me shudder only to think of it. Can the colonel rise from the dead, monsieur? Bonaparte sent an aide-de-camp to inquire for me on his death, and to this day I draw the pension of three thousand francs granted to his widow by the government. I have been perfectly in the right to turn away all the Chaberts who have ever come, as I shall all who may come."

"Happily we are alone, madame. We can tell lies at our ease," said he coolly, and finding it amusing to lash up the Countess' rage so as to lead her to betray herself, by tactics familiar to lawyers, who are accustomed to keep cool when their opponents or their clients are in a passion. "Well, then, we must fight it out," thought he, instantly hitting on a plan to entrap her and show her her weakness.

"The proof that you received the first letter, madame, is that it contained some securities——"

"Oh, as to securities—that it certainly did not."

"Then you received the letter," said Derville, smiling. "You are caught, madame, in the first snare laid for you by an attorney, and you fancy you could fight against justice——"

The Countess colored, and then turned pale, hiding her face in her hands. Then she shook off her shame, and retorted with the natural impertinence of such women, "Since you are the so-called Chabert's attorney, be so good as to——"

"Madame," said Derville, "I am at this moment as much

your lawyer as I am Colonel Chabert's. Do you suppose I want to lose so valuable a client as you are? But you are not listening.''

" Nay, speak on, monsieur," said she graciously.

" Your fortune came to you from M. le Comte Chabert, and you cast him off. Your fortune is immense, and you leave him to beg. An advocate can be very eloquent when a cause is eloquent in itself; there are here circumstances which might turn public opinion strongly against you."

'' But, monsieur," said the Comtesse, provoked by the way in which Derville turned and laid her on the gridiron, " even if I grant that your M. Chabert is living, the law will uphold my second marriage on account of the children, and I shall get off with the restitution of two hundred and twenty-five thousand francs to M. Chabert.''

" It is impossible to foresee what view the bench may take of the question. If on one side we have a mother and children, on the other we have an old man crushed by sorrows, made old by your refusals to know him. Where is he to find a wife? Can the judges contravene the law? Your marriage with Colonel Chabert has priority on its side and every legal right. But if you appear under disgraceful colors, you might have an unlooked-for adversary. That, madame, is the danger against which I would warn you."

" And who is he?"

" Comte Ferraud."

" Monsieur Fearaud has too great an affection for me, too much respect for the mother of his children——"

" Do not talk of such absurd things," interrupted Derville, " to lawyers, who are accustomed to read hearts to the bottom. At this instant Monsieur Ferraud has not the slightest wish to annul your union, and I am quite sure that he adores you; but if some one were to tell him that his marriage is void, that his wife will be called before the bar of public opinion as a criminal——"

" He would defend me, monsieur.''

" No, madame.''

" What reason could he have for deserting me, monsieur?''

" That he would be free to marry the only daughter of a peer of France, whose title would be conferred on him by patent from the King.''

The Countess turned pale.

" A hit!'' said Derville to himself. " I have you on the hip; the poor colonel's case is won. Besides, madame,'' he went on aloud, " he would feel all the less remorse because a man covered with glory—a general, count, grand cross of the Legion of Honor—is not such a bad alternative; and if that man insisted on his wife's returning to him——''

" Enough, enough, monsieur!'' she exclaimed. " I will never have any lawyer but you. What is to be done?''

" Compromise!'' said Derville.

" Does he still love me?'' she said.

" Well, I do not think he can do otherwise.''

The Countess raised her head at these words. A flash of hope shone in her eyes; she thought perhaps that she could speculate on her first husband's affection to gain her cause by some feminine cunning.

" I shall await your orders, madame, to know whether I am to report our proceedings to you, or if you will come to my office to agree to the terms of a compromise,'' said Derville, taking leave.

A week after Derville had paid these two visits, on a fine morning in June, the husband and wife, who had been separated by an almost supernatural chance, started from the opposite ends of Paris to meet in the office of the lawyer who was engaged by both. The supplies liberally advanced by Derville to Colonel Chabert had enabled him to dress as suited his position in life, and the dead man arrived in a very decent cab. He wore a wig suited to his face, was dressed in blue cloth with white linen, and wore upon his waistcoat the broad red ribbon of the higher grade of the Legion of Honor. In resuming the habits of wealth he had recovered his soldierly style. He held himself up; his face, grave and mysterious-looking, reflected his happiness and all his hopes, and seemed to have acquired youth and *empasto*, to borrow a picturesque word from the painter's art. He was no more like the Chabert of the old box-coat than a cart-wheel double sou is like a newly coined forty-franc piece. The passer-by, only to see him, would have recognized at once one of the noble wrecks of our old army, one of the heroic men on whom our national glory is reflected, as a splinter of ice on which the sun shines seems to reflect every beam. These veterans are at once a picture and a book.

When the Count jumped out of his carriage to go into Derville's office, he did it as lightly as a young man. Hardly had his cab moved off, when a smart brougham drove up, splendid with coats-of-arms. Madame la Comtesse Ferraud stepped out in a dress which, though simple, was cleverly designed to show how youthful her figure was. She wore a pretty drawn bonnet lined with pink, which framed her face to perfection, softening its outlines and making it look younger.

If the clients were rejuvenescent, the office was unaltered, and presented the same picture as that described at the beginning of this story. Simonnin was eating his breakfast, his shoulder leaning against the window, which was then open, and he was staring up at the blue sky in the opening of the courtyard enclosed by four gloomy houses.

"Ah, ha!" cried the little clerk, "who will bet an evening at the play that Colonel Chabert is a general, and wears a red ribbon?"

"The chief is a great magician," said Godeschal.

"Then there is no trick to play on him this time?" asked Desroches.

" His wife has taken that in hand, the Comtesse Ferraud,"
said Boucard.

"What next?" said Godeschal.   "Is Comtesse Ferraud
required to belong to two men?"

" Here she is," answered Simonnin.

At this moment the colonel came in and asked for Derville.

" He is at home, sir," said Simonnin.

"So you are not deaf, you young rogue!" said Chabert,
taking the gutter-jumper by the ear and twisting it, to the delight of the other clerks, who began to laugh, looking at the
colonel with the curious attention due to so singular a personage.

Comte Chabert was in Derville's private room at the moment when his wife came in by the door of the office.

"I say, Boucard, there is going to be a queer scene in the
chief's room. There is a woman who can spend her days alternately, the odd with Comte Ferraud, and the even with Comte
Chabert."

" And in leap year," said Godeschal, " they must settle the
count between them."

" Silence, gentlemen, you can be heard!" said Boucard
severely.   "I never was in an office where there was so much
jesting as there is here over the clients."

Derville had made the colonel retire to the bedroom when
the Countess was admitted.

"Madame," he said, "not knowing whether it would be
agreeable to you to meet M. le Comte Chabert, I have placed
you apart.   If, however, you should wish it——"

"It is an attention for which I am obliged to you."

"I have drawn up the memorandum of an agreement of
which you and M. Chabert can discuss the conditions, here
and now.   I will go alternately to him and to you, and explain
your views respectively."

"Let me see, monsieur," said the Countess impatiently.

Derville read aloud—

"'Between the undersigned:

"'M. Hyacinthe Chabert, Count, Maréchal de Camp and Grand Officer of the Legion of Honor, living in Paris, Rue du Petit Banquier, on the one part;

"'And Madame Rose Chapotel, wife of the aforesaid M. le Comte Chabert, *née*——'"

"Pass over the preliminaries," said she. "Come to the conditions."

"Madame," said the lawyer, "the preamble briefly sets forth the position in which you stand to each other. Then, by the first clause, you acknowledge, in the presence of three witnesses, of whom two shall be notaries, and one the dairyman with whom your husband has been lodging, to all of whom your secret is known, and who will be absolutely silent —you acknowledge, I say, that the individual designated in the documents subjoined to the deed, and whose identity is to be further proved by an act of recognition prepared by your notary, Alexandre Crottat, is your first husband, Comte Chabert. By the second clause, Comte Chabert, to secure your happiness, will undertake to assert his rights only under certain circumstances set forth in the deed. And these," said Derville, in a parenthesis, "are none other than a failure to carry out the conditions of this secret agreement. M. Chabert, on his part, agrees to accept judgment on a friendly suit, by which his certificate of death shall be annulled and his marriage dissolved."

"That will not suit me in the least," said the Countess with surprise. "I will be a party to no suit; you know why."

"By the third clause," Derville went on, with imperturbable coolness, "you pledge yourself to secure to Hyacinthe Comte Chabert an income of twenty-four thousand francs on government stock held in his name, to revert to you at his death——"

"But it is much too dear!" exclaimed the Countess.

"Can you compromise the matter cheaper?"

"Possibly."

" But what do you want, madame ? "

" I want—I will not have a lawsuit. I want——"

" You want him to remain dead ? " said Derville, interrupting her hastily.

"Monsieur," said the Countess, "if twenty-four thousand francs a year are necessary, we will go to law——"

"Yes, we will go to law," said the colonel in a deep voice, as he opened the door and stood before his wife, with one hand in his waistcoat and the other hanging by his side— an attitude to which the recollection of his adventure gave horrible significance.

" It is he," said the Countess to herself.

" Too dear ! " the old soldier exclaimed. " I have given you near on a million, and you are cheapening my misfortunes. Very well ; now I will have you—you and your fortune. Our goods are in common, our marriage is not dissolved——"

" But monsieur is not Colonel Chabert ! " cried the Countess, in feigned amazement.

" Indeed ! " said the old man, in a tone of intense irony. " Do you want proofs ? I found you in the Palais Royal——"

The Countess turned pale. Seeing her grow white under her rouge, the old soldier paused, touched by the acute suffering he was inflicting on the woman he had once so ardently loved ; but she shot such a venomous glance at him that he abruptly went on—

" You were with La——"

" Allow me, Monsieur Derville," said the Countess to the lawyer. " You must give me leave to retire. I did not come here to listen to such dreadful things."

She rose and went out. Derville rushed after her ; but the Countess had taken wings, and seemed to have flown from the place.

On returning to his private room, he found the colonel in a towering rage, striding up and down.

"In those times a man took his wife where he chose," said he. "But I was foolish, and chose badly; I trusted to appearances. She has no heart."

"Well, colonel, was I not right to beg you not to come? I am now positive of your identity; when you came in, the Countess gave a little start, of which the meaning was unequivocal. But you have lost your chances. Your wife knows that you are unrecognizable."

"I will kill her!"

"Madness! you will be caught and executed like any common wretch. Besides, you might miss! That would be unpardonable. A man must not miss his shot when he wants to kill his wife. Let me set things straight: you are only a big child. Go now. Take care of yourself; she is capable of setting some trap for you and shutting you up in Charenton. I will notify her of our proceedings to protect you against a surprise."

The unhappy colonel obeyed his young benefactor, and went away, stammering apologies. He slowly went down the dark staircase, lost in gloomy thoughts, and crushed perhaps by the blow just dealt him—the most cruel he could feel, the thrust that could most deeply pierce his heart—when he heard the rustle of a woman's dress on the lowest landing, and his wife stood before him.

"Come, monsieur," said she, taking his arm with a gesture like those familiar to him of old. Her action and the accent of her voice, which had recovered its graciousness, were enough to allay the colonel's wrath, and he allowed himself to be led to the carriage.

"Well, get in!" said she, when the footman had let down the step.

And as if by magic, he found himself sitting by his wife in the brougham.

"Where to?" asked the servant.

"To Groslay," said she.

19

The horses started at once, and carried them all across Paris.

"Monsieur," said the Countess, in a tone of voice which betrayed one of those emotions which are rare in our lives, and which agitate every part of our being. At such moments the heart, fibres, nerves, countenance, soul, and body, everything, every pore even, feels a thrill. Life no longer seems to be within us; it flows out, springs forth, is communicated as by contagion, transmitted by a look, a tone of voice, a gesture, impressing our will on others. The old soldier started on hearing this single word, this first, terrible "monsieur!" But still it was at once a reproach and a pardon, a hope and a despair, a question and an answer. This word included them all; none but an actress could have thrown so much eloquence, so many feelings into a single word. Truth is less complete in its utterance; it does not put everything on the outside; it allows us to see what is within. The colonel was filled with remorse for his suspicions, his demands, and his anger; he looked down not to betray his agitation.

"Monsieur," repeated she, after an imperceptible pause, "I knew you at once."

"Rosine," said the old soldier, "those words contain the only balm that can help me to forget my misfortunes."

Two large hot tears rolled on to his wife's hands, which he pressed to show his deeply rooted affection.

"Monsieur," she went on, "could you not have guessed what it cost me to appear before a stranger in a position so false as mine now is? If I have to blush for it, at least let it be in the privacy of my family. Ought not such a secret to remain buried in our hearts? You will forgive me, I hope, for my apparent indifference to the woes of a Chabert in whose existence I could not possibly believe. I received your letters," she hastily added, seeing in his face the objection it expressed, "but they did not reach me till thirteen months after the battle of Eylau. They were opened, dirty, the writing was unrecognizable; and after obtaining Napoleon's signature to my second marriage contract, I could not help believing that some clever swindler wanted to make a fool of me. Therefore, to avoid disturbing Monsieur Ferraud's peace of mind and disrupting family ties, I was obliged to take precautions against a pretended Chabert. Was I not right, I ask you?"

"Yes, you were right. It was I who was the idiot, the owl, the dolt, not to have calculated better what the consequences of such a position might be. But where are we going;" he asked, seeing that they had reached the barrier of La Chapelle.

"To my country house near Groslay, in the valley of Montmorency. There, monsieur, we will consider the steps to be taken. I know my duties. Though I am yours by right, I am no longer yours in fact. Can you wish that we should become the talk of Paris? We need not inform the public of a situation, which for me has its ridiculous side, and let us preserve our dignity. You still love me," she said, with a sad, sweet gaze at the colonel, "but have I not been authorized to form other ties? In so strange a position, a secret voice bids me trust to your kindness, which is so well known to me. Can I be wrong in taking you as the sole arbiter of my fate? Be at once judge and party to the suit. I trust in your noble character; you will be generous enough to forgive me for the consequences of faults committed in innocence. I may then confess to you: I love M. Ferraud. I believed that I had a right to love him. I do not blush to make this confession to you; even if it offends you, it does not disgrace us. I cannot conceal the facts. When fate made me a widow, I was not a mother."

The colonel with a wave of his hand bid his wife be silent, and for a mile and a half they sat without speaking a single word. Chabert could fancy he saw the two little ones before him.

" Rosine."

" Monsieur."

" The dead are very wrong to come to life again."

"Oh, monsieur, no, no ! Do not think me ungrateful. Only, you find me a lover, a mother, while you left me merely a wife.   Though it is no longer in my power to love, I know how much I owe you, and I can still offer you all the affection of a daughter."

"Rosine," said the old man in a softened tone, "I no longer feel any resentment against you.   We will forget everything," he added, with one of those smiles which always reflect a noble soul ; "I have not so little delicacy as to demand the mockery of love from a wife who no longer loves me."

The Countess gave him a flashing look full of such deep gratitude that poor Chabert would have been glad to sink again into his grave at Eylau.   Some men have a soul strong enough for such self-devotion, of which the whole reward consists in the assurance that they have made the person they love happy.

" My dear friend, we will talk all this over later when our hearts have rested," said the Countess.

The conversation turned to other subjects, for it was impossible to dwell very long on this one.   Though the couple came back again and again to their singular position, either by some allusion or of serious purpose, they had a delightful drive, recalling the events of their former life together and the times of the Empire.   The Countess knew how to lend peculiar charm to her reminiscences, and gave the conversation the tinge of melancholy that was needed to keep it serious.   She revived his love without awakening his desires, and allowed her first husband to discern the mental wealth she had acquired while trying to accustom him to moderate his pleasure to that which a father may feel in the society of a favorite daughter.

The colonel had known the Countess of the Empire; he found her a Countess of the Restoration.

At last, by a cross-road, they arrived at the entrance to a large park lying in the little valley which divides the heights of Margency from the pretty village of Groslay. The Countess had there a delightful house, where the colonel on arriving found everything in readiness for his stay there, as well as for his wife's. Misfortune is a kind of talisman whose virtue consists in its power to confirm our original nature; in some men it increases their distrust and malignancy, just as it improves the goodness of those who have a kind heart.

Sorrow had made the colonel even more helpful and good than he had always been, and he could understand some secrets of womanly distress which are unrevealed to most men. Nevertheless, in spite of his loyal trustfulness, he could not help saying to his wife:

" Then you felt quite sure you would bring me here?"

"Yes," replied she, " if I found Colonel Chabert in Derville's client."

The appearance of truth she contrived to give to this answer dissipated the slight suspicions which the colonel was ashamed to have felt. For three days the Countess was quite charming to her first husband. By tender attentions and unfailing sweetness she seemed anxious to wipe out the memory of the sufferings he had endured, and to earn forgiveness for the woes which, as she confessed, she had innocently caused him. She delighted in displaying for him the charms she knew he took pleasure in, while at the same time she assumed a kind of melancholy; for men are more especially accessible to certain ways, certain graces of the heart or of the mind which they cannot resist. She aimed at interesting him in her position, and appealing to his feelings so far as to take possession of his mind and control him despotically.

Ready for anything to attain her ends, she did not yet know what she was to do with this man; but at any rate she meant to annihilate him socially. On the evening of the third day she felt that in spite of her efforts she could not conceal her uneasiness as to the results of her manœuvres. To give herself a minute's reprieve she went up to her room, sat down before her writing-table, and laid aside the mask of composure which she wore in Chabert's presence, like an actress who, returning to her dressing-room after a fatiguing fifth act, drops half-dead, leaving with the audience an image of herself which she no longer resembles. She proceeded to finish a letter she had begun to Delbecq, whom she desired to go in her name and demand of Derville the deeds relating to Colonel Chabert, to copy them, and to come to her at once to Groslay. She had hardly finished when she heard the colonel's step in the passage ; uneasy at her absence, he had come to look for her.

"Alas ! " she exclaimed, " I wish I were dead ! My position is intolerable——"

" Why, what is the matter ? " asked the colonel.

" Nothing, nothing ! " she replied.

She rose, left the colonel, and went down to speak privately to her maid, whom she sent off to Paris, impressing on her that she was herself to deliver to Delbecq the letter just written, and to bring it back to the writer as soon as he had read it.   Then the Countess went out to sit on a bench sufficiently in sight for the colonel to join her as soon as he might choose.   The colonel, who was looking for her, hastened up and sat down by her.

" Rosine," said he, " what is the matter with you ? "

She did not answer.

It was one of those glorious, calm evenings in the month of June, whose secret harmonies infuse such sweetness into the sunset.   The air was clear, the stillness perfect, so that far away in the park they could hear the voices of some children, which added a kind of melody to the sublimity of the scene.

" You do not answer me ? " the colonel said to his wife.

" My husband——" said the Countess, who broke off, started a little, and with blush stopped to ask him, " What am I to say when I speak of M. Ferraud ? "

" Call him your husband, my poor child," replied the colonel, in a kind voice. " Is he not the father of your children ? "

" Well, then," she said, "if he should ask what I came here for, if he finds that I came here, alone, with a stranger, what am I to say to him? Listen, monsieur," she went on, assuming a dignified attitude, " decide my fate, I am resigned to anything——"

" My dear," said the colonel, taking possession of his wife's hands, " I have made up my mind to sacrifice myself entirely for your happiness——"

" That is impossible ! " she exclaimed, with a sudden spasmodic movement. " Remember that you would have to renounce your identity, and in an authenticated form."

" What ! " said the colonel. " Is not my word enough for you ? "

The word " authenticated " fell on the old man's heart, and roused involuntary distrust. He looked at his wife in a way that made her color, she cast down her eyes, and he feared that he might find himself compelled to despise her. The Countess was afraid lest she had scared the shy modesty, the stern honesty, of a man whose generous temper and primitive virtues were known to her. Though these feelings had brought the clouds to their brow, they immediately recovered their harmony. This was the way of it. A child's cry was heard in the distance.

" Jules, leave your sister in peace," the Countess called out.

" What, are your children here ? " said Chabert.

" Yes ; but I told them not to trouble you."

The old soldier understood the delicacy, the womanly tact

of so gracious a precaution, and took the Countess' hand to kiss it.

"But let them come," said he.

The little girl ran up to complain of her brother.

"Mamma!"

"Mamma!"

"It was Jules——"

"It was her——"

Their little hands were held out to their mother, and the two childish voices mingled; it was an unexpected and charming picture.

"Poor little things!" cried the Countess, no longer restraining her tears, "I shall have to leave them. To whom will the law assign them? A mother's heart cannot be divided; I want them, I want them."

"Are you making mamma cry?" said Jules, looking fiercely at the colonel.

"Silence, Jules!" said the mother in a decided tone.

The two children stood speechless, examining their mother and the stranger with a curiosity which it is impossible to express in words.

"Oh, yes!" she cried. "If I am separated from the Count, only leave me my children, and I will submit to anything——"

This was the decisive speech which gained all that she had hoped from it.

"Yes," exclaimed the colonel, as if he were ending a sentence already begun in his mind, "I must return underground again. I had told myself so already."

"Can I accept such a sacrifice?" replied his wife. "If some men have died to save a mistress' honor, they gave their life but once. But in this case you would be giving your life every day. No, no. It is impossible. If it were only your life, it would be nothing; but to sign a declaration that you are not Colonel Chabert, to acknowledge yourself an impostor, to sacrifice your honor, and live a lie every hour of the day! Human devotion cannot go so far. Only think! No. But for my poor children I would have fled with you by this time to the other end of the world."

"But," said Chabert, "can I not live here in your little lodge as one of your relations! I am as worn out as a cracked cannon ; I want nothing but a little tobacco and the *Constitutionnel.*"

The Countess melted into tears. There was a contest of generosity between the Comtesse Ferraud and Colonel Chabert, and the soldier came out victorious. One evening, seeing this mother with her children, the soldier was bewitched by the touching grace of a family picture in the country, in the shade and the silence ; he made a resolution to remain dead, and, frightened no longer at the authentication of a deed, he asked what he was to do to secure beyond all risk the happiness of this family.

"Do exactly as you like," said the Countess. "I declare to you that I will have nothing to do with this affair. I ought not."

Delbecq had arrived some days before, and, in obedience to the Countess' verbal instructions, the intendant had succeeded in gaining the old soldier's confidence. So on the following morning Colonel Chabert went with the erewhile attorney to Saint-Leu-Taverny, where Delbecq had caused the attorney to draw up an affidavit in such terms that, after hearing it read, the colonel started up and walked out of the office.

"Turf and thunder! What a fool you must think me! Why, I should make myself out a swindler!" he exclaimed.

"Indeed, monsieur," said Delbecq, "I should advise you not to sign in haste. In your place I would get at least thirty thousand francs a year out of the bargain. Madame would pay them."

After annihilating this scoundrel *emeritus* by the lightning look of an honest man insulted, the colonel rushed off, carried away by a thousand contrary emotions. He was suspicious, indignant, and calm again by turns.

Finally he made his way back into the park of Groslay by a gap in the fence, and slowly walked on to sit down and rest, and meditate at his ease, in a little room under a gazebo, from which the road to Saint-Leu could be seen. The path being strewn with the yellowish sand which is used instead of river-gravel, the Countess, who was sitting in the upper room of this little summer-house, did not hear the colonel's approach, for she was too much preoccupied with the success of her business to pay the smallest attention to the slight noise made by her husband. Nor did the old man notice that his wife was in the room over him.

"Well, Monsieur Delbecq, has he signed?" the Countess asked her secretary, whom she saw alone on the road beyond the hedge of a haha.

"No, madame. I do not even know what has become of our man. The old horse reared."

"Then we shall be obliged to put him into Charenton," said she, "since we have gotten him."

The colonel, who recovered the elasticity of youth to leap the haha, in the twinkling of an eye was standing in front of Delbecq, on whom he bestowed the two finest slaps that ever a scoundrel's cheeks received.

"And you may add that old horses can also kick!" the colonel added.

His rage spent, the colonel no longer felt vigorous enough to leap the ditch. He had seen the truth in all its nakedness. The Countess' speech and Delbecq's reply had revealed the conspiracy of which he was to be the victim. The care taken of him was but a bait to entrap him in a snare. That speech was like a drop of subtle poison, bringing on in the old soldier a return of all his sufferings, physical and moral. He came back to the summer-house through the park gate, walking slowly like a broken man.

Then for him there was to be neither peace nor truce! From this moment he must begin the odious warfare with this woman of which Derville had spoken, enter on a life of litigation, feed on gall, drink every morning of the cup of bitterness. And then—fearful thought! where was he to find the money needful to pay the cost of the first proceedings? He felt such disgust of life, that if there had been any water at hand he would have thrown himself into it; that if he had had a pistol, he would have blown out his brains. Then he relapsed into the indecision of mind which, since his conversation with Derville at the dairyman's, had changed his character.

At last, having reached the kiosque, he went up to the gazebo, where little rose-windows afforded a view over each lovely landscape of the valley, and where he found his wife seated on a chair. The Countess was gazing at the distance, and preserved a calm countenance, showing that impenetrable face which women can assume when resolved to do their worst. She wiped her eyes as if she had been weeping, and played absently with the pink ribbons of her sash. Nevertheless, in spite of her apparent assurance, she could not help shuddering slightly when she saw before her her venerable benefactor, standing with folded arms, his face pale, his brow stern.

"Madame," he said, after gazing at her fixedly for a moment and compelling her to blush, "Madame, I do not curse you, I scorn you. I can now thank the chance that has divided us. I do not feel even a desire for revenge; I no longer love you. I want nothing from you. Live in peace on the strength of my word; it is worth more than the scrawl of all the notaries in Paris. I will never assert my claim to the name I perhaps have made illustrious. I am henceforth but a poor devil named Hyacinthe, who asks no more than his share of the sunshine. Farewell!"

The Countess threw herself at his feet; she would have

detained him by taking his hands, but he pushed her away with disgust, saying—

" Do not touch me ! "

The Countess' expression when she heard her husband's retreating steps is quite indescribable. Then, with the deep perspicacity given only by utter villainy, or by fierce worldly selfishness, she knew that she might live in peace on the word and the contempt of this loyal veteran.

Chabert, in fact, disappeared. The dairyman failed in business, and became a hackney-cab driver. The colonel, perhaps, took up some similar industry for a time. Perhaps, like a stone flung into a chasm, he went falling from ledge to ledge, to be lost in the mire of rags that seethes through the streets of Paris.

Six months after this event, Derville, hearing no more of Colonel Chabert or the Comtesse Ferraud, supposed that they had no doubt come to a compromise, which the Countess, out of revenge, had had arranged by some other lawyer. So one morning he added up the sums he had advanced to the said Chabert with the costs, and begged the Comtesse Ferraud to claim from M. le Comte Chabert the amount of the bill, assuming that she would know where to find her first husband.

The very next day Comte Ferraud's man of business, lately appointed president of the county court in a town of some importance, wrote this distressing note to Derville :

" MONSIEUR :—Madame la Comtesse Ferraud desires me to inform you that your client took complete advantage of your confidence, and that the individual calling himself Comte Chabert has acknowledged that he came forward under false pretenses. Yours, etc.,   DELBECQ."

" One comes across people who are, on my honor, too stupid by half," cried Derville. " They don't deserve to be Christians ! Be humane, generous, philanthropical, and a lawyer, and you are bound to be cheated! There is a piece of business that will cost me two thousand-franc notes!"

Some time after receiving this letter, Derville went to the Palais de Justice in search of a pleader to whom he wished to speak, and who was employed in the police court. As chance would have it, Derville went into court number 6 at the moment when the presiding magistrate was sentencing one Hyacinthe to two months' imprisonment as a vagabond, and subsequently to be taken to the Mendicity House of Detention, a sentence which, by magistrate's law, is equivalent to perpetual imprisonment. On hearing the name of Hyacinthe, Derville looked at the delinquent, sitting between two *gendarmes* on the bench for the accused, and recognized in the condemned man his false Colonel Chabert.

The old soldier was placid, motionless, almost absent-minded. In spite of his rags, in spite of the misery stamped on his countenance, it gave evidence of noble pride. His eye had a stoical expression which no magistrate ought to have misunderstood; but as soon as a man has fallen into the hands of justice, he is no more than a moral entity, a matter of law or of fact, just as to statists he has become a zero.

When the veteran was taken back to the lock-up, to be removed later with the batch of vagabonds at that moment at the bar, Derville availed himself of the privilege accorded to lawyers of going wherever they please in the courts, and followed him to the lock-up, where he stood scrutinizing him for some minutes, as well as the curious crew of beggars among whom he found himself. The passage to the lock-up at that moment afforded one of those spectacles which, unfortunately, neither legislators, nor philanthropists, nor painters, nor writers come to study. Like all the laboratories of the law, this anteroom is a dark and malodorous place; along the walls runs a wooden seat, blackened by the constant presence there of the wretches who come to this meeting-place of every form of social squalor, where not one of them is missing.

A poet might say that the day was ashamed to light up this dreadful sewer through which so much misery flows! There is not a spot on that plank where some crime has not sat, in embryo or matured; not a corner where a man has never stood who, driven to despair by the blight which justice has set upon him after his first fault, has not there begun a career, at the end of which looms the guillotine or the pistol-snap of the suicide. All who fall on the pavement of Paris rebound against these yellow-gray walls, on which a philanthropist, who was not a speculator, might read a justification of the numerous suicides complained of by hypocritical writers who are incapable of taking a step to prevent them—for that justification is written in that anteroom, like a preface to the dramas of the morgue, or to those enacted on the Place de la Grève.

At this moment Colonel Chabert was sitting among these men—men with coarse faces, clothed in the horrible livery of misery, and silent at intervals, or talking in a low tone, for three gendarmes on duty paced to and fro, their sabres clattering on the floor.

"Do you recognize me?" said Derville to the old man, standing in front of him.

"Yes, sir," said Chabert, rising.

"If you are an honest man," Derville went on in an undertone, "how could you remain in my debt?"

The old soldier blushed as a young girl might when accused by her mother of a clandestine love affair.

"What! Madame Ferraud has not paid you?" cried he in a loud voice.

"Paid me?" said Derville. "She wrote to me that you were a swindler."

The colonel cast up his eyes in a sublime impulse of horror and imprecation, as if to call heaven to witness to this fresh subterfuge.

"Monsieur," said he, in a voice that was calm by sheer

huskiness, "get the gendarmes to allow me to go into the lock-up, and I will sign an order which will certainly be honored."

At a word from Derville to the sergeant he was allowed to take his client into the room, where Hyacinthe wrote a few lines, and addressed them to the Comtesse Ferraud.

"Send her that," said the soldier, "and you will be paid your costs and the money you advanced. Believe me, monsieur, if I have not shown you the gratitude I owe you for your kind offices, it is not the less there," and he laid his hand on his heart. "Yes, it is there, deep and sincere. But what can the unfortunate do? They live, and that is all."

"What!" said Derville. "Did you not stipulate for an allowance?"

"Do not speak of it!" cried the old man. "You cannot conceive how deep my contempt is for the outside life to which most men cling. I was suddenly attacked by a sickness—disgust of humanity. When I think that Napoleon is at Saint Helena, everything on earth is a matter of indifference to me. I can no longer be a soldier; that is my only real grief. After all," he added with a gesture of childish simplicity, "it is better to enjoy luxury of feeling than of dress. For my part, I fear nobody's contempt."

And the colonel sat down on his bench again.

Derville went away. On returning to his office, he sent Godeschal, at that time his second clerk, to the Comtesse Ferraud, who, on reading the note, at once paid the sum due to Comte Chabert's lawyer.

In 1840, towards the end of June, Godeschal, now himself an attorney, went to Ris with Derville, to whom he had succeeded. When they reached the avenue leading from the high-road to Bicêtre, they saw, under one of the elm-trees by the wayside, one of those old, broken, and hoary paupers who have earned the marshal's staff among beggars by living on at

Bicêtre as poor women live on at La Salpêtrière. This man, one of the two thousand poor creatures who are lodged in the infirmary for the aged, was seated on a corner-stone, and seemed to have concentrated all his intelligence on an operation well known to these pensioners, which consists in drying their snuffy pocket-handkerchiefs in the sun, perhaps to save washing them. This old man had an attractive countenance. He was dressed in the reddish cloth wrapper-coat which the workhouse affords to its inmates, a sort of horrible livery.

"I say, Derville," said Godeschal to his traveling companion, "look at that old fellow. Isn't he like those grotesque carved figures we get from Germany? And it is alive, perhaps it is happy."

Derville looked at the poor man through his eyeglass, and with a little exclamation of surprise he said :

"That old man, my dear fellow, is a whole poem, or, as the romantics say, a drama. Did you ever meet the Comtesse Ferraud ? "

" Yes ; she is a clever woman, and agreeable ; but rather too pious," said Godeschal.

" That old Bicêtre pauper is her lawful husband, Comte Chabert, the old colonel. She has had him sent here, no doubt. And if he is in this workhouse instead of living in a mansion, it is solely because he reminded the pretty Countess that he had taken her, like a hackney cab, on the street. I can remember now the tiger's glare she shot at him at that moment."

This opening having excited Godeschal's curiosity, Derville related the story here told.

Two days later, on Monday morning, as they returned to Paris, the two friends looked again at Bicêtre, and Derville proposed that they should call on Colonel Chabert. Halfway up the avenue they found the old man sitting on the trunk of a felled tree.

"Good-morning, Colonel Chabert," said Derville.

"Not Chabert! not Chabert! My name is Hyacinthe," replied the veteran. "I am no longer a man, I am No. 164, Room 7," he added, looking at Derville with timid anxiety, the fear of an old man and a child. "Are you going to visit the man condemned to death?" he asked after a moment's silence. "He is not married! He is very lucky!"

"Poor fellow" said Godeschal. "Would you like something to buy snuff?"

With all the simplicity of a street Arab, the colonel eagerly held out his hand to the two strangers, who each gave him a twenty-franc piece; he thanked them with a puzzled look, saying:

"Brave troopers!"

He ported arms, pretended to take aim at them, and shouted with a smile:

"Fire! both arms! *Vive Napoléon!*" And he drew a flourish in the air with his stick.

"The nature of his wound has no doubt made him childish," said Derville.

"Childish! he?" said another old pauper, who was looking on. "Why, there are days when you had better not tread on his corns. He is an old rogue, full of philosophy and imagination. But to-day, what can you expect! He has had his Monday treat. He was here, monsieur, so long ago as 1820. At that time a Prussian officer, whose chaise was crawling up the hill of Villejuif, came by on foot. We two were together, Hyacinthe and I, by the roadside. The officer, as he walked, was talking to another, a Russian, or some animal of the same species, and when the Prussian saw the old boy, just to make fun, he said to him, 'Here is an old cavalry man who must have been at Rossbach.' 'I was too young to be there,' said Hyacinthe. 'But I was at Jena.' And the Prussian made off pretty quick, without asking any more questions."

"What a destiny!" exclaimed Derville. "Taken out of

20

the Foundling Hospital to die in the Infirmary for the Aged, after helping Napoleon between whiles to conquer Egypt and· Europe. Do you know, my dear fellow," Derville went on after a pause, "there are in modern society three men who can never think well of the world—the priest, the doctor, and the man of law? And they wear black robes, perhaps because they are in mourning for every virtue and every illusion. The most hapless of the three is the lawyer. When a man comes in search of the priest, he is prompted by repentance, by remorse, by beliefs which make him interesting, which elevate him and comfort the soul of the intercessor whose task will bring him a sort of gladness; he purifies, repairs, and reconciles. But we lawyers, we see the same evil feelings repeated again and again, nothing can correct them; our offices are sewers which can never be cleansed.

"How many things have I learned in the excercise of my profession! I have seen a father die in a garret, deserted by two daughters, to whom he had given forty thousand francs a year! I have known wills burnt; I have seen mothers robbing their children, wives killing their husbands, and working on the love they could inspire to make the men idiotic or mad, that they might live in peace with a lover. I have seen women teaching the child of their marriage such tastes as must bring it to the grave in order to benefit the child of an illicit affection. I could not tell you all that I have seen, for I have seen crimes against which justice is impotent. In short, all the horrors that romancers suppose they have invented are still below the truth. You will know something of these pretty things; as for me, I am going to live in the country with my wife. I have a horror of Paris."

"I have seen plenty of them already in Desroches' office," replied Godeschal.

Paris, *February–March,* 1832.

THE VENDETTA.

Dedicated to Puttinati, Sculptor at Milan.

In the year 1800, towards the end of October, a stranger, having with him a woman and a little girl, made his appearance in front of the Tuileries Palace, and stood for some little time close to the ruins of a house, then recently pulled down, on the spot where the wing is still unfinished which was intended to join Catherine de Medici's Palace to the Louvre built by the Valois. There he stood, his arms folded, his head bent, raising it now and again to look at the Consul's Palace, or at his wife, who sat on a stone by his side.

Though the stranger seemed to think only of the little girl of nine or ten, whose black hair was a plaything in his fingers, the woman lost none of the glances shot at her by her companion. A common feeling, other than love, united these two beings, and a common thought animated their thoughts and their actions. Misery is perhaps the strongest of all bonds.

The man had one of those broad, solemn-looking heads, with a mass of hair, of which so many examples have been perpetuated by the Carracci. Among the thick black locks were many white hairs. His features, though fine and proud, had a set hardness which spoiled them. In spite of his powerful and upright frame, he seemed to be more than sixty years of age. His clothes, which were dilapidated, betrayed his foreign origin.

The woman's face, formerly handsome, but now faded, bore a stamp of deep melancholy, though, when her husband looked at her, she forced herself to smile, and affected a calm expression. The little girl was standing, in spite of the fatigue that was written on her small sunburnt face. She had Italian features, large black eyes under well-arched eyebrows, a native dignity and genuine grace. More than one passer-by was touched by the mere sight of this group, for the persons composing it made no effort to disguise a despair evidently as deep as the expression of it was simple ; but the spring of the transient kindliness which distinguishes the Parisian is quickly dried up. As soon as the stranger perceived that he was the object of some idler's attention, he stared at him so fiercely that the most intrepid lounger hastened his step, as though he had trodden on a viper.

After remaining there a long time undecided, the tall man suddenly passed his hand across his brow, driving away, so to speak, the thoughts that had furrowed it with wrinkles, and made up his mind no doubt to some desperate determination. Casting a piercing look at his wife and daughter, he drew out of his jerkin a long dagger, held it out to the woman, and said in Italian, " I am going to see whether the Bonapartes remember us."

He walked on, with a slow, confident step, towards the entrance to the palace, where, of course, he was checked by a soldier on guard, with whom there could be no long discussion. Seeing that the stranger was obstinate, the sentry pointed his bayonet at him by way of *ultimatum.* As chance would have it at this moment, a squad came round to relieve guard, and the corporal very civilly informed the stranger where he might find the captain of the guard.

" Let Bonaparte know that Bartolomeo di Piombo wants to see him," said the Italian to the officer.

In vain did the captain explain to Bartolomeo that it was not possible to see the First Consul without having written to him beforehand to request an audience. The stranger insisted that the officer should go to inform Bonaparte. The captain urged the rules of his duty, and formally refused to yield to the demands of this strange petitioner. Bartolomeo knit his brows, looked at the captain with a terrible scowl, and seemed to make him responsible for all the disasters his refusal might occasion ; then he remained silent, his arms tightly crossed on his breast, and took his stand under the archway which connects the garden and the courtyard of the Tuileries.

People who are thoroughly bent on anything are almost always well served by chance. At the moment when Bartolomeo sat down on one of the curb-stones near the entrance to the palace, a carriage drove up, and out of it stepped Lucien Bonaparte, at that time minister of the interior.

"Ah ! Lucien, good luek for me to have met you ! " cried the stranger.

These words, spoken in the Corsican dialect, made Lucien stop at the instant when he was rushing into the vestibule ; he looked at his fellow-countryman, and recognized him. At the first word that Bartolomeo said in his ear, he took him with him. Murat, Lannes, and Rapp were in the First Consul's Cabinet. On seeing Lucien come in with so strange a figure as was Piombo, the conversation ceased. Lucien took his brother's hand and led him into a window recess. After exchanging a few words, the First Consul raised his hand with a gesture, which Murat and Lannes obeyed by retiring. Rapp affected not to have seen it, and remained. Then, Bonaparte having sharply called him to order, the aide-de-camp went out with a sour face. The First Consul, who heard the sound of Rapp's steps in the neighboring room, hastily followed him, and saw him close to the wall between the cabinet and the anteroom.

"You refuse to understand me ? " said the First Consul. " I wish to be alone with my countryman."

"A Corsican ! " retorted the aide-de-camp. " I distrust those creatures too much not to——"

The First Consul could not help smiling, and lightly pushed his faithful officer by the shoulders.

"Well, and what are you doing here, my poor Bartolomeo ? " said the First Consul to Piombo.

" I have come to ask for shelter and protection, if you are a true Corsican," replied Bartolomeo in a rough tone.

" What misfortune has driven you from your native land? You were the richest, the most——"

" I have killed all the Porta," replied the Corsican, in a hollow voice, with a frown.

The First Consul drew back a step or two, like a man astonished.

" Are you going to betray me? ". cried Bartolomeo, with a gloomy look at Bonaparte. " Do you forget that there are still four of the Piombo in Corsica ? "

Lucien took his fellow-countryman by the arm and shook him.

" Do you come here to threaten the savior of France ? " he said vehemently.

Bonaparte made a sign to Lucien, who was silent. Then he looked at Piombo, and said, " And why did you kill all the Porta ? "

" We had made friends," he replied ; " the Barbanti had reconciled us. The day after we had drunk together to drown our quarrel I left, because I had business at Bastia. They stayed at my place, and set fire to my vineyard at Longone. They killed my son Gregorio; my daughter Ginevra and my wife escaped ; they had taken the communion that morning; the Virgin protected them. When I got home I could no longer see my house ; I searched for it with my feet in the ashes. Suddenly I came across Gregorio's body ; I recognized it in the moonlight. ' Oh, the Porta have played this trick ! ' said I to myself. I went off at once into the scrub ; I got together a few men to whom I had done some service— do you hear, Bonaparte ?—and we marched down on the Porta's vineyard. We arrived at five in the morning, and by seven they were all in the presence of God. Giacomo declares that Elisa Vanni saved a child, little Luigi ; but I tied him into bed with my own hands before setting the house on

LUCIEN TOOK HIS FELLOW-COUNTRYMAN BY THE ARM.

fire. Then I quitted the island with my wife and daughter without being able to make sure whether Luigi Porta was still alive."

Bonaparte looked at Bartolomeo with curiosity, but no astonishment.

" How many were they?" asked Lucien.

" Seven," replied Piombo. "They persecuted you in their day," he added. The words aroused no signs of hatred in the two brothers. "Ah ! you are no longer Corsicans !" cried Bartolomeo, with a sort of despair. "Good-by. Formerly I protected you," he went on reproachfully. "But for me your mother would never have reached Marseilles," he said, turning to Bonaparte, who stood thoughtful, his elbow resting on the chimney-piece.

" I cannot in conscience take you under my wing, Piombo," replied Napoleon. "I am the head of a great nation ; I govern the Republic ; I must see that the laws are carried out."

"Ah, ha!" said Bartolomeo.

"But I can shut my eyes," Bonaparte went on. "The tradition of the Vendetta will hinder the reign of law in Corsica for a long time yet," he added, talking to himself. "But it must be stamped out at any cost."

He was silent for a minute, and Lucien signed to Piombo to say nothing. The Corsican shook his head from side to side with a disapproving look.

" Remain here," the First Consul said, addressing Bartolomeo. "We know nothing. I will see that your estates are purchased so as to give you at once the means of living. Then later, some time hence, we will remember you. But no more Vendetta. There is no Maquis scrub here. If you play tricks with your dagger, there is no hope for you. Here the law protects everybody, and we do not do justice on our own account."

" He has put himself at the head of a strange people,"

replied Bartolomeo, taking Lucien's hand and pressing it. "But you recognize me in misfortune; it is a bond between us for life and death; and you may command every one named Piombo." As he spoke his brow cleared, and he looked about him approvingly.

"You are not badly off here," he said, with a smile, as if he would like to lodge there. "And you are dressed all in red like a cardinal."

"It rests with you to rise and have a palace in Paris," said Bonaparte, looking at him from head to foot. "It may often happen that I must look about me for a devoted friend to whom I can trust myself."

A sigh of gladness broke from Piombo's deep chest; he held out his hand to the First Consul, saying, "There is something of the Corsican in you still!"

Bonaparte smiled. He gazed in silence at this man, who had brought him as it were a breath of air from his native land, from the island where he had formerly been so miraculously saved from the hatred of the "English party," and which he was fated never to see again. He made a sign to his brother, who led away Bartolomeo di Piombo.

Lucien inquired with interest as to the pecuniary position of the man who had once protected his family. Piombo led the minister of the interior to a window and showed him his wife and Ginevra, both seated on a heap of stones, awaiting his return.

"We have come from Fontainebleau on foot," said he, "and we have not a sou."

Lucien gave his fellow-countryman his purse, and desired him to come again next morning to consult as to the means of providing for his family. The income from all Piombo's possessions in Corsica could hardly suffice to maintain him respectably in Paris.

Fifteen years elapsed between the arrival of the Piombo

family in Paris and the following incidents, which, without
the story of this event, would have been less intelligible.

Servin, one of our most distinguished artists, was the first
to conceive the idea of opening a studio for young ladies who
may wish to take lessons in painting. He was a man of over
forty, of blameless habits, and wholly given up to his art ;
and he had married for love the daughter of a general without any fortune. At first mothers brought their daughters
themselves to the professor's studio ; but when they understood his high principles and appreciated the care by which
he strove to deserve such confidence, they ended by sending
the girls alone. It was part of the painter's scheme to take as
pupils only young ladies of rich or highly respectable family,
that no difficulties might arise as to the society in his studio ;
he had even refused to take young girls who intended to
become artists, and who must necessarily have had certain
kinds of training without which no mastery is possible. By
degrees his prudence, the superior method by which he initi-
ated his pupils into the secrets of his art, as well as the
security their mothers felt in knowing that their daughters
were in the company of well-bred girls, and in the artist's
character, manners, and marriage, won him a high reputation
in the world of fashion. As soon as a young girl showed any
desire to learn drawing or painting, and her mother asked
advice, "Send her to Servin," was always the answer.

Thus Servin had a specialty for teaching ladies art, as Her-
bault had for bonnets, Leroy for dresses, and Chevet for
dainties. It was acknowledged that a young woman who had
taken lessons of Servin could pronounce definitely on the
pictures in the Louvre, paint a portrait in a superior manner,
copy an old picture, and produce her own painting of genre.
Thus this artist sufficed for all the requirements of the aristocracy.

Notwithstanding his connection with all the best houses
in Paris, he was independent and patriotic, preserving with

all alike the light and witty tone, sometimes ironical, and the freedom of opinion which characterize painters.

He had carried his scrupulous precautions into the arrangement of the place where his scholars worked. The outer entrance to the loft above his dwelling-rooms had been walled up; to get into this retreat, as sacred as a harem, the way was up a staircase in the centre of the house. This studio, which occupied the whole of the top story, was on the vast scale which always surprises inquisitive strangers when, having climbed to sixty feet above the ground, they expect to find an artist lodged in the gutter. It was a kind of gallery, abundantly lighted by immense skylights screened with the large green blinds which artists use to distribute the light. A quantity of caricatures, heads sketched in outline with a brush or the point of a palette knife, all over the dark gray walls, proved that, allowing for a difference in the expression, fine young ladies have as much whimsicality in their brain as men can have. A small stove, with a huge pipe that made amazing zigzags before reaching the upper region of the roof, was the inevitable decoration of this studio. There was a shelf all round the room, supporting plaster casts which lay there in confusion, most of them under a coating of whitish dust.

Above this shelf here and there a head of Niobe hanging to a nail showed its pathetic bend, a Venus smiled, a hand was unexpectedly thrust out before your eyes, like a beggar asking alms; then there were anatomical *écorchés*, yellow with smoke, and looking like limbs snatched from coffins; and pictures, drawings, lay figures, frames without canvas, and canvasses without frames, completed the effect, giving the room the characteristic aspect of a studio, a singular mixture of ornamentation and bareness, of poverty and splendor, of care and neglect.

This huge sort of hold, in which everything, even man,

looks small, has a behind-the-scenes flavor; here are to be
seen old linen, gilt armor, odds and ends of stuffs, and some
machinery. But there is something about it as grand as
thought: genius and death are there; Diana and Apollo
side by side with a skull or a skeleton; beauty and disorder,
poetry and reality, gorgeous coloring in shadow, and often
a whole drama, but motionless and silent. How symbol-
ical of the artist brain!

At the moment when my story begins the bright sun of
July lighted up the studio, and two beams of sunshine shot
across its depths, broad bands of diaphanous gold in which
the dust-motes glistened. A dozen easels raised their pointed
spars, looking like the masts of vessels in a harbor. Several young girls gave life to the scene by the variety of
their countenances and attitudes, and the difference in their
dress. The strong shadows cast by the green baize blinds,
arranged to suit the position of each easel, produced a multitude of contrasts and fascinating effects of chiaro-oscuro.

This group of girls formed the most attractive picture in
the gallery. A fair-haired girl, simply dressed, stood at some
distance from her companions, working perseveringly and
seeming to foresee misfortune; no one looked at her nor spoke
to her; she was the prettiest, the most modest, and the least
rich. Two principal groups, divided by a little space, represented two classes of society, two spirits, even in this studio,
where rank and fortune ought to have been forgotten.

These young things, sitting or standing, surrounded by their
paint-boxes, playing with their brushes or getting them ready,
handling their bright-tinted palettes, painting, chattering,
laughing, singing, given up to their natural impulses and revealing their true characters, made up a drama unknown to men;
this one proud, haughty, capricious, with black hair and beautiful hands, flashed the fire of her eyes at random; that one light-
hearted and heedless, a smile on her lips, her hair chestnut,
with delicate white hands, virginal and French, a light nature

without a thought of evil, living from hour to hour; another, dreamy, melancholy, pale, her head drooping like a falling blossom; her neighbor, on the contrary, tall, indolent, with Oriental manners, and long, black, melting eyes, speaking little but lost in thought, and stealing a look at the head of Antinous.

In the midst, like the *Jocoso* of a Spanish comedy, a girl, full of wit and sparkling sallies, stood watching them all with a single glance, and making them laugh; raising a face so full of life that it could not but be pretty. She was the leader of the first group of pupils, consisting of the daughters of bankers, lawyers, and merchants—all rich, but exposed to all the minute but stinging disdains freely poured out upon them by the other young girls who belonged to the aristocracy. These were governed by the daughter of a gentleman usher to the King's private chamber, a vain little thing, as silly as she was vain, and proud of her father having an office at court. She aimed at seeming to understand the master's remarks at the first word, and appearing to work by inspired grace; she used an eyeglass, came very much dressed, very late, and begged her companions not to talk loud. Among this second group might be observed some exquisite shapes and distinguished-looking faces; but their looks expressed but little simplicity. Though their attitudes were elegant and their movements graceful, their faces were lacking in candor, and it was easy to perceive that they belonged to a world where politeness forms the character at an early age, and the abuse of social pleasures kills the feelings and develops selfishness. When the whole party of girl students was complete there were to be seen among them child-like heads, virgin heads of enchanting purity, faces where the parted lips showed virgin teeth, and where a virgin smile came and went. Then the studio suggested not a seraglio, but a group of angels sitting on a cloud in heaven.

It was near noon; Servin had not yet made his appearance.

For some days past he had spent most of his time at a studio he had elsewhere, finishing a picture he had there for the exhibition. Suddenly Mademoiselle Amélie Thirion, the head of the aristocrats in this little assembly, spoke at some length to her neighbor; there was profound silence among the patrician group; the banker faction was equally silent from astonishment, and tried to guess the subject of such a conference. But the secret of the young *ultras* was soon known. Amélie rose, took an easel that stood near her, and moved it to some distance from the "nobility," close to a clumsy partition which divided the studio from a dark closet where broken casts were kept, paintings that the professor had condemned, and, in winter, the firewood. Amélie's proceedings gave rise to a murmur of surprise which did not hinder her from completing the removal by wheeling up to the easel a stool and paint-box, in fact, everything, even a picture by Prudhon, of which a pupil, who had not yet come, was making a copy. After this *coup d'état* the party of the right painted on in silence; but the left talked it over at great length, each one freely expressing themselves against the wisdom of such an act.

"What will Mademoiselle Piombo say?" asked one of the girls of Mademoiselle Mathilde Roguin, the oracle of mischief of her group.

"She is not a girl to say much," was the reply. "But fifty years hence she will remember this insult as if she had experienced it the day before, and will find some cruel means of revenge. She is a person I should not like to be at war with."

"The proscription to which those ladies have condemned her is all the more unjust," said another young girl, "because Mademoiselle Ginevra was very sad the day before yesterday; her father, they say, has just given up his appointment. This will add to her troubles, while she was very good to those young ladies during the Hundred Days. Did she ever say a word that could hurt them? On the contrary, she avoided talking politics. But our *ultras* seem to be prompted by jealousy rather than by party spirit."

" I have a great mind to fetch Mademoiselle Piombo's easel and place it by mine," said Mathilde Roguin. She rose, but on second thoughts she sat down again. " With a spirit like Mademoiselle Ginevra's," said she, " it is impossible to know how she would take our civility. Let us wait and see," and she resumed her work at the easel.

" *Eccola!* " said the black-eyed girl languidly. In fact, the sound of footsteps coming upstairs was heard in the studio. The words, " Here she comes !" passed from mouth to mouth, and then perfect silence fell.

To understand the full importance of the ostracism carried into effect by Amélie Thirion, it must be told that this scene took place towards the end of the month of July, 1815. The second restoration of the Bourbons broke up many friendships which had weathered the turmoil of the first. At this time families, almost always divided among themselves, renewed many of the most deplorable scenes which tarnish the history of all countries at periods of civil or religious struggles. Children, young girls, old men, had caught the monarchical fever from which the government was suffering. Discord flew in under the domestic roof, and suspicion dyed in gloomy hues the most intimate conversations and actions.

Ginevra di Piombo idolized Napoleon; indeed, how could she have hated him ? The Emperor was her fellow-countryman, and her father's benefactor. Baron di Piombo was one of Napoleon's followers who had most efficiently worked to bring him back from Elba. Incapable of renouncing his political faith, nay, eager to proclaim it, Piombo had remained in Paris in the midst of enemies. Hence Ginevra di Piombo was ranked with the " suspicious characters," all the more so because she made no secret of the regret her family felt at the second restoration. The only tears she had perhaps ever shed in her life were wrung from her by the twofold tidings of Bonaparte's surrender on board the *Bellerophon* and the arrest of Labédoyère.

The young ladies forming the aristocratic party in the studio belonged to the most enthusiastically Royalist families of Paris. It would be difficult to give any idea of the exaggerated feelings of the time, and of the horror felt towards Bonapartists. However mean and trivial Amélie Thirion's conduct may seem to-day, it was then a very natural demonstration of hatred. Ginevra di Piombo, one of Servin's earliest pupils, had occupied the place of which they wished to deprive her ever since the first day she had come to the studio. The aristocratic group had gradually settled round her; and to turn her out of a place, which in a certain sense belonged to her, was not merely to insult her, but to cause her some pain, for all artists have a predilection for the spot where they work.

However, political hostility had perhaps not much to do with the conduct of this little studio party of the right. Ginevra di Piombo, the most accomplished of Servin's pupils, was an object of the deepest jealousy. The master professed an equal admiration for the talents and the character of this favorite pupil, who served as the standard of all his comparisons; and, indeed, while it was impossible to explain the ascendency this young girl exercised over all who were about her, she enjoyed in this small world an influence resembling that of Bonaparte over his soldiers. The aristocratic clique had, some days since, resolved on the overthrow of this queen; but as no one had been bold enough to repulse the Bonapartists, Mademoiselle Thirion had just struck the decisive blow so as to make her companions the accomplices of her hatred. Though Ginevra was really beloved by some of the Royalist party, who at home were abundantly lectured on politics, with the tact peculiar to women, they judged it best not to interfere in the quarrel.

On entering, Ginevra was received in perfect silence. Of all the girls who had yet appeared at Servin's studio, she was

the handsomest, the tallest, and the most finely made.   Her
gait had a stamp of dignity and grace which commanded
respect.   Her face, full of intelligence, seemed radiant, it
was so transfused with the animation peculiar to Corsicans,
which does not exclude calmness.   Her abundant hair, her
eyes, and their black lashes told of passion.   Though the
corners of her mouth were softly drawn and her lips a little
too thick, they had the kindly expression which strong people
derive from the consciousness of strength.   By a singular
freak of nature the charm of her features was in some sort
belied by a marble forehead stamped with an almost savage
pride, and the traditional habits of Corsica.   That was the
only bond between her and her native land; in every other
detail of her person the simplicity and freedom of Lombard
beauties were so bewitching, that only in her absence could
any one bear to cause her the smallest pain.   She was, indeed,
so attractive, that her old father, out of prudence, never
allowed her to walk alone to the studio.

The only fault of this really poetic creature came of the
very power of such fully developed beauty.   She had refused
to marry, out of affection for her father and mother, feeling
herself necessary to them in their old age.   Her taste for
painting had taken the place of the passions which commonly
agitate women.

"You are all very silent to-day," she said, after coming
forward a step or two.   "Good-morning, my little Laure,"
she added in a gentle, caressing tone, as she went up to
the young girl who was painting apart from the rest.   "That
head is very good.   The flesh is a little too pink, but it is all
capitally drawn."

Laure raised her head, looked at Ginevra much touched,
and their faces brightened with an expression of mutual affection.   A faint smile gave life to the Italian's lips, but she
seemed pensive, and went slowly to her place, carelessly glanc-
ing at the drawings and pictures, and saying good-morning to

each of the girls of the first group, without observing the unusual curiosity excited by her presence. She might have been a queen amid her court. She did not observe the deep silence that reigned among the aristocrats, and passed their camp without saying a word. Her absence of mind was so complete that she went to her easel, opened her paint-box, took out her brushes, slipped on her brown linen cuffs, tied her apron, examined her palette, all without thinking, as it seemed, of what she was doing. All the heads of the humbler group were turned to look at her. And if the young ladies of the Thirion faction were less frankly impatient than their companions, their side glances were nevertheless directed to Ginevra.

"She notices nothing," said Mademoiselle Roguin.

At this moment Ginevra, roused from the meditative attitude in which she had gazed at her canvas, turned her head towards the aristocratic party. With one glance she measured the distance that lay between them, and held her peace.

"It has not occurred to her that they meant to insult her," said Mathilde. "She has neither colored nor turned pale. How provoked those young ladies will be if she likes her new place better than the old one! You are quite apart there, mademoiselle," she added louder, and addressing Ginevra.

The Italian girl affected not to hear, or perhaps she did not hear; she hastily rose, walked rather slowly along the partition which divided the dark closet from the studio, seeming to examine the skylight from which the light fell; and to this she ascribed so much importance that she got upon a chair to fasten the green baize which interfered with the light, a good deal higher. At this elevation she was on a level with a small crack in the boarding, the real object of her efforts, for the look she cast through it can only be compared with that of a miser discovering Aladdin's treasure. She quickly descended, came back to her place, arranged her picture, affected still to be dissatisfied with the light, pushed a table

21

close to the partition, and placed a chair on it; then she nimbly mounted this scaffolding, and again peeped through the crack. She gave but one look into the closet, which was lighted by a window at the top of the partition, but what she saw impressed her so vividly that she started.

"You will fall, Mademoiselle Ginevra!" cried Laure.

All the girls turned to look at their imprudent companion, who was tottering. The fear of seeing them gather round her gave her courage; she recovered her strength and her balance, and, dancing on the chair, she turned to Laure and said with some agitation:

"Bah! It is at any rate safer than a throne!"

She quickly arranged the baize, came down, pushed the table and the chair far from the partition, returned to her easel, and made a few more attempts, seeming to try for an effect of light that suited her. Her picture did not really trouble her at all; her aim was to get close to the dark closet by which she placed herself, as she wished, at the end near the door. Then she prepared to set her palette, still in perfect silence. Where she now was she soon heard more distinctly a slight noise which, on the day before, had greatly stirred her curiosity, and sent her young imagination wandering over a wide field of conjecture. She easily recognized it as the deep, regular breathing of the sleeping man whom she had just now seen. Her curiosity was satisfied, but she found herself burdened with an immense responsibility. Through the crack she had caught sight of the imperial eagle, and on a camp bed, in the dim light, had seen the figure of an officer of the Guards. She guessed it all. Servin was sheltering a refugee.

She now trembled lest one of her companions should come to examine her picture, and should hear the unfortunate man breathe or heave too deep a sigh, such as had fallen on her ear during yesterday's lesson. She resolved to remain near the door, and trust to her wits to cheat the tricks of fate.

"I had better remain here," thought she, "to prevent some disaster, than leave the poor prisoner at the mercy of some giddy prank."

This was the secret of Ginevra's apparent indifference when she found her easel transplanted ; she was secretly delighted, since she had been able to satisfy her curiosity in a natural manner; and, besides, she was too much absorbed at this moment to inquire into the reason of her exclusion. Nothing is more mortifying to young girls, or indeed to any one, than to see a practical joke, an insult, or a witticism fail of its effect in consequence of the victim's contempt. It would seem that our hatred of an enemy is increased by the height to which he can rise above us.

Ginevra's conduct remained a riddle to all her companions. Her friends and her foes were alike surprised, for she was allowed to have every good quality excepting forgiveness of injuries. Though the opportunities for showing this vice of temper had rarely been offered to Ginevra by the incidents of studio life, the instances she had happened to give of her vindictive spirit and determination had none the less made a deep impression on her companions' minds. After many guesses, Mademoiselle Roguin finally regarded the Italian's silence as evidence of a magnanimity above all praise ; and her party, inspired by her, conceived a plan to humiliate the aristocrats of the studio. They achieved their purpose by a fire of sarcasms directed at the pride and airs of the party of the right.

Madame Servin's arrival put an end to this contest of self-assertiveness. Amélie, with the shrewdness which is always coupled with malice, had remarked, watched, and wondered at the excessive absence of mind which hindered Ginevra from hearing the keenly polite dispute of which she was the subject. The revenge which Mademoiselle Roguin and her followers were wreaking on Mademoiselle Thirion and her party had thus the fatal effect of setting the young *ultras* to discover the cause of Ginevra's absorbed silence. The beautiful Italian became the centre of observation, and was watched by her friends as much as by her enemies. It is very difficult to hide the slightest excitement, the most trifling feeling from fifteen idle and inquisitive girls whose mischief and wits crave only for secrets to guess and intrigues to plot or to baffle, and who can ascribe to a gesture, to a glance, to a word, so many meanings, that they can hardly fail to discover the true one. Thus Ginevra di Piombo's secret was in great peril of being found out.

At this moment Madame Servin's presence produced a diversion in the drama that was being obscurely played at the bottom of these young hearts; while its sentiments, its ideas, its development were expressed by almost allegorical words, by significant looks, by gestures, and even by silence, often more emphatic than speech.

The moment Madame Servin came into the studio her eyes turned to the door by which Ginevra was standing. Under the present circumstances this look was not lost. If at first none of the maidens observed it, Mademoiselle Thirion remembered it afterwards, and accounted for the suspiciousness, the alarm, and mystery which gave a hunted expression to Madame Servin's eyes.

"Mesdemoiselles," she said, "Monsieur Servin cannot come to-day." Then she paid some little compliment to each pupil, all of them welcoming her in the girlish caressing way which lies as much in the voice and eyes as in actions. She immediately went to Ginevra under an impulse of uneasiness, which she vainly tried to conceal. The Italian and the painter's wife exchanged friendly nods and then stood in silence, one painting, the other watching her paint. The officer's breathing was easily audible, but Madame Servin could take no notice of it; and her dissimulation was so complete that Ginevra was tempted to accuse her of willful deafness. At this moment the stranger turned on the bed. The Italian girl looked Madame Servin steadily in the face, and, without be-traying the smallest agitation, the lady said, "Your copy is as fine as the original. If I had to choose, I should really be puzzled."

"Monsieur Servin has not let his wife into the secret of this mystery," thought Ginevra, who, after answering the young wife with a gentle smile of incredulity, sang a snatch of some national canzonetta to cover any sounds the prisoner might make.

It was so unusual to hear the studious Italian sing that all the girls looked at her in surprise. Later this incident served as evidence to the charitable suppositions of hatred. Madame Servin soon went away, and the hours of study ended without further event. Ginevra let all her companions leave, affect-ing to work on; but she unconsciously betrayed her wish to be alone, for as the pupils made ready to go she looked at them with ill-disguised impatience. Mademoiselle Thirion, who within these few hours had become a cruel foe to the young girl who was her superior in everything, guessed by the instinct of hatred that her rival's affected industry covered a mystery. She had been struck more than once by the atten-tion with which Ginevra seemed to be listening to a sound no one else could hear. The expression she now read in the Italian's eyes was as a flash of illumination. She was the last to leave, and went in on her way down to see Madame Servin, with whom she stayed a few minutes. Then, pretending that she had forgotten her bag, she very softly went upstairs again to the studio, and discovered Ginevra at the stop of a hastily-con-structed scaffolding, so lost in contemplation of the unknown soldier that she did not hear the light sound of her compan-ion's footsteps. It is true that Amélie walked on eggs—to use a phrase of Walter Scott's; she retired to the door and coughed. Ginevra started, turned her head, saw her enemy, and colored; then she quickly untied the blind, to mislead her as to her purpose, and came down. After putting away her paint-box, she left the studio, carrying stamped upon her heart the image of a man's head as charming as the Endymion, Girodet's masterpiece, which she had copied a few days previously.

"So young a man, and proscribed! Who can he be?— for it is not Marshal Ney."

These two sentences are the simplest expression of all the ideas which Ginevra turned over in her mind during two days. The next day but one, notwithstanding her hurry to be first at the painting gallery, she found that Mademoiselle Thirion had already come in a carriage. Ginevra and her enemy watched each other for some time, but each kept her countenance impenetrable by the other. Amélie had seen the stranger's handsome face; but happily, and at the same time unhappily, the eagles and the uniform were not within the range of her eye through the crack. She lost herself in conjecture. Suddenly Servin came in, much earlier than usual.

"Mademoiselle Ginevra," said he, after casting an eye round the gallery, "why have you placed yourself there? The light is bad. Come nearer to these young ladies, and lower your blind a little."

Then he sat down by Laure, whose work deserved his most lenient criticism.

"Well done!" he exclaimed, "this head is capitally done. You will be a second Ginevra."

The master went from easel to easel, blaming, flattering, and jesting; and making himself, as usual, more feared for his jests than for his reproofs.

The Italian had not obeyed his wishes; she remained at her post with the firm intention of staying there. She took out a sheet of paper and began to sketch in sepia the head of the unhappy refugee. A work conceived of with passion always bears a particular stamp. The faculty of giving truth to a rendering of nature or of a thought constitutes genius, and passion can often take its place. Thus in the circumstances in which Ginevra found herself, either the intuition she owed to her memory, which had been deeply struck, or perhaps necessity, the mother of greatness, lent her a supernatural flash of talent. The officer's head was thrown off on the paper with an inward trembling that she ascribed to fear, and which a physiologist would have recognized as the fever of inspiration. From time to time she stole a furtive glance at her companions, so as to be able to hide the sketch in case of any indiscretion on their part. But, in spite of her sharp lookout, there was a moment when she failed to perceive that her relentless enemy, under the shelter of a huge portfolio, had turned her eyeglass on the mysterious drawing. Mademoiselle Thirion, recognizing the refugee's features, raised her head suddenly, and Ginevra slipped away the sheet of paper.

"Why do you stay there, in spite of my opinion, Mademoiselle!" the professor gravely asked Ginevra.

The girl hastily turned her easel so that no one could see her sketch, and said, in an agitated voice, as she showed it to her master.

"Don't you think with me that this is a better light? May I not stay where I am?"

Servin turned pale. As nothing can escape the keen eyes of hatred, Mademoiselle Thirion threw herself, so to speak, into the excited feelings that agitated the professor and his pupil.

"You are right," said Servin. "But you will soon know more than I do," he added, with a forced laugh. There was a silence, during which the master looked at the head of the officer. "This is a masterpiece, worthy of Salvator Rosa!" he exclaimed, with an artist's vehemence.

At this exclamation all the young people rose, and Mademoiselle Thirion came forward with the swiftness of a tiger springing on its prey. At this instant the prisoner, roused by the turmoil, woke up. Ginevra overset her stool, spoke a few incoherent sentences, and began to laugh; but she had folded the portrait in half and thrown it into a portfolio before her terrible enemy could see it. The girls crowded round the easel; Servin enlarged in a loud voice on the beauties of the copy on which his favorite pupil was just now engaged; and all the party were cheated by this stratagem, excepting Amélie, who placed herself behind her companions and tried to open the portfolio into which she had seen the sketch put. Ginevra seized it and set it in front of her without a word, and the two girls gazed at each other in silence.

"Come, young ladies, to your places!" said Servin. "If you want to know as much as Mademoiselle di Piombo, you must not be always talking of fashions and balls, and trifling so much."

When the girls had all returned to their easels, the master sat down by Ginevra.

"Was it not better that this mystery should be discovered by me than by any one else?" said the Italian girl in a low tone.

"Yes," answered the painter. "You are patriotic; but even if you had not been, you are still the person to whom I should intrust it."

The master and pupil understood each other, and Ginevra was not now afraid to ask, "Who is he!"

"An intimate friend of Labédoyère's; the man who, next to the unfortunate colonel, did most to effect a junction between the Seventh and the Grenadiers of Elba. He was a major in the Guards, and has just come back from Waterloo."

"Why have you not burnt his uniform and shako, and put him into civilian dress?" asked Ginevra vehemently.

"Some clothes are to be brought for him this evening."

"You should have shut up the studio for a few days."

"He is going away."

"Does he wish to die?" said the girl. "Let him stay with you during these first days of the storm. Paris is the only place in France where a man may be safely hidden. Is he a friend of yours?" she added.

"No. He has no claim to my regard but his misfortunes. This is how he fell into my hands; my father-in-law, who had rejoined his regiment during this campaign, met the poor young man, and saved him very cleverly from those who have arrested Labédoyère. He wanted to defend him, like a madman!"

"And do you call him so!" cried Ginevra, with a glance of surprise at the painter, who did not speak for a moment.

"My father-in-law is too closely watched to be able to keep any one in his house," he went on. "He brought him here by night last week. I hoped to hide him from every eye by keeping him in this corner, the only place in the house where he can be safe."

"If I can be of any use, command me," said Ginevra. "I know Marshal Feltre."

"Well, we shall see," replied the painter.

This conversation had lasted too long not to be remarked by all the other pupils. Servin left Ginevra, came back to each easel, and gave such long lessons that he was still upstairs when the clock struck the hour at which his pupils usually left.

"You have forgotten your bag, mademoiselle," cried the professor, running after the young lady, who condescended to act the spy to gratify her hatred.

The inquisitive pupil came back for the bag, expressing some surprise at her own carelessness; but Servin's attention was to her additional proof of the existence of a mystery which was undoubtedly a serious one. She had already planned what should follow, and could say, like the Abbé Vertot, "I have laid my siege." She ran downstairs noisily, and violently slammed the door leading to Servin's rooms, that it might be supposed she had gone out; but she softly went upstairs again, and hid behind the door of the studio.

When the painter and Ginevra supposed themselves alone, he tapped in a particular manner at the door of the attic, which at once opened on its rusty, creaking hinges. The Italian girl saw a tall and well-built youth, whose imperial uniform set her heart beating. The officer carried his arm in a sling, and his pale face told of acute suffering. He started at seeing her, a stranger. Amélie, who could see nothing, was afraid to stay any longer; but she had heard the creaking of the door, and that was enough. She silently stole away.

"Fear nothing," said the painter. "Mademoiselle is the daughter of the Emperor's most faithful friend, the Baron di Piombo."

The young officer felt no doubt of Ginevra's loyalty when once he had looked at her.

"You are wounded!" she said.

"Oh, it is nothing, mademoiselle; the cut is healing," replied the young officer.

At this moment the shrill and piercing tones of men in the street came up to the studio, crying out, "This is the sentence which condemns to death——" All three shuddered. The soldier was the first to hear a name at which he turned pale.

"Labédoyère!" he exclaimed, dropping on to a stool.

They looked at each other in silence. Drops of sweat gathered on the young man's livid brow; with a gesture of despair he clutched the black curls of his hair, resting his elbow on Ginevra's easel.

"After all," said he, starting to his feet, "Labédoyère and I knew what we were doing. We knew the fate that awaited us if we triumphed or if we failed. He is dying for the cause, while I am in hiding——"

He hurried towards the studio door; but Ginevra, more nimble than he, rushed forward and stopped the way.

"Can you restore the Emperor?" she said. "Do you think you can raise the giant again, when he could not keep his feet?"

"What then is to become of me?" said the refugee, addressing the two friends whom chance had sent him. "I have not a relation in the world; Labédoyère was my friend and protector, I am now alone; to-morrow I shall be exiled or condemned; I have never had any fortune but my pay; I spent my last crown-piece to come and snatch Labédoyère from death and get him away. Death is an obvious necessity to me. When a man is determined to die, he must know how to sell his head to the executioner. I was thinking just now that an honest man's life is well worth that of two traitors, and that a dagger-thrust, judiciously placed, may give one immortality."

This passion of despair frightened the painter, and even Ginevra, who fully understood the young man. The Italian admired the beautiful head and the delightful voice, of which the accents of rage scarcely disguised the sweetness; then she suddenly dropped balm on all the hapless man's wounds.

"Monsieur!" said she, "as to your pecuniary difficulties, allow me to offer you the money I myself have saved. My father is rich; I am his only child; he loves me, and I am quite sure he will not blame me. Have no scruples in accepting it; our wealth comes from the Emperor, we have nothing which is not the bounty of his munificence. Is it not gratitude to help one of his faithful soldiers? So take this money with as little ceremony as I make about offering it. It is only money," she added in a scornful tone. "Then, as to friends—you will find friends!" And she proudly raised her head, while her eyes shone with unwonted brilliancy. "The head which must fall to-morrow—the mark of a dozen guns— saves yours," she went on. "Wait till this storm is over,

and you can take service in a foreign land if you are not forgotten, or in the French army if you are."

In the comfort offered by a woman there is a delicacy of
feeling which always has a touch of something motherly,
something far-seeing and complete; but when such words
of peace and hope are seconded by grace of gesture, and
the eloquence which comes from the heart, above all, when
the comforter is beautiful, it is hard for a young man to resist.
The young colonel inhaled love by every sense. A faint flush
tinged his white cheeks, and his eyes lost a little of the
melancholy that dimmed them as he said, in a strange tone
of voice, "You are an angel of goodness! But, Labédoyère!"
he added, "Labédoyère!"

At this cry they all three looked at each other, speechless,
and understood each other. They were friends, not of twenty
minutes, but of twenty years.

"My dear fellow," said Servin, "can you save him?"

"I can avenge him."

Ginevra was thrilled. Though the stranger was handsome,
his appearance had not moved her. The gentle pity that
women find in their heart for suffering which is not ignoble
had, in Ginevra, stifled every other emotion; but to hear a
cry of revenge, to find in this fugitive an Italian soul and
Corsican magnanimity! This was too much for her; she
gazed at the officer with respectful emotion, which powerfully
stirred her heart. It was the first time a man had ever made
her feel so strongly. Like all women, it pleased her to imagine that the soul of this stranger must be in harmony with
the remarkable beauty of his features and the fine proportions
of his figure, which she admired as an artist. Led by chance
curiosity to pity, from pity to eager interest, she now from
interest had reached sensations so strong and deep that she
thought it rash to remain there any longer.

"Till to-morrow," she said, leaving her sweetest smile
with the officer, to console him.

As he saw that smile, which threw a new light, as it were, on Ginevra's face, the stranger for a moment forgot all else. "To-morrow," he repeated sadly. "To-morrow, Labé-doyère——"

Ginevra turned to him and laid a finger on her lips, looking at him as though she would say, "Be calm, be prudent."

Then the young man exclaimed : "*O Dio ! Chi non vorrei vivere dopo averla veduta !*" ("O God ! who would not live after having seen her !") The peculiar accent with which he spoke the words startled Ginevra.

"You are a Corsican !" she exclaimed, coming back to him, her heart beating with gladness.

"I was born in Corsica," he replied ; "but I was taken to Genoa when very young ; and, as soon as I was of an age to enter the army, I enlisted."

The stranger's handsome person, the transcendent charm he derived from his attachment to the Emperor, his wound, his misfortunes, even his danger, all vanished before Ginevra's eyes, or rather all were fused in one new and exquisite senti-ment. This refugee was a son of Corsica, and spoke its be-loved tongue. In a minute the girl stood motionless, spell-bound by a magical sensation. She saw before her eyes a living picture to which a combination of human feeling and chance lent dazzling hues. At Servin's invitation the officer had taken his seat on an ottoman, the painter had untied the string which supported his guest's arm, and was now undoing the bandages in order to dress the wound. Ginevra shuddered as she saw the long wide gash, made by a sabre-cut, on the young man's forearm, and gave a little groan. The stranger looked up at her and began to smile. There was something very touching that went to the soul in Servin's attentive care as he removed the lint and touched the tender flesh, while the wounded man's face, though pale and sickly, expressed pleasure rather than suffering as he looked at the young girl.

An artist could not help admiring the antithesis of sentiments, and the contrast of color between the whiteness of the linen and the bare arm and the officer's blue and red coat. Soft dusk had now fallen on the studio, but a last sunbeam shone in on the spot where the refugee was sitting, in such a way that his pale, noble face, his black hair, his uniform were all flooded with light. This simple effect the superstitious Italian took for an omen of good-luck. The stranger seemed to her a celestial messenger who had spoken to her in the language of her native land, and put her under the spell of childish memories; while in her heart a feeling had birth as fresh and pure as her first age of innocence. In a very short instant she stood pensive, lost in infinite thought; then she blushed to have betrayed her absence of mind, exchanged a swift, sweet look with the officer, and made her escape, seeing him still.

The next day there was no painting lesson ; Ginevra could come to the studio, and the prisoner could be with his fellow-countrywoman. Servin, who had a sketch to finish, allowed the officer to sit there while he played guardian to the two young people who frequently spoke in Corsican. The poor soldier told of his sufferings during the retreat from Moscow ; for, at the age of nineteen, he had found himself at the passage of the Beresina, alone of all his regiment, having lost in his comrades the only men who could care for him, an orphan. He described, in words of fire, the great disaster of Waterloo.

His voice was music to the Italian girl. Brought up in Corsican ways, Ginevra was, to some extent, a child of nature ; falsehood was unknown to her, and she gave herself up without disguise to her impressions, owning them, or rather letting them be seen without the trickery, the mean and calculating vanity of the Parisian girl. During this day she remained more than once, her palette in one hand, a brush in the other, while the brush was undipped in the colors on the palette ; her eyes fixed on the officer's face, her lips slightly parted, she sat listening, ready to lay on the touch which was not given. She was not surprised to find such sweetness in the young man's eyes, for she felt her own soften in spite of her determination to keep them severe and cold. Thus, for hours, she painted with resolute attention, not raising her head because he was there watching her work. The first time he sat down to gaze at her in silence, she said to him in an agitated voice, after a long pause, "Does it amuse you, then, to look on at painting?"

That day she learned that his name was Luigi. Before they parted it was agreed that if any important political events should occur on the days when the studio was open, Ginevra was to inform him by singing in an undertone certain Italian airs.

On the following day Mademoiselle Thirion informed all her companions, as a great secret, that Ginevra di Piombo had a lover—a young man who came during the hours devoted to lessons—to hide in the dark closet of the studio.

"You, who take her part," said she to Mademoiselle Roguin, "watch her well, and you will see how she spends her time."

So Ginevra was watched with diabolical vigilance. Her songs were listened to, her glances spied. At moments when she believed that no one saw her, a dozen eyes were incessantly centred on her. And being forewarned, the girls interpreted in their true sense the agitations which passed across the Italian's radiant face, and her snatches of song, and the attention with which she listened to the muffled sounds which she alone could hear through the partition.

By the end of a week, only Laure, of the fifteen students, had resisted the temptation to scrutinize Luigi through the crack in the panel, or, by an instinct of weakness, still defended the beautiful Corsican girl. Mademoiselle Roguin wanted to make her wait on the stairs at the hour when they all left, to prove to her the intimacy between Ginevra and the handsome young man by finding them together; but she refused to condescend to an espionage which curiosity could not justify, and thus became an object of general reprobation.

Ere long the daughter of the gentleman usher thought it unbecoming in her to work in the studio of a painter whose opinions were tainted with patriotism or Bonapartism—which at that time were regarded as one and the same thing; so she came no more to Servin's. Though Amélie forgot Ginevra, the evil she had sown bore fruit. Insensibly, by chance, for gossip or out of prudery, the other damsels informed their mothers of the strange adventure in progress at the studio. One day Mathilde Roguin did not come; the next time another was absent; at last the three or four pupils, who had still remained, came no more. Ginevra and her little friend, Mademoiselle Laure, were for two or three days the sole occupants of the deserted studio.

The Italian did not observe the isolation in which she was left, and did not even wonder at the cause of her companions' absence. Having devised the means of communicating with Luigi, she lived in the studio as in a delightful retreat, secluded in the midst of the world, thinking only of the officer, and of the dangers which threatened him. This young creature, though sincerely admiring those noble characters who would not be false to their political faith, urged Luigi to submit at once to royal authority, in order to keep him in France, while Luigi refused to submit, that he might not have to leave his hiding-place.

If, indeed, passions only have their birth and grow up under the influence of romantic clauses, never had so many circumstances occurred to link two beings by one feeling. Ginevra's regard for Luigi, and his for her, thus made greater progress in a month than a fashionable friendship can make in ten years in a drawing-room. Is not adversity the touchstone of character? Hence Ginevra could really appreciate Luigi, and know him, and they soon felt a reciprocal esteem.

Ginevra, who was older than Luigi, found it sweet to be courted by a young man already so great, so tried by fortune, who united the experience of a man with the graces of youth. Luigi, on his part, felt an unspeakable delight in allowing himself to be apparently protected by a girl of five-and-twenty. Was it not a proof of love? The union in Ginevra of pride and sweetness, of strength and weakness, had an irresistible charm; Luigi was indeed completely her slave. In short, they were already so deeply in love that they felt no need either to deny it themselves nor to tell it.

One day, towards evening, Ginevra heard the signal agreed on. Luigi tapped on the woodwork with a pin, so gently as to make no more noise than a spider attaching its thread—thus asking if he might come out. She glanced round the studio, did not see little Laure, and answered the summons; but as the door was opened, Luigi caught sight of the girl, and hastily retreated. Ginevra, much surprised, looked about her, saw Laure, and, going up to her easel, said, "You are staying very late, dear. And that head seems to me finished; there is only a reflected light to put in on that lock of hair."

"It would be very kind of you," said Laure, in a tremulous voice, "if you would correct this copy for me; I should have something of your doing to keep."

"Of course I will," said Ginevra, sure of thus dismissing her. "I thought," she added, as she put in a few light touches, "that you had a long way to go home from the studio."

"Oh! Ginevra, I am going away for good," cried the girl, sadly.

"You are leaving Monsieur Servin?" asked the Italian, not seeming affected by her words, as she would have been a month since.

"Have you not noticed, Ginevra, that for some time there has been nobody here but you and I?"

"It is true," replied Ginevra, suddenly struck as by a remi-

22

niscence. "Are they ill, or going to be married, or are all their fathers employed now at the palace?"

"They have all left Monsieur Servin," said Laure.

"And why?"

"On your account, Ginevra."

"Mine!" repeated the Corsican, rising, with a threatening brow, and a proud sparkle in her eyes.

"Oh, do not be angry, dear Ginevra," Laure piteously exclaimed. "But my mother wishes that I should leave too. All the young ladies said that you had an intrigue; that Monsieur Servin had lent himself to allowing a young man who loves you to stay in the dark closet; but I never believed these calumnies, and did not tell my mother. Last evening Madame Roguin met my mother at a ball, and asked her whether she still sent me here. When mamma said 'Yes,' she repeated all those girls' tales. Mamma scolded me well; she declared I must have known it all, and that I had failed in the confidence of a daughter in her mother by not telling her. Oh, my dear Ginevra, I, who always took you for my model, how grieved I am not to be allowed to stay on with you——"

"We shall meet again in the world; young women get married," said Ginevra.

"When they are rich," replied Laure.

"Come to see me, my father has wealth——"

"Ginevra," Laure went on, much moved, "Madame Roguin and my mother are coming to-morrow to see Monsieur Servin, and complain of his conduct. At least let him be prepared."

A thunderbolt falling at her feet would have astonished Ginevra less than this announcement.

"What could it matter to them?" she innocently asked.

"Every one thinks it very wrong. Mamma says it is quite improper."

"And you, Laure, what do you think about it?"

The girl looked at Ginevra, and their hearts met. Laure could no longer restrain her tears; she threw herself on her friend's neck and kissed her. At this moment Servin came in.

"Mademoiselle Ginevra," he said, enthusiastically, "I have finished my picture, it is being varnished. But what is the matter? All the young ladies are making holiday, it would seem, or are gone into the country."

Laure wiped away her tears, took leave of Servin, and went away.

"The studio has been deserted for some days," said Ginevra, "and those young ladies will return no more."

"Pooh!"

"Nay, do not laugh," said Ginevra, "listen to me. I am the involuntary cause of your loss of repute."

The artist smiled, and said, interrupting his pupil, "My repute? But in a few days my picture will be exhibited."

"It is not your talent that is in question," said the Italian girl; "but your morality. The young ladies have spread a report that Luigi is shut up here, and that you—lent yourself to our love-making."

"There is some truth in that, mademoiselle," replied the professor. "The girls' mothers are airified prudes," he went on. "If they had but come to me, everything would have been explained. But what do I care for such things? Life is too short!"

And the painter snapped his fingers in the air.

Luigi, who had heard part of the conversation, came out of his cupboard.

"You are losing all your pupils," he cried, "and I shall have been your ruin!"

The artist took his hand and Ginevra's and joined them. "Will you marry each other, my children?" he asked, with touching bluntness. They both looked down, and their silence was their first mutual confession of love. "Well," said Servin, "and you will be happy, will you not? Can anything purchase such happiness as that of two beings like you?"

"I am rich," said Ginevra, "if you will allow me to indemnify you——"

"Indemnify!" Servin broke in. "Why, as soon as it is known that I have been the victim of a few little fools, and that I have sheltered a fugitive, all the Liberals in Paris will send me their daughters! Perhaps I shall be in your debt then."

Luigi grasped his protector's hand, unable to speak a word; but at last he said, in a broken voice, "To you I shall owe all my happiness."

"Be happy; I unite you," said the painter with comic unction, laying his hands on the heads of the lovers.

This pleasantry put an end to their emotional mood. They looked at each other, and all three laughed. The Italian girl wrung Luigi's hand with a passionate grasp, and with a simple impulse worthy of her Corsican traditions.

"Ah, but, my dear children," said Servin, "you fancy that now everything will go on swimmingly? Well, you are mistaken." They looked at him in amazement.

"Do not be alarmed; I am the only person inconvenienced by your giddy behavior. But Madame Servin is the pink of propriety, and I really do not know how we shall settle matters with her."

"Heavens! I had forgotten. To-morrow Madame Roguin and Laure's mother are coming to you——"

"I understand!" said the painter, interrupting her.

"But you can justify yourself," said the girl, with a toss of her head of emphatic pride. "Monsieur Luigi," and she turned to him with an arch look, "has surely no longer an antipathy for the King's government? Well, then," she went on, after seeing him smile, "to-morrow morning I shall address a petition to one of the most influential persons at the ministry of war, a man who can refuse the Baron di Piombo's daughter nothing. We will obtain a tacit pardon for Captain Luigi—for *they* will not recognize your grade as colonel. And you," she added, speaking to Servin, "may annihilate the mammas of my charitable young companions by simply telling them the truth."

"You are an angel!" said Servin.

While this scene was going on at the studio, Ginevra's father and mother were impatiently expecting her return.

"It is six o'clock, and Ginevra is not yet home," said Bartolomeo.

"She was never so late before," replied his wife.

The old people looked at each other with all the signs of very unusual anxiety. Bartolomeo, too much excited to sit still, rose and paced the room twice, briskly enough for a man of seventy-seven. Thanks to a strong constitution, he had changed but little since the day of his arrival at Paris, and tall as he was, he was still upright. His hair, thin and white now, had left his head bald, a broad and bossy skull which gave token of great strength and firmness. His face, deeply furrowed, had grown full and wide, with the pale complexion that inspires veneration. The fire of a passionate nature still lurked in the unearthly glow of his eyes, and the brows, which were not quite white, preserved their terrible mobility. The aspect of the man was severe, but it could be seen that Bartolomeo had the right to be so. His kindness and gentleness were known only to his wife and daughter. In his official position, or before strangers, he never set aside the majesty which time had lent to his appearance; and his habit of knitting those thick brows, of setting every line in his face, and assuming a Napoleonic fixity of gaze, made him seem as cold as marble.

In the course of his political life he had been so generally feared that he was thought unsociable; but it is not difficult to find the causes of such a reputation. Piombo's life, habits, and fidelity were a censure on most of the courtiers. Notwithstanding the secret missions intrusted to his discretion, which to any other man would have proved lucrative, he had not more than thirty thousand francs a year in government securities. And when we consider the low price of stock under the Empire, and Napoleon's liberality to those of his faithful adherents who knew how to ask, it is easy to perceive that the Baron di Piombo was a man of stern honesty; he owed his Baron's plumage only to the necessity of bearing a title when sent by Napoleon to a foreign court.

Bartolomeo had always professed implacable hatred of the traitors whom Napoleon had gathered about him, believing he could win them over by his victories. It was he—so it was said—who took three steps towards the door of the Emperor's room, after advising him to get rid of three men then in France, on the day before he set out on his famous and brilliant campaign of 1814. Since the second return of the Bourbons, Bartolomeo had ceased to wear the ribbon of the Legion of Honor. No man ever offered a finer image of the old Republicans, the incorruptible supporters of the Empire, who survived as the living derelicts of the two most vigorous governments the world has perhaps ever seen. If Baron di Piombo had displeased some courtiers, Daru, Drouot, and Carnot were his friends. And, indeed, since Waterloo, he cared no more about other political figures than for the puffs of smoke he blew from his cigar.

With the moderate sum which Madame, Napoleon's mother, had paid him for his estates in Corsica, Bartolomeo di Piombo had acquired the old Hôtel de Portenduère, in which he made no alterations. Living almost always in official residences at the cost of the government, he had resided in this mansion only since the catastrophe of Fontainebleau. Like all simple folks of lofty character, the Baron and his wife cared nothing for external splendor; they still used the old furniture they had found in the house. The reception-rooms of this dwelling, lofty, gloomy, and bare, the huge mirrors set in old gilt frames almost black with age, the furniture from the time of Louis XIV., were in keeping with Bartolomeo and his wife— figures worthy of antiquity. Under the Empire, and during the Hundred Days, while holding offices that brought handsome salaries, the old Corsican had kept house in grand style, but rather to do honor to his position than with a view to display.

His life and that of his wife and daughter were so frugal, so quiet, that their modest fortune sufficed for their needs. To them their child Ginevra outweighed all the riches on earth. And when, in May, 1814, Baron di Piombo resigned his place, dismissed his household, and locked his stable-doors, Ginevra, as simple and unpretentious as her parents, had not a regret. Like all great souls, she found luxury in strength of feeling, as she sought happiness in solitude and work.

And these three loved each other too much for the externals of life to have any value in their eyes. Often—and especially since Napoleon's second and fearful fall—Bartolomeo and his wife spent evenings of pure delight in listening to Ginevra as she played the piano or sang. To them there was an immense mystery of pleasure in their daughter's presence, in her lightest word; they followed her with their eyes with tender solicitude; they heard her step in the courtyard, however lightly she trod. Like lovers, they would all three sit silent for hours, hearing, better than in words, the eloquence of each other's soul. This deep feeling, the very life of the two old people, filled all their thoughts. Not three lives were here, but one, which, like the flame on a hearth, burnt up in three tongues of fire.

Though now and then memories of Napoleon's bounty and misfortunes, or the politics of the day, took the place of their constant preoccupation, they could talk of them without breaking their community of thought. For did not Ginevra

share their political passions? What could be more natural
than the eagerness with which they withdrew into the heart
of their only child? Until now the business of public life
had absorbed Baron di Piombo's energies; but in resigning
office the Corsican felt the need of throwing his energy into
the last feeling that was left to him; and, besides the tie that
bound a father and mother to their daughter, there was,
perhaps, unknown to these three despotic spirits, a powerful
reason in the fanaticism of their reciprocal devotion; their
love was undivided; Ginevra's whole heart was given to her
father, as Piombo's was to her; and certainly, if it is true
that we are more closely attached to one another by our
faults than by our good qualities, Ginevra responded wonderfully to all her father's passions. Herein lay the single defect
of this threefold existence. Ginevra was wholly given over
to her vindictive impulses, carried away by them, as Bartolomeo had been in his youth. The Corsican delighted in
encouraging these savage emotions in his daughter's heart,
exactly as a lion teaches his whelps to spring on their prey.
But as this apprenticeship to revenge could only be carried
out under the parental roof, Ginevra never forgave her father
anything; he always had to succumb. Piombo regarded
these factitious quarrels as mere childishness, but the child
thus acquired a habit of domineering over her parents. In
the midst of these tempests which Bartolomeo loved to raise,
a tender word, a look, was enough to soothe their angry
spirits, and they were never so near kissing as when threatening wrath.

However, from the age of about five, Ginevra, growing
wiser than her father, constantly avoided these scenes. Her
faithful nature, her devotion, the affection which governed all
her thoughts, and her admirable good sense, had gotten the
better of her rages; still a great evil had resulted: Ginevra
lived with her father and mother on a footing of equality
which is always disastrous.

To complete the picture of all the changes that had happened to these three persons since their arrival in Paris, Piombo and his wife, people of no education, had allowed Ginevra to study as she would. Following her girlish fancy, she had tried and given up everything, returning to each idea, and abandoning each in turn, until painting had become her ruling passion; she would have been perfect if her mother had been capable of directing her studies, of enlightening and harmonizing her natural gifts. Her faults were the outcome of the pernicious training that the old Corsican had delighted to give her.

After making the floor creak for some minutes under his feet, the old man rang the bell. A servant appeared.

"Go to meet Mademoiselle Ginevra," said the master.

"I have always been sorry that we have no longer a carriage for her," said the Baroness.

"She would not have one," replied Piombo, looking at his wife; and she, accustomed for twenty years to obedience as her part, cast down her eyes.

Tall, thin, pale, and wrinkled, and now past seventy, the Baroness was exactly like the old woman whom Schnetz introduces into the Italian scenes of his genre-pictures; she commonly sat so silent that she might have been taken for a second Mrs. Shandy; but a word, a look, a gesture would betray that her feelings had all the vigor and freshness of youth. Her dress, devoid of smartness, was often lacking in taste. She usually remained passive, sunk in an armchair, like a Sultana *valideh*, waiting for or admiring Ginevra—her pride and life. Her daughter's beauty, dress, and grace seemed to have become her own. All was well with her if Ginevra were content. Her hair had turned white, and a few locks were visible above her furrowed brow and at the side of her withered cheeks.

"For about a fortnight now," said she, "Ginevra has been coming in late,'

"Jean will not go fast enough," cried the impatient old man, crossing over the breast of his blue coat; he snatched up his hat, crammed it on his head, and was off.

"You will not get far," his wife called after him.

In fact, the outer gate opened and shut, and the old mother heard Ginevra's steps in the courtyard. Bartolomeo suddenly reappeared, carrying his daughter in triumph, while she struggled in his arms.

"Here she is! La Ginevra, la Ginevrettina, la Ginevrina, la Ginevrola, la Ginevretta, la Ginevra bella!" the old Baron joyfully exclaimed.

"Father! you are hurting me!"

Ginevra was immediately set down with a sort of respect. She nodded her head with a graceful gesture to reassure her mother, who was alarmed, and to convey that it had been only an excuse. Then the Baroness' pale, dull face regained a little color, and even a kind of cheerfulness. Piombo rubbed his hands together extremely hard—the most certain symptom of gladness; he had acquired the habit at court when seeing Napoleon in a rage with any of his generals or ministers who served him ill, or who had committed some blunder. When once the muscles of his face were relaxed, the smallest line in his forehead expressed benevolence. These two old folks at this moment were exactly like drooping plants, which are restored to life by a little water after a long drought.

"Dinner, dinner!" cried the Baron, holding out his hand to Ginevra, whom he addressed as Signora Piombellina, another token of good spirits, to which his daughter replied with a smile.

"By the way," said Piombo, as they rose from table, "do you know that your mother has remarked that for a month past you have stayed at the studio much later than usual? Painting before parents, it would seem."

"Oh, dear father——"

"Ginevra is preparing some surprise for us, no doubt," said the mother.

"You are going to bring me a picture of your painting," cried the Corsican, clapping his hands.

"Yes, I am very busy at the studio," she replied.

"What ails you, Ginevra? you are so pale," asked her mother.

"No!" exclaimed the girl with a resolute gesture. "No! it shall never be said that Ginevra Piombo ever told a lie in her life."

On hearing this strange exclamation, Piombo and his wife looked at their daughter with surprise.

"I love a young man," she added in a broken voice. Then, not daring to look at her parents, her heavy eyelids drooped as if to veil the fire in her eyes.

"Is he a prince?" asked her father ironically; but his tone of voice made both the mother and daughter tremble.

"No, father," she modestly replied, "he is a young man of no fortune——"

"Then is he so handsome?"

"He is unfortunate."

"What is he?"

"As a comrade of Labédoyère's he was outlawed, homeless; Servin hid him, and——"

"Servin is a good fellow, and did well," cried Piombo. "But you, daughter, have done ill to love any man but your father——"

"Love is not within my control," said Ginevra, gently.

"I had flattered myself," said her father, "that my Ginevra would be faithful to me till my death; that my care and her mother's would be all she would have known; that our tenderness would never meet with a rival affection in her heart; that——"

"Did I ever reproach you for your fanatical devotion to Napoleon?" said Ginevra. "Have you never loved any one but me ? Have you not been away on embassies for months at a time ? Have I not borne your absence bravely ? Life has necessities to which we must yield."

" Ginevra ! "

" No, you do not love me for my own sake, and your reproaches show intolerable selfishness."

" And you accuse your father's love ! " cried Piombo with flaming looks.

" Father, I will never accuse you," replied Ginevra, more gently than her trembling mother expected. " You have right on the side of your egoism, as I have right on the side of my love. Heaven is my witness that no daughter ever better fulfilled her duty to her parents. I have never known anything but love and happiness in what many daughters regard as obligations. Now, for fifteen years, I have never been anywhere but under your protecting wing, and it has been a very sweet delight to me to charm your lives. But am I then ungrateful in giving myself up to the joy of loving, and in wishing for a husband to protect me after you ? "

" So you balance accounts with your father, Ginevra ! " said the old man in ominous tones.

There was a frightful pause ; no one dared to speak. Finally, Bartolomeo broke the silence by exclaiming in a heart-rending voice : " Oh, stay with us ; stay with your old father ! I could not bear to see you love a man. Ginevra, you will not have long to wait for your liberty——"

" But, my dear father, consider ; we shall not leave you, we shall be two to love you ; you will know the man to whose care you will bequeath me. You will be doubly loved by me and by him—by him, being part of me, and by me who am wholly he."

" Oh, Ginevra, Ginevra ! " cried the Corsican, clinching his fists, " why were you not married when Napoleon had accustomed me to the idea, and introduced dukes and counts as your suitors ? "

"They only loved me to order," said the young girl. "Besides, I did not wish to leave you; and they would have taken me away with them."

"You do not wish to leave us alone," said Piombo, "but if you marry you isolate us. I know you, my child, you will love us no more. Elisa," he said, turning to his wife, who sat motionless and, as it were, stupefied; "we no longer have a daughter; she wants to be married."

The old man sat down, after raising his hands in the air as though to invoke God; then he remained bent, crushed by his grief. Ginevra saw her father's agitation, and the moderation of his wrath pierced her to the heart; she had expected a scene and furies; she had not steeled her soul against his gentleness.

"My dear father," she said in an appealing voice, "no, you shall never be abandoned by your Ginevra. But love me too a little for myself. If only you knew how he loves me! Ah, he could never bear to cause me pain!"

"What, comparisons already!" cried Piombo in a terrible voice. "No," he went on, "I cannot endure the idea. If he were to love you as you deserve, he would kill me; and if he were not to love you, I should stab him!"

Piombo's hands were trembling, his lips trembled, his whole frame trembled, and his eyes flashed lightnings; Ginevra alone could meet his gaze; for then her eyes too flashed fire, and the daughter was worthy of the father.

"To love you! What man is worthy of such a life?" he went on. "To love you as a father even—is it not to live in paradise? Who then could be worthy to be your husband?"

"He," said Ginevra. "He of whom I feel myself unworthy."

"He," echoed Piombo mechanically. "Who? He?"

"The man I love."

"Can he know you well enough already to adore you?" asked her father.

"But, father," said Ginevra, feeling a surge of impatience, "even if he did not love me—so long as I love him——"

"You do love him then?" cried Piombo. Ginevra gently bowed her head. "You love him more than you love me?"

"The two feelings cannot be compared," she replied.

"One is stronger than the other?" said Piombo.

"Yes, I think so," said Ginevra.

"You shall not marry him!" cried the Corsican in a voice that made the windows rattle.

"I will marry him!" replied Ginevra calmly.

"Good God!" cried the mother, "how will this quarrel end? *Santa Virgina*, come between them!"

The Baron, who was striding up and down the room, came and seated himself. An icy sternness darkened his face; he looked steadfastly at his daughter, and said in a gentle and affectionate voice, "Nay, Ginevra—you will not marry him. Oh, do not say you will, this evening. Let me believe that you will not. Do you wish to see your father on his knees before you, and his white hairs humbled. I will beseech you——"

"Ginevra Piombo is not accustomed to promise and not to keep her word," said she; "I am your child."

"She is right," said the Baroness, "we come into the world to marry."

"And so you encourage her in disobedience," said the Baron to his wife, who, stricken by the reproof, froze into a statue.

"It is not disobedience to refuse to yield to an unjust command," replied Ginevra.

"It cannot be unjust when it emanates from your father's lips, my child. Why do you rise in judgment on me? Is not the repugnance I feel a counsel from on high? I am perhaps saving you from some misfortune."

"The misfortune would be that he should not love me."

"Always he!"

"Yes, always," she said. "He is my life, my joy, my thought. Even if I obeyed you, he would be always in my heart. If you forbid me to marry him, will it not make me hate you?"

"You love us no longer!" cried Piombo.

"Oh!" said Ginevra, shaking her head.

"Well, then, forget him. Be faithful to us. After us—— you understand——"

"Father, would you make me wish that you were dead?" cried Ginevra.

"I shall outlive you; children who do not honor their parents die early," cried her father at the utmost pitch of exasperation.

"All the more reason for marrying soon and being happy," said she.

This coolness, this force of argument, brought Piombo's agitation to a crisis; the blood rushed violently to his head, his face turned purple. Ginevra shuddered; she flew like a bird on to her father's knees, threw her arms round his neck, stroked his hair, and exclaimed, quite overcome—

"Oh, yes, let me die first! I could not survive you, my dear, kind father."

"Oh, my Ginevra, my foolish Ginevretta!" answered Piombo, whose rage melted under this caress as an icicle melts in the sunshine.

"It was time you should put an end to the matter," said the Baroness in a broken voice.

"Poor mother!"

"Ah, Ginevretta, mia Ginevra bella!"

And the father played with his daughter as if she were a child of six; he amused himself with undoing the waving tresses of her hair and dancing her on his knee; there was dotage in his demonstrations of tenderness. Presently his daughter scolded him as she kissed him, and tried, half in jest, to get leave to bring Luigi to the house; but, jesting

too, her father refused.   She sulked, and recovered herself,
and sulked again; then, at the end of the evening, she was
only too glad to have impressed on her father the ideas of her
love for Luigi and of a marriage ere long.

Next day she said no more about it; she went later to the
studio and returned early; she was more affectionate to her
father than she had ever been, and showed herself grateful, as
if to thank him for the consent to her marriage he seemed to
give by silence.   In the evening she played and sang for a
long time, and exclaimed now and then, "This nocturne
requires a man's voice!"   She was an Italian, and that says
everything.

A week later her mother beckoned her; Ginevra went, and
then in her ear she whispered, "I have persuaded your father
to receive him."

"Oh, mother! you make me very happy."

So that afternoon, Ginevra had the joy of coming home to
her father's house leaning on Luigi's arm.   The poor officer
came out of his hiding-place for the second time.   Ginevra's
active intervention addressed to the Duc de Feltre, then
minister of war, had been crowned with perfect success.
Luigi had just been reinstated as an officer on the reserve list.
This was a very long step towards a prosperous future.

Informed by Ginevra of all the difficulties he would meet
with in the Baron, the young officer dared not confess his
dread of failing to please him.   This man, so brave in adversity, so bold on the field of battle, quaked as he thought
of entering the Piombos' drawing-room.   Ginevra felt him
tremble, and this emotion, of which their happiness was the
first cause, was to her a fresh proof of his love.

"How pale you are!" said she, as they reached the gate
of the hôtel.

"Oh, Ginevra!   If my life alone were at stake——" exclaimed Luigi, nervously.

Though Bartolomeo had been informed by his wife of this

official introduction of his daughter's lover, he did not rise to meet him, but remained in the armchair he usually occupied, and the severity of his countenance was icy.

" Father," said Ginevra, "I have brought you a gentleman whom you will no doubt be pleased to see. Monsieur Luigi, a soldier, who fought quite close to the Emperor at Mont-Saint-Jean——"

The Baron rose, cast a furtive glance at Luigi, and said in a sardonic tone—

" Monsieur wears no orders?"

" I no longer wear the Legion of Honor," replied Luigi bashfully, and he humbly remained standing.

Ginevra, hurt by her father's rudeness, brought forward a chair. The officer's reply satisfied the old Republican. Madame Piombo, seeing that her husband's brows were recovering their natural shape, said, to revive the conversation, " Monsieur is wonderfully like Nina Porta. Do you not think that he has quite the face of a Porta?"

" Nothing can be more natural," replied the young man, on whom Piombo's flaming eyes were fixed. " Nina was my sister."

" You are Luigi Porta?" asked the old man.

" Yes."

Bartolomeo di Piombo rose, tottered, was obliged to lean on a chair, and looked at his wife. Elisa Piombo came up to him ; then the two old folks silently left the room, arm in arm, with a look of horror at their daughter. Luigi Porta, quite bewildered, gazed at Ginevra, who turned as white as a marble statue, and remained with her eyes fixed on the door where her father and mother had disappeared. There was something so solemn in her silence and their retreat that, for the first time in his life perhaps, a feeling of fear came over him. She clasped her hands tightly together, and said in a voice so choked that it would have been inaudible to any one but a lover, " How much woe in one word ! "

23

" In the name of our love, what have I said?" asked Luigi Porta.

" My father has never told me our deplorable history," she replied. " And when we left Corsica I was too young to know anything about it."

" Is it a Vendetta?" asked Luigi, trembling.

" Yes. By questioning my mother I learned that the Porta had killed my brothers and burnt down our house. My father then massacred all your family. How did you survive, you whom he thought he had tied to the posts of a bed before setting fire to the house?"

" I do not know," replied Luigi. " When I was six I was taken to Genoa, to an old man named Colonna. No account of my family was ever given to me; I only knew that I was an orphan, and penniless. Colonna was like a father to me; I bore his name till I entered the army; then, as I needed papers to prove my identity, old Colonna told me that, help-less as I was, and hardly more than a child, I had enemies. He made me promise to take the name of Luigi only, to evade them."

" Fly, fly, Luigi," cried Ginevra. " Yet, stay; I must go with you. So long as you are in my father's house you are safe. As soon as you quit it, take care of yourself. You will go from one danger to another. My father has two Corsicans in his service, and if he does not threaten your life they will."

" Ginevra," he said, " and must this hatred exist between us?"

She smiled sadly and bowed her head. But she soon raised it again with a sort of pride, and said, " Oh, Luigi, our feel-ings must be very pure and true that I should have the strength to walk in the path I am entering on. But it is for the sake of happiness which will last as long as life, is it not?"

Luigi answered only with a smile, and pressed her hand.

The girl understood that only a great love could at such a moment scorn mere protestations. This calm and con-scientious expression of Luigi's feelings seemed to speak for their strength and permanence. The fate of the couple was thus sealed. Ginevra foresaw many painful contests to be fought out, but the idea of deserting Luigi—an idea which had perhaps floated before her mind—at once vanished. His, henceforth and for ever, she suddenly dragged him away and out of the house with a sort of violence, and did not quit him till they reached the house where Servin had taken a humble lodging for him.

When she returned to her father's house she had assumed the serenity which comes of a strong resolve. No change of manner revealed any uneasiness. She found her parents ready to sit down to dinner, and she looked at them with eyes devoid of defiance and full of sweetness. She saw that her old mother had been weeping; at the sight of her red eyelids for a moment her heart failed her, but she hid her emotion. Piombo seemed to be a prey to anguish too keen, too concentrated to be shown by ordinary means of expres-sion. The servants waited on a meal which no one ate. A horror of food is one of the symptoms indicative of a great crisis of the soul. All three rose without any one of them having spoken a word. When Ginevra was seated in the great, solemn drawing-room, between her father and mother, Piombo tried to speak, but he found no voice; he tried to walk about, but found no strength; he sat down again and rang the bell.

" Pietro," said he to the servant at last, " light the fire, I am cold."

Ginevra was shocked, and looked anxiously at her father. The struggle he was going through must be frightful; his face looked quite changed. Ginevra knew the extent of the danger that threatened her, but she did not tremble; while the glances that Bartolomeo cast at his daughter seemed to proclaim that he was at this moment in fear of the character whose violence was his own work. Between these two everything must be in excess. And the certainty of the possible change of feeling between the father and daughter filled the Baroness' face with an expression of terror.

"Ginevra, you love the enemy of your family," said Piombo at last, not daring to look at his daughter.

"That is true," she replied.

"You must choose between him and us. Our Vendetta is part of ourselves. If you do not espouse my cause, you are not of my family."

"My choice is made," said Ginevra, in a steady voice.

His daughter's calmness misled Bartolomeo.

"Oh, my dear daughter!" cried the old man, whose eyelids were moist with tears, the first, the only tears he ever shed in his life.

"I shall be his wife," she said abruptly.

Bartolomeo could not see for a moment; but he recovered himself and replied, "This marriage shall never be so long as I live. I will never consent." Ginevra kept silence. "But, do you understand," the Baron went on, "that Luigi is the son of the man who killed your brothers?"

"He was six years old when the crime was committed; he must be innocent of it," she answered.

"A Porta!" cried Bartolomeo.

"But how could I share this hatred," said the girl eagerly. "Did you bring me up in the belief that a Porta was a monster? Could I imagine that even one was left of those you had killed? Is it not in nature that you should make your Vendetta give way to my feelings?"

"A Porta!" repeated Piombo. "If his father had found you then in your bed, you would not be alive now. He would have dealt you a hundred deaths."

"Possibly," she said. "But his son has given me more than life. To see Luigi is a happiness without which I cannot

live. Luigi has revealed to me the world of feeling. I have,
perhaps, seen even handsomer faces than his, but none ever
charmed me so much. I have, perhaps, heard voices—no,
no, never one so musical! Luigi loves me. He shall be my
husband.''

"Never!" said Piombo. "Ginevra, I would sooner see
you in your coffin!''

The old man rose, and paced the room with hurried strides,
uttering fierce words, with pauses between that betrayed all
his indignation.

"You think, perhaps, that you can bend my will? Unde-
ceive yourself. I will not have a Porta for my son-in-law.
That is my decision. Never speak of the matter again. I
am Bartolomeo di Piombo, do you hear, Ginevra?''

"Do you attach any mysterious meaning to the words?"
she coldly asked.

"They mean that I have a dagger, and that I do not fear
the justice of men. We Corsicans settle such matters with
God.''

"Well," said the girl, "I am Ginevra di Piombo, and I
declare that in six months I will be Luigi Porta's wife. You
are a perfect tyrant, father,'' she spiritedly added, after an
ominous pause.

Bartolomeo clenched his fists, and struck the marble
chimney-shelf.

"Ah! we are in Paris!" he muttered.

He said no more, but folded his arms and bowed his head
on his breast; nor did he say another word the whole evening. Having asserted her will, the girl affected the most
complete indifference; she sat down to the piano, sang,
played the most charming music, with a grace and feeling
that proclaimed her perfect freedom of mind, triumphing
over her father, whose brow showed no relenting. The old
man deeply felt this tacit insult, and at that moment gathered
the bitter fruits of the education he had given his daughter.

Respect is a barrier which protects the parents and the children alike, sparing those much sorrow, and these remorse.

The next day, as Ginevra was going out at the hour when she usually went to the studio, she found the door of the house closed upon her; but she soon devised means for informing Luigi Porta of her father's severity. A waiting-woman, who could not read, carried to the young officer a letter written by Ginevra. For five days the lovers contrived to correspond, thanks to the plots that young people of twenty-one can always contrive.

The father and daughter rarely spoke to each other. Both had in the bottom of their hearts an element of hatred; they suffered, but in pride and silence. Knowing well how strong were the bonds of love that tied them to each other, they tried to wrench them asunder, but without success. No sweet emotion ever came, as it had been wont, to give light to Bartolomeo's severe features when he gazed at his Ginevra, and there was something savage in her expression when she looked at her father. Reproach sat on her innocent brow; she gave herself up, indeed, to thoughts of happiness, but remorse sometimes dimmed her eyes. It was not, indeed, difficult to divine that she would never enjoy in peace a felicity which made her parents unhappy. In Bartolomeo, as in his daughter, all the irresolution arising from their native goodness of heart was doomed to shipwreck on their fierce pride and the revengeful spirit peculiar to Corsicans. They encouraged each other in their wrath, and shut their eyes to the future. Perhaps, too, each fancied that the other would yield.

On Ginevra's birthday, her mother, heart-broken at this disunion, which was assuming a serious aspect, planned to reconcile the father and daughter by an appeal to the memories of this anniversary. They were all three sitting in Bartolomeo's room. Ginevra guessed her mother's purpose from the hesitation written in her face, and she smiled sadly. At this instant a servant announced two lawyers, accompanied by several witnesses, who all came into the room. Bartolomeo stared at the men, whose cold, set faces were in themselves an insult to souls so fevered as those of the three principal actors in this scene. The old man turned uneasily to his daughter, and saw on her face a smile of triumph which led him to suspect some catastrophe; but he affected, as savages do, to preserve a deceitful rigidity, while he looked at the two lawyers with a sort of apathetic curiosity. At a gesture of invitation from the old man the visitors took seats.

"Monsieur is no doubt Baron di Piombo?" said the elder of the two lawyers.

Bartolomeo bowed. The lawyer gave his head a little jerk, looked at Ginevra with the sly expression of a bailiff nabbing a debtor; then he took out his snuff-box, opened it, and, taking a pinch of snuff, absorbed it in little sniffs while considering the opening words of his discourse; and while pronouncing them he made constant pauses, an oratorical effect which a dash in printing represents very imperfectly.

"Monsieur," said he, "I am Monsieur Roguin, notary to mademoiselle, your daughter, and we are here—my colleague and I—to carry out the requirements of the law, and—to put an end to the divisions which—as it would seem—have arisen —between you and mademoiselle, your daughter—on the question—of—her—marriage with Monsieur Luigi Porta." This speech, made in a pedantic style, seemed, no doubt, to Monsieur Roguin much too fine to be understood all in a moment, and he stopped, while looking at Bartolomeo with an expression peculiar to men of business, and which is half-way between servility and familiarity. Lawyers are so much used to feign interest in the persons to whom they speak that their features at last assume a grimace which they can put on and off with their official *pallium*. This caricature of friendliness, so mechanical as to be easily detected, irritated Bartolomeo to such a pitch that it took all his self-control not to throw Monsieur Roguin out of the window; a look of fury emphasized his wrinkles, and on seeing this the notary said to himself: "I am making an effect."

"But," he went on in a honeyed voice, "Monsieur le Baron, on such occasions as these, our intervention must always, at first, be essentially conciliatory. Have the kindness to listen to me. It is in evidence that Mademoiselle Ginevra Piombo—has to-day—attained the age at which, after a 'respectful summons,' she may proceed to the solemnization of her marriage—notwithstanding that her parents refuse their consent. Now—it is customary in families—which enjoy a certain consideration—which move in society—and preserve their dignity—people, in short, to whom it is important not to let the public into the secret of their differences —and who also do not wish to do themselves an injury by blighting the future lives of a young husband and wife—for that is doing themselves an injury. It is the custom, I was saying—in such highly respectable families—not to allow the serving of such a summons—which must be—which always is a record of a dispute—which at last ceases to exist. For as soon, monsieur, as a young lady has recourse to a 'respectful summons' she proclaims a determination so obstinate—that her father—and her mother," he added, turning to the Baroness, "can have no further hope of seeing her follow their advice. Hence the parental prohibition being nullified —in the first place by this fact—and also by the decision of the law—it is always the case that a wise father, after finally remonstrating with his child, allows her the liberty——"

Monsieur Roguin paused, perceiving that he might talk on for two hours without extracting an answer; and he also felt a peculiar agitation as he looked at the man he was trying to convince. An extraordinary change had come over Bartolomeo's countenance. All its lines were set, giving him an expression of indescribable cruelty, and he glared at the lawyer like a tiger. The Baroness sat mute and passive. Ginevra, calm and resolute, was waiting; she knew that the notary's voice was stronger than hers, and she seemed to have made up her mind to keep silence. At the moment when Roguin ceased speaking, the scene was so terrible that the witnesses, as strangers, trembled; never, perhaps, had such a silence weighed on them. The lawyers looked at each other as if in consultation, then they rose and went to the window.

"Did you ever come across clients made to this pattern?" asked Roguin of his colleague.

"There is nothing to be gotten out of him," said the younger man. "In your place I should read the summons and nothing more. The old man is no joke; he is choleric, and you will gain nothing by trying to discuss matters with him."

Monsieur Roguin therefore read aloud from a sheet of stamped paper a summons ready drawn up, and coldly asked Bartolomeo what his reply was.

"Are there laws in France then that upset a father's authority!" asked the Corsican.

"Monsieur——" said Roguin smoothly.

"That snatch a child from her father?"

"Monsieur——"

"That rob an old man of his last consolation?"

"Monsieur, your daughter belongs to you only so long as——"

"That kill her?"

"Monsieur, allow me."

There is nothing more hideous than the cold-blooded and close reasoning of a lawyer in the midst of such scenes of passion as they are usually mixed up with. The faces which Piombo saw seemed to him to have escaped from hell; his cold and concentrated rage knew no bounds at the moment when his little opponent's calm and almost piping voice uttered that fatal, "Allow me." He sprang at a long dagger which hung from a nail over the chimney-piece, and rushed at his daughter. The younger of the two lawyers and one of the witnesses threw themselves between him and Ginevra, but

Bartolomeo brutally knocked them over, showing them a face of fire and glowing eyes which seemed more terrible than the flash of the dagger.   When Ginevra found herself face to face with her father she looked at him steadily with a glance of triumph, went slowly towards him, and knelt down.

"No, no! I cannot!" he exclaimed, flinging away the weapon with such force that it stuck fast in the wainscot.

"Mercy, then, mercy!" said she.   "You hesitate to kill me, but you refuse me life.   Oh, father, I never loved you so well—but give me Luigi.   I ask your consent on my knees; a daughter may humble herself to her father.   My Luigi, or I must die!"

The violent excitement that choked her prevented her saying more; she found no voice; her convulsive efforts plainly showed that she was between life and death.   Bartolomeo roughly pushed her away.

"Go," he said, "the wife of Luigi Porta cannot be a Piombo.   I no longer have a daughter!   I cannot bring myself to curse you, but I give you up.   You have now no father.   My Ginevra Piombo is buried then!" he exclaimed in a deep tone, as he clutched at his heart.   "Go, I say, wretched girl," he went on after a moment's silence.   "Go, and never let me see you again."

He took Ginevra by the arm, and in silence led her out of the house.

"Luigi!" cried Ginevra, as she went into the humble room where the officer was lodged, "my Luigi, we have no fortune but our love."

"We are richer than all the kings of the earth," he replied.

"My father and mother have cast me out," said she with deep melancholy.

"I will love you for them."

"Shall we be very happy!" she cried, with a gayety that had something terrible in it.

"And for ever!" he answered, clasping her to his heart.

On the day following that on which Ginevra had quitted her father's house, she went to beg Madame Servin to grant her protection and shelter till the time, fixed by law, when she could be married to Luigi. There began her apprenticeship to the troubles which the world strews in the way of those who do not obey its rules. Madame Servin, who was greatly distressed at the injury that Ginevra's adventure had done the painter, received the fugitive coldly, and explained to her with circumspect politeness that she was not to count on her support. Too proud to insist, but amazed at such selfishness, to which she was unaccustomed, the young Corsican went to lodge in a furnished house as near as possible to Luigi. The son of the Portas spent all his days at the feet of his beloved; his youthful love, and the purity of his mind, dispersed the clouds which her father's reprobation had settled on the banished daughter's brow; and he painted the future as so fair that she ended by smiling, though she could not forget her parent's severity.

One morning the maid of the house brought up to her several trunks containing dress-stuffs, linen, and a quantity of things needful for a young woman settling for the first time. In this she recognized the foreseeing kindness of a mother; for as she examined these gifts she found a purse into which the Baroness had put some money belonging to Ginevra, adding all her own savings. With the money was a letter, in which she implored her daughter to give up her fatal purpose of marrying, if there were yet time. She had been obliged, she said, to take unheard-of precautions to get this small assistance conveyed to Ginevra; she begged her not to accuse her of hardness if henceforth she left her neglected; she feared she could do no more for her; she blessed her, hoped she might find happiness in this fatal marriage if she persisted, and assured her that her one thought was of her beloved daughter. At this point tears had blotted out many words of the letter.

"Oh, mother!" cried Ginevra, quite overcome.

She felt a longing to throw herself at her mother's feet, to see her, to breathe the blessed air of home; she was on the point of rushing off when Luigi came in. She looked at him, and filial affection vanished, her tears were dried, she could not find it in her to leave the unhappy and loving youth. To be the sole hope of a noble soul, to love and to desert it —such a sacrifice is treason of which no young heart is capable. Ginevra had the generosity to bury her grief at the bottom of her soul.

At last the day of their wedding came. Ginevra found no one near her. Luigi took advantage of the moment when she was dressing to go in search of the necessary witnesses to their marriage act. These were very good people. One of them, an ex-quartermaster of Hussars, had, when in the army, found himself under such obligations to Luigi as an honest man never forgets; he had become a job-master, and had several hackney carriages. The other, a builder, was the proprietor of the house where the young couple were to lodge. Each of these brought a friend, and all four came with Luigi to fetch the bride. Unaccustomed as they were to social grimacing, seeing nothing extraordinary in the service they were doing to Luigi, these men were decently but quite plainly dressed, and there was nothing to proclaim the gay escort of a wedding. Ginevra herself was very simply clad, to be in keeping with her fortune; but, nevertheless, there was something so noble and impressive in her beauty that at the sight of her the words died on the lips of the good folks who had been prepared to pay her some compliment; they bowed respectfully, and she bowed in return; they looked at her in silence, and could only admire her. Joy can only express itself among equals. So, as fate would have it, all was gloomy and serious around the lovers; there was nothing to reflect their happiness.

The church and the mayor were not far away. The two

Corsicans, followed by the four witnesses required by law, decided to go on foot, with a simplicity which robbed this great event of social life of all parade. In the courtyard of the mayor they found a crowd of carriages, which announced a numerous party within. They went upstairs and entered a large room, where the couples who were to be made happy on this particular day were awaiting the mayor of that quarter of Paris with considerable impatience. Ginevra sat down by Luigi on the end of a long bench, and their witnesses remained standing for lack of seats. Two brides, pompously arrayed in white, loaded with ribbons and lace and pearls, and crowned with bunches of orange-blossoms of which the sheeny buds quivered under their veils, were surrounded by their families and accompanied by their mothers, to whom they turned with looks at once timid and satisfied; every eye reflected their happiness, and every face seemed to exhale benedictions. Fathers, witnesses, brothers and sisters were coming and going like a swarm of insects playing in a sunbeam which soon must vanish. Every one seemed to understand the preciousness of this brief hour in life when the heart stands poised between two hopes—the wishes of the past, the promise of the future.

At this sight Ginevra felt her heart swell, and she pressed Luigi's arm. He gave her a look, and a tear rose to the young man's eye; he never saw more clearly than at that moment all that his Ginevra had sacrificed for him. That rare tear made the young girl forget the forlorn position in which she stood. Love poured treasures of light between the lovers, who from that moment saw nothing but each other in the midst of the confusion.

Their witnesses, indifferent to the ceremony, were quietly discussing business matters.

"Oats are very dear," said the ex-quartermaster to the mason.

"They have not yet gone up so high as plaster in proportion," said the builder. And they walked round the large room.

"What a lot of valuable time we are losing here!" impatiently exclaimed the mason, putting a huge silver watch back into his pocket.

Luigi and Ginevra, clinging to each other, seemed to be but one person. A poet would certainly have admired these two heads, full of the same feeling, alike in coloring, melancholy and silent in the presence of the two buzzing wedding-parties, of four excited families sparkling with diamonds and flowers, and full of gaiety which seemed a mere effervescence. All the joys of which these loud and gorgeous groups made a display, Luigi and Ginevra kept buried at the bottom of their hearts. On one side was the coarse clamor of pleasure; on the other the delicate silence of happy souls: earth and heaven.

But Ginevra trembled, and could not altogether shake off her woman's weakness. Superstitious, as Italians are, she regarded this contrast as an omen, and in the depths of her heart she harbored a feeling of dread, as unconquerable as her love itself.

Suddenly an official in livery threw open the double doors; silence fell, and his voice sounded like a yelp as he called out the names of Monsieur Luigi Porta and Mademoiselle Ginevra Piombo. This incident caused the pair some embarrassment. The celebrity of the name of Piombo attracted attention; the spectators looked about them for a wedding-party which must surely be a splendid one. Ginevra rose; her eyes, thunderous with pride, subdued the crowd; she took Luigi's arm and went forward with a firm step, followed by the witnesses. A murmur of astonishment, which rapidly grew louder, and whispering on all sides, reminded Ginevra that the world was calling her to account for her parents' absence. Her father's curse seemed to be pursuing her.

"Wait for the families of the bride and bridegroom," said

the mayor to the clerk, who at once began to read the contracts.

"The father and mother enter a protest," said the clerk indifferently.

"On both sides?" asked the mayor.

"The man is an orphan."

"Where are the witnesses?"

"They are here," said the clerk, pointing to the four motionless and silent men who stood like statues, with their arms crossed.

"But if the parents protest——?" said the mayor.

"The 'respectful summons' has been presented in due form," replied the man, rising to place the various documents in the functionary's hands.

This discussion in an office seemed to brand them, and in a few words told a whole history. The hatred of the Porta and the Piombo, all these terrible passions, were thus recorded on a page of a register, as the annals of a nation may be inscribed on a tombstone in a few lines, nay, even in a single name: Robespierre or Napoleon. Ginevra was trembling. Like the dove crossing the waters, which had no rest for her foot but in the ark, her eyes could take refuge only in Luigi's, for all else was cold and sad. The mayor had a stern, disapproving look, and his clerk stared at the couple with ill-natured curiosity. Nothing ever had less the appearance of a festivity. Like all the other events of human life when they are stripped of their accessories, it was a simple thing in itself, immense in its idea.

After some questions, to which they replied, the mayor muttered a few words, and then, having signed their names in the register, Luigi and Ginevra were man and wife. The young Corsicans, whose union had all the poetry which genius has consecrated in Romeo and Juliet, went away between two lines of jubilant relations to whom they did not belong, and who were out of patience at the delay caused by a marriage apparently so forlorn. When the girl found herself in the courtyard and under the open sky, a deep sigh broke from her very heart.

"Oh, will a whole life of love and devotion suffice to repay my Ginevra for her courage and tenderness?" said Luigi.

At these words, spoken with tears of joy, the bride forgot all her suffering, for she had suffered in showing herself to the world, claiming a happiness which her parents refused to sanction.

"Why do men try to come between us?" she said, with a simplicity of feeling that enchanted Luigi.

Gladness made them more light-hearted. They saw neither the sky, nor the earth, nor the houses, and flew on wings to the church. At last they found themselves in a small, dark chapel, and in front of a humble altar where an old priest married them. There, as at the mayor's, they were pursued by the two weddings that persecuted them with their splendor. The church, filled with friends and relations, rang with the noise made by carriages, beadles, porters, and priests. Altars glittered with ecclesiastical magnificence; the crowns of orange-blossom that decked the statues of the Virgin seemed quite new. Nothing was to be seen but flowers, with perfumes, gleaming tapers, and velvet cushions embroidered with gold. God seemed to have a share in this rapture of a day.

When the symbol of eternal union was to be held above the heads of Luigi and Ginevra—the yoke of white satin which for some is so soft, so bright, so light, and for the greater number is made of lead—the priest looked round in vain for two young boys to fill the happy office; two of the witnesses took their place. The priest gave the couple a hasty discourse on the dangers of life, and on the duties they must one day inculcate in their children, and he here took occasion to insinuate a reflection on the absence of Ginevra's parents; then having united them in the presence of God, as the mayor had united them in the presence of the law, he ended the mass, and left them.

"God bless them," said Vergniaud to the mason at the church-door. "Never were two creatures better made for each other. That girl's parents are wretches. I know no braver soldier than Colonel Luigi! If all the world had behaved as he did, *L'autre** would still be with us."

The soldier's blessing, the only one breathed for them this day, fell like balm on Ginevra's heart.

They all parted with shaking of hands, and Luigi cordially thanked his landlord.

"Good-by, old fellow," said Luigi to the quartermaster. "And thank you."

"At your service, colonel, soul and body, horses and chaises—all that is mine is yours." ·

"How well he loves you!" said Ginevra.

Luigi eagerly led his wife home to the house they were to live in; they soon reached the modest apartment, and there, when the door was closed, Luigi took her in his arms, exclaiming, "Oh, my Ginevra—for you are mine now—here is our real festival! Here," he went on, "all will smile on us."

Together they went through the three rooms which composed their dwelling. The entrance hall served as drawing-room and dining-room. To the right was a bedroom, to the left a sort of large closet which Luigi had arranged for his beloved wife, where she found easels, her paint-box, some casts, models, lay figures, pictures, portfolios; in short, all the apparatus of an artist.

"Here I shall work," said she, with childlike glee.

She looked for a long time at the paper and the furniture, constantly turning to Luigi to thank him, for there was a kind of magnificence in this humble retreat ; a bookcase contained Ginevra's favorite books, and there was a piano. She

* The other: Napoleon.

24

sat down on an ottoman, drew Luigi to her side, and clasping
his hand, "You have such good taste," said she, in a caressing tone.

"Your words make me very happy," he replied.

"But come, let us see everything," said Ginevra, from
whom Luigi had hitherto kept the secret of this charming
little home.

They went into a bridal chamber that was as fresh and
white as a maiden.

"Oh! come away," said Luigi, laughing.

"But I must see everything," and Ginevra imperiously
went on, examining all the furniture with the curiosity of an
antiquary studying a medal. She touched the silk stuff and
scrutinized everything with the childlike delight of a bride
turning over the treasures of the wedding basket brought her
by her husband.

"We have begun by ruining ourselves," she said in a half-
glad, half-regretful tone.

"It is true ; all my arrears of pay are there," replied Luigi.
"I sold it to a good fellow named Gigonnet."

"Why?" she asked, in a reproachful voice, which betrayed, however, a secret satisfaction. "Do you think I
should be less happy under a bare roof? Still," she went on,
"it is all very pretty, and it is ours!"

Luigi looked at her with such enthusiasm that she cast down
her eyes, and said, "Let us see the rest."

Above these three rooms, in the attics, were a workroom
for Luigi, a kitchen, and a servant's room. Ginevra was
content with her little domain, though the view was limited
by the high wall of a neighboring house, and the courtyard
on which the rooms looked was gloomy. But the lovers were
so glad of heart, hope so beautified the future, that they would
see nothing but enchantment in their mysterious dwelling.
They were buried in this huge house, lost in the immensity
of Paris, like two pearls in their shell, in the bosom of the

deep sea. For any one else it would have been a prison : to them it was paradise.

The first days of their married life were given to love; it was difficult for them to devote themselves at once to work, and they could not resist the fascination of their mutual passion. Luigi would recline for hours at his wife's feet, admiring the color of her hair, the shape of her forehead, the exquisite setting of her eyes, the purity and whiteness of the arched brow beneath which they slowly rose or fell, expressing the happiness of satisfied love. Ginevra stroked her Luigi's locks, never tiring of gazing at what she called, in one of her own phrases, the *beltà folgorante* of the young man, and his delicately cut features; always fascinated by the dignity of his manners, while always charming him by the grace of her own. They played like children with the merest trifles, these trifles always brought them back to their passion, and they ceased playing only to lapse into the day dreams of *far niente*. An air sung by Ginevra would reproduce for them the exquisite hues of their love.

Or, matching their steps as they had matched their souls, they wandered about the country, finding their love in everything, in the flowers, in the sky, in the heart of the fiery glow of the setting sun; they read it even in the changing clouds that were tossed on the winds. No day was ever like the last, their love continued to grow because it was true. In a very few days they had proved each other, and had instinctively perceived that their souls were of such a temper that their inexhaustible riches seemed to promise ever-new joys for the future. This was love in all its fresh candor, with its endless prattle, its unfinished sentences, its long silences, its oriental restfulness and ardor. Luigi and Ginevra had wholly understood love. Is not love like the sea, which, seen superficially or in haste, is accused of monotony by vulgar minds, while certain privileged beings can spend all their life admiring it and finding in it changeful phenomena which delight them?

One day, however, prudence dragged the young couple
from their Garden of Eden ; they must work for their
living.   Ginevra, who had a remarkable talent for copying
pictures, set to work to produce copies, and formed a connection among dealers.   Luigi, too, eagerly sought some
occupation ; but it was difficult for a young officer, whose
talents were limited to a thorough knowledge of tactics, to find
any employment in Paris.   At last, one day when, weary of
his vain efforts, he felt despair in his soul at seeing that the
whole burthen of providing for their existence rested on Ginevra, it occurred to him that he might earn something by
his handwriting, which was beautiful.   With a perseverance,
of which his wife had set the example, he went to ask work
of the attorneys, the notaries, and the pleaders of Paris.
The frankness of his manners and his painful situation greatly
interested people in his favor, and he got enough copying to
be obliged to employ youths under him.   Presently he took
work on a larger scale.   The income derived from this office-
work and the price of Ginevra's paintings put the young
household on a footing of comfort, which they were proud of
as the fruit of their own industry.

This was the sunniest period of their life.   The days glided
swiftly by between work and the happiness of love.   In the
evening after working hard they found themselves happy in
Ginevra's cell.   Music then consoled them for their fatigues.
No shade of melancholy ever clouded the young wife's features, and she never allowed herself to utter a lament.   She
could always appear to her Luigi with a smile on her lips and
a light in her eyes.   Each cherished a ruling thought which
would have made them take pleasure in the hardest toil :
Ginevra told herself she was working for Luigi, and Luigi for
Ginevra.   Sometimes, in her husband's absence, the young
wife would think of the perfect joy it would have been if this
life of love might have been spent in the sight of her father
and mother ; then she would sink into deep melancholy, and

feel all the pangs of remorse ; dark pictures would pass like shadows before her fancy ; she would see her old father alone, or her mother weeping in the evenings, and hiding her tears from the inexorable Piombo. Those two grave, white heads would suddenly rise up before her, and she fancied she would never see them again but in the fantastical light of memory. This idea haunted her like a presentiment.

She kept the anniversary of their wedding by giving her husband a portrait he had often wished for—that of his Ginevra. The young artist had never executed so remarkable a work. Apart from the likeness, which was perfect, the brilliancy of her beauty, the purity of her feelings, the happiness of love, were rendered with a kind of magic. The masterpiece was hung up with due ceremony.

They spent another year in the midst of comfort. The history of their life can be told in these words: "They were happy." No event occurred deserving to be related.

At the beginning of the winter of 1819 the picture-dealers advised Ginevra to bring them something else than copies, as, in consequence of the great competition, they could no longer sell them to advantage. Madame Porta acknowledged the mistake she had made in not busying herself with genre pictures, which would have won her a name ; she undertook to paint portraits ; but she had to contend against a crowd of artists even poorer than herself. However, as Luigi and Ginevra had saved some money, they did not despair of the future. At the end of this same winter Luigi was working without ceasing. He, too, had to compete with rivals ; the price of copying had fallen so low that he could no longer employ assistants, and was compelled to give up more time to his labor to earn the same amount. His wife had painted several pictures which were not devoid of merit, but dealers were scarcely buying even those of artists of repute. Ginevra offered them for almost nothing, and could not sell them.

The situation of the household was something terrible ; the

souls of the husband and wife floated in happiness, love loaded them with its treasures; poverty rose up like a skeleton in the midst of this harvest of joys, and they hid their alarms from each other. When Ginevra felt herself on the verge of tears as she saw Luigi suffering, she heaped caresses on him; Luigi, in the same way, hid the blackest care in his heart, while expressing the fondest devotion to Ginevra. They sought some compensation for their woes in the enthusiasm of their feelings, and their words, their joys, their playfulness, were marked by a kind of frenzy. They were alarmed at the future. What sentiment is there to compare in strength with a passion which must end to-morrow—killed by death or necessity? When they spoke of their poverty, they felt the need of deluding each other, and snatched at the smallest hope with equal eagerness.

One night Ginevra sought in vain for Luigi at her side, and got up quite frightened. A pale gleam reflected from the dingy wall of the little courtyard led her to guess that her husband sat up to work at night. Luigi waited till his wife was asleep to go up to his workroom. The clock struck four. Ginevra went back to bed and feigned sleep; Luigi came back, overwhelmed by fatigue and want of sleep, and Ginevra gazed sadly at the handsome face on which labor and anxiety had already traced some lines.

"And it is for me that he spends the night in writing," she thought, and she wept.

An idea came to dry her tears: she would imitate Luigi. That same day she went to a rich print-seller, and by the help of a letter of recommendation to him that she had obtained from Elie Magus, a picture-dealer, she got some work in coloring prints. All day she painted and attended to her household cares, then at night she colored prints. These two beings, so tenderly in love, got into bed only to get out of it again. Each pretended to sleep, and out of devotion to the other stole away as soon as one had deceived the other. One night Luigi, knocked over by a sort of fever caused by work, of which the burthen was beginning to crush him, threw open the window of his workroom to inhale the fresh morning air, and shake off his pain, when, happening to look down, he saw the light thrown on the wall by Ginevra's lamp; the unhappy man guessed the truth; he went downstairs, walking softly, and discovered his wife in her studio coloring prints.

"Oh, Ginevra!" he exclaimed.

She started convulsively in her chair, and turned scarlet.

"Could I sleep while you were wearing yourself out with work?" said she.

"But I alone have a right to work so hard."

"And can I sit idle?" replied the young wife, whose eyes filled with tears, "when I know that every morsel of bread almost costs us a drop of your blood? I should die if I did not add my efforts to yours. Ought we not to have everything in common, pleasures and pains?"

"She is cold!" cried Luigi, in despair. "Wrap your shawl closer over your chest, my Ginevra, the night is damp and chilly."

They went to the window, the young wife leaning her head on her beloved husband's shoulder, he with his arm round her, sunk in deep silence, and watching the sky which dawn was slowly lighting up.

Gray clouds swept across in quick succession, and the east grew brighter by degrees.

"See," said Ginevra, "it is a promise—we shall be happy."

"Yes, in heaven!" replied Luigi, with a bitter smile. "Oh, Ginevra! you who deserved all the riches of earth——"

"I have your heart!" said she in a glad tone.

"Ah, and I do not complain," he went on, clasping her closely to him. And he covered the delicate face with kisses; it was already beginning to lose the freshness of youth, but the expression was so tender and sweet that he could never look at it without feeling comforted.

"How still!" said Ginevra. "I enjoy sitting late, my dearest. The majesty of night is really contagious; it is impressive, inspiring; there is something strangely solemn in the thought: all sleeps, but I am awake."

"Oh, my Ginevra, I feel, not for the first time, the refined grace of your soul—but, see, this is daybreak, come and sleep."

"Yes," said she, "if I am not the only one to sleep. I was miserable indeed the night when I discovered that my Luigi was awake and at work without me."

The valor with which the young people defied misfortune for some time found a reward. But the event which usually crowns the joys of a household was destined to be fatal to them. Ginevra gave birth to a boy, who, to use a common phrase, was as beautiful as the day. The feeling of motherhood doubled the young creature's strength. Luigi borrowed money to defray the expenses of her confinement. Thus, just at first, she did not feel all the painfulness of their situation, and the young parents gave themselves up to the joy of rearing a child. This was their last gleam of happiness. Like two swimmers who unite their forces to stem a current, the Corsicans at first struggled bravely; but sometimes they gave themselves up to an apathy resembling the torpor that precedes death, and they were soon obliged to sell their little treasures.

Poverty suddenly stood before them, not hideous, but humbly attired, almost pleasant to endure; there was nothing appalling in her voice; she did not bring despair with her, nor spectres, nor squalor, but she made them forget the traditions and the habit of comfort; she broke the mainsprings of pride. Then came misery in all its horror, reckless of her rags, and trampling every human feeling under foot. Seven or eight months after the birth of little Bartolomeo it would have been difficult to recognize the original of the beautiful portrait, the sole adornment of their bare room, in the mother who was suckling a sickly baby. Without any fire in bitter winter weather, Ginevra saw the soft outlines of her face gradually disappear, her cheeks became as white as porcelain, her eyes colorless, as though the springs of life were drying up in her. And watching her starved and pallid infant, she suffered only in his young misery, while Luigi had not the heart even to smile at his boy.

"I have scoured Paris," he said in a hollow voice. "I know no one, and how can I dare beg of strangers? Vergniaud, the horse-breeder, my old comrade in Egypt, is implicated in some conspiracy, and has been sent to prison; besides, he had loaned me all he had to lend. As to the landlord, he has not asked me for any rent for more than a year."

"But we do not want for anything," Ginevra gently answered, with an affectation of calmness.

"Each day brings some fresh difficulty," replied Luigi, with horror.

Luigi took all Ginevra's paintings, the portrait, some furniture which they yet could dispense with, and sold them all for a mere trifle; the money thus obtained prolonged their sufferings for a little while. During these dreadful days Ginevra showed the sublime heights of her character, and the extent of her resignation. She bore the inroads of suffering with stoical firmness. Her vigorous soul upheld her under all ills; with a weak hand she worked on by her dying child, fulfilled her household duties with miraculous activity, and was equal to everything. She was even happy when she saw on Luigi's lips a smile of surprise at the look of neatness she contrived to give to the one room to which they had been reduced.

"I have kept you a piece of bread, dear," she said one evening when he came in tired.

"And you?"

"I have dined, dear Luigi; I want nothing." And the

sweet expression of her face, even more than her words, urged him to accept the food of which she had deprived herself. Luigi embraced her with one of the despairing kisses which friends gave each other in 1793 as they mounted the scaffold together. In such moments as these two human creatures see each other heart to heart. Thus the unhappy Luigi, understanding at once that his wife was fasting, felt the fever that was undermining her; he shivered, and went out on the pretext of pressing business, for he would rather have taken the most insidious poison than escape death by eating the last morsel of bread in the house.

He wandered about Paris among the smart carriages, in the midst of the insulting luxury that is everywhere flaunted; he hurried past the shops of the money-changers where gold glitters in the window; finally, he determined to sell himself, to offer himself as a substitute for the conscription, hoping by this sacrifice to save Ginevra, and that during his absence she might be taken into favor again by Bartolomeo. So he went in search of one of the men who deal in these white slaves, and felt a gleam of happiness at recognizing in him an old officer of the Imperial Guard.

"For two days I have eaten nothing," he said, in a slow, weak voice. "My wife is dying of hunger, and never utters a complaint; she will die, I believe, with a smile on her lips. For pity's sake, old comrade," he added, with a forlorn smile, "pay for me in advance; I am strong, I have left the service, and I——"

The officer gave Luigi something on account of the sum he promised to get for him. The unhappy man laughed convulsively when he grasped a handful of gold-pieces, and ran home as fast as he could go, panting, and exclaiming as he went, "Oh, my Ginevra—Ginevra!"

It was growing dark by the time he reached home. He went in softly, fearing to overexcite his wife, whom he had left so weak; the last pale rays of sunshine, coming in at the dormer window, fell on Ginevra's face. She was asleep in her chair with her baby at her breast.

"Wake up, my darling," said he, without noticing the attitude of the child, which seemed at this moment to have a supernatural glory.

On hearing his voice, the poor mother opened her eyes, met Luigi's look, and smiled ; but Luigi gave a cry of terror. He hardly recognized his half-crazed wife, to whom he showed the gold, with a gesture of savage vehemence.

Ginevra began to laugh mechanically, but suddenly she cried in a terrible voice, "Luigi, the child is cold ! "

She looked at the infant and fainted. Little Bartolomeo was dead.

Luigi took his wife in his arms, without depriving her of the child, which she clutched to her with incomprehensible strength, and after laying her on the bed he went out to call for help.

"Great heaven ! " he exclaimed to his landlord, whom he met on the stairs, "I have money, and my child is dead of hunger, and my wife is dying. Help us."

In despair he went back to his wife, leaving the worthy builder and various neighbors to procure whatever might relieve the misery of which till now they had known nothing, so carefully had the Corsicans concealed it out of a feeling of pride. Luigi had tossed the gold-pieces on the floor, and was kneeling by the bed where his wife lay.

"Father, take charge of my son, who bears your name ! " cried Ginevra in her delirium.

"Oh, my angel, be calm," said Luigi, kissing her, "better days await us ! " His voice and embrace restored her to some composure.

"Oh, my Luigi," she went on, looking at him with extraordinary fixity, "listen to me. I feel that I am dying. My death is quite natural. I have been suffering too much ; and then happiness so great as mine had to be paid for. Yes, my

Luigi, be comforted. I have been so happy that if I had to begin life again, I would again accept our lot. I am a bad mother; I weep for you even more than for my child. My child!" she repeated in a full, deep voice. Two tears dropped from her dying eyes, and she suddenly clasped yet closer the little body she could not warm. "Give my hair to my father in memory of his Ginevra," she added. "Tell him that I never, never, accused him——"

Her head fell back on her husband's arm.

"No, no, you cannot die!" cried Luigi. "A doctor is coming. We have food. Your father will receive you into favor. Prosperity is dawning on us. Stay with us, angel of beauty!"

But that faithful and loving heart was growing cold. Ginevra instinctively turned her eyes on the man she adored, though she was no longer conscious of anything; confused images rose before her mind, fast losing all memories of earth. She knew that Luigi was there, for she clung more and more tightly to his ice-cold hand, as if to hold herself up above a gulf into which she feared to fall.

"You are cold, dear," she said presently; "I will warm you."

She tried to lay her husband's hand over her heart, but she was dead. Two doctors, a priest, and some neighbors came in at this moment, bringing everything that was needful to save the lives of the young couple and to soothe their despair. At first these intruders made a good deal of noise, but when they were all in the room an appalling silence fell.

While this scene was taking place Bartolomeo and his wife were sitting in their old armchairs, each at one corner of the immense fireplace that warmed the great drawing-room of their mansion. The clock marked midnight. It was long since the old couple had slept well. At this moment they were silent, like two old folks in their second childhood, who look at everything and see nothing. The deserted room, to them full of memories, was feebly lighted by a single lamp fast dying out. But for the dancing flames on the hearth they would have been in total darkness. One of their friends had just left them, and the chair on which he had sat during his visit stood between the old people. Piombo had already cast more than one glance at this chair, and these glances, fraught with thoughts, followed each other like pangs of remorse, for the empty chair was Ginevra's. Elisa Piombo watched the expressions that passed across her old husband's pale face. Though she was accustomed to guess the Corsican's feelings from the violent changes in his features, they were to-night by turns so threatening and so sad that she failed to read this inscrutable soul.

Was Bartolomeo yielding to the overwhelming memories aroused by that chair? Was he pained at perceiving that it had been used by a stranger for the first time since his daughter's departure? Had the hour of mercy, the hour so long and vainly hoped for, struck at last?

These reflections agitated the heart of Elisa Piombo. For a moment her husband's face was so terrible that she quaked at having ventured on so innocent a device to give her an opportunity of speaking of Ginevra. At this instant the northerly blast flung the snowflakes against the shutters with such violence that the old people could hear their soft pelting. Ginevra's mother bent her head to hide her tears from her husband. Suddenly a sigh broke from the old man's heart ; his wife looked at him ; he was downcast. For the second time in three years she ventured to speak to him of his daughter.

"Supposing Ginevra were cold ! " she exclaimed in an undertone. " Or perhaps she is hungry," she went on. The Corsican shed a tear. " She has a child, and cannot suckle it, her milk is dried up," the mother added vehemently, with an accent of despair.

" Let her come ; oh, let her come ! " cried Piombo. " Oh, my darling child, you have conquered me."

The mother hastily rose, as if to go fetch her daughter. At this instant the door was flung open, and a man, whose face had lost all semblance of humanity, suddenly stood before them.

" Dead ! Our families were doomed to exterminate each other ; for this is all that remains of her," he said, laying on the table Ginevra's long, black hair.

The two old people started, as though they had been struck by a thunderbolt ; they could not see Luigi.

" He has spared us a pistol-shot, for he is dead," said Bartolomeo deliberately, as he looked on the ground.

PARIS, *January*, 1830.